AUSTRALIA'S ENDANGERED SPECIES

The Extinction Dilemma

AUSTRALIA'S ENDANGERED SPECIES
The Extinction Dilemma

MICHAEL KENNEDY
General Editor

Foreword by
RICHARD MORECROFT

International Comment by
PROFESSOR NORMAN MYERS

Specialist Chapters by
GEOFF WILLIAMS · JOHN BENSON · GRAEME G GEORGE · FRANK ANTRAM

Prentice Hall Press

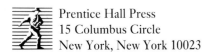

Prentice Hall Press
15 Columbus Circle
New York, New York 10023

First published in Australia in 1990 by
Simon & Schuster Australia
7 Grosvenor Place
Brookvale NSW 2100

Library of Congress Catalog Card Number:
90-60994

ISBN 0-13-053208-8

Typeset in Ehrhardt
by Deblaere Typesetting Pty Ltd
Printed in Hong Kong
First Prentice Hall Press Edition

Produced by Ausworld Publishing for
Simon & Schuster Australia

Kirsty Melville, *Publisher*
Verna Simpson, *Managing Editor*
Vicki Barclay, *Copy Editor*
Leigh Nankervis, *Designer*

Species Research and Text

Stephanie Burton:	The Amphibians
Debbie Callister:	The Fish
Pam Eiser:	The Birds, Reptiles and Marine Mammals
Michael Kennedy:	The Terrestrial Mammals; Parrots; Extinct Species; conservation status assignments; technical editing for all vertebrate species; and section introductions.

ACKNOWLEDGEMENTS

Special thanks to Frank Antram, John Benson, John Briggs, David Cheal,
Peter Copley, Graeme George, Steve Hopper, Bill Laverick, John Leigh,
Richard Morecroft, Norman Myers, Geoff Williams, Alistair Wilson
(Australian Customs Service).
We would also like to thank the following organisations:
Australian National Parks and Wildlife Service for use of threatened invertebrates
list and for permission and help in reproducing the threatened plant list, Ecofund
Australia, Ecology International, World Wildlife Fund (Australia and USA).

Half Title:	Lumholtz's Tree kangaroo	
	M. Cianelli/A.N.T. Photo Library	
Full Title:	Australian Sea Lion	
	Tom and Pam Gardner	
Cover:	Saltwater or Estuarine Crocodile	
	Leo Meier/Courtesy Weldon Trannies	

Contents

Foreword

RICHARD MORECROFT

We humans have a lot to answer for and this book is part of the evidence. It's evidence of the damage that's been done in the past and carries an urgent message about the need for protection in the future. I'm optimistic about the future but it's going to be a long struggle. We're starting to see important changes in attitude towards the environment, but there's a danger that public support and concern will dwindle unless we can get the environmental challenge firmly into perspective and keep it there in the spotlight. We must start to show a genuine respect for the extraordinary system which makes the environment what it is – a tangle of interactions where every type of life has a place, a function and an effect. The balances have been maintained for millions of years, from the primaeval seas through the eras of dinosaurs and the ages of ice. Those balances have swung often and the changes have been enormous, but everything in those environments over the millennia has been part of the same system; every bird, fish, raincloud, rock and fern has been a part of the environmental network of the time and has, so to speak, played it by the rules. But over the last few thousand years, those rules have been badly bent. One particular species has developed so rapidly in its capacity to change the environment that the delicate balance of eons has been dangerously shifted; this particular species has stepped outside the system. No prizes for guessing which species I'm talking about.

Humans are different to any previous life form. We have extraordinary capacities, compared to any other living things (as far as we know), for being able to think about what we're doing, understand how other things work and figure out how to make them work for us. Whatever quirks of evolution have given us these talents, they've allowed us to dominate the planet more rapidly and more completely than any creature has done before. But our success as a species in the short-term carries with it dreadful risks for the long-term health of the whole planet. For most of our history, we have regarded ourselves as a superior form of life and the world around us simply as a resource for our benefit. At last that attitude is starting to be questioned and we're recognising the damage it's caused. In this country, for example, over the past 200 years, well over 50 per cent of the forests have been cleared, nearly 300 species of native birds, animals and plants have been so badly affected that they are considered endangered and at least 130 species have been wiped out altogether; they are already extinct. That sort of environmental plunder has been going on around the world for centuries, but in the last 50 years technology and industry have accelerated at a screaming pace and so have forest clearing and pollution levels. In what is a tiny fraction of time in the vast history of the Earth we have done immeasurable damage to it.

The human approach has been arrogant and destructive and it's time for a change. That change has to come from two things. Firstly, we have to recognise that humans are an animal species on this planet, that we evolved as a part of a balanced environmental system and that we *are* still a part of that system. However we're also separate from it because we're able to affect its balance on a scale that no other creature can. Secondly, we have to do something unnatural. We have to choose to put restrictions on ourselves for

6

the benefit of the environment. No other types of animals or plants consciously control themselves in that way; they look after themselves and environmental forces do the balancing. Goannas don't think about whether they may be eating the eggs of a rare bird and Strangler figs have no sense of responsibility for the trees they imprison. They just do what comes naturally for their own benefit. But we must think differently. We must be prepared to make unprecedented sacrifices and take a special responsibility for the environment around us. Our perspective has to include much more than just our own species. We are able to understand what we've done to the whole planet up to now and we can see the possible effects of future actions. We have absolutely no excuse.

That doesn't mean we can't use our environment at all. There will always be a need for mining, for timber and for manufacturing industries. But those activities need to be carried out with vastly more thought, more forward planning and more respect for the complexity of the environment than there has been in the past. It shouldn't have to be a battle, we can look after the environment and use some of its resources at the same time. Resource management and environmental protection must be more and more closely linked. Inevitably that approach will frustrate some people who want unlimited access to those resources; they will resent the restrictions of environmental legislation. Already there have been cries of 'Greedy Greens!', implying that conservationists are trying to protect too much. But the pendulum has swung so far, during human history, towards a free-for-all use of resources and

Ross Coffey

consequent environmental damage that it has a long way to swing back before we can feel that a balance has been re-established.

Our responsibility is to keep up the momentum towards that balance. Every step is an important one and none more so than identifying which elements in our environment need most urgent help. This book is part of that vital process. While looking at Australia's growing number of endangered species and the threats they face, it makes the need for their protection and the conservation of their habitat absolutely clear.

This book is evidence of the terrible damage we've done to the environment of Australia. I hope it contributes to the sense of urgency we should all feel about looking after what's left.

Richard Morecroft.

The Global Perspective

PROFESSOR NORMAN MYERS

The world faces a profound problem. Species are disappearing at a rate of dozens a day worldwide. Unless we improve our conservation efforts, the demise of at least one third and possibly half of all species, within the lifetime of many readers of this book, is possible.

Fortunately this problem can be turned into a splendid opportunity. There is still time, though only just, to slow and stem the tide of extinctions that is washing over the Earth's wildlife throngs. We have the chance to save species in their many millions. What a challenge!

As Charles Dickens might have put it, this is the worst of times, and it is the best of times too. While the mass extinction could prove to be the greatest wipe-out of species since the first flickerings of life, almost four billion years ago, *it is not inevitable.*

Of course extinction has always been a fact of life. Of the half a billion species that have ever existed, the present 30 million or so represent a mere 6 per cent. But whereas the average 'background' rate during the last 250 million years has been only about one species per year, we are now losing perhaps 50 species per day. By the year 2000 we could be losing ten species with every passing hour, surely the fastest rate that has ever occurred in the Earth's history. Yet another unique feature of the present phenomenon is that it is being caused by a single species. Ironically that species is the only species that has ever existed with the capacity to save other species.

The Scientific Background

What is the scientific evidence for the biological debacle underway? The extinction crisis is centred on tropical forests. Covering only 6 per cent of the land surface, or slightly more than Australia's area, these forests harbour the great bulk of Earth's species, probably 70 per cent and possibly 90 per cent. At the same time, the forests are being depleted faster than any other major

Previous page. The Jaguar (Panthera onca) is an endangered cat that inhabits the rainforests of Central and South America. It is threatened by rainforest destruction and hunting for the fur trade.

Courtesy World Wildlife Fund – US

Rainforest destruction – a threat to human survival.

Courtesy World Wildlife Fund – US

ecological zone. We have already lost half of these forests, and today they are disappearing at a rate of roughly 150,000 square kilometres per year, or nearly 2 per cent of their remaining 8 million square kilometres. Worse, the destruction rate is accelerating, and by the beginning of next century there could be little left apart from two large remnant blocs in the Zaire Basin and the western portion of Brazilian Amazonia, plus two outlier tracts in New Guinea and the Guyana Highlands. Even these 'good news' areas may succumb to population pressures and development processes within a further few decades.

'Hot-Spot' Areas

But species are not evenly distributed throughout tropical forests. Nor is deforestation. A number of localities feature exceptional concentrations of species, and face exceptional threats of destruction. These areas include the forest patches of Madagascar, Atlantic-coast Brazil, western Ecuador, eastern Himalayas, Peninsular Malaysia and north-western Borneo, among others. Ten such hot-spot areas used to comprise 2.2 million square kilometres of forest, now reduced to less than 300,000 square kilometres. While amounting to less than 3.5 per cent of remaining tropical forests, they contain over 34,000 endemic plant species (species found nowhere else) or 13 per cent of all plant species worldwide. These hot-spot localities also feature a minimum of 700,000 endemic animal species, possibly several times more. All such areas may well lose all but fragments of their forests by the year 2000, if present destruction patterns persist. In these areas alone, then, there may be a mini-spasm of species extinctions within the near future.

If conservationists were to concentrate on these areas, where needs are greatest and where the pay-off from safeguard measures would also be greatest, they could engage in a 'silver bullet' attack on the problem of mass extinction. They would get the biggest 'bang' per scarce conservation dollar invested, an altogether more productive approach than the scatter-gun efforts that have often characterised conservation to date.

Rainforest in Papua New Guinea. These vital areas must be protected.

Open Space

There are at least another 15 similar hot-spot areas in tropical forests, including Queensland's wet tropical rainforests, with similarly large stocks of species under terminal threat. In tropical coral reefs there could be at least 12 hot-spot areas; and the same in wetland ecosystems such as the Sudd Swamp in southern Sudan and in the Pantanal Swamp in central Brazil. Still more hot spots occur in Mediterranean-type localities, notably the Cape region of South Africa, California in the United States of America, the Mediterranean Basin itself, and one of the most notable areas of all, south-western Australia.

Putting all these additional hot-spot areas together, there are several million species in dire straits, and virtually all of them can be saved through concentrated safeguard efforts, provided conservationists move fast enough and with clearly targeted strategies.

Economic Benefits of Conserving Forests

The most vulnerable hot-spot areas are largely in tropical countries of the Third World. Not surprisingly, this is where conservation resources are in shortest supply. Scientists and conservationists tend to be few on the ground, and save-species funds are meagre, at best.

But certain areas, such as south-western Australia (a vastly rich floristic region) and California, occur in developed nations. Most remarkable of all, from Australia's stand-point at least, is the wet tropics of northern Queensland, one of the hottest of all hot spots. In just 6,300 square kilometres of rainforest, less than half of what was there 50 years ago, there occur at least 1,165 plant species, of which more than one third are endemic to the area, that is, found nowhere else on Earth. As in many tropical localities, some of these plant species are so restricted that they occur in a single valley or on a single hilltop, that is, they are ultra-vulnerable to elimination through habitat destruction which could occur in a matter of weeks at most. Of the world's 19 oldest flowering-plant families, 13 are represented here, two of them endemic to the area, thus giving the area the highest concentration of such plant families anywhere on Earth. For each plant species we can reckon there are at least 20 and possibly 50 animal species. Fortunately the Australian Government has successfully listed the Queensland forests on the World Heritage List which, by relieving them of all further exploitation, will safeguard them in perpetuity.

In other hot spots too, there are new moves to pull vast numbers of species back from the brink. In Madagascar, for instance, the government, working in conjunction with the World Bank and the World Wildlife Fund, has calculated that the overall costs of deforestation, in terms of fuelwood short-ages, soil erosion, depleted rainfall-catch-ment zones and declining water supplies, is levying a toll on the national economy equiv-alent to US$300 million per year. A rescue operation need cost no more than around US$100 million, making it a thoroughly cost-effective measure and saving huge numbers of species as a bonus.

Not that saving species is a non-economic exercise. Among Madagascar's plants is the Rosy Periwinkle, source of two potent drugs used against Hodgkin's disease, leukaemia and other blood cancers. Sales of these two drugs, in the United States alone, now amount to some US$170 million a year, with economic benefits to American society as a whole, worth some US$400 million a year. Cancer specialists believe there could be at least another 12 plant species in tropical forests with potential to generate similar superstar drugs against cancers of various sorts.

Future of Evolution Knocked off Course?

The economic argument in support of species should not be the only rationale for conservation. There are larger consider-ations that should surely inspire us. The mass extinction unfolding could well entrain severe repercussions for the future course of evolution itself. The forces of natural selection can work only with the species stocks available. If this 'resource base' is drastically reduced, the result is likely to be a depletion of evolution's capacities for speciation (formation of new species), persisting far into the future. The geologic record indicates that five million years elapsed after the dinosaur crash 65 million years ago before there emerged an array of species to match what was there before in numbers and diversity.

The evolutionary outcome, this time, could prove far more drastic than that in the aftermath of the dinosaurs' episode. We must anticipate that many key environments could be eliminated wholesale. As we have seen, they include tropical forests, coral reefs, wetlands and other zones with excep-tional richness of species. These environ-ments have served in the past as pre-eminent cradles of evolution, generating many more species than other environments. Almost every major group of vertebrates and many other large categories of animals appear to have originated in zones with warm, equable climates, and especially in tropical forest zones.

This all means that the 'biotic underpinnings', of basic evolutionary processes, could be severely degraded and depleted. In turn, this means there would not be a compensatory outburst of speciation until after a longer delay than in the past, perhaps even as long as 20 million years.

In short, the mass extinction impending implies that we are conducting an experiment of global scale and unprecedented import. We are not doing it wittingly, still less with purpose aforethought. It is entirely unplanned and uncoordinated. Its workings are mostly undefined and unmeasured. Its results are scarcely anticipated in any detail, even though we know its overall outcome would be wholly irreversible. Yet we pursue our experiment with growing energy and enthusiasm, in all parts of the planet.

This is an experiment of such unrivalled scope and scale that Charles Darwin could hardly have imagined it. In his diaries, we read how Darwin would dearly liked to have spent time, however brief, back in the days of the dinosaurs' decline, not so much to see the dinosaurs as to witness the evolutionary upheaval. How much more would Darwin have preferred to be alive right now, when the extinction spasm is on far greater scale, with the time span more telescoped, and with evolutionary upheavals even more fundamental and far-reaching? Even more to the point, would Darwin not delight to be alive today, when he would be able not only to study species, but to save them?

A Great Creative Challenge

An effort to stem the tide of extinctions is surely not beyond our means. The funding should not be impossible to mobilise, supposing the political leaders, the policy makers and the budget slicers are made aware of what is at stake.

If the prospect seems daunting, let us bear in mind that we are only at the beginning of the trend toward mass extinctions. Our unwitting experiment can still be controlled and eventually contained. *We still have time to save species in immense numbers.*

An opportunity of this sort has never been available to any other community of conservationists. No generation of the past has faced the prospect of mass extinction within its lifetime: the problem has simply never existed before. No generation in the future will ever face a similar challenge: if the present generation fails to come to grips with the task, the problem will be over. Ours is the sole generation that will ever face the prospect: is it not a glorious challenge? Should we not count ourselves a privileged generation, that we are alive at this momentous time?

Both Charles Dickens and Charles Darwin would have had much to say about our present predicament.

Grey Lesser Mouse Lemur – under threat in Madagascar.

Our Biological Heritage

MICHAEL KENNEDY

While many people may be unaware of the enormity of Earth's community of species, society until only recently has always viewed the availability of the natural world as an infinite larder, capable of fulfilling our most rapacious desires.

Australia's share of that guesstimated 'larder' is for the most part biologically unique, and places upon its citizens a responsibility of stewardship that is now being recognised by an increasingly 'environmentally literate' public.

As the table below shows, there could be as many as 30 million different species inhabiting the Earth today. It is anybody's guess how many of these species live in Australia today. No one person really knows the extent of the world's biological tally, but in the past, we have undoubtedly and constantly underestimated the natural diversity and richness of our planet.

At the time Captain Cook arrived in Botany Bay, Australia's wildlife, by now adapted to the changes brought by over 40,000 years of Aboriginal occupation, was as diverse, rich and abundant as a generally harsh climate would permit. The eucalypt forests and rainforests were intact, the fragile deserts free from alien species, and the rivers and harbours sublimely unpolluted. It was a place that had been evolving for millions of years, ever since the final separation of the supercontinent Gondwanaland, that once joined Antarctica, Australia, New Guinea, South America, Africa, Madagascar, India and New Zealand.

In addition to the countless thousands and mostly endemic species of plants, insects and marine molluscs, and over 6,000 vertebrate species comprising freshwater and marine fish, birds, reptiles and amphibians, Australia was the only continent where the marsupials, monotremes and placental mammals (rodents and bats) could be found together. The island of New Guinea, that had evolved for so long joined to the Australian continent, had also developed a similar mammalian component.

Only here in Australia can you find 140 species of marsupials, two monotremes (Platypus and Echidna), and a great diversity of rats, mice and bats. Captain Cook had sailed into a wildlife paradise unequalled anywhere on Earth.

Previous page. Black-footed Rock-wallaby (Petrogale lateralis pupureicollis) *in the Selwyn Range, Queensland. The species is considered vulnerable to extinction.*

Jean-Paul Ferrero/Auscape

KNOWN AND ESTIMATED DIVERSITY OF LIFE ON EARTH

Forms of Life	Known Species	Estimated Total Species
Insects and other arthropods	874,161	30 million insect species.
Higher plants	248,400	Estimates of total plant species 275,000 to 400,000; 10-15 per cent of all plants are believed undiscovered.
Invertebrates	116,873	True invertebrate species may number in the millions; nematodes, eelworms, and roundworms each may comprise more than 1 million species.
Lower plants	73,900	Not available.
Microorganisms	36,600	Not available.
Fish	19,056	21,000, assuming 10 per cent of fish are undiscovered.
Birds	9,040	Probably 98 per cent are known species.
Reptiles and amphibians	8,962	Probably 95 per cent of reptiles, amphibians and
Mammals	4,000	mammals are known species.
TOTAL	**1,390,992**	10 million species considered a conservative estimate; if insect estimates are accurate the total exceeds 30 million.

Source: *Worldwatch Paper 78*, Worldwatch Institute, Washington USA.

The Immensity of the Issue

It is true that the problem of disappearing species represents not only a conservation crisis on a scale never faced before, but also one of the greatest environmental challenges we are ever likely to confront. We hope that this book will convince you of the need, and encourage your participation, in the massive continental effort that will be required if we are to stem the loss of species.

The most serious threat to the continuation of all life on this planet is the loss of biological diversity: the varied living beings that inhabit the globe. As forests are destroyed, water and air polluted, and species removed en masse, inevitable consequences prevail.

It is critical that every person in an essentially affluent Australia realise that something is wrong with our environment, and that the growing number of endangered wildlife species are a clear and ominous warning of things to come. For we not only endanger the enormous wealth of wildlife species as we pursue our everyday lives, but we contribute to an environmental degradation that will ultimately threaten us. We are the one species in 30 million that has brought the world to the edge of devastation and we are the only species that can reverse the process.

But how do we begin to save the countless thousands of species here and around the world? There is no doubt at all that present efforts to conserve species in Australia are far from equal to the task. Unless we shape up today, the myriad Australian species represented in this book may well be gone, tomorrow. Once they have gone, it is forever, never to appear on this Earth again.

It must be clearly understood by all Australians that a link does exist between the survival of our natural heritage, and the health of human society. And if the future impoverishment of our environment, as it will affect wildlife and humans, fails to move society into effective conservation action, then the ramifications could be devastating.

Why Save Wildlife?

It's probably worth asking the question so often put: Why save wildlife? First, it must be recognised that all species on this planet maintain an inalienable right to existence. They must not be seen solely as a resource to be exploited, but as living companions that command equal respect. Humankind must concede that ethical and compassionate considerations are overriding.

Second, species and habitats should simply be maintained in all their diversity for the beauty and pleasure they give. How many people would dispute their intrinsic scientific, educational, cultural and aesthetic values, and that nature's wonders contain mysteries that intrigue us all? The symbolism of wildlife means many things to many people.

Third, species can, and do, provide for humanity a treasure-trove of genetic and other resources that are of inestimable value. Consider everyday items that give us comfort, such as food, clothing and medicines. This rationale however must not be used to justify exploitation for sheer profit motives.

Finally, species and ecosystems provide indirect benefits to society through 'environmental services' that are essential to our survival; air, water, soils, nutrients and other biological ingredients that are a part of an intricate natural web that also supports humankind. If we continue to destroy species and habitats, gradually causing the web to disintegrate, so will be the fate of Homo sapiens.

We have all been seriously interfering with the processes of evolution, the very life forces that created humankind, and the natural resources needed to sustain our teeming billions. So what might be happening now to those evolutionary forces?

The well-known American conservation-biologist Michael Soule answered this question in a very blunt manner in 1982, when he said that '... except for certain temperate, boreal, arctic and oceanic habitats, the speciation process by which new species are created is rapidly becoming inoperative, especially for mammals, birds and many forms of plants. *That the process of creation is virtually finished.*' What better reason could anyone want for stopping the dramatic decline in wildlife species and their habitats than to salvage the very heartbeat of life itself!

Australia's Threatened Species

Our record is not good. In fact it is disastrous. Australia has seen more mammal species go extinct in the last 200 years than any other continent or country on Earth. Already 18 (10 marsupials and 8 rodents) unique species, found nowhere else in the world, have been lost to science and life forever. To this must be added 3 birds, 1 reptile, approximately 100 species of vascular plants and unknown numbers of invertebrates. The unfortunate vertebrate species are listed on page 22, while the list of lost plants can be found in Appendix III.

The large number of plants that have fallen foul of human activities in Australia is also in stark contrast with extinction rates overseas. The European, southern African and United States records come in at 27, 39 and 74 species respectively, way below the extinction rates experienced in Australia.

Those 18 extinct mammals represent a considerable proportion of the total mammal fauna of Australia. They also reflect the enormous impact that European settlement has had upon Australia's arid and semi-arid zones. While no region in Australia has escaped from the inevitable advance of human civilisation, the arid zones, which comprise the largest portion of the Australian land mass, have lost 33 per cent of their mammal species. They have vanished completely. Added to this fact is an estimation by desert scientists, that 90 per cent of all medium-sized desert mammals are either extinct or threatened with extinction.

It has been calculated that all the mammals that are extinct or endangered in the arid regions, weigh between 35 and 5,500 grams. Being a desert mammal in this particular weight range is no fun, and they present Australians with a conservation problem of almost inconceivable proportions.

No area on this enormous continent has remained unscathed after two centuries of colonisation, and though the extinction of so many mammals in the arid zones presents us with the most dramatic example of species loss, the forces of extinction continue around Australia. The tropical and temperate zones species have been hit just as hard, even though the extinction rates have been lower.

The complete lists of Australia's threatened species can be found in Appendices I, II and IV. They contain almost 500 vertebrates, 3,329 plants and over 400 terrestrial and marine invertebrates. It is one of Australia's most depressing statistics. Following here is the list of Australia's top 20 highly endangered vertebrate species.

AUSTRALIA'S MOST HIGHLY THREATENED VERTEBRATES

Southern Right Whale
Humpback Whale
Northern Hairy-nosed Wombat
Rufous Hare-wallaby
Bridled Nailtail Wallaby
Chuditch
Smoky Mouse
Greater Stick-nest Rat
Noisy Scrub-bird
Helmeted Honeyeater
Norfolk Island Boobook Owl
Golden-shouldered Parrot
Broad-headed Snake
Western Black-striped Snake
Lancelin Island Striped Skink
Western Swamp Turtle
Baw Baw Frog
Platypus Frog
Lake Eacham Rainbowfish
Trout Cod

Marine & Coastal Habitats

Marine as well as terrestrial species have suffered sharp declines, though we still know so little about the marine and freshwater ecosystems that surround us and give us life. The Great Barrier Reef, the west coast of Australia, and the Gulf of Carpentaria are just three major regions that have high numbers of threatened marine species. Sharks, giant clams and reef-building corals are just a few examples of marine creatures at risk, and many more are imperilled through excessive commercial harvesting.

Our rivers and coastal lagoons, estuaries, mangrove swamps and other wetlands have borne the brunt of development activities in all areas of coastline where urbanisation, tourism, forestry and mining industries have been seen as the economic priorities.

The south-east and north-east coasts of Australia, south-west Western Australia, north Queensland and the Cape York Peninsula, are all natural regions that have upward spiralling numbers of threatened species.

The wet tropical rainforests of north-east Queensland are particularly important to the conservation of Australia's natural heritage, containing 25 per cent of all plant genera in Australia, 30 per cent of marsupial species, 60 per cent of bat species, 30 per cent of frog species, and 62 per cent of butterflies. A large percentage of these species are unique to the wet tropics, highlighting the vulnerability of this rainforest area that represents no more than a dot on a map of Australia.

Why Have Species Declined?

Those mammal species identified earlier that fall within the weight range 35 to 5,500 grams have been described as 'critical weight range species'. It is believed that these species were particularly susceptible to changes in climatic conditions. They were already living in a harsh arid zone that made living tough enough at the best of times. When droughts came, their distribution contracted to very small areas of suitable and nutritional vegetation. They were continually prone to local extinction.

With the coming of Europeans and their stock animals to the central arid zones, the medium-sized mammals were put under intolerable stress. Their meagre food sources in time of drought and the nutritious food sources further afield after the good rains fell, were decimated by the domestic grazers and introduced rabbits. The mammals virtually had nowhere to go.

The situation was compounded by changing fire regimes in these vast regions. When the Aborigines were moved from their tribal lands to government and religious settlements, many thousands of years of accumulated land management expertise went with them. Scientists have suggested that the frequent burning of large areas of desert by many Aboriginal communities

Mining in Kakadu National Park

Open Space

provided suitable habitats for a large range of small and medium-sized mammals, and that this millennia of natural adaption was abruptly halted when the Aborigines left. As a consequence, uncontrolled wildfires burned large areas, destroying a complex mosaic of vegetation stages spread across the desert zone, vegetation that supplied the ecosystem necessary for the long-term survival of these mammals.

It is also worth contemplating what other species must have been lost in these highly degraded areas: how many plants and invertebrates disappeared with the desert vegetation?

Those populations of mammals that managed to survive in pockets of nutritional vegetation, termed 'refugia' by wildlife scientists, then became very vulnerable to predation by introduced carnivores. The fox, and to some extent the feral cat, have caused tremendous damage to our small and medium-sized mammal populations, and have become the number one enemy in the eyes of many wildlife scientists.

Habitat Degradation and Loss

More than half of Australia's arid land mass is known to be badly degraded through the

19

The endangered Mountain Pygmy-possum
A Smith/NPIAW

heavy agriculture and grazing, places where viable wildlife populations are often unable to survive.

It is probably a combination of factors that eventually drives a species to extinction or near extinction. Clearing of marginal lands, logging, woodchipping, pollution, pesticides, the effects of introduced weeds, direct exploitation for commercial trade or food, illegal hunting, over-fishing and disease, all helped, and are still helping, to bring wildlife populations crashing down.

Not only is it the initial and total loss of habitats in many cases, but more importantly now, the way in which we manage what is left. Australians have destroyed three quarters of our rainforests, and cleared approximately two thirds of the original tree cover, yet we still seem determined to increase this dismal record.

Badly researched and ill managed selective logging operations, woodchipping of old growth eucalypt forests, rainforest destruction, the continuing practice of indiscriminate prescription burning, clearing for agriculture, and the expansion of the grazing industry show no sign of meaningful abatement. Soil erosion and salination have gripped Australia like a plague, yet entirely inappropriate land-management practices persist.

We continue to graze and farm in marginal lands that can never sustain such commercial activities. Our coastal zone remains under immense pressure from 'mega tourist developments', ventures that are economically and socially unsound, and devastating for coastal wildlife. This is all disastrous news for our threatened wildlife species.

The pressures that have combined to besiege our natural heritage, are still very much at work. Many wildlife managers believe that the devastation that has been seen in the arid zones will soon start to show its effects in the tropical north and eastern forested regions, and indeed these pressures are already visible. New threats are also developing to compound the crisis. The possible ramifications of the greenhouse effect are now being researched by scientists. As the world warms up, vegetation regimes will change subtly, rendering habitats

effects of introduced rabbits, domestic stock and other exotic grazers causing enormous habitat destruction. Rabbits, cattle and sheep are not the only species that have been eating and crushing the life from our natural ecosystems; camels, donkeys, buffalo, pigs, goats, horses, and introduced rodents have all played their deadly part. It is the loss of natural vegetation throughout Australia that is the prime cause of wildlife extinctions and endangerment.

As agriculture, grazing and urban development crept slowly across the continent, essential wildlife habitats were swept aside. Massive clearing programs left little but minute habitat fragments in most areas of unsuitable for some species. For instance, the Mountain Pygmy-possum's preferred alpine habitats may disappear completely in time if current predictions are correct.

Moreover, the staggering loss of mammal fauna may soon be repeated with birds and reptiles, and perhaps fish, amphibians, plants and invertebrates, and over far wider areas of the country. Are we about to enter a new era in which we will witness a great spasm of extinctions, or can we all act now to ensure that such a catastrophe never occurs?

Priorities

What about priorities? Why do we have to determine priorities, and how do we arrive at them? The most striking thing about this conservation dilemma is the sheer number of species and the associated habitats involved. Our next consideration is what can we possibly do to help them all survive? The unfortunate reply is that we cannot help them all, at least not directly. The financial and other resources necessary are simply not available to tackle the job entirely. The need for governments to allocate substantially increased budgets to conserve our wildlife is critically important.

This leads to the further and extremely difficult question of which species deserve our priority attention. That this problem must be tackled with great urgency is undoubted, yet no government in Australia has come to grips with the matter. Political attention and public debate are essential.

Allocating priorities to threatened species does not mean an immediate consignment to oblivion for other species on the list. Far from it. Every human effort must be made to conserve life's spectrum of biological diversity. Each and every species is worth saving, and conservation planning must be directed accordingly. This represents the prime goal of all conservationists. Though we must take account particularly of species of conservation concern, we must inevitably monitor all species and habitats; keep a running tab on evolutionary processes so that we are able to react when necessary, and take appropriate remedial and preventative action.

The sad fact is however that the combined list of species under threat in Australia is growing daily. It currently stands at over 4,000 individual species of plants and animals. It is within this unfortunate group that priority actions will have to be decided. The list of criteria that was used in the past to assess which species to help is lengthy, though the degree of threat and particular biological uniqueness of a species are generally used as major priority indicators.

Other criteria include assessing species in terms of their socio-economic values, the likelihood of success of each conservation program, whether or not the species will respond to urgent conservation attention, whether the species would be lost despite help, the species' attractiveness, crisis/symbolic appeal and its political/community support, will the species survive without management attention, is it linked to the survival of other threatened species, and a host of other subjective and scientific markers.

In Australia, however, we are a nation sufficiently affluent to commit ourselves to the goal of conserving every living species. With this clear understanding, priorities should be determined solely upon the degree of endangerment to which each individual species is currently subjected, using other judgements only if unavoidable. But even then, we are still left with a long rollcall of 'endangered' and 'vulnerable' species, particularly in respect to plants. In the latter case, genetic uniqueness criteria may have to be applied.

Protected Areas

Though there is no doubt that many critically endangered species will require direct intervention to save them from certain doom, the largest part of our conservation action must be directed at conserving as much of our remaining natural areas and ecosystems as possible, both on private and public lands.

It must be remembered that national parks and nature reserves cover no more than 5 per cent of our country, and most of these areas cannot in themselves sustain the entire spectrum of species' diversity in Australia. Indeed, research has shown that many of our parks and reserves are too small to support full complements of fauna and flora indefinitely, and are likely to lose species with the passage of time.

Research in the United States has shown that no matter the size of the conservation park allotted for the protection of species and habitats, they have proved far from adequate. Biological diversity continues to be reduced in the largest of areas. American ecologists have recently found that even in parks such as Rocky Mountain (1,049 square kilometres) and Yosemite (2,083 square kilometres) between one quarter and one third of their native mammals have already been lost. These are alarming percentages. Only in the Kootenay-Banff-Jasper-Yoho National Park (20,736 square kilometres) was there no reduction recorded. This park is roughly the size of Kakadu! Further, the majority of Australia's threatened species exist outside national parks and nature reserves, and may never receive such protection.

Therefore, conservation on private land and appropriate management of other government controlled lands to provide secure habitats is critical to conservation in Australia.

By protecting and managing such areas for the benefit of all wildlife and threatened species, we deploy a rescue net that has the very best chance of long-term success. This must become our real priority, coupled with development of management procedures that mitigate against other external threatening processes such as pollution.

What's Being Done?

The conservation of threatened species has never been a glamour campaign in Australia. Wildlife management has always tended to be the poor brother when it comes to conservation priorities. But now, with the realisation that so many species are struggling for survival, both governments and non-government organisations are rising to the challenge.

Despite the low profile given to the conservation of endangered species in the past, there have been many initiatives over the last few years that have significantly helped the lot of critically endangered species.

Many State and Territory wildlife agencies, for instance, have conducted important research and management work on such species as the Bilby in the Northern Territory, the Northern Hairy-nosed Wombat in Queensland, the Numbat in Western Australia, the Greater Stick-nest Rat in South Australia, the Eastern Barred Bandicoot in Victoria, the Parma Wallaby in New South Wales, and a number of other well-known species, the Koala included. Other agencies have spent considerable resources trying to determine the fundamental and underlying causes of extinction, so that appropriate management regimes can be introduced.

Some States have taken the tremendously important step of introducing special legislation which aims to protect the habitats of threatened species and guard them against

AUSTRALIA'S EXTINCT VERTEBRATE SPECIES	
Mammals	**Last Recorded Sighting**
Thylacine	1936
Pig-footed Bandicoot	1907
Desert Bandicoot	1931
Lesser Bilby	1931
Desert Rat-kangaroo	1935
Broad-faced Potoroo	1875
Eastern Hare-wallaby	1891
Central Hare-wallaby	1932
Toolache Wallaby	1924
Crescent Nailtail Wallaby	1930s
Short-tailed Hopping-mouse	1896
Long-tailed Hopping-mouse	1901
Big-eared Hopping-mouse	1843
Darling Downs Hopping-mouse	1840s
White-footed Rabbit-rat	1870s
Lesser Stick-nest Rat	1933
Gould's Mouse	1930
Alice Springs Mouse	1890s
Birds	
Dwarf Emu	1840s
Rufous Bristlebird	1906
Paradise Parrot	1927
Reptiles	
Adelaide Pygmy Bluetongue Skink	1959

The Eastern Barred Bandicoot is highly endangered on the mainland.

JE Wapstra/NPIAW

the external forces that might cause their decline. Victoria's legislation, termed the Flora and Fauna Guarantee Act, is one of the most advanced conservation laws in the world. It aims not only to protect the State's threatened species, but also to conserve the entire range of biological diversity. It is an Act still in its infancy, but is a model to be emulated nationwide. Land clearance controls have also been introduced to complement the Guarantee Act's provisions.

Other notable laws include those in Western Australia governing endangered flora, and in South Australia where land clearance legislation has been in operation for a number of years. In Tasmania, New South Wales and Queensland, governments have promised to introduce specific legislation to protect threatened species and habitats.

Commonwealth Responsibilities

In 1988 the Federal Government established an Endangered Species Advisory Committee (ESAC) whose aim was to develop a national endangered species program, and provide advice to the Minister for the Environment. In 1989, the Advisory Committee (with State and Territory, conservation organisation, scientific, farming community and departmental representation) was given support through the Federal Government's promised ten-year Endangered Species Program.

The Australian National Parks and Wildlife Service will administer the program jointly with ESAC, and implement a 'National Strategy for the Conservation of Species and Habitats Threatened with Extinction'. This strategy must include the introduction of a 'Federal Endangered Species Act'.

International treaties also play an important role in helping conservation in Australia. There are many conventions that directly apply to wildlife, including the Convention on International Trade in Endangered Species of Wild Fauna and Flora (CITES), to which Australia has been a party since 1976. Many of our wildlife species are listed under CITES, covering 31 mammals (not including whales and dolphins), 107 birds, 46 reptiles, 2 amphibians, 1 fish, 3 insects, 6 molluscs, hundreds of reef-building corals and hundreds of plants. Australia is also taking part in negotiations internationally to develop a new 'Convention on the Conservation of Biological Diversity', which aims to protect the world's genetic resources, focusing primarily on tropical rainforests.

These few initiatives do represent the beginning of an era in wildlife management

Central Australian arid zone. At least a third of the mammal species have been lost from these regions.

Open Space

that may help stave off the loss of any more Australian species, but enormous efforts will still be needed. The role of non-government organisations in the conservation of species is becoming increasingly important in this regard, and groups such as World Wildlife Fund Australia, Greenpeace, Australian Conservation Foundation, The Wilderness Society, Trade Records Analysis of Flora and Fauna in Commerce (TRAFFIC) and many others will play a crucial role in the decade ahead.

In the Final Analysis

It is probably the truth, that even the long lists of species to be found in this book do not adequately represent the extent to which wildlife has suffered declines in Australia. This review has taken a national perspective on the crisis, but regionally the situation is often far worse.

Wildlife and habitats are under continuing and immense pressures; yet they are the essential ingredients in the evolutionary game. Keeping them alive has become the 'genetic imperative', convincing Australians of the plight of our wildlife, the 'educational imperative'. The environmental health of a nation and a continent are ultimately in the balance.

This book depicts some of our best known, and most threatened species in Australia, all of which depend upon relatively undisturbed environments for their long-term survival. Even those species that can cope with some degree of human inter-

ference or habitat degradation will inevitably require management in one form or another. Passive management may suffice in the interim, but the eventual fate of species rests entirely upon the activities of their human guardians.

It is not just the deplorable thought of extinctions that should concern Australian society, but the catastrophe that would be represented by the halting of evolutionary processes themselves. As we lose more and more species, so we reduce the gene stocks from which speciation, or the emergence of new species can occur. That global society has reduced nature to such a drastic extent is undoubted.

Securing evolutionary potential for Australia means two things. First, preserving those key environments which undeniably represent cradles of evolution; rainforests, wetlands, mangroves, estuaries, coral reefs and other biotopes that we know to be ecologically complex and species rich. Such reservation and protective management must also be matched by an increasing conservation effort in Australia's arid zones, where wildlife depletion has become quite dramatic. Phasing out the use of marginal lands for grazing and crop production and the retention and extension of tree cover are just two priority targets in achieving this aim. It is also important to note the high conservation value of many of Australia's small coastal islands and their role in providing refuge for a number of critically endangered species.

Second, developing management techniques for wildlife both within and outside protected areas. Implementing management regimes for threatened species and their critical habitats becomes paramount, in tandem with specific reserve declaration whenever possible. This action requires integrated land management that involves many government agencies and conservation groups sharing resources and expertise.

These goals will be substantially helped by strong habitat and species' protection legislation that must be introduced throughout Australia at State, Territory and Federal levels. Governments must also allocate vastly increased resources to ensure that legislation is fully implemented, properly protecting our natural heritage.

We need not just to tackle threatened species problems, park dedication and wilderness preservation. All wildlife and all habitats should be assessed, protected and managed. We must urgently develop a biological diversity conservation plan for deployment throughout Australia – a monitoring process that will let no animal or plant suffer a reduction in its conservation status through wanton destruction or just sheer neglect.

By the year 2000, we should have a good idea of whether or not we will succeed in our long-term task. If we have not put in place sufficient conservation mechanisms by then, it may well be too late. Such mechanisms must include sustainable economic systems, efficient energy use, and a stabilising world population.

The rate of loss of species and habitats is unprecedented in the history of this planet, and unless we are all able to comprehend and embrace the conservation ethic in everyday deeds, then we shall not forestall the looming extinction nightmare. However, we *must* see these times as challenging and exciting, and address the coming years with planning and optimism that ensures this country and our planet will provide a species-rich and healthy environment for centuries to come.

ENDANGERMENT CATEGORIES

The system used throughout this book to describe a species' conservation status is comparatively simple, and partially uses the categories of endangerment employed by the Species Survival Commission (SSC) of the World Conservation Union (WCU) in Switzerland.

The terms used are as follows:

■ ENDANGERED:

These are taxa (species) in danger of extinction and whose survival is unlikely if the causal factors (threats) continue operating.

▨ VULNERABLE:

These taxa (species) are believed likely to move into the 'Endangered' category in the near future if the causal factors (threats) continue operating.

☐ POTENTIALLY VULNERABLE:

This category has been developed by the editor to describe those species that while not currently endangered or vulnerable, are in need of careful research and monitoring to ensure they do not end up in the higher threat categories. They represent the greater number of species in this publication, and are the main indication of the environmental degradation gripping Australia. They may be species that have extremely restricted rainforest distributions, or for whom we have insufficient information to be sure about their status.

Where maps have arrows and black shading, colour denotes former range.

The book highlights a selection of threatened vertebrate species, beginning with the mammals, and proceeding through the birds, reptiles, amphibians and fish. We explain a little about the plight of each, and show you where they are to be found on the Australian continent. A full list of species in trouble is produced in Appendices I, II and IV.

THE THREATENED
Mammals

The large number of mammal species highlighted in the following pages reflects the unpalatable fact that they have been hit the hardest in the 200 years since the arrival of Europeans.

The record of mammal extinctions in Australia is far greater than any other continent or country. We have already lost 18 of our precious mammal species and many more are poised to follow suit. Ten of the original marsupial fauna (7 per cent of the 140 species) have been lost while eight of the rodents (14 per cent of the 58 species) succumbed to similar human-induced pressures.

The bats have not yet been hit by an extinction spasm, but the pressures at play in this modern society are beginning to take their conservation toll. We are only just beginning to understand the important role that bats play in the functioning of many forest ecosystems, pollinating many varieties of flowering plants, and dispersing vast numbers of seeds. All cave-dwelling bats must be considered under threat, and particular concern is now being expressed for our fruit-bats or 'flying fox' species, which are under increasing pressure from forest disturbance, urban sprawl, and persecution by fruit growers.

The marine animals have also yet to suffer a loss of their kind, but this has been by good luck rather than design. Not that you could describe the history of human exploitation of many of these species as good luck. They have suffered immensely through exploitative industries in the past, including sealers and whalers pushing many species to the edge of extinction. The Southern Right and Humpback Whales are only now showing some signs of recovery, and the Australian Sea-lion and Dugong populations remain at a fraction of their former numbers.

There are 123 mammal species listed in this book that are considered to be either endangered, vulnerable, or potentially vulnerable, or nearly half of all Australia's mammalian fauna. We are seeing the gradual depletion of a unique mixture of species, and only recognition of this fact can precipitate the kind of action needed to be taken by us all. There are 65 marsupials, 25 rodents, 18 bats, 14 marine mammals and 1 monotreme that need our help now.

The following represents a selection of those mammals in trouble, and lays clear the known or assumed reason for their decline. It is also an unfortunate truth that many of these species will not receive the direct help they need, for the resources currently available to do so will not suffice. It is necessary therefore to plan conservation actions that will benefit more than one species, and preferably whole ecosystems. Unless this is successfully attempted, many of the species that you will meet in the following pages, may not see out this century.

Previous page. The Brush-tailed Phascogale (Phascogale tapoatafa) has suffered a reduction in its range due primarily to habitat destruction, and has been placed in the potentially vulnerable category.

Leo Meier/ Courtesy Weldon Trannies

Tiger Quoll

M & I Morcombe

PLATYPUS
Ornithorhynchus anatinus

The Platypus is entirely endemic to Australia, to be found nowhere else in the world. Along with the Echidna, its major claim to uniqueness is the amazing capability to lay eggs, the only mammals in the world to do so. Including the Long-beaked Echidna that inhabits the forests of Papua New Guinea and Irian Jaya, these special animals are collectively known as the Monotremes.

The Platypus has also recently been found to employ electrical receptors, as does the Echidna, for detecting its food source of adult and larval invertebrates. Scientists have also been amazed to discover that the species hibernates for long periods.

The animal is distributed all along the eastern seaboard of Australia, from north Queensland to Tasmania, though the range is discontinuous. They can be found in suitable bodies of water within their range, though human population pressures are steadily taking their toll. The Platypus once inhabited parts of South Australia, where it is now extinct, though it has been introduced to Kangaroo Island. The reason for the decline in South Australia is virtually unknown, and investigations are planned to determine the cause.

The Platypus is a solitary animal that has only once been bred in captivity, though many attempts have been made. The Platypus varies significantly in size, those in the south of their range being larger than those in the north. The length varies from 407 to 549 millimetres (measured from tip of beak to tip of tail).

While still common throughout its range, increasing development pressures make the species potentially vulnerable. Human water usage, illegal trapping and industrial pollution will remain the most serious threats. Increased and compatible management of waterways and reserves where the Platypus exists are high priority actions.

POTENTIALLY VULNERABLE

Platypus

HD Millen/NPIAW

KOWARI
Dasyuroides byrnei

The Kowari may be gone from as much as 50 per cent of its original range in the central Australian arid zones. The precise reason for such a decline is uncertain, but habitat destruction through grazing, and predation by the introduced red fox are heavily implicated.

This small carnivorous marsupial is distinguished from its slightly larger relative the Mulgara by a brush of black hairs that completely surround the latter half of the tail. The male Kowari ranges from 140 to 180 millimetres in size with an average tail length between 115 and 120 millimetres. The females are slightly smaller. The Kowari feeds on insects, other small vertebrate species, and also the carrion of much larger animals.

The sparsely vegetated gibber desert regions of south-western Queensland form a major part of the Kowari's remaining range, having become extinct over much of its previously inhabited areas in central Northern Territory and north-eastern South Australia. The Kowari's restricted range, sparse population and dramatic decline, all serve to mark the marsupial as an endangered species, in urgent need of conservation action.

Kowari

Bob Miller/NPIAW

ATHERTON ANTECHINUS
Antechinus godmani

The marsupials in the genus Antechinus are as ferocious as they are small, able to kill other vertebrate species equal their own weight. The Atherton Antechinus is a large antechinus with an average length in the male of 143 millimetres and 122 millimetres for the females, while the long tail can reach 145 millimetres. This small furry mammal has an almost cinnamon rump colour, with rufous belly fur moving to greyish-black on the back.

Once thought to be reasonably common and confused with the Yellow-footed Antechinus, it is restricted to a small area of dense rainforest above 600 metres in elevation, between Cardwell and Innisfail in north Queensland. The Atherton Antechinus has proved to be extremely hard to catch, leaving wildlife managers with little information on its ecology or its precise distribution and abundance. Recent work has shown unusual foraging behaviour, hunting on the forest floor, the tree buttress and stem, and even in the high rainforest canopy itself. The antechinus is also a short lived marsupial, with all the males dying at about 12 months old, immediately after a frenzied mating season in July.

The Atherton Antechinus is the most endangered mammal in tropical Queensland, threatened in part by the cane toad invasions that follow logging activities. It is also considered to be one of the most primitive species of antechinus.

Given the little knowledge available on its ecology, its extremely restricted range (one of the smallest ranges for any Australian mammal – approximately 600 square kilometres) and its fragile rainforest habitat, the species must be considered endangered.

MULGARA
Dasycercus cristicauda

ENDANGERED

The Mulgara is yet another of the central Australian desert mammals that has declined drastically since the arrival of the Europeans. Similar in appearance to the Kowari, being a light sandy brown on the back and greyish-white underneath, it also has a very striking black-haired tail-crest. It ranges in size from 125 to 220 millimetres, with the males at the larger end of the scale, and tails averaging 88 and 100 millimetres in females and males respectively. Like all the small Dasyurids, it is a ferocious hunter often taking insects and other animals as large as itself.

Once widely distributed throughout the central Australian arid regions, encompassing the Northern Territory, Western Australia, South Australia and Queensland, it appears now to be found only in the Northern Territory and Western Australia.

Again, as in the case with its relative the Kowari, the exact reason for the massive loss of range is largely undetermined. So little is known about the species anyway, that scientists and wildlife managers are hard pushed to pinpoint the correct conservation action. This current state of affairs suggests that the species is endangered, demanding intensive ecological research.

CHUDITCH
Dasyurus geoffroii

The Chuditch is also known as the Western Native Cat or Western Quoll, but the former and Aboriginal name is that preferred by wildlife biologists. The Chuditch (a name which refers to its aggressive call) joins a long list of marsupials that has disappeared from most of its former mainland Australian range.

The species used to occur across the southern two thirds of the Australian continent, from Shark Bay in the west, all the way to western New South Wales and Queensland. It is now restricted to the south-west of Western Australia, where its main populations are known to occur in the last broad stands of jarrah forest.

The dramatic loss from almost all of its former range was probably due to changing fire regimes and introduced predators, particularly in the arid zones. In the south-west of Western Australia, that decline was almost certainly precipitated by the loss of large areas of vegetation, with the additional pressure of exotic predators.

The Chuditch is unable to survive in only small pockets of vegetation, and requires continuous forested and perhaps mallee habitat. Similar to other native quolls, the Chuditch can be distinguished by an absence of spots on its 250 millimetre tail, and a first toe on the hindfoot. It is a very efficient

Chuditch

M & I Morcombe

predator, feeding on a great number of small animals, birds, invertebrates and carrion. Averaging 326 millimetres in length, and covered in a thick brown fur dotted with white spots, the adults can weigh greater than 825 grams.

Their conservation situation is precarious, and intensive conservation efforts will be needed to ensure its long-term survival. Improving its endangered status will require the retention of large areas of forest and mallee, combined with research on the effects of fire and logging, and probably captive-breeding programs.

ENDANGERED

ENDANGERED

DIBBLER
Parantechinus apicalis

The Dibbler keeps turning up when least expected! It had previously been unsighted for 83 years, before being rediscovered in 1967, near Cheyne Beach in south-west Western Australia. Since that time, only a few specimens had been recorded, until two other populations were discovered at Fitzgerald River National Park and Torndirrup National Park. Then again in 1988, an amazed wildlife biologist turned up two additional populations on Boullanger Island and Whitlock Island, off the coast of south-west Western Australia. Even so, this still represents a known decline in range of some 90 per cent, having once covered most of south-west Western Australia.

This little marsupial carnivore is approximately 145 millimetres long, with a short, tapered tail averaging 100 millimetres in length. Also aptly known as the Freckled Marsupial Mouse, its brown-grey fur is speckled with white, set against very distinguishable white eye rings.

The Dibbler is a highly endangered species, numbering probably no more than a few hundred animals. It is an insectivorous species that prefers to live in dense coastal heaths, a habitat most prone to be developed. In all probability, the clearing of land, the depravations of introduced predators and inappropriate fire regimes caused such a large contraction in its range.

Dibbler

Babs & Bert Wells/NPIAW

RED-TAILED PHASCOGALE
Phascogale calura

The Red-tailed Phascogale is a very beautiful marsupial. It differs from its near relative, the Brush-tailed Phascogale, by virtue of a very rufous patch at the base of its long, black-brush tipped tail of approximately 144 millimetres. Its general body colour is a rather ash-grey, with a creamy-white underneath. The average head and body length is 113 millimetres for the male and 101 millimetres for the female.

Yet again, we are confronted by an Australian mammal that has experienced a decline of some 90 per cent in range, suffering from clearing of native forests, and predation by cats and foxes. Even as early as the first half of the century the famous naturalist John Gould noted that the only phascogale he had managed to secure in Western Australia had been killed by a domestic cat.

It appears to prefer wandoo and rock oak forest communities in its remaining south-western Western Australia range, and these communities must be protected to help the species endure. These mature vegetation alliances provide the food source for the marsupial, consisting of many invertebrates, small birds and mammals.

Red-tailed Phascogale   J Lochman/NPIAW

The Red-tailed Phascogale was previously patchily distributed throughout southern and central Australia, and is now considered to be highly endangered. Like many of its compatriots, it will be entirely dependent upon the preservation of large tracts of suitable habitat, and the control of foxes and cats.

ENDANGERED

SANDHILL DUNNART
Sminthopsis psammophila

The Sandhill Dunnart is the largest of all the dunnart species, but quite definitely the least observed. Since its discovery in 1894, near Uluru (Ayers Rock) in the Northern Territory, it has proved to be an extremely elusive marsupial. The Sandhill Dunnart was not seen again until 75 years later, only this time much further south, on South Australia's Eyre Peninsula. It is also known from the south-west corner of the Great Victoria Desert and Queen Victoria Spring Nature Reserves in Western Australia, and has now been located in three separate places in the Yellabina sand dunes in South Australia.

This dunnart has a particularly distinctive black pencilling running onto the head ending with a wedge-shaped patch between the eyes, and is otherwise a drab grey colour above. The feet and underside are white with buff-coloured cheeks and flanks. It is distinguished from other dunnarts by a crest of long stiff hairs running the last third of its tail. The species ranges from 91 to 114 millimetres in size, with the tail averaging 120 millimetres.

It is hard to determine the status of an animal that persistently refuses to be trapped by researchers, and when there is virtually no information available on ecological needs. Because our knowledge of the species is so skimpy, and its restricted range, the species must be considered vulnerable to extinction.

VULNERABLE

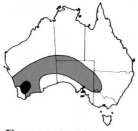

ENDANGERED

NUMBAT
Myrmecobius fasciatus

The Numbat is a fascinating and unique animal. It is the only species in its scientific family, giving the Numbat a very high genetic importance. Once widespread throughout the southern half of Australia from eastern New South Wales, Victoria, southern Northern Territory and central South Australia, it has now contracted to a very small area in south-west Western Australia. This represents a decline of over 90 per cent since the coming of the Europeans.

This most beautiful of marsupials is red-brown above, pale underneath, and has the easily distinguishable set of white bands (six or more) traversing its back. The males range from 202 to 274 millimetres, while the females are slightly smaller at between 210 and 265 millimetres. The average tail length is 178 millimetres. The Numbat's dependence on termites for food contributes further to its restricted habitat availability providing an extra problem for long-term management programs.

The Numbat is a highly endangered species, and its extinction from the greater part of its Australian range has been attributed to massive habitat destruction and degradation, drought, inappropriate fire regimes, and predation by foxes. The species has been the subject of an intensive management and recovery plan by the wildlife authorities in Western Australia over the past several years. The work has included the protection of critical habitats (eucalypt woodlands – wandoo or jarrah forests), captive breeding, and re-introductions and translocations to suitable areas in south-west Western Australia. Such activities must continue well into the future if we are to ensure the species' long-term survival.

Numbat

D Whitford/NPIAW

BILBY
Macrotis lagotis

The Bilby is one of Australia's most highly endangered species, and has often been used by government agencies and conservation organisations to highlight the plight of wildlife species. The Bilby has been lost from probably between 50 and 90 per cent of its former range through the semi-arid regions of Australia, and is extinct in the southern portion of that range.

It is the most unusual looking of all the bandicoot family, with extremely large rabbit-like ears and hind feet, long pale snout, and black and white tail. Its long and amazingly soft blue-grey fur helps impart a fragile and delicate appearance, and you are led to wonder how such an animal could ever survive harsh Australian desert conditions. The Bilby varies in size considerably, from the smallest female of 290 millimetres to the largest male of 550 millimetres, and a tail that can reach a length of 290 millimetres.

Unique among the bandicoots for its ability to construct burrows, the species is omnivorous, eating insects, seeds and fruits etc. Its restricted range includes hummock grasslands and acacia shrublands, including spinifex and tussock grass, and study pro-

Bilby

D Matthews/NPIAW

grams are taking place in Queensland, Western Australia and the Northern Territory.

A variety of influences are thought to have caused the severe reduction in Bilby range and numbers, including vegetation degradation by cattle and rabbits, changes in fire regimes, and the pressures of introduced predators such as the fox. In the Northern Territory great efforts have and are still being made to reintroduce the Bilby to parts of its former range. This project incorporates captive-breeding programs, and is meeting with some success.

ENDANGERED

GOLDEN BANDICOOT
Isoodon auratus

The Golden Bandicoot survives in a range that has been reduced by greater than 90 per cent since the Europeans came to the Australian continent. This immense decline has been attributed to competition from rabbits, predation by foxes and cats, and also the changed fire regimes in the Australian deserts since Aborigines were coaxed onto missionary settlements. These re-occurring causal factors, and their effects on so many of our native mammals, remain for the most part speculative. We can be fairly sure that whatever stresses have been placed upon our wildlife, still continue until this day.

The Golden Bandicoot has a rich golden-brown fur that is pencilled with black, moving to white underneath. Head and body length vary between 190 and 295 millimetres depending upon location, with a maximum tail length of 110 millimetres. Once found inhabiting spinifex and tussock grasslands throughout the arid and semi-arid regions of central, northern and north-western Australia, including Barrow, Middle, and Augustus Islands in Western Australia, it has now been reduced on the mainland to just a small area of the north-west Kimberleys. It can also still be found on Barrow, Middle and Augustus Islands, where it eats invertebrates, turtle eggs and other small animals.

The conservation of the bandicoot will need to include new conservation reserves, captive-breeding and re-introduction programs on the mainland.

ENDANGERED

EASTERN BARRED BANDICOOT
Perameles gunnii

Although the Eastern Barred Bandicoot is still relatively common in Tasmania, the species is highly endangered on the mainland, and has been the subject of an intensive management program.

A very attractive bandicoot, the Eastern Barred has distinctive pale bars across its rump, large ears and a typically elongated bandicoot snout. The species has an average body length of 310 millimetres and average tail length of 94 millimetres, with a slightly smaller average size in Tasmania. The bandicoot's diet consists of earth-dwelling grubs, worms etc, and also selected vegetable materials, including berries and fruits.

It is now restricted to only a fragment of its former range, centred at Hamilton in south-west Victoria, where populations survive in suburban gardens, nearby grasslands and a car dump site. A new captive colony has also been established at Gellibrand in Victoria.

Destruction of its preferred grassland habitat and killing by introduced predators has decimated the mainland population to a point where some biologists believe it may be extinct within 20 years. The Tasmanian population requires further research to properly ascertain its distribution and conservation status, while only continued massive and concerted management (including captive breeding) of the relic Victorian population will ensure the long-term survival of the species.

WESTERN BARRED BANDICOOT
Perameles bougainville

Western Barred Bandicoot   M & I Morcombe

The Western Barred Bandicoot now only survives on Bernier and Dorre Islands off the central coast of Western Australia. These two nature reserves are all that stand between the bandicoot and extinction. Once widespread throughout the semi-arid areas of the southern half of Australia, its extinction on the mainland probably resulted from habitat destruction, competition from rabbits and the assault of foxes.

The bandicoot is identified particularly by its alternating paler and dark stripes across the rump, olive-brown fur above and white below. The average body length is 240 millimetres with a shorter tail of some 90 millimetres. Its habitat on Bernier and Dorre Islands is among sandhills behind beaches, where it feeds in late dusk on insects, roots, herbs, and other small animals.

Its restricted habitat, and the potential for disaster through fire, introduced predator or disease, will always pose a threat to island populations, and steps are being taken to re-introduce the species to the mainland.

M Douglas/NPIAW

Marsupial Mole

MARSUPIAL MOLE
Notoryctes typholops

The Marsupial Mole is one of Australia's most genetically unique and biologically fascinating species.

The mole is blind, has no external ears, has spade-like claws on the fore foot and a heavy shield protecting its snout. The snout is used as an essential burrowing tool, for the mole spends most of its time underground, emerging occasionally to feed on a range of small animals. Its desert range encompasses the arid regions of South Australia, the southern half of the Northern Territory and into the eastern, central and north-west of Western Australia.

The mole reaches a maximum length of 159 millimetres with a short tail extending a further 26 millimetres. Its maximum weight is a mere 70 grams, and it is covered in long, silken sandy-coloured fur.

While the species is apparently common its importance in genetic terms cannot be overstated. We still know virtually nothing of its ecological needs nor about the factors limiting its distribution and abundance. Given the degradation that has affected much of Australia's arid regions, it would be prudent to assume a potential vulnerability and pursue further ecological studies.

POTENTIALLY VULNERABLE

LONG-FOOTED POTOROO
Potorous longipes

The Long-footed Potoroo is a species at the centre of the controversial forestry debate. It is also extremely endangered.

The species is grizzled brown above and grey underneath, and their hind feet are far larger than other potoroos. Its diet is probably similar to that of the Long-nosed Potoroo, which includes grubs, tubers and roots. The species has an average head and body length of approximately 400 millimetres, and a tail of 320 millimetres.

As has occurred with so many species in the last 20 years, the potoroo was only discovered in the late 1970s, with the first live specimens being trapped in 1978, near the town of Bellbird in eastern Gippsland.

Only a very few animals have been collected since then, and it appears to be restricted to an area of only 80 square kilometres of its open forest habitat, that is mostly given over to timber production.

An even more recent discovery, although no animal has yet been sighted, are the signs of the species' presence in the south-east forest of New South Wales Bondi State Forest.

This population is also threatened by commercial forestry activities. While great efforts are being made to conserve and manage the Victorian populations, the authorities in New South Wales appear to be far less sympathetic.

ENDANGERED

ENDANGERED

NORTHERN HAIRY-NOSED WOMBAT
Lasiorhinus krefftii

The Northern Hairy-nosed Wombat is one of Australia's most endangered species. There are only approximately 65 individuals left in the world. These last animals are fully protected in Epping Forest National Park in central Queensland near Clermont. They are the subject of an intensive management program by the Queensland National Parks and Wildlife Service, with support from World Wildlife Fund Australia.

The wombat is a retiring and nocturnal creature, with soft silvery-grey fur, large ears, and as its name suggests, long grey hairs protruding from its nose. The wombat weighs approximately 35 kilograms, is 1000 millimetres in length, and has a tail of some 50 millimetres. Its preferred habitat is acacia and eucalypt woodland and semi-arid grassland, where it lives in burrows, normally on the banks of waterways. Its diet is solely one of grass, which makes the animal very susceptible to droughts and grazing from domestic stock.

The rate of recruitment is critical to the wombat's future, and every effort is being made to ensure the last populations steadily increase. There is little doubt that the decline in population has been caused through habitat destruction and competition from cattle, sheep and rabbits, all of which have been excluded from Epping Forest National Park.

**POTENTALLY
VULNERABLE**

SOUTHERN HAIRY-NOSED WOMBAT
Lasiorhinus latifrons

The Southern Hairy-nosed Wombat is not in the perilous state of his cousin in central Queensland, but nonetheless, has seen its range significantly reduced since the coming of the Europeans. The range in southern South Australia (including the Eyre and Yorke Peninsulas, the Nullarbor Plain and Gawler Ranges) is now very restricted, primarily due to habitat destruction and change, and continual habitat fragmentation. There is also a small population on the Western Australian side of the Nullarbor Plain.

The wombat is smaller than his northern counterpart, ranging from 772 to 934 millimetres, and weighing between 19 and 32 kilograms. The tail can extend from 25 to 60 millimetres. The diet is also different to the Queensland species, consisting of a range of grasses and selected herbs and shrubs, all to be found in its semi-arid environment.

Their decline has been brought about in the manner that has affected so many of our other native mammals, by way of excessive clearing for agriculture, grazing, and the devastating effects of the introduced rabbit. The species is also shot by farmers who believe it causes damage to their properties. The species requires more intensive ecological research and increased management activities.

Southern Hairy-nosed Wombat

Graeme Chapman

BURROWING BETTONG
Bettongia lesueur

The Burrowing Bettong or Boodie had one of the largest mainland distributions of any Australian mammal, covering most of Western Australia, South Australia, the southern half of the Northern Territory and well into New South Wales and Victoria. Today, however, the species is totally extinct on the continent, probably having gone completely by the 1940s. It still survives on a number of Western Australian islands (Barrow, Bernier and Dorre) though is now also extinct on Dirk Hartog and Boodie Islands.

This dramatic decline mirrors the fate of so many of Australia's small marsupial species. The Burrowing Bettong was thought to have suffered due to competition with rabbits for its burrows, predation by cats and foxes, and the results of changed fire regimes.

The species is yellow-grey above and light grey to cream underneath with a lightly haired and fat tail which is considerably shorter than the head and body. Its former wide distribution resulted in a great variation in size, ranging from 215 to 400 millimetres.

Burrowing Bettong

K Johnson/NPIAW

Strictly nocturnal, the Burrowing Bettong emerges from its sometimes extensive burrow system, on rocky island habitat, to feed on seeds, roots, invertebrates and fruits.

The remaining island populations are still endangered, and programs are needed to re-introduce the species to the mainland.

ENDANGERED

TASMANIAN BETTONG
Bettongia gaimardi

The Tasmanian Bettong became extinct in Victoria and South Australia during the first quarter of this century. It had disappeared from New South Wales as early as 1840, and has not been sighted in Queensland since the late 1860s. The probable cause can never be known with certainty, but it seems likely that massive habitat destruction, aided by the rabbit and predation by foxes, helped tip the scales against mainland survival. It had previously ranged from coastal southern Queensland right around coastal south-east Australia to South Australia. Still surviving in eastern Tasmania, where the fox is absent and the rabbit less prevalent, it is nonetheless faced with continued habitat destruction by forestry operations, 1080 poisoning programs and the depravations of wild dogs and cats.

The Tasmanian Bettong has brown-grey fur above, beautifully pencilled with white, while the undersurface is a much paler grey. The tail is long, an average of 326 millimetres, with a head and body length of around 323 millimetres. The bettong's preferred habitat in Tasmania was open grassy plains, but intensive agricultural developments have forced the species to utilise open, dry sclerophyll forests that have grassy understoreys. The diet is primarily one of grasses, roots, other vegetation, and probably small animals.

Prevailing conditions certainly represent a future threat to the bettong's range and abundance, and steps must be taken to monitor its population status.

POTENTIALLY VULNERABLE

ENDANGERED

NORTHERN BRUSH-TAILED BETTONG
Bettongia tropica

There has been considerable debate about the scientific status of this isolated population of bettongs in northern Queensland, with much confusion over whether it should be considered a full species or subspecies. Whatever the agreed outcome, the fact remains that the population is extremely isolated (its relative being found in south-west Western Australia), little known, and extremely important.

The bettong is approximately 400 milli-metres head and body length, with a tail only slightly shorter. There is an urgent need to find out a great deal more about the species' biology and the factors that limit its range and abundance. Highly restricted in its rain-forest habitat on the western edge of the North Queensland Wet Tropics World Heritage area, such a small and localised population is vulnerable to both natural and man-made perturbations, which renders it endangered.

POTENTIALLY VULNERABLE

MUSKY RAT-KANGAROO
Hypsiprymnodon moschatus

The Musky Rat-kangaroo is both the smallest and most primitive of all the macropod species. It is also one of the least known, with an extremely restricted rain-forest range and sparse population. These attributes combined, serve to make the species potentially vulnerable to both natural and man-made disturbances.

On the positive side, the entire range of the animal appears to be within the North Queensland Wet Tropics World Heritage area, now protected from logging and other development activities. The precise range of the rat-kangaroo is thought to cover an area of only 320 kilometres by 65 kilometres, near Cooktown in north Queensland.

The Musky Rat-kangaroo has rich brown fur that turns to grey-brown on the head, and is a mere 231 millimetres average length, plus a tail of approximately 140 millimetres. The species feeds mainly on rainforest fruits and invertebrates. As with other rat-kangaroos, it regularly gives birth to twins.

We still need to find out a lot more about its social habits and ecological requirements, in an effort to secure its long-term future.

POTENTIALLY VULNERABLE

LUMHOLTZ'S TREE-KANGAROO
Dendrolagus lumholtzi

The Lumholtz's Tree-kangaroo is slightly smaller than its close relative Bennett's Tree-kangaroo, and while it also inhabits the rainforest of north Queensland, the ranges of the two species do not appear to overlap. Its coastal rainforest habitat is to be found at altitudes of over 300 metres, between Ingham and Mossman, and within the confines of the North Queensland Wet Tropics World Heritage area.

The females are considerably smaller than the males, averaging 480 and 555 milli-metres respectively, with a tail length of approximately 700 millimetres. Lumholtz's Tree-kangaroo is a nocturnal and normally solitary animal, a clumsy but efficient climber, and feeds on a variety of rainforest leaves and fruit. Both the sexes are similar in colour, with a dark face and muzzle, surrounded by a light grey band on the forehead and sides of the face. Its blackish-brown back turns lighter on the lower part of the back and very pale grey underneath.

This spectacular animal has lost much of its preferred habitat through extensive clear-ing of lowland rainforest, and its resultant restricted range and rarity leaves it poten-tially vulnerable to a variety of pressures.

SPECTACLED HARE-WALLABY
Lagorchestes conspicillatus

POTENTIALLY VULNERABLE

The Spectacled Hare-wallaby is one of many Australian marsupials that also has secure island populations, in this case Barrow Island in northern Western Australia. The species has experienced a substantial decline, formerly inhabiting most of the northern arid and semi-arid parts of Australia from the Pilbara in Western Australia right through to northern and central Queensland. It is now very rare in the Pilbara district and has all but disappeared from the Great Sandy Desert and the south-eastern parts of its range in the Northern Territory. This decline probably occurred due to the effects of feral cats and foxes, degradation of habitats by and competition with rabbits, and changed fire regimes.

The wallaby is one of the most attractive of the family of hare-wallabies with a particularly distinctive bright orange ring surrounding the eyes. The body colour is brown to rufous above and pale below and its feet are pale grey-brown. Weighing between 1.6 to 4.5 kilograms and with a head and body length of approximately 435 millimetres and the tail the same again, its small size makes this wallaby particularly susceptible to predation by foxes and cats.

Living in spinifex, hummock and tussock grasslands, forest, wood and shrub lands throughout its northern range, the animal feeds on the same species that provides its cover. The drastic decline in its range and the continuing clearance of vital habitats pose a threat to this species' future and stable conservation status.

Spectacled Hare-wallaby

H & J Beste/NPIAW

BENNETT'S TREE-KANGAROO
Dendrolagus bennettianus

POTENTIALLY VULNERABLE

The tree-kangaroos are among some of Australia's most unusual and beautiful marsupials. One of two Australian species, Bennett's Tree-kangaroo still remains relatively unknown in a biological and ecological sense.

This aboreal animal is known to make the occasional foray to the forest floor, and has been observed making leaps of 18 metres from tree tops to ground. This species has an overall dark brown fur, with a greyish tinge around its head and shoulders, and easily distinguishable black fore and hindfeet.

The male tree-kangaroo is approximately 650 millimetres in length, with the females considerably smaller, and a long tail that can reach 940 millimetres.

Confined to a restricted belt of highland and lowland rainforest in north Queensland, where it feeds on leaves and fruit, the species is rare and sparsely distributed. Its current range is situated within the North Queensland Wet Tropics World Heritage area, approximately between Mossman and Cooktown, though the species remains potentially vulnerable.

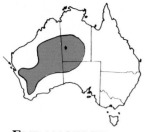

ENDANGERED

RUFOUS HARE-WALLABY
Lagorchestes hirsutus

The Rufous Hare-wallaby is another of the marsupial species that has suffered a greater than 90 per cent decline in its mainland range, and remains highly endangered. It is also a species that has found some but not assured security on Western Australian islands (Bernier and Dorre). Until recently, there were two remaining and isolated populations in the Tanami Desert in the Northern Territory, but one colony was completely wiped out by what was thought to be a single fox. Needless to say this was a great blow to the conservation efforts of the Northern Territory Government. The remaining colony consists of approximately 30 animals.

The species once occupied greater than 25 per cent of continental Australia. This vast area took in much of the arid and semi-arid lands from the Western Australian wheat-belt, extending east and north to eastern central Northern Territory and south to the north of South Australia. Spinifex hummock grasslands were its preferred habitat in the sand plain and sand-dune deserts throughout its former range. The major reasons for the dramatic loss of range and populations have been ascribed to the changing fire regimes that resulted when Aborigines were moved on to missionary settlements. The fires they frequently lit provided ideal vegetation mosaics that benefited arid-zone mammal species, including the Rufous Hare-wallaby. Then the fox began to take its deadly toll.

The wallaby averages 330 millimetres in length in the males and 375 millimetres in the females, with an approximate tail length of 275 millimetres.

As its name suggests, the species is rufous above and paler below with long, soft fur, and a head that is dark rufous in the Tanami population. Digging short burrows to protect themselves from the heat of the day, they feed on spinifex seeds, perennial shrubs and sedges.

Concerted efforts by governments and conservation groups are continuing to save the mainland population from extinction.

ENDANGERED

BANDED HARE-WALLABY
Lagostrophus fasciatus

The Banded Hare-wallaby is yet another species that has completely disappeared from the mainland of Australia. It survives only on Bernier and Dorre Islands off the coast of Western Australia. It has also been lost from Dirk Hartog Island. These islands have now become crucial conservation zones for some of Australia's most highly endangered species.

As its name implies, the wallaby has quite distinctive black and white bands across its rump, set against a grizzled-grey back and pale undersides. Head and body length average around 430 millimetres with a tail extending a further 370 millimetres.

On Bernier and Dorre Islands, the wallaby inhabits dense acacia scrub in which it shelters during the day, emerging at night to feed on grasses, scrubs and other plants. The loss of its previous mainland range (and Dirk Hartog Island), stretching from Shark Bay in Western Australia down the coast to the southern shorelines of the State, is thought to have been due to predation by cats, and competition from rabbits. Efforts are now underway to re-introduce the species to Dirk Hartog Island and the mainland.

Banded Hare-wallaby   G Robertson/NPIAW

C Andrew Henley/NPIAW

Bridled Nailtail Wallaby

BRIDLED NAILTAIL WALLABY
Onychogalea fraenata

There are three species of Nailtail Wallabies. The Bridled Nailtail is endangered, the Crescent Nailtail is extinct, and the Northern Nailtail is apparently stable. Reduced to less than 10 per cent of its former range, the Bridled Nailtail was once thought extinct, until a population was discovered near the town of Dingo, in central Queensland, in 1973. The species is now found solely on Tauntan Scientific Reserve, declared specifically for the wallaby's protection. It is also closely managed by the Queensland National Parks and Wildlife Service.

The Bridled Nailtail is one of the most beautiful of Australia's wallaby species. The white 'bridle' line running from the centre of the neck down to the side of the body is clearly identifiable. Male wallabies can attain a length of some 700 millimetres, while females have a maximum size of approximately 540 millimetres. The tail, which has a distinguishing and horny pointed 'nail' at the tip, measures up to 540 millimetres in the male.

Once common on the slopes and plains of the western side of the Great Dividing Range, all the way south to the extreme eastern parts of South Australia, its decline has been dramatic. The probable causes stem from the effects of the pastoral industry and resultant habitat destruction, competition with rabbits and perhaps through predation by introduced carnivores. The species' preferred habitat appears to be brigalow scrub, open grassy woodland and eucalypt forest, where it normally grazes.

ENDANGERED

43

POTENTIALLY VULNERABLE

PARMA WALLABY
Macropus parma

The Parma Wallaby provides good stories for the telling. Once thought to be extinct in Australia, not having been seen for some 50 years, it was rediscovered in forests near Gosford in New South Wales in 1967. Previous to this date great efforts were being

J McCann/NPIAW

Parma Wallaby

made to translocate animals, that had been found thriving on Kawau Island in New Zealand, to Australia. The hope was to arrange a successful repopulation program. The species had been taken to Kawau Island almost a century before, and had since become a forestry pest. Those efforts became misplaced after the 1967 rediscovery, and still further populations were found on the northern coast of New South Wales. More recently, an ambitious re-introduction program had attempted to put the Parma Wallaby back into areas formally inhabited in the south of the State, but tragically foxes killed all the released animals.

The species range remains limited to high rainfall areas of New South Wales, on the eastern side (coastal belt) of the Great Dividing Range. The wallaby prefers wet sclerophyll forest with a scrubby understorey, and is primarily nocturnal, feeding on grasses and herbs. The species is generally greyish-brown above with a white throat and chest, measuring a maximum 528 millimetres in males and 527 millimetres in females. The tail is about the same length again with 50 per cent of animals having a white tip.

Its restricted range, the continuing pressures on its forest habitat, and its susceptibility to predation by foxes, make this wallaby potentially vulnerable to extinction.

VULNERABLE

BRUSH-TAILED ROCK-WALLABY
Petrogale penicillata

The Brush-tailed Rock-wallaby inhabits suitable rocky areas in the sclerophyll forests of south-eastern Australia, where it feeds on grasses and herbs.

A very attractive animal, the species has a light coloured cheek stripe and a black dorsal stripe from behind the eyes to the back of the head. Brown above moving to rufous on the rump, it has a long tail averaging 601 millimetres and has the distinctive brush at its terminus. The male rock-wallaby averages 540 millimetres head and body, with the female slightly smaller at 500 millimetres.

Current distribution extends up to Rockhampton in Queensland, and down to The Grampians in the south. The species' range has been severely reduced in western and southern New South Wales, and in Victoria, where the populations are considered to be endangered. The major causes of decline are competition with feral goats, sheep and rabbits, and hunting pressure from the European fox.

The species is considered to be vulnerable, and requires further ecological studies and careful management.

YELLOW-FOOTED ROCK-WALLABY
Petrogale xanthopus

The Yellow-footed Rock-wallaby is a very beautiful animal that frequents rocky outcrops in dry country, often in association with permanent fresh water, and a dominant vegetation of mulga scrub. Here the species feeds on grasses and herbs, tubers, bark and foliage.

The largest of the rock-wallabies, it reaches a length of 650 millimetres in males, with a strikingly yellow and brown ringed tail, 690 millimetres in length. It has a brilliantly ornamented long, soft and silky coat, with a beautiful white muzzle stripe, a dark brown dorsal stripe from its crown to mid back and a white stripe from the back of the shoulder down to the hip.

In the early days of European settlement the beauty of the animal attracted the hunter's gun and it wasn't long before sizeable shipments of skins were heading for England. However, the pressures of trade were not those that would eventually cause significant decline in its range. Extensive competition from feral goat populations, habitat destruction, competition with grazing stock and possible predation by foxes and cats, have now threatened the species' survival, especially in New South Wales and Queensland.

Once found extensively in the Flinders and other ranges in South Australia, extending through the north-west corner

Yellow-footed Rock-wallaby

A Fox/Auscape

of New South Wales into south-western Queensland, the species is now only found in any significant numbers in South Australia. Considered to be potentially vulnerable to extinction, the species requires strong protection in its remaining colonies, and long-term management plans to be implemented.

POTENTIALLY VULNERABLE

PROSERPINE ROCK-WALLABY
Petrogale persephone

The Proserpine Rock-wallaby is truly one of the most amazing wildlife discoveries of this century. Secluded and completely hidden to the world in its rainforest habitat, near the central Queensland town of Proserpine, the first animal was not collected until 1976! It had previously been known to members of the Proserpine branch of the Wildlife Preservation Society of Queensland. How the species had managed to stay undiscovered for so long is a mystery in itself.

Closely related to the Yellow-footed Rock-wallaby, the species measures between 520 and 640 millimetres with a maximum tail length of 680 millimetres. It is a dark grey rock-wallaby with black feet and a white tip to its tail.

Only a few animals have been collected to date, and combined with its extremely restricted range, and our scant knowledge of its conservation requirements, it must be regarded as an endangered species.

ENDANGERED

EXTINCT

CRESCENT NAILTAIL WALLABY
Onychogalea lunata

The Crescent Nailtail Wallaby was an extremely attractive animal, with thick ash-grey silky fur, matched against rich rufous colouring on the back and sides of the neck. It had pale, crescent-shaped markings on the shoulders, with similar coloured shading over the eyes, cheeks and hips, and a clearly defined dark stripe running down its back. It was not unlike its extant but endangered cousin, the Bridled Nailtail Wallaby, with the horny tail-tip common to the genus.

The wallaby was once widespread from south-west Western Australia, across central and eastern parts of that state, into the central ranges of the Northern Territory and north South Australia. Its habitat was thickets in eucalypt and mulga woodlands.

The species has not been positively recorded in Australia since the 1930s. The reasons for the species' decline are only speculative but it seems probable that drastic changes to its preferred habitat through the introduction of domestic grazing stock and rabbits, predation by foxes and the effects of persecution by farmers, combined to ensure the wallaby's demise.

The species was reported to have been seen in the Northern Territory in 1957 and a dead animal, supposedly killed by a fox was found near Warburton, Western Australia in 1964. It is possible the wallaby survived into the late 1950s and while the species is now presumed extinct, it may still survive somewhere in the central deserts.

POTENTIALLY VULNERABLE

LEMUROID RINGTAIL POSSUM
Hemibelideus lemuroides

The Lemuroid Ringtail Possum appears to be the most sensitive of all rainforest possums to canopy disturbance and fragmentation of its rainforest habitat. This unfortunate fact may help biologists determine better the overall effects of rainforest destruction.

This aboreal and nocturnal possum has a long bushy tail averaging 355 millimetres, that ends in a finger-like bare tip. It has a thick fur coat, woolly grey above moving to a yellowish tinge underneath, with an average head and body length of approximately 330 millimetres.

Its rainforest haunts are to be found above the altitude of 450 metres between approximately Cardwell and Mossman in north Queensland. Its range is inside the boundaries of the North Queensland Wet Tropics World Heritage area. This extremely agile animal feeds almost exclusively on a wide range of leaves.

Given the further studies needed into population dynamics of the possum, its restricted rainforest range, and its susceptibility to disturbance, it must be considered as potentially vulnerable.

Lemuroid Ringtail Possum

Frithfoto/Olympus

CENTRAL AUSTRALIAN BRUSHTAIL POSSUM
Trichosurus vulpecula

ENDANGERED

It may come as a surprise to find an 'endangered' tag assigned to the Brushtail Possum that we all know so well. Often thought of as a pest in the suburbs of cities in eastern States, the species is nonetheless in some trouble in central Australia. Taking the entire range of the possum into account, the dramatic reduction of populations in central Australia, where only six animals have been observed in recent years, represents a national decline of perhaps some 25 per cent. Biologists believe that a rapid decline took place in the 1930s, and that this is still continuing.

It is rare in its extremely restricted range in the central deserts, and appears confined to isolated populations along watercourses and in sheltered gullies. Determining the cause of the decline becomes a major goal for researchers and managers. Part of the recovery plan procedures include the re-introduction of the species into parts of their former range in central Australia, including Uluru (Ayers Rock) National Park.

H & J Beste/NPIAW
Herbert River Ringtail Possum

HERBERT RIVER RINGTAIL POSSUM
Pseudocheirus herbertensis

POTENTIALLY VULNERABLE

The Herbert River Ringtail Possum is another species that has an extremely restricted rainforest distribution in the north of Queensland. There are two subspecies of possum that differ markedly in fur colour.

The Herbert River Ringtail Possum has an almost black body, contrasted by a prominent white chest and belly, with a long tapered tail. Head and body length average 349 millimetres with a tail that is slightly longer. Living at an altitude in excess of 300 metres in dense rainforest between the towns of Ingham and Cairns in north Queensland, it rarely ventures to the ground, feeding in the canopy on a diet of rainforest tree leaves.

The species' potential vulnerability stems from its restricted habitat, and the need for information on ecological requirements.

DAINTREE RIVER RINGTAIL POSSUM
Pseudocheirus herbertensis cinereus

The Daintree River Ringtail Possum is the northern subspecies of the Herbert River Ringtail Possum described previously. Though both are restricted to a tiny portion of the northern tropical rainforests, their ranges never overlap.

This possum is found between about Mossman and Bloomfield in north Queensland, in rainforest above 500 metres in elevation. Most of its distribution is contained within State forests and national parks of the North Queensland Wet Tropics World Heritage area. Its size and habits are similar to its southern relation, though the species colouration is not. The Daintree River Ringtail Possum has a much lighter, pale fawn fur, with a longitudinal dark stripe on its head. This species is also thought to be potentially vulnerable due to its restricted rainforest habitat and little known ecology.

M & I Morcombe

Green Ringtail Possum

GREEN RINGTAIL POSSUM
Pseudocheirus archeri

Confined to dense upland rainforest, above 300 metres in elevation, the Green Ringtail Possum is a remarkably beautiful animal, with a truly distinctive 'green' fur. Combined with distinguishing white patches below the eyes and ears, and two silvery stripes running down its crown and back, it presents a most striking appearance. The possum has an average head and body length of 364 millimetres, with a slightly shorter white-tipped tail that is broad at the base.

The Green Ringtail lives mostly on a diet of leaves, and avoids descending to the forest floor, only doing so to breach gaps between trees. Its preferred rainforest habitat seems fairly secure in the North Queensland, Wet Tropic World Heritage area, and can also withstand a certain amount of forest disturbance. Nonetheless, its restricted range, around Mossman in north Queensland, and the need to determine more about the species' ecological requirements, suggests that the species should still be considered potentially vulnerable.

YELLOW-BELLIED GLIDER
Petaurus australis

The Yellow-bellied Glider is the largest of the gliders. It is heavily dependent on tall, mature eucalypt forests, both temperate and subtropical, of eastern Australia. Its range stretches from just south of Mackay in central Queensland, down the east coast and into the extreme edge of western Victoria. There is also an isolated population on the edge of the North Queensland Wet Tropics World Heritage area, between Ingham and Mossman.

This latter population is considered vulnerable due to past timber extraction operations. The southern populations are considered to be potentially vulnerable, due to their patchy distribution, the past effects of serious bushfires (Ash Wednesday in 1983) and the continuing commercial pressures upon mature forests in the south-east. These essential forests provide the glider with a varied diet of insects, nectar, and pollen, and the sap of eucalypts, obtained by biting patches of tree trunk.

The coat of the Yellow-bellied Glider is quite variable, with long, fluffy fur ranging from dusky-brown to grey on its back, and creamy-white to yellow underneath. Attached to the wrist and ankle is the skin membrane, used for spectacular feats of gliding, helped by a long bushy tail which averages 433 millimetres.

Many more forest reserves need to be set aside for this species, and further research work is required to determine the on-going effects of forestry practices.

Yellow-bellied Glider

R Whitford/NPIAW

POTENTIALLY VULNERABLE

WESTERN RINGTAIL POSSUM
Pseudocheirus occidentalis

As in the case of the Central Australian Brushtail Possum, people little expect to see a tag of 'endangered' associated with the Ringtail Possum. Although the Ringtail is widely distributed around the country one particular population is now in considerable conservation trouble.

The Western Australian subspecies is considered endangered by biologists, a state of affairs they think was brought about by the combined effects of predation by foxes, inappropriate fire regimes, and the continued fragmentation of its forest habitats through agricultural expansion.

The species appears to prefer peppermint gums, but also paperbark forests and eucalypt woodlands.

The species is also rare within its Cape York range, though the precise reasons are unknown. The Western Australian population requires urgent study and positive conservation action.

ENDANGERED

ENDANGERED

LEADBEATER'S POSSUM
Gymnobelideus leadbeateri

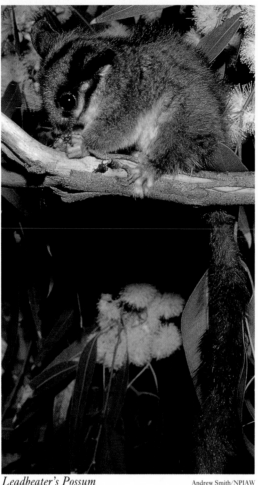

Leadbeater's Possum   Andrew Smith/NPIAW

With a prominent dark dorsal stripe running the length of its back, and set against a soft grey-brown fur, Leadbeater's Possum is an extremely attractive and highly endangered mammal. Its length ranges between 150 and 170 millimetres, while its distinguished bushy tail, which is broader and black at its tip, averages 172 millimetres. It requires mature trees that provide both nesting holes and sufficient food of insects and gum.

The possum has been the topic of some controversy. Its known and extremely restricted range is entirely within mountain ash forests in Victoria's central highlands, forests that are destined to be completely logged. Unless appropriate reserves are set aside for this species and forestry practices are altered accordingly, the possum could decline to minimal numbers and, in fragmented populations, be unable to survive.

Victoria now has in place a Flora and Fauna Guarantee Act, which theoretically ensures the protection of threatened species such as Leadbeater's Possum, and it remains to be seen whether the law can now save this species from extinction.

ENDANGERED

MOUNTAIN PYGMY-POSSUM
Burramys parvus

The Mountain Pygmy-possum is the only Australian mammal species that is restricted to alpine and sub-alpine regions. It occurs on both the Victorian and New South Wales sides of the border. The first specimen was not discovered until 1966, where it was collected in a ski hut on Mount Hotham in Victoria. There are at least four small sub-populations at Mount Kosciusko, Mount Bogong, Bogong High Plains and Mounts Lock and Higginbotham, with an estimated breeding population of some 2,300 animals.

This small marsupial (though largest of the pygmy-possums) attains a length in the region of 100 to 115 millimetres, with the tail extending a further 140 millimetres or so. It has grey-brown, dense fur above, but lighter grey to cream below, depending on the population location.

Its high altitude habitat of low scrubs and grasses is covered in snow for at least three months of the year, during which times it survives among boulders. The possum eats fruits, seeds, vegetable matter and insects, with a particular fondness for Bogong moths. Its extremely restricted alpine habitat has suffered destruction at the most densely populated areas, due to the development of ski resorts.

Efforts have been made by the Victorian wildlife authorities to alleviate pressure on fragmented populations by building a 'tunnel of love' under the road at Mount Hotham permitting proper social organisation. Coupled with the potential for further and serious loss of habitat through the greenhouse effect, the species must be considered endangered.

M & I Morcombe

Honey-possum

HONEY-POSSUM
Tarsipes rostratus

The Honey-possum is one of our smallest marsupials ranging between 40 and 98 millimetres with a long prehensile tail measuring as much again. Its uniquely adapted and almost trunk-like snout is used (in combination with a long brush-like tongue) for extracting nectar and pollen from banksias and other flowers. It has light brown to grey fur above, with a prominent central dark stripe running down its back, flanked by paler bands.

The Honey-possum lives in the south-west of Western Australia, where it is dependent upon very fragile and increasingly fragmented sandplain heathland habitat. Susceptible to inappropriate fire regimes and the depravations of foxes and cats, the species is potentially vulnerable.

POTENTIALLY VULNERABLE

G Schick/NPIAW

KOALA
Phascolarctos cinereus

POTENTIALLY VULNERABLE

It is thought that when the Europeans first came to Australia that Koala populations gained some benefit from their presence. The theory is that the species was released from earlier hunting pressures by Aborigines. However, it was not to be long before this situation changed quite dramatically.

Both the Koala's habitat and its skin were eagerly sought by an ever increasing human population. In the 1920s and 1930s millions of koala skins found their way onto the export market, and concern soon spread about the species' conservation status. While the trade was to eventually come to an end, the continuing and massive habitat destruction did not. Primarily for this reason the Koala has disappeared from greater than 50 per cent of its original range. This habitat contraction and fragmentation is believed to

have caused the rise in the occurrence of the disease *Chlamydia*, a matter of serious conservation concern.

The Koala varies significantly in size, those in the south of their range (once extending from the south-east tip of South Australia through central and coastal Victoria, New South Wales and as far as north Queensland) being much larger than those in the north. Victoria's Koalas can reach a length of 782 millimetres and weigh up to nearly 12 kilograms.

The species remains potentially vulnerable to extinction. Retention and restoration of the Koala's open forest and woodland habitat are the essential ingredients for its long-term survival, especially given that the species feeds predominantly on a restricted range of eucalypt leaves.

EXTINCT

THYLACINE OR TASMANIAN TIGER
Thylacinus cynocephalus

Next to the Koala the Thylacine is Australia's most celebrated animal. The last captive Thylacine died in Hobart Zoo in 1936 but since that time there have been numerous but uncollaborated sightings from many parts of Tasmania. Regular reports are also received of sightings on the mainland, particularly in Western Australia.

The Thylacine was once found throughout mainland Australia and New Guinea. Biologists believe that it became extinct in these regions perhaps two to three thousand years ago primarily due to competition with the dingo. The animal survived in Tasmania when rising seas caused separation from the mainland some 12,000 years ago, where it was able to thrive in the absence of dingos.

The Thylacine, or 'Tasmanian Wolf' as it was once known, was our largest modern marsupial carnivore. It was indeed wolf-like in appearance stemming from the shape of its head and forequarters and very 'canine' teeth. Over a metre in length the Thylacine had sandy-brown coarse hair, marked with the highly distinguishable broad dark bands across its back which lead to its European 'tiger' tag. Preying primarily on kangaroos and wallabies the species utilised open forests and woodlands across the majority of the island state.

The Thylacine's demise has been attributable mainly to intensive destruction programs instigated by the pastoral industry concerned over stock losses and supported officially by the Tasmanian Government. Some scientists believe that this persecution alone could not have accounted for the species' extinction and speculate that a disease epidemic that had earlier afflicted the Tasmanian Devil may be implicated.

Great efforts have been made by individuals, organisations and governments over the past decade to try to prove the Tasmanian Tiger still exists, but all to no avail – so far! Many remain convinced that the animal still lurks secretively in untouched forest areas. If the tiger ever emerges again it will be the greatest wildlife 'rediscovery' of the century.

CENTRAL ROCK-RAT
Zyzomys pedunculatus

Like some species of lizards, the Central Rock-rat is reputed to have the ability to lose part of its tail if frightened, though the species is so rare, we may never know for certain. First collected in 1896 in central Australia, it has been recorded on only five occasions since, the last time being in 1960. This makes the Central Rock-rat one of Australia's most elusive rodents, a true mammalian mystery.

Its known range centres on the Macdonnell Ranges, Reynolds Range and Davenport Range, around Alice Springs in the Northern Territory. Its assumed preferred habitat are the rocky ranges in these arid zones, where the predominant vegetation is sparse low shrubs and trees, sparse grasses and perhaps spinifex.

The Central Rock-rat has very soft, yellow-brown fur above, ranging from cream to white below, and is particularly distinguished by its swollen tail, common to all species in its genus. Head and body length have been recorded at a maximum of 140 millimetres with a hairy tail reaching the same length again.

It has not been possible to determine the reasons for the species' rarity; whether it was human induced or a natural phenomena. In any event, it remains one of our most rare and vulnerable species and if rediscovered must be given the fullest protection.

ENDANGERED

VULNERABLE

HEATH RAT
Pseudomys shortridgei

The Heath Rat was first known to exist in the south-west corner of Western Australia, but has not been seen since 1906, and was therefore presumed to be extinct. But in 1961, it joined the ranks of many other 'rediscovered' Australian species, when a population was identified in western Victoria. The species inhabits heath scrublands in The Grampians and is uniquely adapted to life in these fragile habitats.

The Heath Rat is entirely dependent upon fire regimes which produce the environmental variables needed for its existence. It colonises patches that are regenerating after fire, where it feeds on flowers, seeds and berries, switching to less digestible grasses as the preferred food source disappears. It is a large animal with grizzled, grey-brown fur above, and much paler colouring below, reaching a head and body length of 120 millimetres maximum. The short tail is hairy, a maximum of 95 millimetres, dark above and lighter below.

Heathlands have always been among the first habitats to be extensively cleared by human development, and even today such habitats are under extreme pressure. The fire regimes that the animal depends upon have also changed drastically since European occupation. These factors continue to be a threat to the species which is considered to be highly vulnerable.

VULNERABLE

FALSE WATER-RAT
Xeromys myoides

The False Water-rat inhabits tropical coastlines in southern Queensland and the top end of the Northern Territory, where it prefers tidal mangroves and grassy swamps, areas where shallow water can be found. Very few animals have been collected since it was first discovered in the late nineteenth century, and most of those within the last 20 years. Its restricted range and apparent rarity is thought by some to be a simple reflection of insufficient searching, though its coastal habitats are under pressure from developments of all kinds.

The species has short, slate-grey fur, white underneath, short ears, small eyes, and a long smooth tail ranging from 93 to 99 millimetres. Head and body length range between 115 and 127 millimetres. It had always been assumed this little carnivore preyed on crabs and in the early 1980s biologists finally observed this. The animal deftly dismembered the crab's claws, and then proceeded to bite each leg off, before turning it over and devouring it almost completely.

Habitat degradation, clearing and disturbance all pose potential threats to the False Water-rat, and its vulnerability must be accounted for.

False Water-rat

H & J Beste/NPIAW

C Kemper/NPIAW

GOLDEN-BACKED TREE-RAT
Mesembriomys macrurus

This tropical rodent is a very distinguishable animal. It has an orange-brown stripe running down the length of its back (head and body length averages 220 millimetres), contrasting against an overall grey fur. Its long tail, which averages 315 millimetres, is white for the last two thirds terminating in a white brush. It is thought to eat vegetable matter and insects, though not a great deal is known about its biology.

It is a coastal tree dweller that has been lost from a large part of its former range, which extended from the Kimberleys in the west to the eastern top end of the Northern Territory. The species can be found in a variety of habitats, from eucalypt woodlands with tussock grass understorey, to coastal beaches and mangrove swamps. It has not been seen in the Northern Territory since 1969, and is generally sparsely distributed.

While some populations are secure in national parks and uninhabited islands, its loss of range and sparse distribution suggest that it should be monitored carefully.

POTENTIALLY VULNERABLE

PREHENSILE-TAILED RAT
Pogonomys mollipilosus

This little known species inhabits the rainforests of north-east Queensland, and the tip of Cape York Peninsula. The long tail which measures up to 208 millimetres is used as its name implies, to grip onto twigs and branches as it forages for leaves and nuts. It has soft, brown-grey fur above changing to pure white below, and has a distinguishing narrow black eye ring. Head and body length reaches a maximum of 138 millimetres.

This rodent has only been collected a few times since it was first discovered in Australia in 1974, when it was brought to Lake Barrine tourist lodge on the Atherton Tableland, by a domestic cat. All that is known about the species' biology is derived from observations of the species in its Papua New Guinean habitat. Given its apparent rarity, restricted rainforest locations, and our paucity of knowledge regarding its ecological needs, it must be regarded as potentially vulnerable.

POTENTIALLY VULNERABLE

Babs & Bert Wells/NPIAW

Shark Bay Mouse

SHARK BAY MOUSE
Pseudomys praeconis

VULNERABLE

The Shark Bay Mouse was first discovered on the Peron Peninsula, Shark Bay, Western Australia in 1858. Since that time no other animal has been seen on the mainland, and survives only on Bernier Island off the central Western Australian coast. Only a few specimens were recorded on Bernier Island between the turn of the century and 1975, when a number of animals were caught by wildlife biologists.

The Shark Bay Mouse is fairly small, attaining a maximum length of 115 milli-metres, with the fully furred tail extending a further 125 millimetres. It has a long shaggy coat that is grizzled, dark brown above, graduating to white on the underside, with large ears and eyes. Inhabiting coastal dune vegetation, it burrows underneath spinifex tussocks, and feeds mainly on flowers such as daisies.

The species may yet be rediscovered on the mainland, but until that time, its restricted distribution on one offshore island dictates its vulnerability.

SMOKY MOUSE
Pseudomys fumeus

ENDANGERED

The distribution of the Smoky Mouse has contracted considerably in the last 200 years. Once occurring in south-east New South Wales, and more extensively throughout eastern Victoria, it is now confined to heathlands and dry forest in The Grampians, and the coastal woodlands of eastern Gipps-land including some protected areas.

The mouse has long, soft, smoky-grey fur becoming greyish-white below. The ears are distinctly purple, while the feet are pink with white fur. The species has an average body length of 90 millimetres and a tail of 140 millimetres.

It is a species that has specific ecological requirements in its restricted fire generated habitat, relying on seeds of shrubby legumes, berries and Bogong moths in summer, and a winter survival strategy that involves eating underground fungi.

It is necessary therefore to be able to manage habitats to improve the species' conservation chances, but this also neces-sitates securing appropriate protected areas. Until this can occur, the species remains highly vulnerable to extinction.

HASTINGS RIVER MOUSE
Pseudomys oralis

The Hastings River Mouse was first described by scientists in 1921, after its initial collection in the 1840s with one specimen being labelled 'Hastings River, New South Wales'. The species was not seen again until 1969, when a third animal was trapped near Warwick in Queensland, a long way from the Hastings River.

In more recent years, a number of mice have been located from the upper Hastings River, and an area near Dorrigo in New South Wales. The population from the upper Hastings River is now apparently secure in a national park, while other populations are generally scattered about the northern tablelands of New South Wales.

Its preferred habitat seems to be in open forest, near creek banks with bracken and grass ground vegetation. The Hastings River Mouse has a head and body length extending to a maximum 170 millimetres with a slightly shorter tail. It is covered in soft, brown-grey fur that turns to greyish-white underneath, with distinctly white feet and protruding eyes.

Despite the recently identified locations of this mouse it must be regarded as vulnerable.

VULNERABLE

GREATER STICK-NEST RAT
Leporillus conditor

Once found across the entire southern half of the Australian continent from Shark Bay in the west, extending to the extreme north-west corner of Victoria and western portions of New South Wales, the Greater Stick-nest Rat has not been seen on the mainland since 1933.

The causes of such a drastic decline are, as with so many Australian mammal species, fairly speculative, but probably accurate. Competition and habitat destruction from introduced grazing animals and rabbits, severe effects of drought and fire regimes altered by European presence, and in later years, the final straw of predation by an alien carnivore, the fox.

Remaining only on the Franklin Islands off the coast of South Australia there are perhaps no more than 1,000 Greater Stick-nest Rats still surviving. Its habitat is found in semi-arid/arid areas consisting of low shrubland and shrub steppe, where it builds large above-ground nests from sticks, nests that can be as much as 1 metre high and 1.5 metres in diameter.

The species is entirely herbivorous, preferring the leaves and fruits of succulent plants. It is a large animal, that can reach 260 millimetres, not including the furred 170 millimetre tail. It is distinguished by large ears and eyes, and fine, soft, yellowish-brown fur above, changing to creamy-white below.

The species remains highly vulnerable in its sole island domains.

ENDANGERED

Greater Stick-nest Rat

H Aslin/NPIAW

H & J Beste/NPIAW

Western Mouse

WESTERN MOUSE
Pseudomys occidentalis

VULNERABLE

The Western Mouse was not discovered until 1930 and is still known only from a very few specimens in the south-west corner of Western Australia.

Whilst apparently preferring shrublands and woodlands on sandy soils, the mouse exists on a diet of mostly plant material, though beetles are also consumed, perhaps accidentally.

Once more widespread than today, it has been hit hard by extensive clearing practices in the Western Australian wheat-belt, where it is rare, and now remains on only a few isolated vegetation remnants. Its dark grey head and body averages 97 millimetres in length with greyish-white fur below and white paws. Its tail is considerably longer at between 120 and 140 millimetres.

This little known rodent whose conservation dilemma is acute, is certainly vulnerable to extinction unless carefully monitored and managed.

PILLIGA MOUSE
Pseudomys pilligaensis

VULNERABLE

Only discovered in 1975, the Pilliga Mouse has remained a very elusive rodent. Captured in the Pilliga Scrub in north-eastern New South Wales, in an area dominated by cypress pine forests and sandy soils with heathy understorey, the species remains a mystery to biologists. Only a very few animals were recorded between 1975 and 1980, but then in 1987, a new population was discovered in the same area.

Like many of the rodents, they are primarily creatures of the night, and appear to live in burrows. Apart from some minimum breeding data, this is all we know of the mouse, and ecological studies are badly needed. The animals so far recorded have an average head and body length of 71 millimetres and tail length of 68 millimetres. It has grey fur on its back, leading to russet on the flanks and white underneath.

While the population size could remain underestimated, it must be considered vulnerable until we can determine the reasons restricting its distribution and abundance.

DUSKY HOPPING-MOUSE
Notomys fuscus

The Dusky Hopping-mouse has suffered a greater than 90 per cent decline in its original range since European settlement. It is found today in the sand-dune systems in extreme south-west Queensland, and in an adjacent part of South Australia, near the border with New South Wales and Queensland.

An active burrower, the Dusky Hopping-mouse is one of the more attractive and striking of our endemic rodents. It is orange to grey on the back and white underneath, although its colours can vary greatly. It has large hindfeet, large ears, a large throat pouch and a long tail which averages 140 millimetres. Head and body length range from 80 to 115 millimetres. Like other hopping-mice it does not drink water, but obtains fluid from seeds, plants and insects.

The Dusky Hopping-mouse is a very rare animal, with little known of its breeding habits or ecological requirements, and is considered to be vulnerable to extinction.

VULNERABLE

Dusky Hopping-mouse

C Andrew Henley/NPIAW

59

VULNERABLE

NORTHERN HOPPING-MOUSE
Notomys aquilo

Groote Eylandt in the Northern Territory contains the only known and stable population of Northern Hopping-mice in Australia. While a specimen was apparently collected on Cape York in the late nineteenth century, and then again near the Cadell River on mainland Northern Territory in 1973, they have not been seen since. Groote Eylandt therefore remains a critically important refuge for the species. Here they are found in areas of stabilised dunes, covered mainly by a single acacia species, with an understorey of spinifex hummocks where they live in groups in large burrows.

The Northern Hopping-mouse has a small throat pouch, typical of all the hopping-mice, and reaches a length of 112 millimetres, with a tail extending a maximum of 173 millimetres. Its fur is relatively thin, being sandy-brown on the back and white underneath.

Its restricted distribution, not withstanding its possible occurrence on Cape York and in the Northern Territory, renders the species vulnerable to environmental catastrophe and must be protected.

H & J Beste/NPIAW

Lakeland Downs Mouse

POTENTIALLY VULNERABLE

LAKELAND DOWNS MOUSE
Leggadina lakedownensis

As with many other rodent populations the Lakeland Downs Mouse is thought to experience dramatic explosions in numbers when environmental conditions are favourable. It was this type of phenomenon that saw the first recording of the species from Lakeland Downs in north-eastern Queensland, southern Cape York Peninsula.

The mouse was first found in 1969 on 'William Island', an area periodically cut off from flooding of the Bizants and North Kennedy Rivers in north Queensland. A specimen has also been recently recorded as having been found on the other side of Cape York Peninsula in 1933.

The habitat at Lakeland Downs consists of woodland with kangaroo and spear grass, covering basalt red and brown soils. Here it is assumed to feed on the seeds of native and introduced grasses. The animal has a very short tail between 40 and 45 millimetres, small ears and a head and body length of between 60 and 75 millimetres. Its fur is a light fawn colour changing to white underneath.

Given that so little is known of its biology, its apparent disappearance, and its restricted habitat, the species must be considered potentially vulnerable until further information can be ascertained.

EXTINCT

LESSER STICK-NEST RAT
Leporillus apicalis

The Lesser Stick-nest Rat was last seen for certain in 1933, south of the Mann and Musgrove Ranges in South Australia. It once held a vast range across the Australian continent, widespread throughout central and southern Australia, extending from the coast of Western Australia, across and down into the north-east and south-west corners of Victoria and New South Wales respectively. Its near relative, the Greater Stick-nest Rat is also extinct on mainland Australia, though thankfully still survives on Franklin Island off the South Australian coast.

The species is renowned for building large nests of sticks and stones, both in caves and at the base of trees and shrubs. The early settlers would have been able to find nests all through the semi-arid shrublands, rocky range and mulga woodland habitats used by the animal.

The Lesser Stick-nest Rat was, as its name implies, smaller than the Greater Stick-nest Rat. It was of a lighter build with a longer tail ending in a white tip, prompting one of its alternative common names, the White-tipped Stick-nest Rat.

Little was ever recorded of the ecology of this species, though early explorers noted its nocturnal, aboreal and gregarious habits. The cause of the demise of the Lesser Stick-nest Rat can never be known for sure but clearly this herbivorous species was never able to compete for food with the hordes of sheep, cattle and rabbits that gradually overran a good portion of its natural range. It is thought that it also suffered severe predation by introduced foxes and cats. Reported sightings still occur in the desert regions and given our history of 'rediscovered species' some hope remains that it might still survive.

LESSER WART-NOSED HORSESHOE-BAT
Hipposideros stenotis

Though this bat was first described in 1895, very little has been learnt of its habits or distribution since, and only a very few specimens have been recorded.

The Lesser Wart-nosed Horseshoe-bat utilises caves and rock cracks in sandstone cliffs and gorges on the Arnhem Land plateau in the Northern Territory, where waterholes are bordered by paperbark trees. Other specimens have been recorded in the Kimberleys in Western Australia and north-west Queensland, near Mount Isa, often in disused mines.

This insectivorous bat is covered in brown fur, darker on top and lighter below. It has large pointed ears and as the name implies it has a 'wart' on the end of its nose. The body and head length is approximately 45 millimetres, the tail measures some 30 millimetres and the forearm length varies from 42 to 45 millimetres.

Lesser Wart-nosed Horseshoe-bat   G Baker/A.N.T. Photo Library

POTENTIALLY VULNERABLE

Endemic and rare, the species is considered potentially vulnerable, until more information can be obtained on its distribution, biology and conservation status.

GREATER WART-NOSED HORSESHOE-BAT
Hipposideros semoni

This species is considered to be an outlier of the main Papua New Guinean population and is rare in Australia. It is nonetheless an important part of our Australian bat fauna, though we have yet to learn a great deal about its habits.

Horseshoe-bats are normally characterised by elaborate noseleafs. The name horseshoe comes from the U-shaped lower portion of the noseleaf, which was said to resemble a horseshoe. The Greater Wart-nosed Horseshoe-bat has a small 'wart' on the centre of the upper noseleaf, from which its own name was derived. The biological purpose of both leaflets and wart are still unknown.

Its fur is brown above, graduating lighter beneath with a head and body and tail length averaging 45 and 15 millimetres respectively. The forearm averages 44 millimetres.

Its primary habitat appears to be tropical rainforest and woodland along north-eastern coastal Queensland. A nocturnal species, the Greater Wart-nosed Horseshoe-bat roosts in caves by day, foraging close to the ground in the evenings to prey upon slow-moving insects.

Once again, this particular species is not well known to Australian biologists, and we need to make more stringent efforts to discover its survival requirements. Its rarity, restricted range and rainforest habitat, suggest a vulnerability that should be taken into account in conservation planning.

GB Baker/A.N.T. Photo Library

Fawn Horseshoe-bat

FAWN HORSESHOE-BAT
Hipposideros cervinus

Restricted to the eastern tip of Cape York Peninsula, the Fawn Horseshoe-bat is formerly thought to have occurred in greater numbers, but appears to have declined. It is a rare animal that roosts dotted about the ceilings of its cave, preferring not to cluster together. An adept hunter, the bat flies close to the ground seeking out its invertebrate prey, and in its rainforest habitat, does so through echolocation effective within a range of 3 metres.

Biologists have noted that the species can sometimes have three colour phases in the one colony, ranging through grey-brown to orange. Its unusual 'noseleaf' distinguishes this species from other horseshoe-bats. The bat grows to 55 millimetres in length. The tail and forearm can reach 30 and 46 millimetres respectively.

The Fawn Horseshoe-bat is more common outside of Australia, though the Australian population, restricted and uncommon as it is, should be regarded as in need of constant monitoring.

ORANGE HORSESHOE-BAT
Rhinonicteris aurantius

The Orange Horseshoe-bat is one of Australia's most spectacular endemic mammals. Not only is the species rare, but also genetically unique, being the only member of its genus. Found across the top end of northern Australia, ranging from the Kimberleys in the west, through the Northern Territory and into Queensland in the east, it inhabits monsoon forest, dry sclerophyll forest and woodlands.

It has magnificent orange fur, which darkens around the eyes, and has easily identifiable 'scalloping' on its upper nose. The species can reach a length of 53 millimetres with an additional 25 millimetre tail. The forearms measure approximately 48 millimetres and look particularly red set against the transparent wings.

The Orange Horseshoe-bat roosts in caves that sometimes contain colonies comprising several hundred animals. It emerges from the cave in the evenings to hunt for moths, beetles and many other invertebrate species.

It is also a species that is clearly and disastrously affected by human interference, and there have been instances when entire colonies have abandoned their roosts. With increasing development pressures at the top end of Australia, especially those associated with tourism, the bat faces an uncertain future.

Far more needs to be discovered about its ecological requirements and all roosts given full protection wherever they are located. It is a very vulnerable species.

Orange Horseshoe-bat

GB Baker/A.N.T. Photo Library

VULNERABLE

TUBE-NOSED INSECTIVOROUS BAT
Murina florium

The Tube-nosed Insectivorous Bat has the dubious distinction of being the rarest mammal recorded alive within Australia. Only one specimen has been taken, and it is apparently only the sixteenth time it has ever been captured worldwide (others known from Sumbawa, Flores, Buru and Seram). The Australian specimen was trapped on the Atherton Tableland in north Queensland in 1981, and has not been seen since.

It appears to be uniquely adapted to life in high altitude, mist-shrouded rainforests. It is thought that besides its diet of rainforest insects, it may also be adapted to extract nectar from rainforest flowers. The recorded animal had a head and body length of 47 millimetres, a tail measuring 34 millimetres and a forearm extending to 35.7 millimetres. The bat has long, brown fur, paler below, and the distinctive 'tubular nostrils'.

A peculiar trait of these bats is the method they have devised for resting in damp conditions. It wraps the leathery wings around its body, and holds them away, so as to form an umbrella shape. While resting in this posture, the fine spray and water runs down the wings and flows off away from the body, an ideal way for keeping dry.

Further surveys are required to locate this species to learn more of its ecological needs.

POTENTIALLY VULNERABLE

GOLDEN-TIPPED BAT
Phoniscus papuensis

The Golden-tipped Bat was thought at one time to be extinct throughout Australia. A period greater than 80 years passed between the last Australian recording in 1897 (the first was in 1884) and its subsequent rediscovery in 1981, near Cairns in north Queensland.

Since 1981, the bat has been collected in several other locations in coastal forests of eastern Australia, stretching from the very tip of Cape York in northern Queensland, all the way south to the New South Wales and Victorian borders.

The bat has apparently adapted to tropical, subtropical and temperate coastal habitats where it glides through the upper rainforest canopy in search of its insect prey.

It is able to fly both fast and slow, and is even known to hover, utilising one of the quietest echolocation calls recorded among Australian bats. They are also known to roost among palm fronds in their rainforest habitat, and in human dwellings.

The Golden-tipped Bat has a head and body length of between 50 and 60 millimetres, a tail extending almost the same again, and an average forearm length of 37 millimetres. The species' name is derived from its dark brown fur which is tipped gold.

Still very little is known about the biology and ecological requirements of this very rare bat. Coupled with the continuing pressures upon the forests of coastal eastern Australia, the species is particularly vulnerable.

LITTLE BENT-WING BAT
Miniopterus australis

The distribution of the Little Bent-wing Bat stretches along the east coast of Australia from Cape York in the north all the way down to central New South Wales. It roosts communally in caves and tunnels and flies out in the evenings to look for insects, preferring to forage among a canopy of thickly timbered habitats. The bat only reaches a length of 48 millimetres with the

tail accounting for another 48 millimetres. It has a very distinctive chocolate-brown colour, becoming paler beneath. The forearms average approximately 38 millimetres.

The species has also gained partial fame through association with the Ghost Bat, as both species utilise the bat caves at Mount Etna in north Queensland. These caves are one of the very few maternity sites for the species in Australia. Sometimes numbering in excess of 100,000 individuals, they make a spectacular sight as they emerge for the long evening task of finding food, often becoming prey themselves as pythons and Ghost Bats literally pluck the Little Bent-wing Bats from the air.

They are also subject to the vandalism perpetrated by the limestone mining company who persist, despite all protestations, to blow up valuable bat roosting sites.

While the species remains common overall, its reliance upon so few maternity sites is a major conservation problem, and all efforts must be made to fully protect those sites known to science, and any others that may come to light. The species must be considered potentially vulnerable.

Little Bent-wing Bat

Michael Cermak/A.N.T. Photo Library

P German/A.N.T. Photo Library

Large Forest Eptesicus

LARGE FOREST EPTESICUS
Eptesicus sagittula

While the main population of this very small bat is centred primarily in the south-east of Australia, including Tasmania, there is one isolated population to be found on the Atherton Tableland in northern Queensland. The species is normally found in large cracks or hollow limbs of trees in dense wet and dry eucalypt forests of the south-east.

It is the largest bat in a family of rather tiny bats and roosts singly or in colonies of up to 60 individuals. The species forages for insect food through the forests in the evenings, but we generally know little about the species' reproduction or ecology. The bat averages 50 millimetres in length with a tail slightly shorter. The forearm of this dark brown forest bat is no more than 36 millimetres long, and is distinguished from others in the family by 'tri-colour' hairs on its belly.

The Large Forest Eptesicus needs hollow trees, which these days are at a premium in the south-east forests. The threats posed to this species by current logging practices render it extremely vulnerable.

POTENTIALLY VULNERABLE

BARE-BACKED FRUIT-BAT
Dobsonia moluccense

The Bare-backed Fruit-bat is the only member of Australia's 'megabat' fauna that is known to roost in caves. While in Indonesia and Papua New Guinea, the species is far more numerous and can be found roosting in colonies of thousands of individuals, the Australian population is far more sparse and limited. It only occurs in north-east coastal Queensland on Cape York Peninsula.

Normally found roosting in dark areas such as disused mines, boulder piles and even abandoned houses, the species is immediately disitinguishable from other large fruit-bats. This is apparent from behind when roosting, as the wing membranes appear to meet in the middle of the back, giving the impression of a hairless bat. There is however a large 'pocket' between the membrane and furred back. The bat is dark brown appearing black, and is approximately 300 millimetres in length, with a tail accounting for another 30 millimetres. The forearm measures 155 millimetres.

Its restricted range and rainforest habitat dictate that the species requires regular monitoring, in a region under increasing development pressure.

POTENTIALLY VULNERABLE

Ghost Bat

G Anderson/A.N.T. Photo Library

VULNERABLE

GHOST BAT
Macroderma gigas

The endemic Ghost Bat is probably Australia's most well-known bat species, if only for unfortunate reasons. Perhaps the species' most famous roosting and nesting sites, and largest colonies, are at Mount Etna caves, near Rockhampton in Queensland. This critical bat habitat has been under pressure for many years because of the activities of limestone mining. This came to prominent public attention recently when the limestone mining company, with the full permission of the Queensland Government, blew up one of the main roosting caves. This action shocked scientists, conservationists and the public alike.

The Ghost Bat is a large animal with head and body measuring up to 115 millimetres, and a wingspan of about 500 millimetres. It has a light grey almost bleached appearance, paler beneath, and large long ears that are joined at the base. It is distributed widely but patchily across the northern half of Australia and is found in a variety of habitats including rainforests. It is also Australia's only carnivorous bat, eating large insects, reptiles, frogs, birds, small mammals and sometimes other bat species.

Having diminished in range and numbers, and remaining sparse and rare, with roosting sites and habitats under increasing pressure, the species must be considered vulnerable to extinction.

SOUTHERN RIGHT WHALE
Eubalaena australis

So called by the early whalers who regarded it as the 'right' whale to hunt, being a slow swimmer, yielding high blubber and oil and floating even when dead, Southern Right Whales were already vastly reduced in numbers by the turn of this century. In Australia they were heavily exploited from shore-based whaling stations. They have been protected since 1935 and are still regarded as endangered.

These whales are basically black in colour with a large stocky body and growing to an average of 15 metres in length. They have large flippers which are roughly triangular in shape but no dorsal fin. The head is rounded and their mouth is strongly arched with long baleen plates. White, barnacle-covered 'bumps' or callosities appear on the top of the head, along the jaw and around the eye. These are different for each animal and serve as a means of identification. Calves can be almost white in colour.

The twin blowholes of this whale are separated and angled outwards giving the characteristic V-shaped blow.

Right Whales swim on the surface with their mouths slightly open sieving plankton and other small fish from the water. Mating occurs in early spring and after ten months a single calf is born in the shallow, warm waters. Females appear to breed every three years.

Southern Right Whales migrate from the Antarctic feeding grounds to the southern coasts of Australia in winter where they can be seen in shallow waters just beyond the surf line.

Southern Right Whale

DJ James/NPIAW

ENDANGERED

BRYDE'S WHALE
Balaenoptera edeni

These are also known as Tropical Whales and bear a close resemblance in both general shape and form to the Sei Whale. They are smaller in size than the Sei Whale being an average of 12 metres for males and 13 metres for females. The dorsal fin is more erect, pointed and distinctly curved towards the tail. Instead of the usual one ridge running from the blowhole to the tip of the snout, the Bryde's Whale has three. The colour is normally a uniform dark bluish-grey, darker on the back and paler on the underside.

Bryde's Whales occur in tropical and sub-tropical waters and are rarely found in waters where the temperature drops below 20°C. They are found mainly near the shore. They occur in all waters in Australia except the colder more southerly ones off Victoria and Tasmania and are often seen from Stradbroke Island, Queensland.

They feed all the year round on a primary diet of small schooling fish such as mullet and sardines. They are deep divers. Almost nothing is known about their behaviour although mating and breeding seem to take place all year round. While usually congregating in small groups of five or six, they will sometimes gather in large concentrations.

They have not been subjected to intensive whaling activity, but as with many other marine mammals, they are very vulnerable to the effects of marine debris and pollution.

VULNERABLE

ENDANGERED

SEI WHALE
Balaenoptera borealis

During the mid-1960s, these whales constituted the major part of the Antarctic whale catch. Their numbers were seriously reduced by hunting and the stock finally had to be protected. New estimates for large whales in the Antarctic put their numbers at 1,498. This presents grave conservation fears.

They are a large whale varying in length from 15 to 20 metres. They have a steely, dark grey colour, lighter underneath with whitish throat grooves. The metallic appearance is enhanced by the light and dark mottlings on the flanks and belly. The dorsal fin is tall and hooked and situated further forward than that of either the Blue or Fin Whale. Flippers are small and the baleen plates are black with a fine white fringe.

The fineness of the baleen plates allows the Sei Whale to feed on smaller prey species than any other whale. They specialise in plankton but eat small schooling fish as well. They usually skim their prey from the water.

Sei Whales are widely distributed in all oceans although they generally avoid areas close to the ice and while they do frequent coastal waters they usually remain some 100 metres offshore. No authenticated record of strandings by this species exists in Australia. The pair bond seems to be important and they are believed by some to be monogamous.

VULNERABLE

MINKE WHALE
Balaenoptera acutorostrata

The history of modern whaling has been one of decimation of one species of whale after another starting with the largest. The Minke Whale is the smallest of the so-called 'Great Whales' and was the mainstay of the whaling industry in the late 1970s and 1980s. Even today, despite the moratorium on commercial whaling, several hundred Minke Whales are being killed annually, supposedly in the name of science. Although the most abundant of the baleen whales, their future is far from secure.

Minke Whales occur worldwide and are found right up to the icepack. More than any other baleen whale, they will venture into rivers and inland seas. They may occur in all waters around Australia where they are often seen.

They vary from 8 to 10 metres in length, with the female slightly larger than the male. They are a dark bluish-grey in colour, tending to lighter underneath. They have a distinctive narrow pointed head with a prominent central ridge. The dorsal fin is in the last third of the back and is tall and curved. There is a bright white patch across the middle of the upper surface of the flipper.

More than any other baleen whale, the Minke Whale specialises its diet on small schooling fish such as anchovy and herring but they do certainly consume planktonic crustaceans as well. These whales live for about 50 years. They can reproduce faster than any other of the baleen whales as it is possible for them to breed every 18 months.

Minke Whale   DJ James/NPIAW

BLUE WHALE
Balaenoptera musculus

The Blue Whale is the largest animal to have ever inhabited the earth. It has an average length of 25 metres for males and 26 metres for females with a maximum recorded length of 33.58 metres. Their weight averages 80,000 to 130,000 kilograms and calves weigh about 7,250 kilograms at birth and measure about 7 metres. Sexual maturity is reached at about 22 years. They are monogamous, pairing perhaps for life. Calves are fed 600 litres of an incredibly rich and concentrated milk (50 per cent fat) per day and can double their weight in a week. Blue Whales breed once every two or more commonly three years and may live for as long as 100 years. When feeding they eat 3,600 kilograms of krill per day.

As the name suggests, Blue Whales are blue-grey or slate-blue in colour with some body mottling. They are long and streamlined and there is a single ridge extending from the twin blowholes to the snout. The small, low dorsal fin is crescent-shaped and placed well back on the body. The belly is often covered by a yellowish film of cold water algae.

Blue Whale

Ken Balcomb/Courtesy World Wildlife Fund

Blue Whales occur in all major oceans of the world but prefer colder waters and open seas and do not concentrate in coastal areas. The Northern and Southern Hemisphere stocks do not mix.

With the development of modern whaling Blue Whales were heavily exploited. In one Antarctic season alone, 1930-31, over 30,000 were slaughtered. The species faced extinction but was not protected until 1967 and is still endangered today. From an initial population estimate for the Antarctic of some 150,000-200,000 whales, most recent estimates put their numbers at 453.

ENDANGERED

FIN WHALE
Balaenoptera physalus

Fin Whales occur in all oceans of the world although they tend to avoid the icepack. They migrate towards the equator and their tropical breeding areas during the winter. They can occur in all waters surrounding Australia.

Varying from 17 to 26 metres in length they are second only to the Blue Whale in both size and weight. They are dark grey on the back and white underneath with a sharp line of demarcation between the two. The head is unusually coloured, being asymmetrical. There is a distinct ridge running from the back to the dorsal fin which is about 60 centimetres high and is angled sharply backwards.

In the Antarctic, these whales eat mostly krill which they take by gulping huge mouthfuls of water which is then expelled: the krill and any small fish being strained out on the inside of the baleen and swallowed whole.

Fin Whale stocks have been decimated by commercial whaling activities. Due to their fast speed (over 20 knots) and strength they were not caught by the early whalers but were in modern times. From an initial estimate of population size of some 448,000 before commercial whaling, their numbers were reduced to an estimated 70,000-80,000 and there was optimism about the ability of the whale to recover numbers. Recent estimates, however, give cause for alarm as they put the size of the Antarctic population at 2,096.

ENDANGERED

Humpback Whale

ENDANGERED

HUMPBACK WHALE
Megaptera novaeangliae

This is one of the most recognisable whales. They are a large whale varying in size from 14 to 19 metres. Colouration is generally shiny black above with white underneath. The flippers, which are almost one third of the total body length, are mottled black and white above and almost pure white below. Both the leading edge of the flipper and the trailing edge of the tail are scalloped. The whale is not really humpbacked at all but shows a stiffly arched tail stock when diving.

Humpback Whales migrate from their polar summer feeding grounds to their winter breeding grounds in the warmer tropical waters. The Northern and Southern Hemisphere populations rarely mix. In Australia Humpback Whales can be seen migrating along both the east and west coasts. In the south they live mostly on swarming crustaceans such as krill and feed by rushing on their prey from below.

Humpback Whales are famous for their songs which can go on for over half an hour with all whales in one area singing the same song. Little however is known about who sings or why.

This species was heavily exploited from whaling stations around Australia until it was afforded protection in 1963. From an original stock size in the Southern Hemisphere of 100,000 its numbers were reduced to less than 3,000 with the most recent estimate for the Antarctic stocks being 4,047.

There is increasing tourist interest in observing this species, particularly on breeding and feeding grounds, however this needs to be controlled in order to avoid disturbing the whales.

SPERM WHALE
Physeter macrocephalus

For many people, this is the archetypal whale. The large square head (up to one third of the total body length), small under-slung jaw and the powerful tail flukes are unmistakeable. It has a number of hump-like ridges on its lower back, the largest of which resembles a dorsal fin which is otherwise absent. Body colour is grey and the skin around the lips is usually white. There may be various other light patches present and the frequency and area of these seems to increase with age. It has a maximum length of 20 metres for males and 17 metres for females. It is further characterised by its distinctive blow which is a single spout angled forward at 45°.

The majority of these whales spend most of their lives in warm seas between 40°N and 40°S. They favour the edges of ocean trenches and points where strong currents flow in opposite directions and occur in all Australian waters.

Their main diet is squid for which they can dive quickly to great depths. They are polygamous. Females often occur in harem groups with young animals, and several older males and bachelor males often form herds. There is evidence of strong social relation-

Sperm Whale   P J Mannell/NPIAW

ships. They are one of the more frequent species to strand, often in whole herds. Sight is not as important as their ability to echolocate.

In Australia, Sperm Whales were one of the two main species to be commercially exploited and the last whaling station only closed in 1978. They were hunted for their oil and the spermaceti. Whale populations around Australia were decimated and recent estimates put their numbers now in the Antarctic at just 3,059 from an initial worldwide population of some 950,000+. Apart from the still-present threat of future exploitation, these whales are also susceptible to all sorts of marine debris which can entangle them or be ingested.

ENDANGERED

PYGMY SPERM WHALE
Kogia breviceps

The Pygmy Sperm Whale is found in the warmer waters of the world including Australia and it may migrate from tropical to slightly more temperate waters in summer.

The body of the Pygmy Sperm Whale is steelish grey in colour tending towards a lighter grey underneath. They average about 3 metres in size, with an average weight of 363 kilograms. The head is conical in shape and the dorsal fin is small and low. The whale has a tiny underslung jaw and a head to total body length ratio of some 15 per cent. The flippers are short and broad and located far forward. Some paler markings either in front of the eye and/or between the flipper and the eye may be present.

Like its larger relative, the giant Sperm Whale, the Pygmy Sperm Whale is believed to dive deep for its food. As well as squid, the whale also feeds on fish and crabs, some of which are caught in quite shallow water. Diving is believed aided by the spermaceti organ. Pygmy Sperm Whales often strand.

They are rarely seen at sea and no estimates of total population size are available. It would appear to be uncommon. Further studies are needed to determine the effects of subsistence killing and the level and effect of incidental kills both in coastal fisheries (particularly since the introduction of monofilament gillnets) and in the large pelagic trawl fisheries.

POTENTIALLY VULNERABLE

POTENTIALLY VULNERABLE

DWARF SPERM WHALE
Kogia simus

In many respects the Dwarf Sperm Whale is similar to its relative the Pygmy Sperm Whale. It is smaller in size however, with an average length of 2.4 metres and an average weight of 154 kilograms. Both species are similar in colour, steelish grey tending to paler underneath, and the belly is suffused with a pink tinge. Like its relative it has a slightly bulbous head and small, underslung jaw. It too can have the pale 'false gill' mark but does not have the pale mark in front of the eye. Unlike the Pygmy Sperm Whale, however, its dorsal fin is large.

This whale occurs in the warmer seas of the world but tends to be slightly more common in the tropics than its relative. It may frequent the edge of the continental shelf.

It dives deep and spends long periods submerged and feeds on squid and various fish species. It is a shy, unobtrusive animal that is regarded as relatively uncommon though potentially vulnerable. It also strands on the Australian coast.

As for the Pygmy Sperm Whale, further studies are needed to determine the effects on this species of subsistence killing and the level and effect of incidental kills both in coastal fisheries (particularly since the introduction of monofilament gillnets) and in the large pelagic trawl fisheries.

ENDANGERED

AUSTRALIAN SEA-LION
Neophoca cinerea

The male Australian Sea-lion is a bulky, heavy animal about 2 to 2.5 metres from nose to tail and weighs up to 300 kilograms. Adults are a rich chocololate-brown colour with slightly longer and rougher hair around the neck giving the appearance of a collar. The hairs on the nape of the neck are white. In contrast, females are more slender with a nose to tail length of 1.7 to 1.8 metres and weigh 80 kilograms. They are silvery grey to fawn on the back with a cream underside.

The animals can be quite aggressive. During the breeding season the males actively herd their cows and can be quite rough in so doing. Territorial fights often occur. The pups too can be subjected to quite vicious attacks from larger animals, often for no apparent reason, and these can result in their death.

Their range extends from Kangaroo Island in South Australia to Houtman Abrolhos, islands on the west coast of Western Australia. They inhabit marine inshore waters, colonising sandy beaches or rocky shores of the coast and small offshore islands.

The population is estimated to be in the order of 3,500 to 5,000 but the trend in numbers are not known, although there is a suggestion that they are declining. Australian Sea-lions were heavily hunted last century. Their breeding sites are sensitive to human disturbance and require protection and any potential trade in the species or parts thereof must be closely monitored. The species must be considered far from secure, and requires strong protection and the implementation of appropriate management regimes.

Australian Sea-lion

M & I Morcombe

B Cropp/NPIAW

Dugong

DUGONG
Dugong dugon

Undisturbed, the Dugong lives a slow-paced peaceful life. It is the only existing herbivorous mammal that is strictly marine and feeds almost exclusively on seagrasses. They reach lengths up to 3 metres and weights of about 400 kilograms. It is believed that it was the Dugong that gave rise to the mermaid legend.

Dugongs occur in warm, shallow inshore waters throughout the Indian Ocean. In Australia its main range is from Shark Bay in Western Australia north to Moreton Bay in southern Queensland. On the east coast stray dugongs have been recorded as far south as Botany Bay in Sydney, New South Wales.

Dugongs have a spindle-shaped body 3 metres in length and thick, brown to grey coloured skin. The large round head merges into the neck. The fleshy lips are very large with small bristly hairs. Animals tend to live alone or occasionally in small family groups and one young is produced.

Dugongs have been subjected to quite heavy exploitation and they have certainly been seriously depleted. Australia has the largest surviving populations of Dugong, with current estimates suggesting a population in excess of 50,000 animals.

The major threats to Dugongs are from direct hunting (they are protected in Australian waters following extensive exploitation last century), from incidental captures in shark and fish nets, and in the long term, from the destruction of coastal habitat and pollution. In Australia subsistence hunting by Aborigines and Torres Strait Islanders living in native communities is permitted.

Further surveys to determine the full extent of Dugong distribution in Australia are needed, along with research into their population dynamics.

Management plans must also be developed, combined with identification and protection of essential Dugong habitat.

VULNERABLE

73

THE THREATENED
Birds

The birds, perhaps through their increased mobility, have managed so far to escape the depravations visited upon the mammals, but many believe that the forces moving species to extinction will soon prey more forcefully upon them.

The impact of European settlement upon our varied avian fauna has been significant, if often, unrecognised.

There are about 720 species of birds in Australia. The range of families is immense, including the parrots, waders, birds of prey, honeyeaters, waterfowl, flightless birds and many others. Of these species, 70 per cent are endemic to Australia, that is, they are found nowhere else in the world. Three species are known to have become extinct in modern times, though at least 100 are of conservation concern, including many that are on the brink.

However the extinction record for birds is far worse if we include species that have gone extinct on our small island territories. For example, Lord Howe Island and Norfolk Island, off the east coast of Australia, have lost 15 bird species between them and at least a further five species are threatened.

The Dwarf Emu used to occur on King Island, Kangaroo Island and Tasmania when the Europeans first arrived, but the celebrated naturalist John Gould remarked on its virtual disappearance in the early

nineteenth century. The Rufous Bristlebird has not been seen in Western Australia since 1906, and must now be presumed extinct, while there have been no confirmed sightings of the Paradise Parrot in south-east Queensland since 1927.

The Australian parrots are amongst the most diverse in the world, but an alarming proportion of them are in some kind of conservation dilemma. Perhaps Australia's most spectacular bird, the Cassowary, restricted to the rainforest of north Queensland, has also suffered greatly due to the continuing destruction of its rainforest habitat, and now requires urgent conservation action. These and many other species of threatened Australian birds are described in the pages that follow.

One of the lessons to be learnt about birds is that we must not assume frequent sightings are a sign that all is well. The habitat loss and degradation that affects all other vertebrate species, equally affects the birds. Urgent conservation action must be implemented before they go the way of so many Australian mammals.

Previous page. Lesser Sooty Owl (Tyto multipunctata) in threat display. This beautiful owl inhabits rainforests on the east coast of Australia and is potentially vulnerable.

Frithfoto/Olympus

POTENTIALLY VULNERABLE

GOULD'S PETREL
Pterodroma leucoptera

Gould's Petrel breeds only on Cabbage Tree Island, 3.2 kilometres off the coast from Port Stephens, New South Wales. It is here where, between the months of October and April, the bird makes its nest on the steep western slopes of the Island in the hollow trunks of fallen trees, in short burrows or in rock piles under the fallen fronds of the Cabbage Tree Palm. A single egg is laid between late November and early December with the chick hatching in January.

This is a smallish petrel, growing to about 300 millimetres in length with a wingspan of

some 710 millimetres. It is predominantly slate-black in colour with white forehead, underparts and underwing. The tail and rump are blue-grey with a darker tip.

Total population of this petrel is probably about 1,000 birds. Such a restricted distribution on an island makes the bird extremely susceptible to habitat modification and predation by introduced cats and rats. Rabbits may also pose some threat through denudation of vegetation. Effective controls on introduced species need to be implemented and maintained.

ABBOTT'S BOOBY
Sula abbotti

Abbott's Booby is a pelagic bird, being sighted over a wide area of the Indian Ocean. Its sole breeding area however is on Christmas Island where it builds a substantial nest high up in emergent rainforest trees and shrubs.

Easily identified, Abbott's Booby is a predominantly white bird with some black on the wing, tail and rump and conspicuous black skin around the eye. Both the male and female have black-tipped bills. It grows to around 750 millimetres and weighs about 1.4 kilograms.

Its major food is flying fish and squid. The bird has been threatened by phosphate mining on the island which results in clearing of forests, including its breeding trees. Apart from the direct removal of nest sites by the clearing of trees, studies indicate that the breeding success of the bird has also been affected by wind turbulence downwind of forest clearings.

As Abbott's Booby is a slow-breeding bird, producing only one chick every two

Abbott's Booby

G Robertson/NPIAW

years, it is essential for its long-term survival that adequate reserves of suitable nesting habitat be provided. The species has been the subject of a long-term research and management program conducted by the Australian National Parks and Wildlife Service.

ENDANGERED

PROVIDENCE PETREL
Pterodroma solandri

Although known by a number of other names, the common name Providence Petrel is a reference to the part played by the bird in supplementing the food supply of the struggling convict colony on Norfolk Island. In a three month period during 1790 it is recorded that 171,362 birds were killed on the Island for food. Such wholesale slaughter, combined with the effect of introduced stock animals on the bird's habitat led to the extinction of the Providence Petrel on Norfolk Island.

Until recently its only breeding colony was thought to be on Lord Howe Island where large numbers of the birds build their nests on the steep forested slopes of Mounts Lidgbird and Gower. It may previously have occurred on lower parts of the Island but has been eradicated from there by goats and pigs. In 1985 a small colony was discovered

nesting on the cliff tops of Philip Island.

General plumage of the bird is dark grey with conspicuous white patches under the wings, noticeable when in flight. The face is scalloped white. The underparts are a paler grey. Size is about 400 millimetres in length with a 940 millimetre wingspan. Its diet consists mainly of cephalopods with some small fish.

Providence Petrels are rarely seen at sea and its oceanic range remains a mystery although it has been sighted in Japanese waters during summer.

It is considered one of the great bird-watching experiences to see these birds returning to the Island and watch as they gather above the forest canopy, wheeling and diving. As with any strictly island breeding species, it has an inherent vulnerability and must be constantly monitored.

POTENTIALLY VULNERABLE

G Robertson/NPIAW

Christmas Island Frigatebird

CHRISTMAS ISLAND FRIGATEBIRD
Fregata andrewsi

ENDANGERED

Like the Greater Frigatebird, the Christmas Island Frigatebird is black in colour but is distinguished from it by a white abdomen and, in the female, a white breast. Common to all frigatebirds, the male has a bright red throat pouch. It is a large bird reaching up to a metre in length.

It is found along coasts and on oceanic islands in tropical seas. Its only known breeding area is on Christmas Island in the Indian Ocean and its range extends to the surrounding seas including around Malaysia and Indonesia. Confirmed sightings of it have been made in Darwin in the Northern Territory but it is considered a vagrant to this area. It may also occur infrequently elsewhere along the north-west Australian coast.

The Christmas Island Frigatebird builds its nests several metres up in trees of the rainforest. Its diet consists mainly of flying fish but it also eats squid and carrion.

It has only a small total population and there is some evidence to suggest that its numbers are still declining. It has previously been exploited for food. Reserves on Christmas Island do offer protection to some of its breeding areas but it is nevertheless threatened by rainforest clearing (phosphate mining) and other habitat disturbance. Tourism development may also provide a potential threat to it on the Island.

LESSER NODDY
Anous tenuirostris

VULNERABLE

The Lesser Noddy is 330 millimetres long, including 105 millimetres of tail, and has a wingspan of 630 millimetres. Its overall plumage is sooty-brown with the top of the head greyish-white. There is a white arc below the eye. The tail is almost square with a central notch.

The Australian subspecies is confined around Houtman Abrolhos Islands of Western Australia where it nests in large colonies.

The bird feeds on fish, plankton, molluscs and jellyfish. It is sometimes observed diving through the crests of waves. It nests in colonies on the limbs of trees, often in mangroves, where it builds a nest of wet seaweed cemented with excrement.

The bird has a very restricted range and is thus vulnerable to habitat disturbance, marine pollution and introduced predators. Monitoring programs are essential.

(AUSTRALIAN) LITTLE TERN
Sterna albifrons sinensis

The Little Tern has a worldwide distribution with the Australian subspecies *sinensis* having a range extending from Broome in Western Australia round the north and eastern coasts to Tasmania, with sightings also in parts of South Australia. It occurs in coastal waters, bays and shallow inlets and on salt or brackish lakes. It even occurs on sewage farms near the coast.

This is the smallest of the Australian terns varying in size from 205 to 255 millimetres. The back, wings and tail are a pale pearl-grey with the underparts white. White markings on the forehead extend over the eyes in a thin line making a V-shape. The tail is forked and the yellow bill is tipped with black.

The tern feeds mainly on fish which it dives for in shallow waters.

Population numbers have been severely reduced in the south-east. Encroaching vegetation; human activity, both industrial and recreational, and predation are all threats. Future planning should avoid developments near nesting sites and human disturbance should be controlled if the species is to recover.

VULNERABLE

Jack & Lindsay Cupper/Auscape

Grey Falcon

GREY FALCON
Falco hypoleucos

This is one of Australia's rarest raptors. It is predominantly blue-grey in colour with its tail barred with darker bands. The face and the underparts are white and eye-ring cere and legs are conspicuously yellow. Males are 340 millimetres in length with the females appreciably larger at 430 millimetres.

The falcon is not found outside Australia where it is distributed throughout the inland and drier coastal parts of all States. Its habitat consists of the more open, lightly-timbered and grassy inland plains and it particularly frequents timbered watercourses. It is rarely seen.

When hunting, the Grey Falcon swoops low over open country or perches in trees. It can soar to great heights from which it drops at great speed on its prey of birds, small mammals and reptiles. It also feeds on insects, particularly grasshoppers.

When breeding, believed to be in late spring, it takes over the old nest of another hawk or crow which it proceeds to line with animal hair or bark. Two to four eggs are laid and the gestation period is approximately five weeks.

While undoubtedly uncommon, the status of the species is unknown. It is only partly protected in reserves and potential threats include overgrazing, degradation of riparian habitats and pesticides. In addition to further research into the status of the species there is a need for stricter controls on the use of pesticides.

POTENTIALLY VULNERABLE

79

VULNERABLE

PEREGRINE FALCON
Falco peregrinus

To watch a Peregrine Falcon in flight is a memorable experience. It soars with flat wings and tail fanned and the quick and shallow beating of its wings is interspersed by glides. When it sights its prey it swoops at speeds in excess of 300 kilometres per hour. Its prey consists of any small to medium-size birds, rabbits and other mammals that occur in the open during the day.

The falcon is generally slate-blue in colour with a black head, nape and cheeks. Distinguishing marks include the unmarked, cream throat and chestnut-buff chest and the chestnut-buff lower breast and trousers which are finely-banded black. The black-tipped bill is blue-grey in colour. Females are 480 millimetres and males 380 millimetres, with a wingspan of some 900 millimetres.

Although generally uncommon, the Peregrine Falcon can be found in a variety of habitats including cliffs and gorges, timbered watercourses, open woodland, pastures, swamps and rivers throughout Australia. An estimated 3,000 to 5,000 pairs occur in Australia of a worldwide population estimated to be in the order of 12,000 to 18,000 pairs.

Like other birds of prey, this falcon is susceptible to pesticide poisoning which can cause birth defects and the thinning of its egg shells. Further, in Australia, it has been shot as a pest and is also subject to illegal trade. Conservation action must include research, public education and protection of nesting sites, particularly as a disturbed bird may not return to its nest to continue incubation or feeding of the chicks.

Peregrine Falcon
Jack & Lindsay Cupper/Auscape

VULNERABLE

RED GOSHAWK
Erythrotriorchis radiatus

The Red Goshawk is basically red-brown in colour with bold black streaks. Its cheeks are grey and the cere is yellow. The tail is greyish with darker bars. It has rufous trousers and is identified by its large, bright yellow legs. Females are larger than the males and tend to have bolder streaking. They vary in size from 450 to 580 millimetres.

It is rare and occurs in open forest, woodlands and along tree-lined watercourses in coastal and sub-interior regions of northern and eastern Australia, south to northern New South Wales. It once occurred as far south as Sydney but urbanisation and tourist development has seen its range contract. It is perhaps most common in the Kimberleys and coastal Northern

Territory.

It catches its prey either in the air or on the ground. It hunts other birds up to the size of cockatoos, small mammals and reptiles.

Its nest is built high in a tree away from human disturbance. It is a large, rough structure of sticks and twigs and it will sometimes rebuild an abandoned nest of another species. It lays two to three bluish-white eggs.

Habitat destruction, illegal egg collecting, pesticide use and mining activities (particularly Kakadu) present possible threats to the species. Essential breeding habitats must be protected, and stronger enforcement of laws relating to egg stealing and pesticide application must be initiated.

LORD HOWE ISLAND WOODHEN
Tricholimnas sylvestris

The Lord Howe Island Woodhen is found only on Lord Howe Island, 790 kilometres north-east of Sydney, where it is now confined to the summits of Mount Gower and Mount Lidgbird. It is one of the rarest birds in the world.

It has no natural predators on Lord Howe Island and was common throughout the Island when the first European settlers arrived. Large numbers were killed for food and many of the remaining birds fell victim to habitat destruction and to predation of chicks and eggs by wild pigs, cats, dogs and rats. They would have become extinct as many other endemic island species except that they had managed to colonise the inaccessible mountain tops and it was here that they survived. The total population was reduced to a handful of animals. A captive-breeding program was instituted and efforts made to remove introduced predators. Captive-bred animals have now been released back on to the slopes of the mountains.

The Woodhen is a flightless bird with strong legs and a strong slightly downward curving beak. It is mainly olive-brown in colour with chestnut and black barring on the wings. It is strongly territorial and feeds on insects, snails and worms. These ground-nesting birds are naturally curious and have little sense of fear.

To ensure the bird's survival an active management program, including the removal of feral animals, will need to be maintained. Additional secure areas of habitat on the island must be available so that its population can expand. While the population remains so low any predator can have catastrophic effects.

ENDANGERED

Lord Howe Island Woodhen   Tom & Pam Gardner

PLAINS WANDERER
Pedionomus torquatus

The Plains Wanderer is now considered endangered throughout its range and is rarely seen. It was once however quite common across the grassy plains of eastern Australia and in inland New South Wales. The causes of its rapid decline were the conversion of its habitat for wheat production and the grazing of sheep and cattle. The introduction of rabbits and goats may also have changed its native habitat while shooting, and predation by feral cats, dogs and foxes may have been contributory factors to its decline.

If a food supply of seeds and insects is assured all year round the birds tend to be sedentary; otherwise they may be nomadic.

The Plains Wanderer tends to be more upright than other quails. The female is larger and more colourful than the male, being 175 millimetres long compared to his 165 millimetres. The plumage of both birds is pale brown-grey and they have a general mottled appearance. The female is characterised by a black and white spotted collar which sits on a chestnut bib: both are absent in the male. Bill, legs and feet are rich-yellow particularly during breeding.

The Plains Wanderer is particularly tame and is reluctant to fly even when threatened. The effects of pesticides have also been implicated in the species' decline.

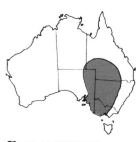

ENDANGERED

VULNERABLE

AUSTRALIAN CASSOWARY
Casuarius casuarius

The second largest bird in Australia, standing some 1.5 to 2 metres tall, the Australian Cassowary is unmistakeable. The glossy black hair-like feathers of the mature animal, the bare head and blue neck, the bright red wattles hanging from the neck and the horny helmet leave no doubt as to its identity. A large spike on the inside of each foot makes a formidable, if seldom used, weapon.

Australian Cassowary

Frithfoto/Olympus

The Australian Cassowary occurs in the rainforests of north-eastern Queensland from Cape York to Townsville. It can also occur in the canefields.

It is a sedentary, solitary bird which appears to maintain a territory. When disturbed it puts its head down and charges off into the dense vegetation.

The female lays four lustrous green eggs which are incubated by the male. He also raises the chicks which are, for the first few months, striped yellow and black. The bird feeds on fallen fruits in the rainforest. When necessary, it will also eat cultivated fruits and many other foods, including snails.

It is important for its long-term survival that large continuous tracts of rainforest be retained as it needs to move around to take advantage of the various fruits as they come into season.

Many questions remain unanswered about the Cassowary, including its present status, the full extent of its range, its population size and factors influencing its decline. The listing of Queensland's Wet Tropical Rainforests on the 'World Heritage List' will certainly help the species' future survival chances, but the species must still be considered vulnerable.

VULNERABLE

FRECKLED DUCK
Stictonetta naevosa

The Freckled Duck is considered one of the rarest waterfowl in the world and is believed to be a primitive form closely related to the ancestors of waterfowl before they differentiated into swans, geese and ducks.

Plumage is darkish-brown to black in colour with fine pale-buff to whitish spots. The underside is paler. The bill has a markedly scooped-out look and, in the male, turns orange-red at the base during the breeding season. The timing of the breeding season seems to vary depending on the availability of water but this is not fully understood.

Its main food is algae, which it filters, as well as a few insects and crustaceans.

While recorded sporadically in most parts of Australia, its main breeding distribution is restricted to the Murray-Darling River Basin and a small area in the southwest of Western Australia.

The Freckled Duck's survival depends on permanent, heavily vegetated freshwater swamps or creeks. It is threatened by habitat changes, including drainage programs, other water conservation schemes and salinity. It associates inconspicuously with other ducks and this has resulted in it being illegally shot during waterfowl open seasons in Victoria and New South Wales. Its future is not secure, and enforcement of hunting laws and regulation of grazing activities on dry lakebeds are urgently required management actions.

Graeme Chapman

Radjah Shelduck

RADJAH SHELDUCK
Tadorna radjah

The Radjah Shelduck is a very vocal bird and a rattling cry usually announces its presence before it has been seen. It occurs in tropical Australia where it once ranged from northern New South Wales around the coastline to northern Western Australia. Its range has contracted since then and it is now seldom found on the east coast except in northern Queensland. It also occurs on islands within its range. The bird prefers mudbanks and mangrove areas although it will visit freshwater swamps and lagoons and during the dry season concentrates on permanent water sources.

The bird has a white head, neck, breast and belly. Its back changes from deep rich chestnut to black at the tail and there is a chestnut band across its chest. It has a bright green speculum and the bill and legs are both flesh-coloured. The nest is constructed in large hollow trees close to the water. They probably mate for life. It feeds in the shallows of the swamps on a variety of molluscs, algae, insects and sedges.

Unlike most other ducks its major threat has not been destruction of habitat for agricultural purposes but its vulnerability to the duck hunter. The birds are slow to react and easy to see and therefore easy to shoot. Any proposed development in its remaining habitat would also need to be assessed in terms of impact on the duck.

POTENTIALLY VULNERABLE

LORD HOWE ISLAND CURRAWONG
Strepera graculina crissalis

The Lord Howe Island Currawong is a subspecies of the common Pied Currawong, which is distributed extensively along the eastern mainland of Australia. Like its close relative, it is also a large, noisy, black bird touched with white on the wings and at the tip of the tail.

As the name implies, it is found only on Lord Howe Island which is about 790 kilometres north-east of Sydney. On the island it inhabits both forests and pasture lands where it can be seen hopping along the ground in search of insects. It also eats fruits. The bird nests high in trees of tall forests. Its nest of sticks is lined with bark and grass.

It is considered endangered, its population having been reduced to a critically small number. The reason for this decline is however unknown although humans and introduced animals have taken a heavy toll on the landbird population of the island. Further research is needed if this population trend is to be reversed, though future habitat destruction must be avoided at all costs.

ENDANGERED

Frithfoto/Olympus

Australian Bustard

AUSTRALIAN BUSTARD
Ardeotis australis

POTENTIALLY VULNERABLE

The Australian Bustard stands 1.2 metres tall with a wing span of 2.3 metres. The back, wings and tail of the bird are all dark brown with light brown markings and the wing-coverts are brown with white and black markings. The breast is pale grey, the belly white and there is a black band across the chest. The crown and nape are both black.

The male has a distinctive, spectacular display and in this posture struts around roaring and booming. It does not have an established breeding season across its whole range but breeds when grass growth is at its greatest.

Although thought of as ground-dwelling birds, they can fly for some distance. They are nomadic, moving with the rainfall and feed on insects, small vertebrates, seeds and fruits.

The bird could once have been seen almost anywhere in open-type country but is now only common on Cape York Peninsula, the Barkly Tablelands and in the Kimberleys. Many factors have contributed to this decline including: modification of habitat by grazing; predation by foxes; and widespread shooting. Its habitat includes grasslands, light scrublands and woodlands, pastoral country, and croplands.

The pressures that have plagued the Australian Bustard are still very much at work, and it is essential that wildlife authorities across the country institute appropriate management regimes, including long-term monitoring programs.

NORFOLK ISLAND SILVEREYE
Zosterops albogularis

Also known as the White-breasted White-eye, this bird occurs only on Norfolk Island. The last observations of this endemic species were made in the 1970s. It is confined to the upland rainforests and is protected within the Norfolk Island National Park.

This is the largest of the white-eyes. It is 140 millimetres long with a green head and olive-brown to olive-green back with the clear white underparts which distinguish it from other silvereyes found on the island. It has a characteristic white eye ring.

Little is known about the species but it feeds on olives, fruit and insects in the tall trees of the forest. It is solitary and breeds from October to December and rarely calls. Its habits and habitat preference make it difficult to observe or trap and it is possible that very small numbers may persist undetected.

At the beginning of the century, it was fairly common but its numbers have declined rapidly, so that it is highly endangered and on the verge of extinction. Factors contributing to its decline include the introduction of the Grey-breasted Silvereye, extensive clearing of the native forest on which it depends and predation by rats and cats.

ENDANGERED

MALLEEFOWL
Leipoa ocellata

Mostly found in mallee and other dry scrubs of inland southern Australia, the Malleefowl is a large sedentary bird, about 600 millimetres long and weighing about 15 kilograms. Its wings and back are mottled black, brown and white with a white underside and a prominent broad band of black extending from the neck to the breast.

The birds mate for life and breed between spring and autumn. While the female forages for food, the male builds and maintains the large nesting mound, measuring 2 to 5 metres in diameter and up to a metre high, in which the eggs incubate. He does this by filling an excavation in the sand with dry leaves, twigs and bark. Following winter rains, this vegetation begins to ferment, heating the mound and warming the eggs. In summer, he adds sand to the mound to cool it and, by adding or removing sand as necessary, maintains a constant 33°C temperature which he tests with his tongue. The female lays her eggs singly into an opened mound. The chicks are born underground and dig their way to the surface and are independent from birth.

While the Malleefowl normally lives without water it is dependent upon the mallee scrub for its food and nesting materials. Its numbers and range have therefore been affected by land clearance for farming, particularly wheat, by food competition from sheep, goats and rabbits and predation of eggs and chicks by foxes. Inappropriate fire regimes and hunting are also implicated in the species' decline.

Habitat loss and introduced predators still severely threaten the species. Intensive management programs are in progress but retention of large areas of essential habitat and control of foxes is critical to the long-term survival of the species.

VULNERABLE

Malleefowl   Tom & Pam Gardner

85

BUSH THICK-KNEE
Burhinus magnirostris

Also known as the Bush Stone-curlew among other names, the Bush Thick-knee is a large, long-legged bird about 550 millimetres in length including a 45 millimetre bill and 180 millimetre tail. Its feathers are dark grey to mid-brown above with black streakings and blotchings, and buff and white below, again with conspicuous dark streaks. It has a large, heavy-lidded, yellow eye. Its colouring can make it hard to see

Bush Thick-knee   Frithfoto/Olympus

providing good camouflage, particularly when in shadow.

It inhabits grassy, open woodland where its distinctive call can be heard at night, but can also be found in sandy scrub near beaches, in mangrove fringes, on country golf courses and in orchards and plantations, in some areas. Its distribution has changed over time, presumably as a result of urban development. While occurring unevenly throughout most of Australia, it is most common in the sub coastal areas of the Northern Territory and on Cape York Peninsula where land use is at low intensity, and is generally rare or extinct in closely-settled areas.

These ground-living birds prefer to 'freeze' rather than fly if disturbed, however, they are capable of strong flight. Its food is primarily invertebrates, such as insects and spiders, although it will occasionally take small vertebrates and fruits if available.

The major threats are urban development, intense cultivation, burning and overgrazing. The species requires careful conservation monitoring.

NORFOLK ISLAND PARROT
Cyanoramphus novaezelandiae cookii

The Norfolk Island Parrot is one of Australia's most endangered birds, perilously close to the edge of extinction. In 1983, there were no more than 17 to 30 birds remaining on Norfolk Island, halfway between the Australian and New Zealand coastlines, and desperate measures were needed to help them survive.

It is a very beautiful, bright green parrot becoming rather lighter and yellow beneath, and reaches a length of 300 millimetres. It has a highly distinguishable red patch covering the forehead and crown and through each eye. On Norfolk Island the bird lives in the meagre remnants of Norfolk Island pine forests primarily in Mount Pitt Reserve, where it feeds on seeds, berries and buds.

Other subspecies of this parrot formerly ranged through Lord Howe and Macquarie

Islands, though these species are now extinct. Many pressures have been brought to bear on the Norfolk Island Parrot including habitat destruction, disease, predation by rats and cats and competition from the introduced Crimson Rosella.

The Australian National Parks and Wildlife Service in association with other government and private organisations, including the New Zealand Department of Conservation, jointly mounted a rescue operation beginning in 1983. Based on a captive-breeding program, starting with hand reared chicks taken from the wild, several early attempts at breeding resulted in infertile eggs. Success was finally achieved in late 1988, when two chicks were born. The long-term aim of the program is to release progeny back into the wild population.

PALM COCKATOO
Probosciger aterrimus

The Palm Cockatoo is a very spectacular bird. Their large size, magnificent head crest and red face patch combine to make this black cockatoo much sought after by illegal bird traffickers and collectors. They can reach 580 millimetres in length and are the only cockatoos in Australia that lack a distinctive colour band on their tail feathers.

They are dependent on rainforest habitat and have an extremely restricted range at the very tip of Cape York in Queensland from the north of Princess Charlotte Bay on the east coast across to the Archer River on the west coast. They are mainly found in coastal areas where they utilise the fringes between rainforest and eucalypt woodlands. They live on a diet of seeds, nuts and fruits, and normally feed at the very tops of tall trees, rarely coming to the ground.

Although the Palm Cockatoo is locally common it cannot be considered safe. Their very limited range, restricted and essential rainforest habitats, pressure for new developments in the area, and the ever-present threat from bird traders, renders the species potentially vulnerable.

POTENTIALLY VULNERABLE

Palm Cockatoo

Frithfoto/Olympus

D Watts/NPIAW

Orange-bellied Parrot

ENDANGERED

ORANGE-BELLIED PARROT
Neophema chrysogaster

One of Australia's most endangered species, the Orange-bellied Parrot numbers only a few hundred. It has been luckier than most species in the same predicament however, with four Australian Governments combining to help try and save it from extinction.

The parrot measures some 210 millimetres including a long slender tail. Its upper parts are best described as bright grass-green with a yellow belly that graduates to an obvious orange patch in the centre. It has a striking frontal band of blue between the eyes, and a similar colouring on the leading edge of the wings.

The species has an extremely restricted coastal distribution at only a few localities in South Australia and Victoria. A small population was known from near Sydney at the end of the last century, but is now extinct. In summer, the parrots migrate from the mainland to Tasmania where they nest and breed in the South West National Park and at other locations in the region. It occupies a variety of coastal habitats, including heathlands, sedgelands and grasslands, where it feeds on seeds, fruits and berries.

Loss and degradation of winter habitats in South Australia and Victoria, competition for food and a critically small population remain as serious problems for the species' future. Additionally, illegal trapping persists, and wildfires in their Tasmanian breeding grounds continue to pose difficult management problems.

The combined efforts of wildlife authorities in Tasmania, South Australia, Victoria and Canberra have had limited success, but the species is a long way from being removed from the endangered species list. Protection of critical habitats is essential, and adequate reserves have yet to be fully realised.

GOLDEN-SHOULDERED PARROT
Psephotus chrysopterygius

The Golden-shouldered Parrot is a bird under pressure. It has already disappeared from a large part of its original range, and unless the threats that have operated in the past are curbed quickly, it may not survive long into the next century.

Habitat loss and degradation caused by the activities of the pastoral industry and fire have resulted in the bird's drastic decline. Grazing results in the replacement of the bird's preferred food source, mostly native seeds, with introduced pasture plants. These effects are further compounded by the illegal bird trade. Golden-shouldered Parrots are highly prized by collectors here and internationally, where many thousands of dollars are eagerly paid for these highly coloured birds. Despite strong national and international legislation to prohibit and control trade, the parrots still find their way onto illegal markets.

The parrot is found only in remote parts on the western side of Cape York Peninsula in north Queensland. Restricted now to a very small area in the north-east part of its former range, the bird survives in open savannah woodland where it nests in termite mounds.

Approximately 260 millimetres in length, with the male far more colourful than the female, it is easy to understand the attention paid to them by smugglers. The male has a pale lemon-yellow forehead set against a black crown. Its name is derived from the brilliant golden shoulder patch on the wing, with turquoise underparts and scarlet feathers on the lower belly.

Drastic action is needed now to secure its long-term survival. As a sedentary bird, reservation is a viable option, and yet it is currently far from adequately protected in conservation areas. A management plan should be developed and implemented as soon as possible, protecting key habitats and guarding against the future effects of tourism and development in the Cape York area.

ENDANGERED

EXTINCT

PARADISE PARROT
Psephotus pulcherrimus

The Paradise Parrot is almost certainly extinct, though many naturalists still hold out some hope that it may turn up one day to prove the pessimists wrong. The famous ornithologist John Gould named the bird 'pulcherrimus', meaning 'very beautiful', but it was his assistant John Gilbert who discovered the species in 1844. This first sighting probably marked the beginning of the end for this splendid bird. Although it was last seen in 1927, rumours of the parrot's continued existence persist in its old Queensland haunts, though a thorough search by World Wildlife Fund in 1981 failed to produced any firm evidence.

It was a magnificent parrot. A medium-sized bird 30 centimetres long, including the tail, the male displayed a staggering range of colours. A black crown capped the frontal red band running between the eyes, while its back and wings were an earth-brown colour. Its wing shoulders and underbelly were scarlet, face and throat turquoise green graduating to turquoise blue on the breast and flanks. The beauty of this bird helped push it to extinction as it was an irresistible prize for trappers and collectors.

The Paradise Parrot inhabited savannah woodland and scrubby grasslands. It ranged perhaps as far as the Mitchell River in the north of Queensland but was certainly locally common in central Queensland between Rockhampton, inland to the Darling Downs and into northern New South Wales.

It is assumed that the pressures of the bird trade, grazing and severe droughts sent the Paradise Parrot into a population decline from which it was never to recover.

POTENTIALLY VULNERABLE

GLOSSY BLACK COCKATOO
Calyptorhynchus lathami

The Glossy Black Cockatoo is smaller and less spectacular than other black cockatoos, but is nonetheless distinctive. Approximately 500 millimetres in length it is uniform dark brown-black with a band of bright red tail feathers. The females have clearly identifiable yellow patches on the head and neck.

Glossy Black Cockatoo   Graeme Chapman

The species' range extends the length of the east coast of Australia from Mackay in north Queensland down to central and coastal Victoria, with an isolated population on Kangaroo Island off the South Australian coast. Within this range the species can be found in closed forests and open woodlands, primarily among stands of casuarinas. The casuarinas provide the Glossy Cockatoos with their main source of food, in the form of casuarina seeds, expertly extracted from cones. The only sign of their presence in the forest will often be the soft 'clik clik clik' as the bill negotiates the casuarina cones.

The species apparent dependence on healthy stands of casuarina forests form the basis of conservation problems. The cockatoo has never been a common species, though the past destruction and continued clearing of casuarina forests on the east coast has reduced populations and still threatens its long-term future. It is a sedentary species that is not adequately protected in reserves and for which no management plans have been developed.

Conservation of casuarina habitats are essential for this species' survival and until adequate reserves have been established and a management regime put in place this bird must be considered potentially vulnerable.

NORFOLK ISLAND BOOBOOK OWL
Ninox novaeseelandiae undulata

ENDANGERED

The Norfolk Island Boobook Owl is extremely rare being found only in the Norfolk Island National Park. Its loud and distinctive call, the persistent 'boobook' characteristic of its species may carry for several kilometres under favourable conditions but is only rarely heard.

The bird is nocturnal, roosting amongst the dense foliage of the reserve during the day and hunting at night. Its diet consists of insects, small birds and mice.

About 350 millimetres in length, the bird is dark brown above with buff and white flecks and underparts a lighter brown with quite noticeable white flecks. A thin band of white feathers over the brow forms a V-shape.

In 1987 only one female survived on the Island. The reasons for the species' decline are probably the removal of native forest and the scarcity of suitable old nest trees. Only the national park where it remains has been unaffected by such clearance. Predation by rats and the activities of bird collectors in the past may also have contributed to the decline of the species.

The species is the subject of an intensive recovery program by the Australian National Parks and Wildlife Service, which has involved the introduction of two male birds from New Zealand as possible mates for the sole surviving bird. In late 1989 the first two chicks were hatched.

EASTERN GRASS OWL
Tyto longimembris

The Eastern Grass Owl is seldom seen which reflects its very rare status. It is generally found in grassy areas along the Queensland coast and in north-eastern New South Wales but at least one record for it exists in every State.

Little is known about this owl although it does eat small rodents and insects including grasshoppers. Its movements may be related to the occurrence of the small rodents on which it feeds. They live in loose communities with some distance between individual birds or breeding pairs. It builds its nest under the cover of substantial tussocks and roosts on the ground during the day.

The upperparts of the owl are a mottled dark grey or dark chocolate-brown and the facial disc is creamish. The underparts vary from cream to a pale orange buff and are lightly spotted.

This is Australia's rarest owl although it may be more common than present records indicate. It lives in tall grass tussocks in extensive swampy areas and among the sedges and dense stands of cumbungi on the bore plains. Its movements are nomadic and this may give some distortion in the picture concerning range and status.

Eastern Grass Owl

Frithfoto/Olympus

The predominantly coastal habitat and range of the species clearly pose a threat to its conservation status. Recognition of this fact by wildlife authorities is required, and further research and management programs instituted.

POTENTIALLY VULNERABLE

RUFOUS SCRUB-BIRD
Atrichornis rufescens

The Rufous Scrub-bird is very difficult to observe. It is shy and retiring and stays well hidden in the dense forest that characterises its range. It is very rare with extremely low numbers remaining.

Its range extends from northern New South Wales to just across the Queensland border, usually in the highlands. It lives in thick undergrowth in the rainforest and adjacent eucalypt forest.

The Rufous Scrub-bird rarely flies, preferring to spend its time amongst the leaf litter where it forages for the small insects, larvae and other invertebrates that make up its food supply. The male is known for his distinctive song and is also a good mimic. The bird is territorial. The nest is only used once and it is probable that the female incubates the eggs and feeds the chicks without assistance.

Its size is about 160 millimetres. The bird is rufous-brown in colour with fine black barring, a whitish throat, black breast in the male and brown breast in the female and undertail-coverts rufous.

Even at the time of European settlement in Australia it is doubtful that there was more than fragmented populations. Subsequent clearing of rainforest for agriculture, grazing or timber production reduced its available habitat further and destroyed some of the remaining populations. Habitat loss and burning remain as serious threats to this species which must be considered vulnerable.

VULNERABLE

ENDANGERED

NOISY SCRUB-BIRD
Atrichornis clamosus

The Noisy Scrub-bird has an extraordinary voice and can often be heard calling loudly for a long time. While easy to hear the bird is extremely difficult to see and is usually very secretive. The female is rarely heard.

The bird is brown above with a dull-white breast changing to yellow-buff on the belly. A white throat above a black upper breast forms an inverted V-shape. The rump and undertail are rufous. Its size is about 210 millimetres. It feeds on large insects such as crickets and cockroaches, soft-bodied invertebrates and slaters which it finds in the leaf litter. It is a feeble flier, preferring to run through the undergrowth.

Protected in the Two Peoples Bay Nature Reserve the Noisy Scrub-bird is found only in the area of Mount Gardner, east of Albany in Western Australia. Here it lives among the eucalypts in steep, damp and heavily vegetated gullies. Too frequent use of fire affected the bird's invertebrate food supply and it was not reported between 1889 and 1961 during which time it was presumed extinct. There are about 100 breeding pairs surviving and this may not be a viable population. The bird is also particularly susceptible to droughts. Despite concerted conservation efforts the bird remains highly threatened.

ENDANGERED

GOULDIAN FINCH
Erythrura gouldiae

The Gouldian Finch, 140 millimetres in size, is a colourful and extremely attractive bird. It has green wings and back, a blue rump, black chin and throat, a long, black tail, lilac breast and yellow belly. The bill is cream with a red tip. The female is generally duller than the male. Three different types of head colour occur: black, red and yellow. Black-headed birds are the most common, followed by red-headed, with yellow-headed birds quite rare. The three types occur in flocks together.

As with many other native Australian birds, it has declined both in range and numbers especially around the Gulf of Carpentaria. It occurs across north and north-eastern Australia where it inhabits eucalypt woodland with a grassy understorey and adjacent clearings near a permanent water source. It is partly migratory, moving north to south through its range from the dry to the wet season. It avoids well-settled areas.

The bird feeds mainly on grass seeds which it extracts from the seedheads while clinging to the grass stems. During the breeding season insects form an important part of its diet.

The birds breed from December to August. They build a nest in a hollow in the branch of a tree or in a termite mound. Several pairs may use the same tree or hollow. Unlike many other birds they are active during the heat of the day.

Reasons for its decline are not known but it could be related to trapping for the bird trade (which is now prohibited) and the annual burning of grasses that occurs in northern Australia. Other potential threats include grazing and mining when this occurs within its direct range. Increased State and federal co-operation are needed to conserve this endangered bird, including control of clearing and burning practices.

Gouldian Finch

Jean-Paul Ferrero/Auscape

ALBERT'S LYREBIRD
Menura alberti

Like the Superb Lyrebird, Albert's Lyrebird also sings and displays but its tail is less spectacular. It is both smaller and darker than its relative. Its general plumage is a dark chestnut brown with the rump and undertail-coverts a rich chestnut. Its underparts are pale. The tail is glossy black but without the outer lyre-shaped plumes. It varies in size from 650 millimetres for the female to the male's 900 millimetres.

It inhabits dense subtropical rainforests and scrubs and has a small range confined to the north-eastern corner of New South Wales and south-eastern corner of Queensland.

The male sings with a voice that is loud and clear. He sings and displays on a platform that he builds by trampling down the dense vegetation. During display, he inverts his tail over his back and droops his wings. The nest is large and often located on rocks or cliff faces, or else in the trees perhaps on a stump. The female does all the work: building the nest; incubating the egg; brooding and feeding the chick.

The only two species of lyrebirds in the world are endemic to Australia. Although once plentiful, they were driven close to extinction through hunting by early settlers for their tail feathers.

The species has suffered some reduction in its already restricted rainforest range. A management regime must include protection of all essential habitats on freehold land, and other remaining pockets of its original rainforest habitat. Until such conservation measures are put in place, there is little likelihood that Albert's Lyrebird will find relief from its vulnerable status.

Albert's Lyrebird

W Lawler/NPIAW

VULNERABLE

MARBLED FROGMOUTH
Podargus ocellatus

The Marbled Frogmouth is rarely seen, even by ornithologists, so not much is known about it. It is restricted to rainforests and two subspecies occur in Australia: *Podargus ocellatus marmoratus* on Cape York Peninsula in northern Queensland; and *Podargus ocellatus plumiferus* across the Queensland-New South Wales border. It is also found in Papua New Guinea and the Solomon Islands.

Both a red-brown and a grey form of the bird occur. The marbled effect, that gives the bird its common name, is the result of irregular white blotches scattered throughout its plumage.

The bird is believed to roost in the thick scrub of the rainforest during the day and to hunt for the insects that form its diet during the night.

It appears that the Marbled Frogmouth was once more common, particularly on Cape York Peninsula and it has been suggested that the decline in the southern population was as a result of rainforest clearing. While the New South Wales habitat of this species could be said to be a little more secure, Cape York is coming under increasing development pressure and populations must be fully protected and managed.

VULNERABLE

**POTENTIALLY
VULNERABLE**

YELLOW-LEGGED FLYCATCHER
Microeca griseoceps

The Yellow-legged Flycatcher is an example of a bird that has a very restricted distribution and for which there is only limited information available. The bird is restricted to the tropical rainforests of Cape York Peninsula, Queensland where it inhabits the outermost branches of the crowns of rainforest trees. They are thus difficult to observe and identify.

The bird is distinguished from others of its genus by its pale orange or yellow legs. Common to others in its genus it has a flat broad bill that is dark above and cream below. Its upperparts are olive-green to brown; the throat and upper breast are almost white with the rest of the underparts lemon. Its head is grey. It is very small, being no more than 130 millimetres in size.

It feeds on insects which it flushes from the outer foliage and vine-covered branches high in the rainforest trees. The nest and eggs have not been described and there are no measures of its abundance.

The restricted range of the species, lack of biological information, and presence in an area under increasing pressure from development interests, leaves it particularly vulnerable.

VULNERABLE

RED-LORED WHISTLER
Pachycephala rufogularis

The Red-lored Whistler is restricted to isolated patches of mallee in inland areas of south-western New South Wales, north-western Victoria and south-eastern South Australia. This mainly ground-feeding bird eats insects and occasionally berries. It tends to be rather shy and elusive and is usually seen singly except when breeding.

The upperparts are generally grey with the flight feathers edged with cream. The lores, throat and through to the vent are rufous red, with a band of grey-brown across the lower breast. The female is generally paler in colour. They are about 220 millimetres in length with a longish tail.

The range of the Red-lored Whistler has contracted since European settlement. The bird depends on mallee and its associated native pines and broombush. This habitat has been greatly reduced by conversion to agricultural and pastoral land. While fire has been a part of the natural Australian system for centuries, a new type of fire regime characterised by frequent low intensity burning has also had a deleterious effect on the bird. Its habitat is partly protected in a series of reserves and these may be sufficient for the bird's long-term survival.

The reserves and private lands where the species now survives must be adequately managed. Until such a management regime is put in place, the species will remain vulnerable to extinction.

Red-lored Whistler   Graeme Chapman

WESTERN WHIPBIRD
Psophodes nigrogularis

The Western Whipbird is extremely shy and elusive, inhabiting dense thickets of heath, mallee scrub and coastal dune scrub. It exists only in five isolated populations that range from north-western Victoria to southern Western Australia. Three subspecies of the bird are recognised: *nigrogularis* which occurs in the south-west region of Western Australia and on the tip of the Eyre Peninsula in South Australia; *leucogaster* which occurs in the Murray-Darling region of South Australia and Victoria; and *pondalowiensis* which occurs on the tip of Yorke Peninsula and possibly on Kangaroo Island, South Australia. Of these *nigrogularis* and *leucogaster* were both once more widespread. Increasing aridity, clearing of habitat and fire have all helped to reduce the species' range.

While there may be some colour and tone variation between the different subspecies, the general plumage of the birds is olive-green above and grey below. The throat is black with white sides and the tail feathers are also tipped white. The bird has a grey crest. Total body length varies from 240 to 255 millimetres.

The song of the Western Whipbird is not like the characteristic whipcrack of the Eastern Whipbird but is nonetheless loud and distinctive. It feeds on insects and small invertebrates, including snails. Breeding takes place between July and November and

Western Whipbird   R Garstone/NPIAW

the male and female share incubation and feeding of the chicks.

The species remains susceptible to mallee clearing and inappropriate fire regimes and still requires increased management efforts. These factors collectively pose a threat to its continued existence.

VULNERABLE

BLACK GRASSWREN
Amytornis housei

First discovered in 1901, the Black Grasswren was not sighted again for some 67 years until it was rediscovered in July 1968. It is one of the largest of the grasswrens reaching 210 millimetres in length. The head and back are finely streaked white on black and the tail is also black. The rump and uppertail-coverts are chestnut and the underparts are black streaked with white. The female is similar but has chestnut streaking on the breast.

The bird is known from only a few areas in the north-west Kimberleys in Western Australia where it lives in rough sandstone country among boulders, spinifex and other small bushes. Its colour allows it to blend in well with the sandstone. The bird seldom flies. It is assumed that it breeds in the wet season but this is not known for sure and no nest has yet been found.

There are no measures of the bird's abundance and as it has rarely been observed, its habits are not well known. This lack of knowledge combined with restricted habitat dictate that it be treated as potentially vulnerable.

POTENTIALLY VULNERABLE

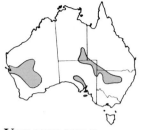

VULNERABLE

THICK-BILLED GRASSWREN
Amytornis textilis

The Thick-billed Grasswren is 165 to 190 millimetres in length and is generally darkish brown in colour, the underparts being paler than the upperparts, and is streaked with white. It has a long tail and a stout conical bill. The female is similar to the male but with chestnut flanks.

Three subspecies, occurring in isolated populations are generally recognised, although many writers refer only to two, giving it a discontinuous distribution. *Amytornis textilis textilis* occurs in Western Australia and South Australia, *Amytornis textilis modestus* is found in the Northern Territory, South Australia and New South Wales and *Amytornis textilis myall* occurs on the Eyre Peninsula in South Australia.

Its habitat is characterised by large shrubs which provide ground-level shelter for the bird. This varies from saltbush, bluebush and nitrebush on the sandy and gibber plains to clumps of canegrass *Zygochloa paradoxa*, often along watercourses.

The bird is secretive in nature and often difficult to observe. It feeds mainly on seeds, small berries and small beetles.

At least two of the subspecies have seen marked population declines this century. Grazing and trampling have been major causal factors in this decline. It is also vulnerable to introduced predators. The Western Australian subspecies is a particularly vulnerable bird, absent from most of its previous range and extinct on Dirk Hartog Island. Areas where this species still persists must be managed with its long-term survival as a priority goal.

Thick-billed Grasswren   R Garstone/NPIAW

VULNERABLE

EASTERN BRISTLEBIRD
Dasyornis brachypterus

The Eastern Bristlebird is rich brown above tending to an olive-brown towards the long graduated tail. Its underparts are more grey-brown and there is a pale buff-coloured line extending above the eye. Its wings are short and rounded. There are three bristles on either side of its bill but these can be difficult to see except at close quarters. It is 210 to 220 millimetres in size. It breeds from August to January and lays two eggs.

This sedentary bird is rare and shy but has a loud, distinctive call. Its range was once more continuous but it is now found only in isolated pockets extending from Cunningham's Gap in southern Queensland to the New South Wales–Victoria border. The bird occurs in both coastal and montane heathlands but is restricted to the coastal areas towards the southern end of its range. It is fairly common locally in both Barren Grounds and Nadgee Nature Reserves.

Essentially a ground-dwelling bird, it can fly a few metres if necessary but it usually runs fast along the ground with its tail raised and often fanned. It forages in the dense heath among the leaf litter for its food of insects and seeds.

Factors relevant to its decline include habitat destruction or modification associated with the spread of settlement, agricultural and mining activities and the effects of fire. These causal factors are still present within the species' coastal range and appropriate management regimes must be devised.

Graeme Chapman

Western Bristlebird

WESTERN BRISTLEBIRD
Dasyornis longirostris

The Western Bristlebird differs from the eastern species in that it is slightly smaller (180 to 220 millimetres); has a slightly longer bill; a darker crown; and is distinctly dappled grey across the head, nape and mantle.

Although generally shy and secretive it will perch on a twig above the vegetation but dives for cover at the slightest sound of disturbance.

The bird lives in dense coastal shrubs and heaths and its range once extended from Perth around the south coast of Western Australia to Albany. As a result of extensive land clearing for agriculture it is now rare and restricted to a narrow coastal strip from Two Peoples Bay to the Fitzgerald National Park. Its population increased in the Two Peoples Bay Fauna Reserve.

Like the Eastern Bristlebird it is sedentary and ground dwelling but manages a short, feeble flight if necessary. It breeds from August to January and lays two eggs. It feeds on insects and seeds which it collects on the ground.

Fire poses a particular threat to the bird along with continued habitat destruction and degradation. Intensive management of remaining habitat is required.

ENDANGERED

RUFOUS BRISTLEBIRD
Dasyornis broadbenti

Three separate subspecies of the Rufous Bristlebird are recognised: *broadbenti* (Eastern), *whitei* (Western) and *litoralis* (Southwest). Of these, *litoralis* occurs in the southwest region of Western Australia but no reliable record of it has been made since 1906 at the beginning of extensive burning to create grazing land, and is probably extinct. The other two subspecies occur along a narrow coastal stretch from Anglesea in Victoria to the mouth of the Murray River in South Australia. Within this range *broadbenti* occurs east of 141°E and *whitei* occurs west of 141°E. It is believed to extend into the Otway Ranges in Victoria.

It is a ground-living bird which can, but rarely flies, preferring to dart through the undergrowth. It has a varied diet which includes beetles, berries, caterpillars, earthworms, moths and seeds. It builds a nest close to the ground in dense shrub. Both birds feed the chicks and the incubating bird is fed by its mate.

The back is grey-brown with slightly darker wings and tail. The throat and breast and belly are mottled grey-brown. It has a grey patch around and in front of the eye and the crown and face are rufous.

Clearing of habitat and the increased use of fire that comes with settlement have already proven to have a deleterious effect on the bird. In the east it is also potentially vulnerable to disturbance by recreational vehicles on the coastal dunes it inhabits.

POTENTIALLY VULNERABLE

D Watts/NPIAW

Forty-spotted Pardalote

ENDANGERED

FORTY-SPOTTED PARDALOTE
Pardalotus quadragintus

Sadly, this species may already be heading inexorably towards extinction. It is endemic to Tasmania and the Bass Strait islands. Although probably never common previously, it certainly had a more widespread distribution. Probably less than 2,500 individuals remain in about six or seven relict populations. There are populations on islands like Maria Island National Park, and on peninsulas such as Tinderbox Peninsula.

As its name suggests, the Forty-spotted Pardalote has approximately 40 spots: 20 on each wing. Its head and back are a dull olive-green and wings are brownish-black with the white spots. The tail is also black. The breast and belly are yellow-grey tending to grey and it has a pale yellow face and undertail-coverts. It is about 100 millimetres in size.

It inhabits wet and dry eucalypt forests and woodlands. It feeds in the white gums *Eucalyptus viminalis*, on a variety of insects such as small beetles, flies and spiders. Other food in its diet, includes termites and weevils. It breeds between September and January when it lays three to five lustrous white eggs.

Habitat destruction, unsuitable fire regimes and competition from other pardalotes for nest hollows remain as continuing threats to the species.

POTENTIALLY VULNERABLE

CHESTNUT-BREASTED WHITEFACE
Aphelocephala pectoralis

The Chestnut-breasted Whiteface was not seen from the time it was first described by John Gould in 1871 until it was rediscovered in 1914. The species inhabits gibber plain country where there are shrubs and ranges in an area of central South Australia which extends north from Port Augusta to Oodnadatta and west between Cooper Pedy and Lake Frome.

The bird is about 100 millimetres in length, and has a grey crown with white undersides. It is distinguished by its chestnut markings including a broad band across its breast. It is a shy bird which feeds on the ground on seeds and insects.

While undoubtedly rare and uncommon, there is some uncertainty as to the exact status of the bird given the sparsely-populated country which it inhabits. It is unknown whether grazing activities are a threat in its arid habitats, but the species must be considered potentially vulnerable.

HELMETED HONEYEATER
Lichenostomus melanops cassidix

The Helmeted Honeyeater is one of four subspecies of the Yellow-tufted Honeyeater and has been considered by some as a separate species. It is the largest and most brightly coloured of the subspecies.

The back varies from brown-olive to yellow-green and a black patch extends from the bill to the ear. It has a yellow ear tuft. Underparts are yellow-green with dark streaks. It is distinguished by the short fixed crest or helmet of golden feathers on its forehead and reaches up to 230 millimetres in length. Its diet consists of nectar and insects, which it catches in the forest canopy or takes from the tree bark.

Once more widespread across the ranges and along watercourses east of Melbourne, Victoria, the bird's habitat has been destroyed by settlement and it is now reduced to a tiny area along the Woori Yallock, Cockatoo and Cardinia Creek systems in the Dandenong Ranges. Here it lives among the forest of swamp gums, manna gums and tea-tree thickets. It is estimated that less than 200 individuals may remain and doubt has been expressed as to whether the Cardinia Creek population survives at all.

Helmeted Honeyeater

Frithfoto/Olympus

Apart from destruction of its habitat by clearing, the bird is also susceptible to the effects of fire. Further, it is facing dislocation from its breeding areas by Bell Miners. The bird is subject to an intensive management program conducted by Victorian wildlife authorities.

ENDANGERED

REGENT HONEYEATER
Xanthomyza phrygia

This bird is thought to be decreasing both in range and in overall numbers. It lives in eucalypt forest and woodland across south-eastern Australia from Rockhampton in Queensland to the Mount Lofty Ranges in South Australia. Its main occurrence is from the Hunter River Valley in New South Wales to central Victoria and it does not occur in the south Gippsland area or Otway Ranges of Victoria. It is a highly nomadic bird and may reappear in areas after a long absence and quickly disappear again.

The bird feeds on the nectar of flowering trees including those in urban areas and flocks of them follow the flowering of trees such as eucalypts and banksias. They will go into orchards where they can cause damage by eating the cultivated fruits, particularly if in large flocks. They also eat insects.

The Regent Honeyeater is 200 to 225 millimetres in size with the female often much smaller than the male. They are mostly black in colour with distinctive yellow scalloping on the breast and back. The brilliant yellow patches on the wings and on the tail feathers stand out well in flight. The bird has an area of bare pinkish skin around the eye.

As a nomadic species the Regent Honeyeater requires large areas of suitable habitat. Reserves need to be declared, along with extensive re-planting programs and general habitat retention education programs.

ENDANGERED

THE THREATENED
Reptiles

People tend not to think about reptiles in terms of their endangerment – a reptile is a reptile. Most do not realise that Australia has one of the world's most spectacular and diverse range of reptilian fauna – a treasure little appreciated.

There are around 700 species of reptiles in Australia, comprising the lizards, snakes, turtles and crocodiles. A staggering 88 per cent of these are found only on our island continent.

To date only one species appears to have been lost for ever. The Adelaide Pygmy Bluetongue Skink has not been sighted since 1959. While a time period of 50 years is normally required before declaring a species extinct, many believe that this Bluetongue has gone. However, given the number of times that a species once thought extinct on the mainland has been subsequently rediscovered, there may still be hope.

The fact that the reptiles have not suffered the degree of extinctions reflected by the mammals does not mean that they have eluded the effects of 200 years of development. Over 150 threatened reptiles require our conservation management attention.

Many have certainly come near to extinction, such as the Saltwater Crocodile, the Western Swamp Turtle, and the Broad-headed Snake. These and many others are still far from being described as safe, with the pressures of habitat destruction and exploitation still working against them. The Western Swamp Turtle is critically near the edge, surviving in only two small swamps near the city of Perth. It has recently been given a further lease of life through the successful hatching of a number of young turtles, captive bred at Perth Zoo, though its future in the wild is still extremely tenuous.

It is essential to remember that the decline experienced by many of our unique vertebrate species in the last 50 years is very likely to continue, unless we can mitigate against those destructive elements. Without urgent remedial conservation action, we can expect population crashes and possible extinctions to accelerate to a point where any future help may simply be too late.

Previous page. The Green Python (Chondrophython viridis) *is one of Australia's most spectacular reptiles, often sought after by wildlife smugglers. The species is potentially vulnerable.*

Frithfoto/Olympus

FRESHWATER OR JOHNSTON'S CROCODILE
Crocodylus johnstoni

POTENTIALLY VULNERABLE

As its name implies, the Freshwater Crocodile lives in large permanent freshwater rivers and waterholes. It occurs from the Kimberley region in the north-west across the coast and hinterland of north and north-eastern Australia to the Burdekin River in Queensland.

The Freshwater Crocodile is smaller than its saltwater relative, growing to about 3 metres in length. Its snout is long, smooth and slender and the reptile is grey or olive-brown in colour with darker mottling and whitish below. Its diet is varied consisting of a combination of fish, frogs, crustaceans, small reptiles, birds and mammals for which it forages at night.

Like the Saltwater Crocodile, it too was extensively netted and hunted for leather production during the 1960s. As population numbers fell and concern was expressed for its long-term viability the crocodile was given legal protection. Viable populations are today believed to exist in a number of protected areas that occur within its range. Its present status is unknown although there is some suggestion that its numbers may be increasing based on its ability, in recent years, to colonise areas previously occupied by Saltwater Crocodiles. It is still uncommon and numbers and distribution should be carefully monitored as the species is still exploited for the export trade.

SALTWATER OR ESTUARINE CROCODILE
Crocodylus porosus

The Saltwater Crocodile is the largest living reptile in the world. While they can grow to a length of 7 metres or more, they rarely exceed 5 metres in length. It is light grey-brown above with darker markings and lighter below. It has a relatively broad snout.

This crocodile is found in estuaries, large streams, lakes, swamps and coastal waters, extending from the open sea to inland, from the Kimberleys in northern Western Australia to Cape York in Queensland and extending almost the entire length of the eastern seaboard of Queensland. Its diet consists of crustaceans, fish, reptiles, birds and mammals. It is largely nocturnal. During the wet season it lays approximately 60 eggs in river banks.

The Saltwater Crocodile was heavily exploited in the 1950s and 1960s, only to receive total protection in the early 1970s. Professor Harry Messel of Sydney University has spent many years studying crocodile populations in northern Australia and the results of his most recent surveys suggest population levels of 10,000 for the Northern Territory, 2,500 for the Kimberleys in Western Australia, and 3,000 for Queensland.

The species is exploited in ranching operations in the Northern Territory, the

Saltwater or Estuarine Crocodile

Leo Meier/Courtesy Weldon Trannies

products exported primarily to Japan. In the three regions where the species occurs, there has developed a dangerous trend towards the removal of so-called 'rogue' animals from lakes and rivers. These crocodiles are normally transported to private and commercial tourist operations, with absolutely no benefit to the species' conservation prospects.

Urgent protection must be given to Queensland's crocodiles, and large protected areas set aside across the north of Australia. Further research and conservation management is clearly required.

VULNERABLE

LOGGERHEAD TURTLE
Caretta caretta

The Loggerhead Turtle is the only species in its genus. It is found throughout the world in tropical and warm temperate waters where it inhabits coastal and offshore areas. Only an occasional specimen enters southern Australian waters but it occurs elsewhere, including the Great Barrier Reef.

It mainly lays its eggs between October and May, although it can do so at any time of the year. Approximately 100 small, round, parchment-shelled eggs are laid.

The Loggerhead Turtle grows to about 1.5 metres in length. Above it is dark reddish-brown and there are sometimes darker brown markings. The shell, which is white, cream or yellowish on the underside, is somewhat elongated and more or less heart-shaped. Unlike other marine turtles its upper jaw does not project forward to form a hooked beak. It is further distinguished by the five costal shields on the upper shell.

Although still widely distributed, populations appear to be declining everywhere except in Australian waters. This decline is believed to be a result of the collection of its eggs for human consumption, though increasing pollution of its marine environment and destruction of nesting beaches remain as serious threats. A turtle conservation plan is urgently needed in Australia.

POTENTIALLY VULNERABLE

HAWKSBILL TURTLE
Eretmochelys imbricata

The Hawksbill is a carnivorous turtle and can be found foraging on coral reefs. It inhabits coastal waters and while it is found throughout tropical and warm temperate waters, it is only abundant in Australia. Here its range extends from mid-western Western Australia to southern Queensland.

The turtle is smallish, being no more than 1 metre in length. The upper shell is basically olive-green or brown but is marked with irregular patches of reddish-brown, dark brown and black. It is paler underneath. The scales of the head, which is rather small, are often dark and strongly contrasting. The shell is narrow and distinctly heart-shaped.

Its usual nesting place in Australia is on the islands of Torres Strait although it has nested on mainland beaches further south. It has been observed, for example, nesting in the Gulf of Carpentaria.

Reasons for its continuing decline are twofold. First, it was heavily exploited for its shell but this use was largely superseded when plastics were introduced; more recently turtles have been further exploited by countries for a variety of products. They are also increasingly susceptible to marine debris and pollution.

JC Wombey

Flatback Turtle

FLATBACK TURTLE
Chelonia depressa

The dorsal surface of the Flatback Turtle is grey, grey-green or olive in colour and it is creamy-yellow underneath. It has a moderate-sized head. The broadly oval shell is covered by a thin layer of fleshy skin and turns up at the sides in the adults. It grows to about 1.2 metres in length.

This turtle has a much more restricted range than other marine turtles being confined to the shallow coastal waters of northern Australia from the Kimberley region in Western Australia to the Torres Strait. It can also occur on the Great Barrier Reef. It breeds throughout its range and has previously been described as rare, and in need of conservation monitoring.

It is perhaps not quite as vulnerable as other marine turtles as it is not so sought after for its meat. However, large numbers of its eggs are collected and eaten by Aborigines.

Dean Lee/Courtesy Weldon Trannies

Green Turtle

GREEN TURTLE
Chelonia mydas

The Green Turtle has been mercilessly exploited throughout the world for centuries and is now rare except in the waters of northern Australia. Occurring in all tropical waters it can be found along the tropical coasts of Australia. Unlike the Hawksbill Turtle, however, it does breed throughout its range in Australia and produces about 100 small round eggs.

It is olive-green above with brown, reddish-brown and black patterning. The head is average in size and the upper eyelid has a series of large scales. It grows to about 1 metre in length. Hatchlings are con-trastingly black on top and white below. This turtle is unusual in that the adults are believed to be almost entirely herbivorous while the young are carnivorous.

The Green Turtle is considered a delicacy and is sought for turtle soup. It has also been valued for its oil, shell and skin which is used for leather making. As the last stronghold for the turtle it is important that Australia provides protection of its breeding grounds.

Concern for this and other species of marine turtle is particularly acute. They cannot sustain the high level of exploitation by our near neighbour, Indonesia.

POTENTIALLY VULNERABLE

PACIFIC RIDLEY TURTLE
Lepidochelys olivacea

This relatively large turtle is distributed throughout the tropical seas of the world although not necessarily in great numbers. In Australia it seemingly occurs right along the north coast but reliable records only exist from Torres Strait and Coburg Peninsula in the Northern Territory. From this latter location is also the only reliable nesting records for the species in Australia. This turtle lays up to 100 large round eggs.

It grows to about 1.5 metres in length with a large head. In colour it is grey or olive-grey and there are no conspicuous markings. It is whitish underneath. The shell is heart-shaped.

In Central American countries it seems to have heavier concentrations and is taken for food, leather and oil. Otherwise, it is uncommon throughout the rest of its range including Australia where its conservation status requires further investigation.

POTENTIALLY VULNERABLE

ENDANGERED

LEATHERY TURTLE
Dermochelys coriacea

The Leathery Turtle is the largest turtle in the world, growing up to 3 metres in length. It is very dark brown to black with a series of fine dots running in rows down its back. Its sides are edged with pale cream or yellow spots. It is whitish underneath. The heavy, paddle-shaped limbs are clawless.

This species occurs in all tropical and temperate waters throughout the world and extends further south to colder waters than any other sea turtle species. It inhabits coastal waters, including larger bays, estuaries and rivers. In Australia, it can be found in coastal waters, with most sightings being in the temperate waters and more commonly along the eastern seaboard. Minor nesting is known to occur along a short stretch of the central Queensland coast. These turtles have been observed feeding on jellyfish and blue-bottles along the coast of New South Wales.

Although rare in Australia, the species is considered endangered internationally and is regarded thus by Australian authorities. It is threatened by the taking of eggs for human consumption. It has a small number of breeding grounds worldwide which are heavily pillaged. This species must be given full protection in Australian waters.

Robert WG Jenkins

Pig-nosed Turtle

POTENTIALLY VULNERABLE

PIG-NOSED TURTLE
Carettochelys insculpta

Confined in Australia to the Northern Territory, it has been found in only the Daly, Victoria and Alligator River systems. Within these it is found in the freshwater reaches, at the tidal mouth and in large waterholes and lagoons.

Little is known in Australia of its nesting habits although pregnant females have been taken here. Its diet appears to consist of figs, pandanus, snails and small fish.

It is essentially grey-toned along its back and white through cream to yellow below. There is a light band extending behind its eye. This turtle is distinguished by its pitted shell, large, two-clawed flipper and long fleshy snout. It grows to 70 centimetres.

It is the only species in both its genus and family and much work is needed to determine its conservation status and management requirements.

WESTERN SWAMP TURTLE
Pseudemydura umbrina

Also known as the Western Swamp Tortoise, this turtle has a squarish shell, about 15 centimetres long, which is brown above and lighter yellow or olive-brown below. It has a short neck and its broad, flat head has a horny covering and is the only species in its genus.

The Western Swamp Turtle is considered to be Australia's most endangered reptile. Fewer than 50 animals remain in its natural habitat and its numbers are declining. It is a swamp dweller and is found only in two small ephemeral swamps at Bullsbrook, near Perth, Western Australia. Ellenbrook and Twin Swamps Nature Reserves were dedicated and the area has now been fenced and is actively managed for the species.

In addition, there is an active conservation project involving population monitoring and breeding research in progress. A captive-breeding program seems to offer the only hope for this animal's long-term survival, particularly as there may be very few females remaining in the wild.

Success in breeding this highly endangered species was achieved in 1989 when young turtles were born in captivity in Perth Zoo.

ENDANGERED

STEPHEN'S BANDED SNAKE
Hoplocephalus stephensi

As its name suggests, this snake is banded with broad, irregular dark bands alternating with thinner, lighter ones. Occasionally, the bands may be missing altogether. It has a total length of about 45 centimetres.

The snake is found along the ranges and coast from Gosford, near Sydney, in New South Wales to Canungra in southern Queensland where it inhabits the wetter sclerophyll forests and rainforests. It is at least partly tree dwelling.

It feeds on lizards, birds and small mammals and bears its young alive, which range from three to eight at a time.

Continuing threat from commercial timber production in areas of State forest and the fragmentation of its habitat, have lead to it being regarded as vulnerable.

VULNERABLE

Stephen's Banded Snake

Glen Threlfo

107

BROAD-HEADED SNAKE
Hoplocephalus bungaroides

This snake, with a total length of up to 60 centimetres, is confined to the Hawkesbury sandstone country near Sydney where it occurs both on the coast and ranges. It is usually found under large rock slabs, or in rocky crevices. While areas of its habitat are represented in several national parks, its occurrence so close to major population centres is considered a matter for concern.

The Broad-headed Snake is basically black in colour, with yellow spots on its head and bands of bright yellow scales around its body, forming an irregular stripe along its side. Its underside is grey-black. Mainly feeding on lizards and frogs, the snake bears its young alive.

Its bite, while not considered lethal, can nevertheless produce severe symptoms and this has led to it being deliberately killed. This killing, together with habitat disturbance (including the removal of sandstone blocks for suburban gardens and vandalism) and collection by reptile fanciers has led to it being regarded as endangered.

Robert WG Jenkins

Western Black-striped Snake

WESTERN BLACK-STRIPED SNAKE
Neelaps calonotus

Appearing overall reddish-orange in colour with a prominent black stripe, the Western Black-striped Snake is found in coastal and near-coastal areas in a strip running from Lancelin to Rockingham and inland for about 90 kilometres in south-western Western Australia. It is a small snake, with a total length of about 25 centimetres. Its scales are cream, edged reddish-orange, except for those forming a narrow stripe down its back which are black edged. Its underside is white or cream and it has a black-tipped snout and black patches on the head and neck. The Western Black-striped Snake is a burrowing snake which feeds on lizards and lays eggs.

With a restricted distribution, and occurring as it does so close to Perth, there is concern for this species. Loss of habitat, through urban development, for example, could fragment the populations and increase pressure from predators. To ensure its future it is necessary to determine the adequacy of existing protected areas and create further ones if these prove inadequate.

Commercial trade in this species combined with the other pressures threaten its future survival. The inland population is probably already extinct and urgent management is required to ensure its continued existence.

JC Wombey

Diamond Python

DIAMOND PYTHON
Morelia spilota spilota

This is one of two subspecies of *Morelia spilota*. It has a relatively restricted distribution, being found only in the rainforests and dense eucalypt forests in coastal districts of New South Wales. The other subspecies, the Carpet Snake, is much more widespread extending from the rainforests of the east to the deserts of the centre.

It is a beautiful snake which makes it attractive to reptile fanciers. With an average length of 2 metres, although a maximum of 4 metres is possible, the Diamond Python is glossy black above with cream or yellow spots on individual scales forming together to create a series of diamond-shaped patterns.

Underneath, it is cream or yellow with some dark grey markings. It is mostly nocturnal and has a varied diet of terrestrial vertebrates.

Although this is a non-venomous snake, it has not stopped people from killing it in the mistaken belief that it is deadly. The snake is believed to be uncommon as a result of forest clearing, predation and competition, collecting by traders and deliberate killing. As with most snakes an extensive public education campaign is needed to overcome inbred fears, while protection and urgent management of essential habitats must be given high priority.

VULNERABLE

Frithfoto/Olympus

Boyd's Forest Dragon

**POTENTIALLY
VULNERABLE**

BOYD'S FOREST DRAGON
Gonocephalus boydii

Boyd's Forest Dragon is found only in the rainforests of north-east Queensland between Townsville and Cooktown. Although it is reasonably common in some areas, its distribution is nevertheless restricted and this makes it particularly vulnerable. An extremely attractive lizard, it has a high potential value in the overseas reptile trade.

The lizard has total length from snout to vent of some 150 millimetres, with a tail twice as long again. Its back is a rich chocolate-brown colour sometimes with a green tinge. It has a number of splashes and stripes of yellow, cream or black including a series of yellow scales on the flanks. Its ventral surface is pale brown or off-white although the throat may be darker brown and its large head is wedge-shaped.

This tree-dwelling lizard is well camouflaged and is usually only seen when foraging in more open areas. The species requires monitoring in its restricted rainforest habitat.

SOUTHERN ANGLE-HEADED DRAGON
Gonocephalus spinipes

Active during the day, this tree-living lizard is confined to the rainforests and adjoining wet sclerophyll forests of north-eastern New South Wales and south-eastern Queensland. It has a snout to vent length of about 11 centimetres and a tail twice this length again.

It is grey, grey-brown or chocolate-brown in colour overspread with green. Often it has dark brown markings and spots. Its colouring serves well as camouflage and it is usually seen only when foraging on roadsides, tracks or stream edges.

The Southern Angle-headed Dragon is considered vulnerable. This is both as a result of its limited distribution and its potential value in the reptile trade.

Southern Angle-headed Dragon   Frithfoto/Olympus

POTENTIALLY VULNERABLE

JC Wombey   *Ring-tailed Gecko*

RING-TAILED GECKO
Cyrtodactylus louisiadensis

This is a most striking reptile. Arboreal, with a voracious appetite, it is found along the coast and on the ranges in north-eastern Queensland extending as far south as the Atherton Tableland, where it has been recorded from caves and rock fissures.

The gecko is pale brown in colour with broad purplish-brown bands edged with white which extend down its back to the long curling thin tail. A distinctive white-edged skin fold runs along its side. It has a broad flat head and is considered a large gecko with a snout to vent length of 16 centimetres.

Further research is needed to determine the status of the species. Until such information is known it should remain a concern.

POTENTIALLY VULNERABLE

VULNERABLE

LINED BURROWING SKINK
Lerista lineata

This animal is found under rocks and logs only in south-western Western Australia at Freemantle and on nearby islands.

The Lined Burrowing Skink is grey-brown in colour with two thin black stripes extending from the neck to the tail, with a snout to vent length of approximately 50 millimetres.

Species in the genus *Lerista* are generally burrowing animals that feed on ants, termites and other small insects.

The adequacy of protected areas for this species is uncertain and its proximity to Perth is likely to have had some effect on the natural distribution of its population.

The isolation of small populations can also have long-term consequences for the integrity of the species through the restriction placed on gene flow which is potentially a problem for this species' future survival.

VULNERABLE

LORD HOWE ISLAND SKINK
Leiolopisma lichenigera

Restricted to Lord Howe Island and nearby islets including Ball's Pyramid, the Lord Howe Island Skink is rich bronze or olive in colour with prominent stripes running down its side from the eye to the base of the tail with a pale underside. It has a snout to vent length of about 80 millimetres.

In winter, the skink is active during the daytime and has been observed feeding on seabird eggs which it has cracked open by rolling on the rocks. In summer, it is active at night when it feeds on small marine crustaceans, insects and other organisms.

Habitat disturbance and introduced animals have led to a decline in its numbers. Usually found on grassy-stony slopes under rocks, boulders and fallen timber the Lord Howe Island Skink is now uncommon on Lord Howe Island itself although it still occurs in greater numbers on the offshore islets.

The species has also disappeared from Norfolk Island apparently due to the introduction of rats.

Although the species still occurs on small islands off the coast it must be regarded as vulnerable.

Lord Howe Island Skink

JC Wombey

Robert WG Jenkins

Pedra Branca Skink

PEDRA BRANCA SKINK
Pseudemoia palfreymani

The Pedra Branca Skink is found only on Pedra Branca Rock, a small uninhabited island off the southern coast of Tasmania, in the South West Tasmania National Park.

It is dark brown to black in colour with a spotted head and lighter stripes. It has a snout to vent length of about 75 millimetres and a tail of about 90 millimetres.

Pedra Branca Rock is a small, barren, rocky island less than 60 metres above sea level. It is assumed that the skink basks on the exposed rock surfaces on the island and shelters around rocky crevices.

While seemingly secure, given the remoteness of its location, this may not necessarily be the key factor in its long-term survival. The skink is apparently dependent on large colonies of seabirds on the island which are, in turn, dependent on regular schools of mackerel. Interference with the supply of mackerel may therefore have a flow-on effect on the integrity of the seabirds and thus of the skink itself.

Population monitoring must continue to ensure any adverse population trends can be quickly detected.

POTENTIALLY VULNERABLE

EXTINCT

ADELAIDE PYGMY BLUETONGUE SKINK
Tiliqua adelaidensis

Bluetongue lizards are extremely familiar reptiles to many Australians. They are often found in suburban gardens or sunbaking in the middle of roads. It will surprise many to know however that the only species of reptile in Australia that is believed to be extinct is in fact one of our nine species of bluetongues. The last reliable record of the Adelaide Pygmy Bluetongue Skink dates back to 1959.

As its name implies, this reptile was the smallest of all the bluetongues reaching a snout to vent length of only 90 millimetres, compared to the common Eastern Blue-tongue at 300 millimetres. The species was grey or grey-brown above, graduating paler on its flanks. The limbs and tail were marked with darker spots and blotches against paler scales.

Though the species was recorded mostly from the general vicinity of Adelaide little is known of its true distribution or biology. The reason for the Bluetongue's demise is unclear though it is assumed that because the Adelaide region has been subjected to substantial modification and degradation to allow for urban development its necessary habitat was severely disrupted.

LANCELIN ISLAND STRIPED SKINK
Ctenotus lancelini

Another species with a restricted distribution, the Lancelin Island Striped Skink is found only on the small, uninhabited coastal Lancelin Island, about 100 kilometres north of Perth. It is found around and under rocks, rocky outcrops and under decaying logs.

While variable in both colour and pattern, the skink is generally brown above with darker brown speckling. It has yellow legs with blackish-brown markings.

The snout to vent length is approximately 80 millimetres.

The effects of the introduction of exotic animals, such as rats and cats, on native wildlife on islands is well documented. The skink could similarly be vulnerable and it has been suggested that its long-term future may well depend on the ability of the authorities to keep Lancelin Island free of introduced predators. While the Island is a nature reserve, access to it is not restricted and its proximity to Perth and the mainland generally places the species at further risk from such factors as habitat disturbance.

MANGROVE MONITOR
Varanus indicus

Growing to a total length of about 1 metre this attractive lizard is distributed throughout the rainforests and coastal mangrove forests of eastern Cape York Peninsula and the Torres Strait Islands. It has also been recorded from coastal mangrove forests in Arnhem Land, Northern Territory. Outside Australia, it is found also on parts of the Indo-Papuan Archipelago.

The Mangrove Monitor's colour is dark purplish-brown with many cream, yellow or yellow-green flecks and spots. Underneath, it is cream or white.

Its diet consists of insects, fish, reptiles, birds and mammals which it forages for around forest streams and tidal mangrove areas. It can both swim and climb.

Its status is uncertain and, having a very restricted distribution, must warrant monitoring and further research. Development proposals for Cape York Peninsula make this need for further research more urgent.

Mangrove Monitor

Frithfoto/Olympus

BRONZE-BACKED LEGLESS LIZARD
Ophidiocephalus taeniatus

This lizard is the only member of its genus. Until recently it was known only to occur in the vicinity of Charlotte Waters in the Northern Territory but it has now been reported from a few locations on the western fringe of the Simpson Desert. It may in fact have a much wider distribution throughout the arid shrublands that surround the Simpson Desert. Intense monitoring is needed to define both their distribution and abundance in greater detail.

The Bronze-backed Legless Lizard has a snout to vent length of 102 millimetres. It is a rich fawn colour above with a darker brown band providing a clear demarcation from the upper surface to the grey-brown under-surface. It is distinctively patterned. The head is grey and the tail is longer than the body. It has a small external ear opening.

The best protection for this lizard may in fact be the remote and inhospitable nature of the terrain in which it lives. It may also be vulnerable from the destruction of its microhabitat or disturbance by livestock.

VULNERABLE

Robert WG Jenkins

Unnamed Legless Lizard (Aprasia parapulchella)

UNNAMED LEGLESS LIZARD
Aprasia parapulchella

Occurring in the southern tablelands, the south-western slopes in New South Wales and the Australian Capital Territory, the Legless Lizard can be found around granite outcrops. Recorded specimens were found under weathered granite rocks on a grazed grassy riverside slope.

The Legless Lizard has a light grey body with a darker brown head and neck. It is whitish underneath. Its body is slender and it has a snout to vent length of 14 centimetres with a tail nearly as long again.

It is currently regarded by authorities in Australia as threatened but they must be surveyed more intensely to define their distribution and abundance in greater detail. Although its occurrence in several areas within Canberra Nature Park gives it some protection, overall the lizard may be vulnerable to habitat disturbance by the removal of the rocks, on which it depends, for suburban gardens. Its closeness to suburban Canberra also renders its habitat vulnerable.

VULNERABLE

115

Amphibians

Something is happening to the frogs. In the last ten years or so perhaps a dozen species of frogs have vanished from their rainforest habitats all down the east coast of Australia.

No-one really knows why. The same dramatic disappearances have occurred in North America, Central and South America and Europe. They may be a frightening indicator of environmental degradation, or the victims of subtle changes to our climate.

Are they a sign that the greenhouse effect is nearer than we think, or is it a tragic combination of all these factors? Even if we are to concede that the disappearances may be a part of a normal climatic and species' cycle, can such natural cycles complete their normal course in an environment so irrevocably changed by modern society?

Whatever the causes, and many frogs have suffered at the hands of human development, the fact remains that a large number of amphibians require our immediate attention. The high level of frog endemism (94 per cent are found nowhere else in the world), and the great paucity of information about their biological requirements, serve to increase the urgency with which we must take conservation action.

Australian frogs provide us with some marvellous examples of nature at work. Among their ranks, they have the only species which incubates its young in its stomach, and one of the only two amphibian species on the entire planet to use body language to communicate with one another.

The frogs for which we express grave concern are all extremely small, nondescript and live in highly restricted and vulnerable habitats. They present a particularly demanding conservation problem, and one that must be solved before the passage of time prevents remedial action.

Of the total frog fauna of Australia, now approaching 180 species, 41 are listed in this book. There are probably many more frogs yet to be discovered in Australia, and many more that may need to be added to the list of threatened species.

Previous page. Inhabiting rocks and logs in swift mountain streams, Litoria rheocolus *is restricted to rainforest areas in north-east Queensland, and has been listed as potentially vulnerable.*

H & J Beste/Auscape

POTENTIALLY VULNERABLE

Loveridge's Frog

Robert WG Jenkins

LOVERIDGE'S FROG
Kyrannus loveridgei

This frog burrows in soft, moist soil or moss or sits in moss-lined cavities beside streams. Male frogs call from underground. It lives in rain and Antarctic beech forests as well as wet sclerophyll forests. These forests are found in the McPherson and Gibraltar ranges of the Queensland-New South Wales border area above 1000 metres.

Loveridge's Frog has a dark brown back with a white or light orange belly. The throat area is heavily dotted with dark brown. It is about 30 millimetres in length.

Although the population may be stable its very restricted range in an area under increasing development pressure renders the species vulnerable.

Note: To measure the length of a frog you measure from the tip of its nose or snout to the end of its backside or vent.

JC Wombey

Pouched Frog

POUCHED FROG
Assa darlingtoni

The Pouched Frog is also known as the 'hip pocket frog' and the 'marsupial frog', because the male incubates the young in a pair of pouches on either side of his body. The male lowers himself over the egg mass which liquefies. The embryos climb their way over his mucous slippery body into the pouches. The male helps by sweeping his feet and hands to scoop up lost embryos. It takes about 48 days for froglets to emerge.

This frog is the only species in its genus. It is about 30 millimetres long. The colour of its back may vary from grey to reddish-brown, usually with dark patches and streaks on the head and flanks. Underneath it is cream-coloured with heavy motley brown patches.

It is known only in the McPherson Range and nearby mountainous areas on the border between New South Wales and Queensland. It can be found under rocks, leaf litter and rotting logs in rainforest and close by Antarctic beech forests.

The species' vulnerability stems from its extremely restricted range and the threat of habitat destruction.

VULNERABLE

ROUND FROG
Arenophryne rotunda

This is a burrowing frog which spends most of its time underneath the surface of coastal sand-dunes. Other burrowing frogs burrow backwards into the ground using only their feet. The Round Frog burrows head first into the sand. To do this it has broad fingers with a very short outer finger. The frog burrows into the sand at dawn where it absorbs moisture through its skin. It surfaces at night to feed mainly on ants. Males and females pair at the beginning of winter, mate underground and remain below the surface for at least five months. Round Frogs change from eggs to baby frogs entirely within the egg capsule and don't swim in water as tadpoles.

This frog is short and fat with short limbs. On top it is a dull cream colour with patches of brown. Underneath it is a paler cream colour with a few smaller dark patches. It is about 30 millimetres long.

Round Frogs are only known from the False Entrance Well site on coastal sand-dunes on Carrarang Station near Denham in Western Australia where they are particularly vulnerable to habitat disturbance.

VULNERABLE

WALLUM FROGLET
Crinia tinnula

The call of this frog is said to sound like the tinkling of a small bell. It can be found in acid paperbark swamps of southern Queensland and coastal areas of northern New South Wales.

The belly of this frog is often white on light brown with some darker flecks. The back of the male is white with heavy black flecks. The female is white with lighter flecks. The Wallum Froglet is distinguished by a line of white dots on the middle of its throat, similar to the Common Eastern Froglet. This frog is approximately 30 millimetres in length.

The species is potentially vulnerable due to its restricted coastal habitats in regions under immense development pressure.

Baw Baw Frog

JC Wombey

BAW BAW FROG
Philoria frosti

The Baw Baw Frog is under severe threat, even though it is largely within a national park, because it has to compete with a ski resort. It is found under logs and rocks near streams and in tunnels in sphagnum bogs at altitudes about 1500 metres on Mount Baw Baw in Victoria.

Its back is usually dark brown with black markings and white patches. Underneath it is a motley creamy-yellow on brown. A distinct feature is small warts on the sides of the back and the rump. Its belly and throat is smooth. The females are about 50 millimetres in length and the males are smaller at 45 millimetres.

The Baw Baw Frog is one of the few frogs that scientists agree is actually endangered due to habitat destruction by man's activities.

SPHAGNUM FROG
Philoria sphagnicolus

Although the Sphagnum Frog seems to appear in a confusing range of colour shades, it is fairly easy to identify because it lives in beds of moist sphagnum moss.

Its upper surface comes in a variety of colours from cream or orange to black, with darker patches associated with small warts. However, the most constant marks are a pair of dark stripes which may meet in front. The undersurface is usually white with brown flecks on the throat. The fingers and toes lack webbing. The average length is 35 millimetres.

The Sphagnum Frog is known only in ranges more than 700 metres above sea level in New South Wales near Ebor and Dorrigo down to Barrington Tops, which are areas of high rainfall. Its habitat has been extensively cleared and development pressures still remain.

POTENTIALLY VULNERABLE

CORROBOREE FROG
Pseudophryne corroboree

This is possibly the easiest frog to identify because of its very beautiful contrasting colour pattern of black and bright yellow stripes. The undersurface ranges from yellow, yellow and pale blue, to white and black. The skin on the back can be granular with low warts which tend to form a pattern of low ridges. It is about 30 millimetres long.

It is found in the Australian Alps area above 1500 metres where there are extensive sphagnum bogs. The frog lays its eggs in nests in deep burrows in the sphagnum moss. Below the tree line it will use fallen logs and debris for shelter.

The Corroboree Frog is considered potentially vulnerable because of its commercial potential as an aquarium animal and its restricted distribution.

POTENTIALLY VULNERABLE

Corroboree Frog

JC Wombey

JC Wombey

Southern Toadlet

**POTENTIALLY
VULNERABLE**

SOUTHERN TOADLET
Pseudophryne dendyi

This frog was named in 1892 but it is still uncertain as to what distinguishes it from a very similar species called the Brown Toadlet. If the frog is found above 1300 metres in the Snowy Mountains, then it is likely to be a Southern Toadlet. The Southern Toadlet is about 35 millimetres in length and is a very dark brown-black colour on the back with patches of bright yellow near the rear and on the upper limbs. Its belly is marbled in black and white.

It is found in south-eastern New South Wales and eastern Victoria where its restricted and patchy distribution combined with ever-present habitat threats render the species potentially vulnerable.

**POTENTIALLY
VULNERABLE**

EUNGELLA TORRENT FROG
Taudactylus eungellensis

There have been only two reports in the world of frogs using body language to communicate. One is the Australian Eungella Torrent Frog. Dr Michael Tyler witnessed an extremely rare example of frog body language in 1985 when he saw two Eungella Torrent Frogs. One was making a series of tiny hops and then waving its arm and leg like a circus clown. This frog seemed to be focusing its attention on another frog which was sitting about one metre away and looking totally unmoved by the whole performance. Eventually the active frog swam to join the inactive frog and began to stroke its head and body. The pair then dived into the water and swam off together.

A likely explanation for this behaviour is that it is all part of a courtship pattern useful in an area where the background noise is so high that having a vocal sac would be of no use.

This is slightly larger than the Mount Glorious Torrent Frog being approximately 35 millimetres long. Its call has been likened to a little hammer tapping on a metal plate.

It would be easy to confuse this frog with the Mount Glorious Torrent Frog because the colours are almost the same. However this frog has an X-shaped dark mark on the back behind the head. The belly and thighs are entirely spotless.

The Eungella Torrent Frog is only known from Eungella and Finch Hatton Gorge, west of Mackay in Queensland and this particularly limited range places the frog at risk.

MOUNT GLORIOUS TORRENT FROG or DAY FROG
Taudactylus diurnis

The Mount Glorious Frog was once abundant in southern Queensland but has not been seen for a number of years. It is considered endangered. It is aptly named because it has an amazing ability to hang onto rocks and in crevices in very fast-flowing torrents of water. It is also found in pools and swift flowing streams but when frightened, will quickly jump into a waterfall or torrent to escape.

For many years, it was thought that this frog was mute because the adult males lack vocal sacs. Their call is now described as a barely audible, very soft clucking sound, repeated a few times in quick succession.

The back of this frog is greyish-brown with darker spotting. There is a very distinctive 'H' of colour between the shoulders, with a darker bar between the eyes. The belly is cream or pale yellow with large light grey spots. The females are longer than the males being approximately 30 millimetres.

This frog's limited rainforest habitat at Mount Glorious and Konadilla in south-eastern Queensland renders the frog endangered.

ENDANGERED

SHARP-SNOUTED TORRENT FROG
Taudactylus acutirostris

This is also referred to as the Tinker frog because of the metallic 'tink, tink' of its call, which sounds like a glass being tapped with a spoon.

It is found in rainforest, in debris, vegetation and rocks near and in small mountain streams. The Sharp-snouted Torrent Frog is known only in the rainforest areas of the ranges in the Cairns-Innisfail area of north-eastern Queensland.

Its back is coloured greyish-brown to dark brown. The sides are dark grey to black. The back and the sides are separated by a very clearly marked black stripe which starts at the snout and continues nearly to the groin. There is a very pale stripe just above the black stripe. The belly and throat are greyish-white with a black edging along the lower jaw. The tops of the limbs are striped. It is about 30 millimetres in length.

The species is thought potentially vulnerable due to its restricted rainforest range.

POTENTIALLY VULNERABLE

Sharp-snouted Torrent Frog

Tom & Pam Gardner

PLATYPUS FROG or GASTRIC BROODING FROG
Rheobatrachus silus

This amazing frog was only discovered in 1973 and tragically it may already be extinct. A female was observed to open her mouth and give birth to baby frogs which hopped from her tongue. The reproductive habits of this genus are unique in the whole of the animal kingdom.

The tadpoles develop in the stomach of the female after the eggs are swallowed. They are eventually regurgitated as fully formed froglets. The frog's stomach shuts down production of acid and also halts the crushing movements of the stomach. A few days after the birth of the last baby, the mother resumes eating in the normal way, as she does not eat at all while the babies are in her stomach. The mother gives birth to about 25 babies in the one pregnancy!

The female is about 50 millimetres in length and the males are smaller at 40 millimetres. On top, the frogs are browny-black with browny-black streaks and patches. The belly is whitish with some bright orange on the limbs. The eyes are quite prominent and directed upwards.

The frogs hide under rocks in boulder-strewn, fast-flowing creeks in rainforests. The Platypus Frog is known only in the Blackall and Conondale Ranges in south-eastern Queensland. The species has not been seen for a number of years and while clearing has occurred within its forested range the precise reasons for its drastic decline is unknown.

Platypus Frog or Gastric Brooding Frog

Robert W G Jenkins

JC Wombey

Unnamed Gastric Brooding Frog (Rheobatrachus vitellinus)

UNNAMED GASTRIC BROODING FROG
Rheobatrachus vitellinus

This is the second species of the genus Rheobatrachus. It was discovered in 1984 and as yet it has no distinctive common name. It is simply referred to as the second species of Gastric Brooding frog. *Rheobatrachus vitellinus* also broods its young in its stomach and gives birth through the mouth.

The range of this frog is 800 kilometres north of the Platypus Frog and inhabits fast-flowing rainforest creeks in the Clarke Range of Eungella National Park near Proserpine in Queensland.

R. vitellinus ranges in length from 62 to 70 millimetres for the females and 55 millimetres for the males. It is much longer than the other Gastric Brooding frog. They are similar in colouring except that this frog has an extensive area of vivid yellowish-orange on the belly and the undersurface of the arms. The back is a pale brown with obscure darker patches.

This frog has not been seen in the wild since soon after its discovery and biologists cannot explain its disappearance.

ENDANGERED

ROCK-DWELLING ELEGANT MICROHYLID
Cophixalus saxatilis

The Rock-dwelling Elegant Microhylid is known only in the Black Mountain area near Cooktown in northern Queensland. This frog lives in warm, humid cracks between enormous rocks typical of this area.

Viewed from above, this frog is brown with irregular darker brown markings. There is usually a darker coloured bar between the eyes and a W-shaped mark between the front legs. The colour underneath the frog is creamy-white with some dark spots on chin, front legs, palms and soles. The third finger disc is wider than that of the fourth toe. This frog is about 30 millimetres long.

Although the habitat of the Rock-dwelling Elegant Microhylid is generally protected within the Black Mountain National Park, the actual area in which the frog can be found, is extremely small and therefore the species is vulnerable.

VULNERABLE

125

THE THREATENED
Fish

An alarmingly large proportion of Australia's endemic freshwater fish species are threatened with extinction. The following pages highlight 16 of the estimated 79 species that are considered to be at risk.

It is an extremely sad state of affairs, and yet one that seems to attract little, if any, public attention. Governments and their responsible agencies still persist in undertaking activities that threaten our native fish to an even greater extent. Perhaps the most obvious example is the release of exotic fish species into many of our freshwater systems for the sole purpose of providing fisherman with something to catch.

While we may not know a great deal about the biological requirements of the majority of our freshwater fish, we certainly know enough to understand that such introductions have been one of the main factors causing the drastic decline in native fish populations. Fishermen don't like timid fish to catch, they like the aggressive predators, and these are the species that compete all too successfully with the original inhabitants of Australia's lakes and streams.

The major reasons for the sorry conservation status of native freshwater fish stems from the pollution and destruction of natural habitats. There are only about 200 species of freshwater fish in Australia, and our main preoccupation must be concerned with reversing these ever-threatening trends.

You may be surprised to learn that the Great White Shark is giving marine biologists increasing cause for conservation concern. If we know little about the needs of our freshwater fish, then we know even less, and certainly seem to care even less about the marine fishes. They too have felt the heavy hand of human development.

Scientists are also concerned about the conservation status of the Grey Nurse Shark, Herbst's Shark, the Black Cod, and the Southern Bluefin Tuna. Doubtless there are many other marine species currently in jeopardy.

Previous page. Concern has been expressed by Australian fish biologists as to the conservation status of the Grey Nurse Shark (Eugomphodus taurus), and it is listed in this book as potentially vulnerable.

Kev Deacon/Auscape

VULNERABLE

MACQUARIE PERCH
Macquaria australasica

Renowned for its angling and eating qualities, the Macquarie Perch has suffered considerable declines in distribution and abundance. Although once widely distributed throughout the Murray-Darling and south-east coast river systems, it is now confined to the upper reaches of the Murray-Darling system and some New South Wales coastal rivers such as the Shoalhaven.

Adults can reach a weight of 3.5 kilograms but are more commonly 200 millimetres long and weigh about 400 grams. The head is deep and laterally compressed, with a tapered snout. The tail fin is rounded. Back colouration varies from black, dark brown or bluish-grey to green-brown, becoming lighter along the sides; the belly is white. Juveniles are often mottled on the back and

sides. Adults are carnivorous and the larvae and very young fish feed on zooplankton. The species is most abundant in large lakes fed by suitable shallow spawning streams.

Population declines are attributed primarily to siltation, which destroys the preferred habitat of deep rock pools with considerable cover and smothers spawning sites; trout may also compete with it for food and eat juveniles. Dam construction, over-fishing, local pollution and river improvement have also been suggested as factors contributing to its decline. Techniques have been developed to successfully induce breeding in artificial conditions. As a result, the New South Wales State Fisheries have been able to restock some habitat areas, considerably improving its survival prospects.

EASTERN FRESHWATER or CLARENCE RIVER COD
Macullochella ikei

There has been a dramatic decrease in the distribution and abundance of this freshwater cod since the 1900s. It was formerly found throughout the Clarence River system in New South Wales but is now confined mostly to the Nymboida River. During the 1950s specimens were known to reach 22 kilograms but those in the small remnant population now average 1 kilogram. The largest specimen ever caught weighed 49.5 kilograms.

Preferred habitat is clear, rocky waters. Growth is slow. Fish become reproductively mature at four to five years when they weigh around 1 kilogram. Spawning occurs when water temperatures rise above 18°C.

Declines in the population of this species are thought to be associated with large floods and mining pollution that occurred during the 1940s. There is considerable concern for the survival of this cod.

As a result, a fishing ban has been imposed on this species. Whilst this is a positive step, unless it is widely publicised and actively enforced, its conservation benefit would be questionable.

ENDANGERED

OXLEYAN PYGMY PERCH
Nannoperca oxleyana

A poorly known species, the Oxleyan Pygmy Perch is only known from a few sites in northern New South Wales and southern Queensland. Its range extends northwards from the Richmond River system towards the dune lakes between the Maroochy and Noosa River systems.

Adults will reach up to 75 millimetres. Known habitats include reedy and weedy lake edges and slow-flowing rivers with a sandy bottom. Physical characteristics include: a compressed elongated body; enlarged teeth at the front of the lower jaw; a deeply notched single dorsal fin; and a straight ended tail. The back is olive with dark scale margins; sides are paler with indistinct rows of darker, brownish blotches; the belly is whitish and eyes are blue. There

Oxleyan Pygmy Perch   GE Schmida

are blue markings on the gill covers and a black spot with orange margins at the base of the tail.

Too little is known about this species to accurately identify specific threats to its survival, however its limited distribution certainly suggests vulnerability.

POTENTIALLY VULNERABLE

DRYSDALE HARDYHEAD
Craterocephalus n. sp.

This newly discovered species has not yet been described to science. Body length is commonly 50 to 60 millimetres, but some specimens reach up to 70 millimetres. It is a thin fish, reaching a maximum body depth of about one fifth of its length. There are two dorsal fins, both of equal height, but the first

slightly smaller than the second. The tail is slightly forked and there is a silvery line and darker spots along its side.

The Drysdale Hardyhead is found in the Drysdale River, Western Australia. It appears to be rare, with very few collected. Habitat and diet are not well known.

POTENTIALLY VULNERABLE

POTENTIALLY VULNERABLE

DALHOUSIE HARDYHEAD
Craterocephalus dalhousiensis

Another small fish with a very restricted distribution, the Dalhousie Hardyhead has a deep body, thick fleshy lips, a small mouth and two similar sized dorsal fins. The back is dark brown, with two or three rows of brown spots along the lower sides. Specimens reach a maximum length of 70 millimetres, with males generally being slightly shorter than females. They are omnivorous.

Distribution is restricted to the Dalhousie Springs in the Finke River system, approximately 120 kilometres north of Oodnadatta, South Australia. This species is interesting because it is the only species of hardyhead that is known to be permanently sexually dimorphic, that is, with separate male and female individuals. Other hardyheads only exhibit temporary sexual differences during the breeding season.

The primary threat to this species lies in its extremely restricted distribution and requires constant monitoring.

POTENTIALLY VULNERABLE

PRINCE REGENT HARDYHEAD
Craterocephalus n. sp.

Another undescribed, newly discovered hardyhead, the Prince Regent Hardyhead is only known from two sites in the Roe River system, Western Australia.

Specimens are known to reach 70 millimetres and have two equal sized dorsal fins. The back is deep green to olive and back and side scales are barred or blotched with black. A black stripe runs from the eye to the snout and all fins are straw-coloured. Habitat is known to be clear flowing waters with a sandstone bottom.

So little is known about this species that it is difficult to identify specific threats, however its apparent rarity and restricted distribution are cause for concern.

POTENTIALLY VULNERABLE

BLIND GUDGEON
Milyeringa veritas

A poorly known species confined to subterranean waters in Western Australia, the Blind Gudgeon has only been sighted at nine localities between 1944 and 1980. It is well adapted to cave-dwelling, lacking eyes and most skin pigmentation and having a well developed system of sensory papillae on the head and sides, through which it is thought to feel. The body is grey, the forehead pale yellow, fins flesh-coloured and there is a purplish area above the gills. It is known to reach 45 millimetres.

The known distribution is subterranean waters between North West Cape and Yardie Creek, Western Australia. It is thought to be a carnivore but may also eat algae. Specimens have been observed to swim slowly near the surface of limestone wells, especially at night, where they are thought to feed on insects and the like which fall onto the well surface.

So little is known about the biology, population and specific habitat requirements of this species that it is difficult to predict likely threats and suggest appropriate conservation action.

Blind Gudgeon 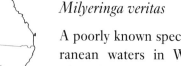 GE Schmida

SLENDER GUDGEON
Hypseleotris ejuncida

This species has only been collected from one locality in the Prince Regent River, Western Australia. Here it was inhabiting a quiet, clear pool with a sandstone bottom. Known maximum length is around 50 millimetres. The Slender Gudgeon has a very slender, compressed body, a small mouth and two dorsal fins; the first smaller than the second. The body is tan. All body scales have a dark brown edge, which forms a diamond pattern on the sides. There are white spots and wavy bands on the second dorsal fin and four to six wavy bands of dark spots on the tail fin. Other fins are clear to dusky although there is a dark bar across the base of the pectoral fin. Males have a dark brown head. Females are smaller and lighter coloured. Little is known about the biology of this species but it is presumed that breeding behaviour is similar to other gudgeons, with the male undertaking parental care by guarding the eggs until they hatch.

The known distribution of this species is within the Prince Regent Nature Reserve. Gudgeons are becoming increasingly popular aquarium species and it is likely that this species would also enter trade if specimens were available.

POTENTIALLY VULNERABLE

BARNETT RIVER GUDGEON
Hypseleotris kimberleyensis

This gudgeon has a very restricted distribution and is only known from the Manning Creek Gorge, near Mount Barnett Station, Western Australia. Here it is common in small, clear rocky pools, with a moderate flow, and 1 to 2 metres deep.

This species has a very slender body and reaches lengths of up to 50 millimetres. The back and body are golden brown. The outer margins of the second dorsal and tail fins are whitish; pectoral and pelvic fins are white. Differences between the sexes are not as pronounced as in other closely related gudgeons. Males are usually darker than females; the end of the tail fin is rounded in males and straight in females.

There could be some demand for this species in the aquarium trade if specimens became available. The known distribution does not fall within any protected area.

POTENTIALLY VULNERABLE

SWAN GALAXIAS
Galaxias fontanus

This small minnow-like fish has an extremely restricted distribution, being found only in the headwaters of the Swan River, Tasmania, above Hardings Falls. Specimens are commonly 65 millimetres long but individuals have been recorded up to 96 millimetres.

It has a broad, flat head, a slightly forked tail and, like all its close relatives, only one dorsal fin. The belly is cream-coloured to white; the back and sides bear irregular blotching or banding. There are no distinctive markings on the fins. The Swan Galaxias stays in freshwater throughout its life, where it spawns in spring or early summer. It inhabits shallow spring-fed waters, densely shaded by riverine scrub and is not found where banks and river beds have been disturbed by roading activity.

Declines in the population of this species are primarily thought to be due to the introduction of an exotic predator, the Brown Trout. If Brown Trout are introduced into the Swan River above Hardings Falls (the remaining range of the Swan Galaxias), then grave fears are held for its survival. The Swan Galaxias has no special protection in Tasmania. Protection of the headwaters of the Swan River would be a positive step towards trying to save this species.

ENDANGERED

VULNERABLE

SADDLED GALAXIAS
Galaxias tanycephalus

This is another rare species of Tasmanian minnow with a restricted distribution. It has a stout body; long head tapering to a long, slender snout; large mouth with equally developed jaws and a distinctly forked tail.

Back colouration is olive-green with saddle-grey bars across the back and sides. Spots sometimes replace the back bars. The belly varies from olive to silvery and fins have a purplish sheen. Specimens are usually 65 to 80 millimetres long but have been known to reach 147 millimetres.

This rare species is found among boulders at the water's edge in Arthurs Lake, Woods Lake and the upper reaches of Lake River below Woods Lake Dam, Tasmania. It lives in freshwater throughout its life and is thought to spawn in late winter to spring.

This species is at risk because of its small population and restricted distribution. Specific threats likely to further endanger the population have not been documented.

Saddled Galaxias

GE Schmida

ENDANGERED

CLARENCE GALAXIAS
Galaxias johnstoni

Another small minnow-like fish, the Clarence Galaxias is one of Australia's most endangered fish. It has a stout tubular body, with a large mouth reaching well below the eye. Specimens are commonly over 70 millimetres long with the largest recorded reaching 98 millimetres. Colour on the back and upper sides is dark greyish-black, varying from olive to silvery on the lower sides and belly. The sides are marked with irregular brownish bands and blotches.

This species is found only in the Clarence Lagoon, associated tributaries, and the upper Clarence River, in the Derwent River system, Tasmania. It has been found in both still and flowing waters and appears to be a solitary, furtive species, probably living on the bottom of streams. Although the biology of the species is not well known, it is reported to be carnivorous, taking aquatic insects and their larvae. Spawning probably occurs in spring and the fish are thought to remain in freshwater throughout their life.

Exact threats to the species are not known, but its apparent rarity and extremely limited distribution makes it very vulnerable.

POTENTIALLY VULNERABLE

PYGMY RAINBOWFISH
Melanotaenia pygmaea

Unlike other closely related rainbowfish, this small fish has an extremely limited distribution. It is found only in the Prince Regent River system, Western Australia, with most specimens being collected from Cascade Creek, above King's Cascade.

Males are usually less than 50 millimetres long and females reach up to 35 millimetres. Both sexes become sexually mature at 23 millimetres. It has the characteristic pointed head of rainbowfish, a bright orange lower surface of the belly and yellowish fins. It is found in fast-flowing streams with frequent cascades or rapids. In these streams it inhabits deeper pools, often at the base of waterfalls, which have clear water and a solid rock bottom with little or no vegetative cover.

The known distribution of this fish lies within the Prince Regent Nature Reserve which should help in its conservation.

ARTHUR'S PARAGALAXIAS
Paragalaxias mesotes

This small minnow-like fish has a restricted range and is uncommon throughout this range. Arthur's Paragalaxias is found only in Arthurs Lake, Woods Lake and the Lake River downstream of Woods Lake in Tasmania.

It has a stout body with a long head sloping to a blunt long snout, a large mouth and a slightly forked tail fin. Back colouration is dark green or grey, sides grey to olive-gold and the belly silvery-grey. The dark back colour extends down the sides in irregular bands and patches and the fins are amber coloured with darker pigmentation along the rays. Specimens are commonly up to 60 millimetres long but have been recorded up to 78 millimetres. A carnivorous species, it appears to prefer still waters. Adults breed in freshwater in either spring or summer.

Any disturbance to areas within its limited distribution is likely to place this uncommon species at unacceptable and further risk.

Arthur's Paragalaxias   GE Schmida

POTENTIALLY VULNERABLE

NON-PARASITIC LAMPREY
Mordacia praecox

The Non-parasitic Lamprey has a number of unique features which make it of scientific interest. It is the first example from the Southern Hemisphere of a lamprey that spends its entire life cycle in freshwater and lacks a parasitic phase. A member of the primitive group of 'jawless fishes', this rare lamprey is restricted to the Moruya and Tuross Rivers in New South Wales. Adults are 120 to 150 millimetres long and breed in their first year during August to October. The number of eggs produced is the lowest recorded for this type of fish. There is no published description of its habitat.

Until more is known about this species it is difficult to identify specific risk, however, its restricted distribution immediately suggests vulnerability.

POTENTIALLY VULNERABLE

BLIND CAVE EEL
Ophisternon candidum

Since its discovery in 1959, only four specimens of the Blind Cave Eel have been collected, and it has only been sighted or collected at three locations. It lives in subterranean waters, where it probably inhabits dark caverns and fissures. This species shows some of the typical characteristics of cave-adapted species, lacking both eyes and body pigmentation.

The body is slender, reaching a maximum of 400 millimetres in length; there are no fins except a very thin membrane around the tip of the tail.

It is thought to occur throughout the subterranean system below the coastal plain between North West Cape and Yardie Creek, Western Australia.

This species appears extremely rare, but because its habitat is so inaccessible, population numbers are difficult to assess.

VULNERABLE

133

Invertebrate Conservation

GEOFF WILLIAMS

Invertebrates are those groups of animals that do not possess a backbone. Examples are the sponges, molluscs or snails, spiders, the crustaceans, the various worm phylla, insects and all the varied host of related creatures that scuttle about below our feet, fly high in the forest canopies overhead or float as zooplankton in the world's oceans.

Estimates for the total number of insect species alone range from three to over 30 million species and are considered to comprise 70 per cent of the world's fauna. The vertebrates total only some 5 per cent.

In Australia insect fauna is believed to contain approximately 140,000 species with less than 50 per cent formally named. A significant proportion of these species are endemic. Possibly one third of Australian terrestrial invertebrates are confined to the tropical forests of northern Queensland.

Of the total estimated Australian invertebrate fauna, only some 1 per cent has been studied in detail and this has generally been prompted by their economic or agricultural significance. Better known insect families include the butterflies, dragonflies, beetles, some flies, the mosquitoes and biting midges.

Only in Europe, and to a lesser extent North America, is the invertebrate fauna relatively well studied, although this holds true more for the state of taxonomic understanding than for insights into the ecology and population status of individual species.

Invertebrates in Ecosystems

Generally invertebrates occupy a fundamental and critical position in the operation and function of terrestrial ecosystems.

Many plants depend on invertebrates for pollination. Some plants permit pollination by a wide range of invertebrates. Other plants are reliant on only a few species and in some cases only one insect is responsible for pollination.

Invertebrates aid the distribution of organic matter and nutrients thereby influencing the soil's structure and profile and the spatial patterns of plant species and plant communities. In some instances both the plants and insects benefit from their relationship. Some acacias, for example, provide a nutrient reward for ants, while the ants influence or restrict herbivore attacks on the plant.

Invertebrates also effect decomposition of plant material through ingestion or by breaking woody or fibrous tissues up into smaller fractions. The resultant increase in surface area helps facilitate physical decomposition and leaching.

Many invertebrates are phytophagous, that is, feed on plants. This may involve adults and larvae but not necessarily both. Some species do not feed as adults.

This herbivore pressure has resulted in strong evolutionary interaction between plants and phytophagous invertebrates. Consequently structure and shape of individual plants species has resulted in reproductive, chemical and physical defence strategies aimed at mitigating against herbivore pressure. Herbivore pressure can also influence the structure of plant communities, and the responses between particular plants and their associated suite of herbivores is considered to be the major generator of terrestrial organic diversity.

Invertebrates make a major contribution to food chains and, as such, underpin healthy ecosystems. Many animals, both with and without backbones, are wholly or partially insectivorous and are inextricably reliant on invertebrates. Many carnivorous animals are indirectly linked to invertebrates by virtue that their prey may, in their turn, depend on invertebrates as a food source. Many carnivorous vertebrates may switch to invertebrate prey when their normal prey sources are absent or are at low densities.

Invertebrates also possess intrinsic values involving form, colour, adaption, diversity and uniqueness. Their genetic diversity represents a major potential biocontrol and pharmaceutical resource and they are a source of aesthetic enrichment and creative inspiration to human cultures.

General Impacts

The size of invertebrate species allows them to exploit subtle changes and opportunities within the environment to a far greater degree than that allowed most other animals.

Invertebrates generally undergo relatively rapid life cycles or possess capabilities that allow them to either circumvent unsuitable seasonal impacts, or to rapidly recover population levels in suitable environmental conditions.

Apart from the determining role of climate, latitude, photoperiod (response by animals and plants to length of day and night), topography and vegetation type, invertebrates also respond to soil type, the amount and condition of leaf litter and fallen logs on forest floors, the diversity of understorey plants, the frequency and intensity of fire, the frequency of site flooding, the presence of suitable hosts and much much more.

Changes in the nature of these bring about modifications in individual invertebrate populations and in the composition of the invertebrate community. This may result in individual species or whole assemblages being pushed out of habitats or disadvantaged in favour of others.

Richmond Birdwing Butterfly   Glen Threlfo/Auscape

Removing the shrub layers from forest systems, will remove all the invertebrates (and vertebrates) dependent, for whatever reason, on that shrub layer. Regular burning of vegetation communities also destroys the old rotting logs on the forest floor and thus precludes, from that ecosystem, the invertebrates (for example, beetles, various bugs, cicadas, cockroaches and planarian worms) dependent upon them as cover or food sources. Removing the sandy strand lines along foreshores through engineering works similarly destroys the habitat for shore-dependent species that use the strand zones for foraging, shelter or reproduction.

Taking away one particular plant species can displace a whole suite of invertebrates dependent on it. Likewise, removing a single vegetation stratum by burning or clearing can so impoverish the biological values that, in effect, landscapes approach more the roles played by urban parkland. Aesthetically more desirable than treeless plains, it consequently possesses an impoverished representation of the original invertebrate complexity.

Assessing Conservation Status

Given the rich nature and diversity of our fauna and the subtle changes in habitats required to bring about their demise, the conservation of invertebrates presents some problems. In addition to the poor state of knowledge on the ecology of individual species, basic distributions are only presumed whilst many species new to science are annually discovered and named. Even the much-heralded rainforests of our east coast have been poorly surveyed for invertebrates. Thus, it is difficult to give more than a handful of species the label of 'rare and endangered' when they may be inadequately sampled, highly localised or undergo quite natural and regular population fluctuations. The term rare and endangered implies a knowledge of population status, distribution and ecology, which is simply not possessed for the vast majority of Australian species. Conservation ranking of invertebrates based upon 'endemicity' and species at least tentatively considered to be localised, and thus potentially 'vulnerable', may provide more useful criteria.

Butterflies represent a relatively well-studied invertebrate group but are generally an exception. Some crepuscular scarab beetles as adults fly for short time periods once every two to three years, whilst the presence of certain adult buprestid beetles may be punctuated by periods of apparent absences of six to ten years. Hence, the

	Percentage named spp.	Percentage known species not yet named	Estimated percentage spp. not yet collected	Total number estimated spp.
Collembola (springtails)	10	10	80	2,500
Protura	30	20	50	100
Diplura	33	17	50	100
Archaeognatha	30	20	50	10
Thysanura (silverfish)	34	16	50	70
Ephemeroptera (mayflies)	10	60	30	300
Odonata (dragonflies)	80	8	12	300
Blattodea (cockroaches)	50	20	30	640
Isoptera (termites)	64	16	20	310
Mantodea (praying mantids)	45	35	20	160
Dermaptera (earwigs)	30	5	65	200
Plecoptera (stoneflies)	40	20	40	150
Orthoptera (grasshoppers, crickets)	27	51	22	2,840
Phasmatodea (stick insects)	55	30	15	160
Embioptera (web-spinners)	31	19	50	130
Psocoptera (psocids, booklice)	30	30	40	410
Phthiraptera	8	2	90	3,600
Hemiptera (bugs, cicadas)	37	23	40	9,400
Thysanoptera (thrips)	32	18	50	1,500
Megaloptera (alderflies)	36	50	14	25
Neuroptera (lacewings)	60	22	18	510
Coleoptera (beetles)	55	8	37	33,550
Strepsiptera	7	68	25	150
Mecoptera (scorpion-flies)	81	10	9	30
Siphonoptera (fleas)	72	9	19	110
Diptera (flies, mosquitoes, midges)	49	21	30	10,110
Trichoptera (caddis-flies)	36	24	40	470
Lepidoptera (moths, butterflies)	47	21	30	21,870
Hymenoptera (ants, wasps, bees, sawflies)	41	16	43	18,166

Table 1. *Taxonomic knowledge of Australian insects and related fauna after Taylor 1983*

chances of an entomologist encountering them at all, let alone sufficiently, to gauge their distribution and population status, is not especially outstanding. Many insect species are known from only single specimens or from small, inadequately labelled series collected last century. The substantial taxonomic obstacles with the Australian fauna means that names cannot readily be applied to animals encountered. In addition, a few site-specific studies are available with data scattered throughout the scientific literature so that, in Australia, the study of many invertebrates is a frontier science.

Invertebrate Habitats

Habitat destruction is most commonly cited as the major cause of population decline of invertebrate species but the impact of introduced animals on native invertebrates by direct predation (for example, rodents), or displacement pressure by related exotic species (for example, introduced snails and slugs), is poorly known. Where rats have

been introduced to islands the impact on flightless native faunas has been disastrous. For flightless and endemic faunas restricted to mountain tops or limited vegetation remnants the surrounding 'sea' of differing and unsuitable habitat creates an 'island-like' vulnerability.

Whilst being able to identify individual species that warrant conservation concern, some complete faunas are also vulnerable, either because their habitat is restricted spatially, is subject to development pressure and weed invasion, or because they are highly specialised. These include cave faunas, species occupying mountain tops and alpine zones, host-specific animals, invertebrates of coastal rainforest remnants and maritime vegetation, and invertebrates only recorded from vegetation relics in intensively-farmed regions. Also, many species are flightless and have limited capacity for dispersal. When local populations of any given species are removed from ecosystems by modifications or changes to land use, even of a temporary nature, then the ability of these species to re-establish from near-adjoining sites is restricted.

Habitats at Risk

Many invertebrate species are at risk because the habitats upon which they are dependent are, themselves, at risk. This may be because the habitats are geological remnants of once more extensive ecosystems, were once relatively extensive but have undergone substantial reduction in area and fragmentation since European settlement, have been further degraded by exotic weed infestation, and localised unsympathetic land usage or, whilst still extensively represented, have been subject to chemical, physical and biotic modifications which have altered or removed conditions suitable for occupation.

The examples listed below are not exhaustive but are merely intended to draw attention to the range of habitats and vegetation remnants which are vulnerable to further degradation and loss of associated invertebrate populations. In most cases, little ecological or census data are available on vegetation-invertebrate interactions or species present.

It is relatively safe to assume that undocumented invertebrate species have already been lost through microhabitat destruction and more general ecosystem clearance.

Riverine Rainforests These occupied the rich alluvial flood plains of the central eastern and south-eastern coastline. In New South Wales the remaining riverine rainforest remnants represent little more than 100 hectares. All are disjunct in distribution, often exist in otherwise heavily-cleared landscapes and frequently adjoin centres of settlement. All remaining riverine rainforest remnants need active management and rehabilitation if they are to be retained. Floristically, they are composed of typically subtropical rainforest species and trees typical of dry rainforests. The invertebrates are predominantly Indo-Malayan in origin. Some invertebrate species are only known from these remnants.

Littoral Rainforests Littoral rainforests occur as disjunct, yet floristically distinct rainforests, along the east coast of Australia and are particularly well represented on the mid-north coast of New South Wales. Some distinctive structural features of the rainforests are the pronounced wind shearing and dwarf growth patterns of tree species forming the windward, frontal barriers.

Habitat destruction is the major threat to invertebrate conservation. Open Space

Some tree species that may achieve canopy heights of more than 10 metres in sheltered landward positions may barely grow higher than 20 centimetres where individuals grow along exposed seaward margins.

Littoral rainforest represents approximately 5 to 7 per cent, or 1,300 hectares, of the remaining rainforests in New South Wales and a considerably smaller percentage of the remaining rainforests in Queensland. All have been significantly cleared for agriculture, sand-mining, residential and tourist development. All have been further degraded by exotic weed invasion and unsympathetic land usage and most require some form of active management and rehabilitation.

A major single threat to littoral rainforests, and their invertebrate faunas, is the introduced South African shrub Bitou Bush. Originally introduced to stabilise beach dunes, it has invaded both disturbed and undisturbed coastal vegetation.

Insects presently recorded only from littoral rainforests include the beetles *Maoraxia littoralis*, the monotypic *Trachys blackburni* and *Helferella miyal* and *Helferella manningensis;* the last two species known only from two small rainforest remnants on the New South Wales north coast. The southern subspecies of the Regent Skipper Butterfly also occurs in littoral rainforests.

Vine Thickets Vine thickets occur on the outer margins, often fire-prone boundaries, of dry rainforest and as distinctive low vegetation scrubs.

In northern Queensland additional vine thickets occur as discrete vegetation stands surrounded by fire-prone sclerophyll woodlands (for example, Forty-Mile Scrub, Toomba, Barrakas Scrub). These rainforest-related thickets are assumed to be geological refugia composed of fire-sensitive plant species requiring soils of higher nutrient status, although the general dynamics and requirements are poorly understood.

The thickets are prone to fire impacts, may be subject to clearing throughout most of their distribution, are degraded by feral and domestic stock and are poorly represented in reserves. Little information on the associated invertebrate fauna is available.

Brigalow Woodlands These woodlands are characteristically dominated by *Acacia harpophylla* and extend southward from the vicinity of Townsville, northern Queensland, into the central western region of New South Wales. The southerly occurrences are more fragmented.

At European settlement it was considered that brigalow lands occupied approximately 6 million hectares. Since settlement brigalow has been subjected to massive clearing for agriculture, and consequential exposure and desiccation (which modifies plant associations), weed invasion, degrading of vegetation relics by livestock ingress, erosion, modification of nutrient cycles and fire.

137

Important stream habitats can be severely disturbed by clearing of adjacent vegetation.   Geoff Williams

more southerly latitudes, being either relatively uncommon or totally absent from the northern half of Australia.

Whilst they are structurally simple vegetation communities, existing in zones of highly dynamic environmental stress (for example, exposure to salt, periodic tidal and flood inundation), their associated terrestrial invertebrate fauna has been subjected to heavy destruction through coastal development pressure, clearing and regular burning for agriculture, trampling and grazing by livestock, as land-fill sites, through discharges of residential and industrial wastes, fertiliser run-off from farmlands and the use of insecticides.

● **Coastal** *Casuarina* **and** *Melaleuca* wetlands have been subjected to heavy clearing, mainly for agricultural development and drainage. Both forest types are relatively undiverse when compared with the richness of plants and vegetation structures found in eucalypt forests and rainforests. However, such comparisons are a little unfair, because the various plant communities are really quite distinct entities and possess different, often unique habitat opportunities for different animals. Again, the invertebrate fauna of *Casuarina* and *Melaleuca* wetlands have been poorly studied, yet the respective ecosystems are still subject to destruction and degradation.

If the worst of the greenhouse scenarios come to pass, then the various maritime vegetation types, and the littoral and riverine rainforest remnants, will suffer degrees of partial or complete *inundation* – a polite term for drowning.

The many brigalow associations are poorly represented in nature reserves and the original mosaic of associated invertebrate communities has already undergone considerable obliteration and modification.

Maritime Communities A number of distinctive vegetation communities are restricted to the coastline, estuaries and associated lower river systems of Australia. These include mangroves, saltmarshes and transitional reed swamps, *Casuarina* (she-oaks) and *Melaleuca* (paperbark) forests.

● **Mangroves** exhibit greater structural and floristic diversity along the northern coastline and, to some degree, have acted as refugia and dispersal corridors for some rainforest-associated fauna. Along the east coast, the mangrove forests increasingly become less diverse to the extent that only River Mangrove and Grey Mangrove are commonly encountered south of the New South Wales north coast.

The terrestrial invertebrate fauna of mangroves, particularly in the more southern latitudes, is almost unknown. Historically, however, mangroves have been cleared and felled for harbour development, oyster growing and channel, canal estate projects, tourist and residential development. They are also subject to chemical pollution.

● **Saltmarshes** are tidally-prone transitional vegetation zones, most commonly developed in association with mangrove and seagrass communities, in estuaries and coastal rivers. They are better represented in

Alpine Zones The opportunities for the establishment of truly alpine vegetation in Australia are very limited. Alpine vegetation, as such, is presently restricted to eastern Victoria, the Kosciusko region of southern New South Wales and areas of Tasmania. It comprises a mosaic of distinct and intergrading types of plant communities consisting of heaths, woodlands, herbfields, fens, bogs and feldmarks (characterised by dwarfed, prostrate species).

They are prone to trampling, compaction, grazing pressure and burning. Grazing by livestock can result in selective feeding on, and consequent reduction or elimination of individual plant species. Alpine communities may be heavily reduced or eliminated should adverse greenhouse impacts occur. This will result in widespread loss or reduction to populations of specialised, and alpine-restricted, invertebrates en masse.

Specific alpine invertebrates already considered to be threatened are the syncarid crustaceans, the Large Blue Lake Mayfly, the Mount Kosciusko Wingless Stonefly, the Mount Donna Buang Wingless Stonefly and the moths *Acalyphes philorites*, *Dirce aesiodora* and *Dirce oriplancta*. They are threatened by fire, livestock trampling and development.

Mountain Fauna Environmental conditions existing on mountains are distinct from surrounding lowlands, creating an insular condition for invertebrate faunas. Many mountainous areas and individual mountain tops contain relic vegetation communities or species of limited distribution. Over time, they have acted as refuge areas for plants and animals displaced from previously wider distributions. The resulting fragmentation of the populations resulted in the increasing speciation of reproductively isolated faunas. The fauna is often highly specialised and frequently lacks any significant capacity for wider dispersal.

These mountain faunas are vulnerable to climatic change through loss of suitable microhabitat and the vegetation is threatened by displacement or modification to the existing complement of species. Individual vegetation communities and associated invertebrates are also vulnerable from fires.

Streams and Lakes Australia is a relatively dry continent and possesses a much-reduced capacity for the development of a rich and diverse freshwater fauna. However, this is not meant to imply that the invertebrate fauna is without any outstanding or distinctive features.

Such habitats are important for the retention of many insects and these form the basis of higher food chains. Insect groups typical of streams and lakes include the dragonflies and damselflies, caddisflies, stoneflies, mayflies and a number of freshwater adapted bugs which include 'water boatmen', 'water striders' and giant 'water bugs'.

Whilst the different insect orders and families may be found widely across the continent wherever suitable water bodies occur, many individual species are restricted to small geographically restricted regions, individual river and stream systems, or even just a single section of one stream only.

Other invertebrate groups also frequent freshwater streams. Several families of bivalve molluscs, the Hyriidae, Sphaeriidae and Corbiculidae, often occur where suitable sediments exist. The Sphaeriidae or 'peashells' are small animals that are widely distributed through a range of habitats including flowing streams and quiet pondages, such as dams and alpine bogs.

The Corbiculidae are restricted to flowing freshwater habitats and may become occasional pests infesting irrigation and town water pipes. The Hyriidae are larger mussels and are found in both still and flowing water.

They are important food sources for aquatic and semi-aquatic mammals (for example, Platypus, Water-rat).

A number of species of freshwater crustaceans occur in streams. These include the freshwater shrimp, yabbies and various spiny crayfish. There are nine genera of Australian freshwater crayfish and all are placed, with other crayfish species known from the Southern Hemisphere, in the family Parastacidae. Many species have a requirement for cold, highly-oxygenated water and as a consequence are restricted to fast-flowing mountain streams, where considerable speciation of the fauna has occurred with individual species occupying discrete stream areas and confined geographic distributions. This leaves individual species vulnerable to localised environmental perturbations and the fauna, as a whole, is vulnerable to changes in water quality (for example, fertiliser run-off, contamination from livestock faeces), flow rate, loss of catchment, temperature changes, fragmentation of populations due to selective habitat loss and alteration to shading resulting from vegetation removal.

Parastacidae crayfish with very limited geographic distributions are tabled in Appendix II. The list is somewhat arbitrary and conservative but it should be mentioned that it encompasses the greater majority of known parastacid species and all genera. Genera such as *Euastacus*, *Cherax* and

Australian freshwater lakes have rich and diverse invertebrate fauna.

Regent Skipper Butterfly populations have been fragmented by habitat loss. Frithfoto/A.N.T. Photo Library

Engaeus have undergone considerable speciation in zones of major human growth and development, and less adaptable species should encounter increasing threats to their habitats.

One species of *Astacopsis*, the Giant Tasmanian Freshwater Crayfish (*A. gouldi*), is vulnerable to overfishing and streamside clearing.

In addition to the relatively advanced parastacids, a number of very primitive crustaceans, the Syncarida, are found in freshwater bodies in Tasmania. Three genera, *Allanaspides*, *Anaspides* and *Paranaspides* are vulnerable to habitat disturbance, flooding and predation by exotic Brown Trout and are listed in the International Union for Conservation of Nature and Natural Resources (IUCN) Invertebrate Red Data Book.

Remnant Bushland Much, sometimes all, of the original native vegetation is now urbanised, and intensively farmed agricultural areas have been cleared, fragmented into isolated vegetation patches with little possibility of faunal interchange, or the remnants exist as degraded vegetation 'islands' in city and urban districts with no hope of recolonisation when faunal elements are displaced. Massive regions of central Queensland, the central western districts of New South Wales, the western mallee of Victoria, the south-east quarter of South

Australia and the wheat-belt region of southern and south-western Australia have been converted to biotically simplified agro-ecosystems. These offer very limited opportunity for occupation by all but the most mobile, adaptive, often cosmopolitan, invertebrates. Any invertebrates restricted to these regions, with overspecialised habitat requirements and dependency upon a small range of, or even single, host plants is in danger of extinction. Thus, for many species the often only remaining and suitable habitats exist as roadside verges, stock reserves, council reserves, railway verges and cemeteries.

Selective invertebrates at risk include the primitive ant genus *Nothomyrmecia* and the jewel beetle subgenus *Themognatha* which occurs as a very conspicuous and seasonal fauna in mallee districts. The spiders *Idiosoma nigrum*, *Kwonkan wonganensis*, *Kwonkan moriarti* and *Kwonkan eboracum*, are threatened by agricultural developments in South Australia and Western Australia, and the grasshoppers *Keyacris scurra* and *Genurellia cylindrica*, from eastern Australia, are threatened by livestock grazing and agricultural clearing respectively.

Some invertebrates may have already achieved extinction in these intensively farmed and settled areas *prior* to European settlement. Not necessarily through natural evolutionary displacement but by the contentious proposal that the arrival of Aboriginal man in Australia, and his

commensurate hunting and burning practices, brought about the demise of at least some mammalian megafauna species (*Diprotodon*, *Procoptodon*, *Zygomaturus*, *Sthenurus* and the like). These were large animals, well-adapted to the climatic influences and vegetation present during the known occupation of the continent by Aboriginal peoples. Perhaps their demise was the result of combinations of change, that is increasing aridity, increasing environmental restrictions and hunting pressure, by chance all operating at the same time.

All these giant browsing kangaroos, rhinoceros-like grazers, omnivores and carnivorous marsupials would have been host to particular invertebrate ecoparasites, internal parasites, commensals and animals associated with their faeces and carcasses that may have been specifically adapted to these now-extinct hosts. Their grazing impacts alone would have modified plant communities to which less directly influenced invertebrates would have responded. What now-vanished native dung beetles may have enthusiastically rolled away the droppings of lost diprotodonts! Fantasy? Not at all. In Africa at this moment similarly related beetles selectively adapted to the massive quantities of by-products from elephants and rhinoceros are faced with similar extinction over part, or all, of their previous range.

Cave faunas Australian cave systems contain many rare species but offer limited opportunities for colonisation by invertebrates. Any resident fauna is subject to unpredictable variation of outside food influxes and may be subjected to periodic flushing which washes out or destroys populations. Species reliant on bat guano have to contend with the variable availability of the resource because of seasonal fluctuations in bat populations. More recently, bat-reliant cave faunas are confronted with more permanent reductions in bat populations due to destruction of suitable roosting caves for mining purposes (for example, limestone extraction). Therefore, as populations of the 'guanophilic' invertebrates may be subjected to natural fluctuations in populations as a response to natural fluctuations in mammal populations, many localised populations may be faced with a more insidious restriction and possible extinction.

Three general groups of cave-frequenting insects and arachnids are recognised. Truly troglobitic species are obligate inhabitants, their morphological and physiological adaptions restricting them to a cavernicolous (cave-inhabiting) existence. Most troglobitic species are predacious and the restriction of troglobites to the southern, particularly Tasmania, sections of Australia is correlated with glaciation events during the Pleistocene period (approximately 2 million to 0.1 million years ago) with temperate cave systems offering refuge to species only capable of tolerating narrow temperature ranges (stenothermic). Truly troglobitic invertebrates occurring in highly localised cave systems in Tasmania comprise the carabid beetle genera *Tasmanotrechus* (one species from northern Tasmania), *Indacarabus* (two species restricted to southern Tasmania), and *Goedetrechus* (two species restricted to southern Tasmania).

Troglophiles are animals capable of existing in caves all their lives but not visibly exhibiting any modifications specifically adapted for cave life. Unlike troglobites, which are adaptive captives of their cave environment, troglophiles are less restricted and more mobile and can exist above ground if suitable conditions, for example, food resources for cave life, cease to exist. Relatively more numerous troglophitic beetles are recorded from the Australian mainland. Also recorded from southern caves is the beetle family Jacobsoniidae, represented by a new genus and species from bat guano.

A third group found in caves are trogloxenes; species which use the caves for shelter but derive most, if not all, of their food from surface (epigean) sources.

A number of cave-inhabiting invertebrates are thought to be particularly vulnerable. The silver fish *Trinemura russendensis* from site flooding and *Trinemura anenome* from tourism and trampling, the slaters or isopods *Abebaioscia troglodytes*, *Armadillo cavernae*, *Echinodillo cavaticus*, a new species of *Styloniscus* and the trapdoor spider *Troglodiplura lowryi*, all from tourist-related impacts.

Invertebrate cave faunas, generally, are sensitive and vulnerable to changes in light, changes in food resources, ventilation changes, desiccation and substrate compaction by trampling. Recreational and tourism developments are a major threat. Even just widening cave entrances and modifying their capacity to receive surface-fed detritus pose threats to these environmentally-insular cave faunas.

The preceding examples are by no means exhaustive and the invertebrates of even more spatially-extensive ecosystems are vulnerable. The microhabitat mosaics of tropical rainforests, lagoon and catchment systems in the Northern Territory and the

THE BIG SCRUB REMNANTS

Ecosystem Approaches to Invertebrate Conservation

Prior to the European settlement of New South Wales, one of the largest expanses of lowland subtropical rainforest extended north-east from Lismore in the far north of the state to the vicinity of Rosebank and Byron Bay, and south-east towards Ballina and Meerschaum Vale.

Estimated at approximately 75,000 hectares in size, it was cleared so that only a small remnant of isolated pockets remained. Today these small remnant rainforests survive at Davis Scrub, Victoria Park Nature Reserve, Hayter's Hill, Johnson Scrub, Big Scrub Flora Reserve, Booyong and Boatharbour Nature Reserve. Several other small remnants also persist.

All the known remnants were weed infested, suffered soil compaction and unrestricted access and, although not islands in the strict sense, all were vulnerable to the stress and degradation suffered by true islands.

Even in that degraded state, the rainforest remnants preserved what they could of the original Big Scrub invert-

ebrate community. In the last decade there has been an increasing awareness of the need to preserve and restore these remnants, and rainforest remnants more generally. Many of the surviving pockets of rainforest vegetation have been the subject of ongoing community regeneration programs.

In working towards these goals the rainforests receive active management: degrading exotic weeds are removed, usage is rationalised, canopies are restored and replanting programs extend the future rainforest area and restore habitat.

In so doing, the viability of these rainforest remnants is enhanced and the relic animal communities within have an increased chance of survival, in vegetation that would have ultimately been lost.

Rare and visually resplendent invertebrates known to occur in the Big Scrub rainforest remnants include the Regent Skipper Butterfly, the Richmond Birdwing Butterfly and the Grey Christmas Beetle. As with many other vegetation relics, the less obvious fauna awaits even a basic assessment or has already been lost without record.

little explored rainforests of the Kimberley region of north-west Australia all contain arguably 'rare', inadequately-documented and geographically restricted species.

Invertebrates at Risk
Whilst whole faunas may be threatened because the habitats to which they are thought to be restricted are threatened, some individual species and some unrelated groupings of invertebrates are also vulnerable.

Cryptozoic Fauna These include taxonomically unrelated, ecologically homogenous invertebrates found under logs, stones and fallen bark. Included are the planarian worms, predatory nemertines, velvet worms, land molluscs, many annelid worms and most arthropod orders; spiders, harvestmen, insects, amphipods. All are at risk through widespread fire impacts and modifications to habitat from agricultural and residential developments.

Three nemertine species, *Argonemertes australiensis*, *A. hillii* and *A. stocki* are listed as rare. Even where the species are common, their distribution is often highly localised due to both natural and human-induced fragmentation of habitats.

Worms The majority of Australia's diverse native earthworm fauna placed within the family Megascolecidae, which includes the Giant Gippsland Earthworm, are considered to be vulnerable. Other giant earthworms, in the genus *Digaster*, are recorded from New South Wales but the ecology and distribution of the fauna generally is poorly known.

Most native species are unable to persist in areas under cultivation and the greater majority of earthworms encountered in urban gardens and farmlands are introduced species, usually lumbricids. The Lumbricidae can displace native species and have been introduced into Lord Howe Island which supports a rich native annelid fauna.

Native species are sensitive to changes in soil structure, desiccation and detritus. Feral pigs pose a threat to insular faunas.

Terrestrial Snails Gastropod land snails are a conspicuous element of the ground fauna where suitable habitat exists. They are particularly well represented in rainforest and wet sclerophyll forests. Species requiring calcium carbonate for shell production can be prolific in moist forests developed on soils derived from calcarious parent rock.

The fauna includes species that are herbivores, general omnivores and non-selective carnivores. They are vulnerable to loss of habitat through clearing, erosion, desiccation, destruction of habitat by fires and predation by feral animals. A number of exotic species have been introduced.

Destruction of habitat by feral animals and some direct predation has had a severe impact on the highly endemic fauna of Lord Howe Island. Many, once abundant, species have been reduced in number and distribution and are locally extinct in several formerly occupied areas. Many are almost extinct or are thought to now be extinct, for example, *Placostylus cuniculinsulae* from Rabbit Island. Some species such as the large *Platocostylus bivaricosus* and *Gudeoconcha sophiae*, apparently once widespread and abundant, now survive only in isolated colonies.

As with most of Australia's invertebrate fauna, knowledge of life histories, interactions with other fauna and possible predators is very poor.

Arthropods This heterogeneous group of articulate-jointed animals contains many of the invertebrates that historically have suffered from 'bad press' – the centipedes, spiders, scorpions, beetles, fleas and bedbugs. Yet, all have their place in native ecosystems and trying to categorise them

into rankings of 'friend or foe' is an irrelevant exercise.

The arthropods dominate the terrestrial biota and contain such numerically massive numbers of species that there is no shortage of variously threatened and endangered candidates for inclusion in lists of animals at risk.

Many species are at risk for the very reasons of habitat vulnerability outlined earlier. Some specific individuals have already been noted and, rather than attempt to draw attention to the many orders that justifiably could be considered, comments are restricted to some of the more conspicuous insect orders.

Butterflies Butterflies have specific host plants and include many species and subspecies with localised populations. Increasing urbanisation and agricultural activities are major causes for population decline and species acknowledged as being threatened can be found in Appendix II. The list could be widened to include other very rare butterflies, for example, *Hesperilla choastala choastala* from the Blue Mountains in New South Wales or species that are common but whose populations have been fragmented by habitat loss, for example, Regent Skipper and Richmond Birdwing, although now rela-

tively well represented in nature reserves and national parks.

The conservation and management of a number of the Lycaenid butterflies is compounded because they have an obligatory association with certain ant species. Thus, any conservation strategy has to account for the interrelationship of ant, butterfly and specific butterfly host plants.

Examples of Lycaenid butterflies associated with ants and with very localised and restricted populations are *Paralucia spinifera*, first named in 1978. *P. spinifera* is only known from a very small area east of Bathurst, New South Wales. Larvae intially feed on *Bursaria spinosa* but older larvae and pupae are associated with ants. The Small Brown Azure has a very disjunct range and occurs as geographically isolated populations in southern Western Australia, western New South Wales, north-western Victoria and south-east South Australia. The larvae feed on plants of *Choretrum glomeratum* and larvae and pupae are found in the nests of sugar ants. Illidges Ant-blue is confined to a very small area of south-east Queensland, from Brisbane to Burleigh Heads. The larvae is found in the nests of the ant *Crematogaster laeviceps* upon which they may be predatory. Attempts at rearing the butterfly larvae, in the absence of the ants, have been unsuccessful.

This nemertine worm Argonemertes hillii *is rare and threatened by agricultural and residential development.*

Geoff Williams

Dragonflies These have an association with water bodies and many populations are also very localised in distribution. Species over which some concern for the viability of the populations has been expressed include *Austroaeschna hardyi* (Tasmania), *Agriocnemis kunjina* (Western Australia), *Austroagrion pindrina* (Western Australia), *Neurobasis australis* (Queensland), *Archipetalia auriculata* (Tasmania), and *Hemiphlebia miribilis* (Victoria). Threats include habitat drainage and changes to water quality and chemistry.

Stick insects These include many highly sedentary species with localised populations within suitable areas of habitat. The combination of sedentary habits with localised populations presents many species with both reproductive problems and vulnerability to predation and land use practices, for example, prescribed burning of forests.

The large stick-insect *Dryococelus australis* was eliminated from Lord Howe Island within a few years by the accidental introduction of rats. Extinct on Lord Howe Island, the species may still survive on Ball's Pyramid and is a candidate for intense field assessment of any remaining populations, ecology and (hopefully) breeding programs if ever there was one. That the similarly vulnerable Lord Howe Island Woodhen was the subject of intensive conservation programs illustrates the tiered approach to vertebrate conservation versus invertebrate conservation.

Beetles Beetles occupy an apparently favoured place in the scheme of things. There are over 300,000 formally named species in the world and in Australia there are over 20,000 named species.

Many· species are highly localised, are flightless and are vulnerable to habitat clearance, fires and agricultural and forestry practices. Very little is known about the ecology and habitat requirements of individual animals.

Species considered to be threatened include the King Christmas Beetle by coastal and urban development, ground-frequenting localised Lucanidae, some jewel beetles or Buprestidae by agriculture and urban development, predatory Carabidae beetles restricted to particular substrates, aquatic species (for example, the hygrobiids *Hygrobia niger* and *H. australasiae*), and the Hoop Pine Weevil.

The selection of vulnerable invertebrates and their vulnerable habitats considered above represents a very small fraction of the threats that need to be addressed if we are to retain the present level of terrestrial and freshwater invertebrate diversity.

The marine invertebrates are also suffering from the effects of human exploitation and pollution, and a list species thought to be

This beetle, Xyroscelis crocata *is from a primitive and endemic genus.*　　Geoff Williams

of conservation concern is provided by Ecofund Australia in Appendix II.

Invertebrate Conservation Requirements

The marked biological diversity of the invertebrate fauna dictates that, no matter how broadly habitat reserves are drawn, notable invertebrate taxa, and widely-spaced individual populations, will be left outside the boundaries. Therefore, it is obligatory to consider the wider application of smaller reserves, refuge systems and species-specific site registers. In some rural areas, no Crown land now remains and thus the conservation of many relic populations depends upon the sympathetic management of privately-owned lands, council-controlled reserves and roadside verges. There also needs to be an increase in resources allocated to studying the Australian fauna.

Nature conservation policies directed primarily at preserving plant and vertebrate diversity in the serendipitous hope that sufficient invertebrate taxa will somehow be included within the final boundary line, fail to address the role of invertebrates within ecosystems. Such policies are likely to fall substantially short of conserving both individual invertebrate species and genetic diversity throughout known distributions and geographically isolated populations.

An invertebrate conservation Action Plan for Australia needs to be developed with some urgency. Organisations and individuals are now working towards this goal.

THE FATE OF THE LORD HOWE ISLAND PHASMID

LORD HOWE ISLAND PHASMID
Dryococelus australis

In 1918 the supply ship *Makambo* went aground at Ned's Beach in the far northeast corner of Lord Howe Island. From the grounded ship came the Black Rat and in less than five years the predation by this highly adept climber had brought a further five species of the island's endemic birds to extinction.

Prior to the introduction of the rats, Lord Howe Island was also home to the large and slow-moving Lord Howe Island Phasmid (or Tree Lobster), a flightless stick-insect that once inhabited tree hollows and was common. The species occurred nowhere else. Being large,

flightless and slow-moving it fell as easy prey to the rats and is now extinct on Lord Howe Island.

Approximately 20 kilometres to the south rises the spectacular 550 metres high spire that is Ball's Pyramid. Totally isolated, and to date without rats, the spire has been the subject of a number of scientific surveys. In 1964 a dead specimen of the thought-to-be-extinct Lord Howe Island Phasmid was found and this gave hope that the species was not extinct, not yet.

Whilst the Lord Howe Island Woodhen was to eventually be the subject of a breeding and reintroduction program, the Phasmid has failed to engender a similar response.

Australia's Threatened Plants

JOHN BENSON

Plants are our predecessors as well as our companions on this planet; they are also the cornerstone of life. We cannot survive without them because they are the factories that transform sunlight and water into the basic substances required by other living organisms: sugars, proteins, vitamins and, of course, oxygen.

Think of how we rely on plants for cotton, grains, fruit and vegetables; wood for construction and paper. The range of chemicals in plants is astounding and most species have not yet been tested for compounds that may be useful to humans. Many of our medicines owe their origin to plants including one of the most important drugs, aspirin. Even coal is derived from the decomposition of plants in ancient swamps. And since animals depend on plants we could add wool, meat, leather, oil and its derivative fuels to the list.

Plants have been instrumental in moulding the Earth's environment. Oceanic algae appeared over 2,000 million years ago and began breathing oxygen into the atmosphere. This helped build up the Earth's ozone layer which in turn provided protection from ultraviolet radiation for land-colonising plants and animals. Fossil evidence indicates that the first land plants existed 420 million years ago. Seed plants such as conifers evolved 300 million years ago while flowering plants first appeared 150 million years later.

The greenhouse effect, causing us so much concern at present, is directly related to plants. Burning fossil fuels and forests releases carbon dioxide into the atmosphere, which results in an increased retention of heat in the oceans and atmosphere, a consequent climate change and rise in sea levels. A solution to this problem must involve plants, after all they are effective hoarders of carbon.

Modern crop production relies on monocultures of plants. With an increasing worldwide tendency of growers to use patented new breeds of grains, fruit, vegetables and garden plants, there is a narrowing of the genetic base. Therefore, when diseases arise the damage can be catastrophic. In terms of human self-interest, this is one very important reason to conserve, in their natural habitat, viable populations of the original plants and closely-related species from which cultivars have been or in the future could be derived. One example involved the interbreeding of a 'wild' wheat, native to the Middle East, with cultivated varieties of wheat. This successfully diminished the blight of wheat-rust.

Aboriginal Australians listed hundreds of species of Australian plants for food, fabric, weapons and medicine.

The limitless potential use of plants is clear. In addition, there are aesthetic and moral reasons to maintain genetic diversity on Earth. Plant species have a right to exist and to evolve naturally. We would not be truly human without experiencing the form and colour that plants provide. There is an innate human feeling and need for plants, as expressed in our art and design.

Over 250,000 species of flowering plants have been described by science and about 10 per cent of these are threatened. The threatened list is growing as landscapes are altered at an ever-increasing rate on our overpopulated planet.

For so many reasons we should be concerned to conserve all plants and their habitats. In this chapter we will be looking at the special problems facing the rare or threatened flora of Australia.

A Unique Flora

Australia now receives less precipitation than any other continent except Antarctica. Semi-arid or arid environments cover two thirds of the land mass. Much of the north is subjected to 'wet' and 'dry' seasons; the south-west and south of the continent have a typically Mediterranean climate with wet, cool winters and dry, hot summers; the eastern seaboard is wet, hot in the north and cool in the south. It is understandable that a range of vegetation communities exist on a continent with such contrasts.

Scientists have described over 16,000 native vascular plant species (spore-bearing plants with water and food-conducting tissues, that is, ferns, herbs, shrubs and trees that dominate the landscape) in 262 families as living in these vegetation communities. It is considered that this figure will rise to over 20,000 after more species have been discovered and as plant taxonomists continue to revise present classifications. When we add non-vascular plants (liverworts, mosses, algae, fungi and lichens) to these figures, it is likely the total number of plant species known to exist in Australia will rise beyond 50,000.

While there are few plant families unique to Australia, 80 per cent of vascular plant species are endemic. Our endemic flora are a privilege which brings with it a responsibility. It follows that the conservation of this large number of plant species can only be achieved by Australians in Australia.

The Evolution of Australia's Flora

To explain today's flora we need to go back 135 million years ago to the time of the southern supercontinent, Gondwanaland, that bound Antarctica, South America, Africa, Madagascar, India and New Zealand to what is now Australia and New Guinea.

An undescribed spider-orchid, known from one plant only on Mt Canobolas near Orange.

Colin Bower

The primitive flowering plant Idiospermum australiense.

John Williams

There are strong botanical links particularly at the family level between these now distant land masses. For example, the sedge family, Restionaceae, and the family that contains the waratah and banksia, the Proteaceae, are major components of both the African and Australian flora. There are also links at the generic level. The genus of the southern beeches, *Nothofagus* and the associated southern conifer genera *Podocarpus* and *Araucaria* are common to South America, New Zealand and Australia.

During a warm, wet period 60 million years ago, rainforest covered much of Australia and Antarctica which was then still attached. This was a period of great diversification of the flowering plants, the ancestral base from which much of the modern flora was derived. Between 40 and 30 million years ago Australia and Antarctica finally separated and Australia's flora was left alone to radiate and adapt to changing climatic conditions as the continent moved northward into the mid-latitudes. Rainforest retracted to coastal zones as aridity increased. There is debate about the timing of the onset of aridity, however some evidence (such as high quantities of grass pollen in dated cores) suggests there may have been an arid zone in Australia at least 10 million years ago.

The most recent events (on the geological scale of time) that have moulded Australia's flora have been the several ice ages that have come and gone over the last two million years. Pollen evidence suggests that aridity increases during an ice age and decreases during the interglacial periods. During climatic change, at any one place, vegetation has adjusted its species composition and structure. Some flora managed to survive the upheaval of climatic change by retreating to favourable topographical locations termed 'refugia'. For moisture-loving species these included places, where there existed altitudinal gradients and/or protective aspects, that allowed species to survive inhospitable periods. The eastern escarpment of the Great Dividing Range has been critical to the survival of some of the ancient Gondwana elements including very primitive flowering plants, such as the unique and threatened *Idiospermum australiense* at Cape Tribulation in northern Queensland.

The most recent ice age lasted from about 30,000 to about 12,000 years ago. Since then, the treeline has risen and forests have expanded, but the predominantly hard, dry form of the vegetation has remained.

Natural Rarity

Species have always appeared and disappeared through evolutionary processes and there have been fluctuations in the rate of speciation and extinction. Some plant species are naturally rare due to their specialised adaptation to uncommon niches in the environment. For example, several species of cushion plants present in alpine regions of New South Wales and Tasmania are rare because their habitats are very restricted in area.

Plants may be rare because they are relics of past ecosystems that were once more widespread and have been largely displaced by climatic change. The palm *Livistona*

mariae survives at Finke Gorge in central Australia and the dwarf conifer *Microstrobos fitzgeraldii* clings precariously to life on cliffs in the Blue Mountains of New South Wales.

Some rare plant species may be newly evolved not yet having spread over large areas nor having developed large populations.

In what appears to be a paradox, many rare plants require frequent disturbance to survive. For example, Menindee Nightshade, one of the native 'tomatoes' in western New South Wales appears on the beds of a number of lakes after flooding recedes. It grows rapidly, flowers and fruits, then dies off, hardly to be seen again until the next flood.

In today's world, because of an unprecedented level of destruction of natural habitats around the globe, we are witnessing the greatest rate of species extinction (and therefore loss of genetic diversity) in the Earth's history. This comparison includes the catastrophic period that lead to the extinction of the dinosaurs 65 million years ago.

The Impact of the Aborigines on Australia's Flora

Aboriginal people arrived in Australia at least 40,000 years ago and the impact they have had on the flora is still being debated. Although Aborigines did not carry out widespread cultivation of crops there is evidence to suggest they increased the population of edible plants through deliberate plantings or selective management. Historical accounts of Aborigines using fire support modern views that the vegetation has been substantially modified by Aboriginal burning. For example, it is probable that the monsoon rainforest of the Northern Territory was greatly reduced in extent by Aboriginal burning. The remaining small patches of this type of rainforest contain a number of rare plants including the endangered palm *Ptychosperma bleeseri* which occurs near Darwin.

The impact of burning, whether Aboriginal or not, was profound, as much of Australia's contemporary sclerophyllous flora has adjusted to certain fire 'regimes'. Changes in these regimes since European settlement have in themselves been an endangering process for quite a number of plant species.

Aboriginal burning in conjunction with the quite drastic climatic changes of the glacial and interglacial periods over the last 40,000 years undoubtedly influenced the evolution and the distribution and abundance of Australia's flora and fauna.

Modern Threats to Australia's Flora

There are few places in Australia that have not been directly or indirectly affected by 200 years of European settlement. The major ways in which Europeans have degraded natural ecosystems and native flora have been clearing land for agriculture and settlements, introducing alien plants and animals, intensively logging forests, polluting watercourses (thus harming aquatic plants), altering the structure and nutrient status of soils, altering natural disturbances, for example, floods or fire, over-collecting plants or their seeds for trade and introducing alien pathogens, for example, root fungi.

In general terms the major areas of disturbance are the two isolated temperate zones, one on each side of the continent, with their flat to undulating landscapes and arable soils. It is estimated that at least half of Australia's forests and woodlands have been cleared since European settlement. In the eastern grain-belt, over 90 per cent of the native vegetation has been removed and replaced by introduced pastures and monocultures of crops.

Concurrently, many of the last stands of tall eucalypt forests in the eastern and south-western parts of Australia that escaped the early settler's axe, are being subjected to intensive forestry practices such as wood-chipping or are being cleared and replaced with single-species plantations. This not only alters the physical and age class structure of the forest trees but also greatly effects understorey species.

Most other parts of Australia have been grazed to various degrees by domestic stock or introduced, feral animals. In Australia's vast semi-arid and arid inland this grazing is having a devastating impact on vegetation. What we are seeing there is an aging flora and an insidious loss of palatable trees, shrubs and herbs through senescence or other factors, together with the failure of seedlings to establish. Besides sheep and cattle, rabbits, goats, horses and donkeys also cause substantial damage to Australia's vegetation.

In the arid centre and tropical savannah grasslands and woodlands of northern Australia, unnatural fires threaten a number of plant species. Not far from Darwin, in a small rainforest remnant, is found the only population of the endangered palm *Ptychosperma bleeseri* which became rare because fire destroyed much of its habitat. Subsequently, *P. bleeseri* has suffered from grazing including rummaging by pigs.

This is not the only threatened plant affected by feral pigs. The largest Australian ground orchid *Phaius tancarvilliae*, which occurs on the coastal sand plains of Queensland and northern New South Wales, produces ground tubers that are prized by pigs for food. Their destructive rooting of the swampy ground has damaged some populations of the orchid. Put in

perspective, however, this damage is minor compared to that caused by coastal sand-mining and the invasion of exotic weeds that remain the greatest threat to Australia's temperate coastal flora.

Mining and quarrying affect a relatively small part of Australia but their impact can be absolute, wiping out all vegetation. It is thought that the bauxite mining at Weipa on Cape York Peninsula may have severely depleted the population of the grass *Heterachne baileyi*. In Western Australia the vulnerable Chittering Grass Wattle, *Acacia anomala*, and in South Australia the endangered *Ptilotus beckeranus* are both threatened by roadside gravel quarries.

Over 85 per cent of Australians live in towns and cities and the population continues to grow. Urban development is rapidly engulfing some of the richest environments on the continent, especially along the subtropical and temperate eastern seaboards. It is therefore not surprising that high numbers of threatened plants are recorded from such places as the New South Wales and southern Queensland coasts.

For example, the habitat of the Downy Wattle is the eucalypt box and ironbark forests on Wianamatta Shales in western Sydney. This region is being rapidly urbanised to the extent that there are now only a few populations of this wattle remaining. The fate of the largest population of Downy Wattle, which occurs at Long Neck Lagoon near Windsor, is in the hands of State politicians who are deliberating on the future land use of the area.

Another example of the impact of urban expansion comes from Canberra. As the city's sprawl continues to envelop the Monaro valley, one of the last populations of the endangered 'pea' *Swainsona recta*, is being pushed closer to extinction. In a concession to conservation the Canberra authorities left two house blocks free of development and constructed a two-metre cyclone fence around the few plants. Fortunately, there are three other populations of *S. recta* elsewhere but these are endangered by grazing and other factors.

Our inquisitiveness and attraction to plants also threatens some of our rare flora. Collection of native plants and seed are threatening many plant species, particularly orchids, palms and some of the attractive shrubs and mallee trees in south-west Western Australia. The endangered palm *Ptychosperma bleeseri*, cited above, is now further threatened by people collecting its seeds. The rarest eucalypt in Australia, *Eucalyptus recurva*, with a population of only

The endangered palm Ptychosperma bleeseri.

John Benson

Eucalyptus recurva, *Australia's rarest eucalypt.*

John Briggs

involved in this are justified considering the increasing use of the list by all levels of government and the public at large.

The Distribution of Rare or Threatened Plants in Australia

A comprehensive statistical analysis of the distribution of ROTAP species is presented here.

A total of 3,329 species of vascular plants are listed as rare or threatened in Australia. This accounts for approximately 17 per cent of the nation's vascular flora, similar to the situation in Europe but higher than that of the United States of America where only 10.3 per cent of flora are listed.

Distribution Category	X	E	V	R	K	Total	% of Total
1	46	2	10	3	111	172	5.2
2	36	148	495	763	398	1,840	55.2
3	15	59	279	601	363	1,317	39.6
Total	97	209	784	1,367	872	3,329	
% of Total	2.9	6.3	23.5	41.1	26.2		

Table 1. *Overall summary of the number of Australian plant species in each coding (from Briggs and Leigh 1988) (see Appendix IV for an explanation of the codes)*

The distribution of all ROTAP species by botanical divisions in Australia is shown in Figure 1. Cape York Peninsula contains the largest number of listed ROTAP species but when only the most threatened 993 species (E and V) are considered, it is clear that the regions of greatest concern are the heaths and forests of south-west Western Australia; the subtropical coast of northern New South Wales and south-eastern Queensland where many threatened rainforest plants exist in small remnants, and Cape York Peninsula, a region of immense diversity coming under threat from mining, tourism, space-station development and illegal collection of plants.

Other regions with high numbers of flora at risk include the central coast of New South Wales including Sydney; the western plains of Victoria; South Australia's Eyre Peninsula and the east coast of Tasmania.

Conservation Achievements

While 65 per cent of Australia is subjected to cropping and grazing, about 5 per cent of its landmass has been set aside for nature conservation.

Only 53.2 per cent of ROTAP plants are conserved in reserves to some degree. This inadequacy is further clouded by the fact that only 20 per cent of these are adequately reserved. Therefore only 11 per cent of the 3,329 species of Australia's rare or threatened plants are known to be amply represented in the nation's conservation

a few individuals at one site on the southern tablelands of New South Wales, is threatened by tourists who, attracted by its novelty, trample around its roots and collect specimens! The cushion plants mentioned previously and other delicate alpine flora are also threatened by trampling, particularly in Tasmania. It seems tragic that its very rareness makes a species even more endangered.

A National List of Rare or Threatened Plants

In response to a growing concern about the plight of endangered species during the 1960s and 1970s the IUCN began drawing up lists of plants and animals considered to be threatened with extinction.

The first significant list of rare and threatened plant species of Australia was prepared in 1974. In 1975 an ad hoc Working Group on Endangered Flora was established under the auspices of the Council of Nature Conservation Ministers (CONCOM) which represents all Australian States and Territories. Their first task was to

develop a list of Australian plants that warranted listing under CITES.

Based on the plant collections held in the major herbaria around the country and the opinions of expert field botanists, several editions of the list of Rare or Threatened Plants (ROTAP) have been developed.

This list is reproduced in a modified form in Appendix IV.

The ROTAP list is crucial because it highlights those plants most deserving special consideration when planning for conservation reserves or when considering land-use issues. It is not unusual for the species listed on the ROTAP list to be tabled as evidence during legal proceedings over development proposals.

As information comes to hand the ROTAP list is updated. In the past, this vital task survived only due to grants from the World Wildlife Fund and Commonwealth Government agencies. Fortunately, the Commonwealth Scientific and Industrial Research Organisation (CSIRO) has now agreed to maintain the list. The costs

reserve network. If we are generous and predict that a further two thirds of the 1,160 plants of unknown reserved status (see Table 2) are adequately reserved this figure rises to 36 per cent, still a rather poor statistic.

Adequacy of Reservation	Conservation Status					% of total of reserved species
	EC	VC	RC	KC	Total	
a	5	51	263	9	327	19.1
i	31	145	45	10	231	13.4
–	15	194	746	205	1,160	67.5
Total	51	390	1,054	224	1,719	

Table 2. *Summary of the numbers of ROTAP plants reserved (from Briggs and Leigh 1988) (see Appendix IV for an explanation of the codes)*

Tasmania, Victoria and New South Wales each have 80 per cent of ROTAP species reserved to some degree while the figures for other States and Territories range between 40 and 55 per cent.

To label a ROTAP species as adequately reserved, the figure of 1,000 individuals located in reserves has been chosen. This may need qualifying depending on the nature of the plant, the habitat and threats. We know little about the minimum population size required for plants to avoid inbreeding and subsequent loss of genetic variation; and this will vary between species.

Plants differ from vertebrate animals in having the capacity to expand their populations vegetatively, that is, to clone. With some threatened plants, for example the Downy Wattle, it is difficult to discern genetically distinct individuals from those that have sprouted from rootstocks. A patch of a rare grass may have thousands of seemingly independent plants spread over a few square metres but, in fact, each of these may be derived from the same parent. Therefore, to adequately conserve plants that exhibit vegetative growth we should aim to protect the largest available, disparate populations.

Another factor that should not be ignored, when assessing the conservation status of a plant species, is whether the range of its distribution is sampled in reserves. Although the ideal arrangement would be to sample populations over the full range of their distribution the most important objective should be to sample, substantially, populations in the centre of its range, as in most cases the bulk of a species variation should be present there.

The principal prerequisite for conserving rare or threatened Australian plants remains the protection of the largest possible populations of each species, but even this can fail for some endangered plants if follow-up management is inadequate. And sound management relies on knowledge about the biology and ecology of the plants and their habitats.

Research and Management

It is self-evident that rare species can be difficult to survey and research because they have small populations of very restricted occurrences. However, rare plants do have an advantage over animals in that they are stationary. Knowing where rare plants have previously been collected and carrying out surveys of their occurrences are prerequisites to conserving them. A comprehensive survey should highlight the best places to establish reserves and yield hypotheses about the species' biology or ecology that can be tested by future research. Yet only a minority of Australia's most threatened plants have been thoroughly surveyed and more surveys need to be carried out so they can form the basis of long-term monitoring of key populations.

Monitoring rare plants allows us to assess the population trend of a species. Some rare plants are difficult to monitor because their life cycles lack regular patterns. They have inconsistent seed production or growth depending on climate or other factors. Nevertheless, monitoring should highlight those plants with falling populations and it is these species that should receive more extensive research.

Only when field managers can predict with some confidence what will happen to a species under a given set of circumstances can we be assured of maintaining viable populations of rare or threatened plant species.

To predict successfully how a population of a plant will respond, after a fire or drought or under certain grazing pressures, we need to learn about its survival and reproduction, that is, its life cycle, the seed bank in the soil, the establishment of new individuals and maturation of the individual. Studies of the habitat as a whole and of the way the plant specialises in its niche and interacts with its neighbours, complements the knowledge we gain solely by studying the species itself.

Genetic variability can also be important when considering the minimum population required to be protected and managed. Plants, unlike most animals, are modular in design and their units of construction such as a leaf and internode can produce a new individual plant. Horticulturalists use cuttings as often as they use seeds!

Unfortunately, there are limited resources to study rare or threatened plants. It will take decades to complete research on even the threatened plants, that is, those listed as endangered or vulnerable, 993 species in all.

Once some insight has been gained into how a plant is threatened and what it requires to survive, it is the responsibility of managers to implement suitable programs. Scientific endeavour is wasted if research results are not effectively translated to managers,

Figure 1 *Total number of threatened plant species for each region of Australia (from Briggs and Leigh 1988)*

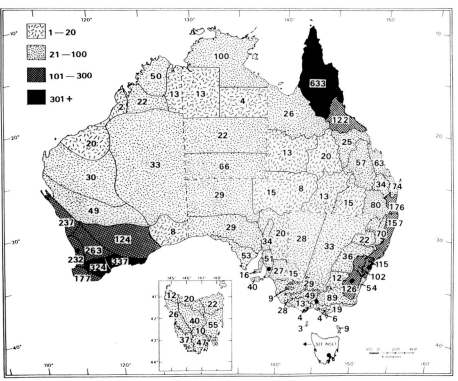

whether the latter be park rangers or private landholders.

One of the most cost-effective means of protecting rare or threatened plants, both inside and outside reserves, is to establish a thorough database of locational records. This allows wildlife managers to make better informed inputs to land-use issues and can greatly mitigate the loss of populations of our threatened flora.

Botanic Gardens and Cultivation

The primary aim of conservation must be to conserve in the wild, habitats with their constituent species, as this is the only means by which nature will continue to evolve and adapt to long-term changes in the environment. Situations do arise, however, when propagation or seed storage can play a crucial role in preventing extinctions of plants by providing a bank from which recovery in the wild can be realised.

In instances where only a few individuals of a species remain in the wild there may be no choice but to attempt to grow individuals in botanic gardens from cuttings or seed.

The subtropical rainforest tree *Diplogottis campbellii* grows on low-altitude alluvial plains in the Richmond-Tweed Rivers region on the far north coast of New South Wales, in remnants of what was once Australia's largest area of subtropical rainforest. It has a total known wild population of about 25 mature plants, most of which survive as isolated trees in cleared paddocks on private land. Even if one or more of the paddocks where it is found were acquired and fenced off, it is unlikely that this would result in a recovery of the species because the habitat has been so grossly modified. It is near to impossible for a non-colonising rainforest seedling to establish in a field dominated by kikuyu grass. Fortunately however, the plight of this ornamental tree with edible fruit has been given wide publicity. The wild population of *D. campbellii* is being augmented by propagation from cuttings in both local nurseries and botanic gardens. Propagated specimens from several different populations have been planted into the Mount Warning National Park arboretum as a means of 'capturing' a vulnerable genetic stock that lies outside the reserve system.

This is a case where to do nothing would probably result in its extinction within a few decades; therefore propagation and transplantation were the correct options to apply in this instance.

There is an encouraging trend in botanic gardens towards emphasising rare plants in their education, propagation and seed storage programs. The Canberra Botanical Gardens now grow most of Australia's endangered plants. They have also undertaken research into genetic variation of some acutely threatened species. An example is the Philip Island Hibiscus which had only a few individuals surviving after the island's vegetation was denuded by rabbits (Philip Island is a small island off Norfolk Island in the South Pacific). Now that the rabbits have been eliminated, it is possible that the population of the hibiscus will recover, although the erosion on the island has been such that it is unlikely the vegetation will return to its original form and diversity.

The establishment of seed stores in major botanic gardens and by the CSIRO means that, at least for those endangered plants that produce storable seeds, there is a last line of defence against extinction.

While botanic gardens and wider cultivation can play a role in conserving rare plants, problems do arise. The genetic integrity of plants propagated in captivity can be polluted through hybridisation with other species, or crossing with individuals of the same species that have been derived from different populations in the wild. This is particularly troublesome if enrichment plantings aimed at bolstering wild populations of rare plants are proposed. Also, such transplanting programs are costly.

Present Legislation

The most effective flora protection laws in Australia are in Western Australia and Victoria.

Western Australia has one of the world's most diverse floras. Under the amended Wildlife Conservation Act (1950-1980), plants substantiated as being threatened may be declared by the Minister as rare flora and notified in the Government Gazette. By the end of 1988, 227 taxa were listed. The listed taxon is protected on private and public land and cannot be taken without consent of the Minister. The Department of Conservation and Land Management has a significant budget for fencing, which is often the most urgent action required to protect a population of a threatened plant. Populations of gazetted flora are still 'accidentally' destroyed and there are inconsistencies in the gazetted list as many endangered species are not yet listed.

A remarkable piece of legislation came into being in Victoria in 1988, titled the Flora and Fauna Guarantee (FFG). With a few exceptions the legislation covers all native Victorian flora and fauna. The Act deals with recovery and prevention. Species at risk are given special attention for management through a listing process under Schedule 2 of the Act. Listing is not restricted to a species but can also include an assemblage of species (that is, habitat) and a potentially threatening process (for example, pollution, weed invasion). It is this last aspect that

The vulnerable Tasmanian plant Milligania johnstonii.

John Benson

makes this legislation unique. In urgent situations an Interim Conservation Order (ICO) can be applied to critical habitats.

Future Legislation

The following features are important for inclusion in laws drawn up to protect threatened plants and their habitats:

- schedules that contain species in the greatest need of protection and monitoring;
- improved regulations to control the taking of protected flora – encouraging propagation and discouraging picking from the wild;
- an Australia-wide listing of threatened and exploited species requiring national protection, thereby overcoming the 'free trade between States' barrier of the Australian Constitution;
- interim conservation orders that can be applied immediately and allow time for the pursuit of permanent protection of species and their habitats;
- the onus of proof for persons caught possessing threatened flora suspected to have been illegally taken should lie with the defendant;
- highly threatened species, that is, all endangered (E) and vulnerable (V) species, should not be allowed to be taken from the wild on any land tenure except where stock is taken, under a licence from a conservation agency, as a basis for a propagation program that is designed to relieve the pressure on wild populations;
- voluntary conservation agreements with appropriate financial support to encourage landholders to protect critical habitats;
- the legislation should bind the Crown, that is, all government agencies.

Even the best laws will not be effective unless they are enforced and this can only be achieved through the commitment of people and funds to carrying out conservation programs in the various wildlife agencies around Australia. The main priority should be to boost compensation/land acquisition funds beyond their present paltry amounts.

Conclusion

We do not want to increase the number of plant species in Australia listed as rare or threatened. That is why there is an urgent need to protect, in reserves or by other means, representative samples of ecosystems containing both rare and common species. The fact that over 50 per cent of ROTAP

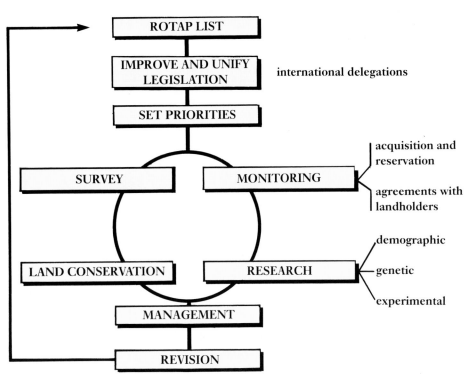

Figure 2 *Major programs for the conservation of rare or threatened Australian plants*

species are not yet adequately reserved indicates greater effort is required in establishing reserves. The larger the reserves and the more complete the catchments contained within them, the better the chance of success in long-term conservation, even in the face of abrupt events such as fire or disease and the better the chance of adapting to long-term changes in the environment.

A prerequisite in choosing places to reserve is to assimilate the locational records of ROTAP species and then to survey them. Subsequent to survey a conservation strategy can be constructed with recommendations for reservation, research and management.

Unfortunately many rare plants only persevere in isolated remnants and their conservation and management can be tedious and expensive. The co-operation of landholders is often critical to a species' survival. There is a need for better education of farmers about conservation of habitats and rare species. Tax concessions could play a larger role in encouraging this co-operation. This would mean changing existing federal laws and regulations.

Since it is not possible to work toward protecting all rare plants concurrently, priorities need to be established based on criteria such as degree of threat and genetic 'uniqueness'. This in turn requires extensive but directed activities such as the development of databases, survey, research and monitoring programs.

The programs paramount to the conservation of rare or threatened plants are illus-

trated in Figure 2.

Even with all these efforts it is certain that some plant species will become extinct due to human interference. We must do all that is possible to turn the tide of extinctions and in doing so with enthusiasm, set an example to other less-developed nations. We can start by involving and educating the public and by improving and unifying the laws that govern the protection of flora in Australia.

WHAT CAN I DO?

- Don't pick native plants from natural areas.
- Grow native plants and join a native plant society, botanic garden or conservation group.
- Take an interest in your local bushland.
- Join a bushland weeding group.
- Persuade politicians and local councils to protect important sites.
- If you are a farmer with a rare plant or important habitat on your property do what you can to prevent its deterioration by fencing it off from stock, you will probably be able to get assistance from government authorities.
- Urge governments to give incentives to landholders willing to fence off natural remnants or plant trees.
- Grow plants native to your area preferably using seed or cuttings from local plants.

Captive Breeding
of Endangered Species

GRAEME G GEORGE

Breeding in captivity is becoming an indispensable part of efforts to halt the decline in populations of threatened species all over the world. There are several pressures on wild animal populations currently threatening many of them with extinction. Wild animals are losing their living space through habitat changes, such as clearing of forest for agriculture. Many are hunted for their meat, hides, horns, feathers or eggs, at rates which are unsustainable and often illegal. Many face competition from introduced species for living space and resources, such as food, as well as facing predation by introduced carnivores. Conservation programs designed to save threatened species from extinction usually require considerable effort to reverse the factors causing decline of the species in its natural habitat. Establishing secure captive-breeding populations can often buy some time while longer term programs are implemented. Captive breeding is not a solution to the problem of conserving threatened species. Ultimately, this can only be achieved in the species' natural habitat, but conservation can be assisted by establishing captive-breeding populations of rare and threatened species.

Captive breeding for conservation purposes has two primary functions: multiplication of reduced populations to provide the numbers to re-establish viable wild populations and preservation of a sample of the gene pool in case of the total loss of the wild population.

A classic example of a species being saved from total extinction because of established captive populations, is Père David's Deer which became extinct in China during the

Boxer Rebellion in 1900. It survives today because a few individuals, taken out of China last century, were successfully bred at Woburn Abbey in the United Kingdom. Similarly, zoo populations of the European Bison, the American Bison and the Hawaiian Goose were also used to re-establish wild populations of these species. The captive population of the Mongolian Wild Horse (Przewalski) has been managed over recent decades for eventual re-establishment in the steppes of central Asia and plans are currently being made to release surplus captive-bred animals into suitable parts of their former range. The Thylacine of Tasmania was not so lucky. Although kept in many zoos around the world, around the turn of the century, no captive breeding was ever recorded and the last captive specimen died in a private Hobart zoo in 1936.

These few success stories are due to the fact that captive-breeding populations were present in zoological collections at a time when the wild populations were found to have become extinct, or were on the verge of becoming so. More recently, the last remaining individuals of several critically endangered species overseas have been deliberately captured to establish captive-breeding populations, to prevent their imminent extinction. The first of these was the international effort to rescue the Arabian Oryx which was being hunted to extinction on the Arabian Peninsula in Saudi Arabia. The last few remaining wild oryx were rounded up in 1962 and brought together with animals from several zoos to form the nucleus of a world herd at the Phoenix Zoo in Arizona, where they commenced breeding. Progeny of this group, some 20 years later, were successfully re-introduced to Oman and others have since been returned to Jordan. More recently, the last remaining Black-footed Ferret and Californian Condor

were brought into captivity in the United States of America in 1986 to establish breeding groups. Without this action, hotly debated among conservationists and government biologists at the time, neither species had a chance of avoiding extinction.

A Conservation Tool

Captive breeding as a conservation tool has long been seen as a last resort, with the prevailing sentiment being that, as long as a species was still breeding in the wild, it had a better chance of surviving there than if it were removed to the artificial conditions of captivity with all its attendant risks. This may once have been a justified view but techniques for captive-animal husbandry and reproduction have improved tremendously over recent decades. Our understanding of the dynamics of wild populations, and the processes that are causing their decline on a global scale, has also increased dramatically, so that captive breeding has rather suddenly become accepted as a legitimate and frequently essential step in saving an increasing number of species from extinction. The dramatic growth in scientific knowledge of how small populations behave biologically has resulted in a new scientific discipline being recognised, that of Conservation Biology. This new area of scientific endeavour focuses on the management of small populations both in captivity and the wild. It has become increasingly evident that many populations of wild animals in national parks and other nature reserves are isolated in virtual 'islands' of habitat and will need to be managed in a similar manner to populations held in captivity.

The basis for our concern about small populations is both demographic and genetic. Obviously the smaller a population is, the more likely it is to go extinct, but a population's size and its genetic structure are

These two chicks were raised by the last Norfolk Island Boobook Owl. It is still perilously close to extinction despite this success with controlled breeding.

John Hicks

interlinked. This is all to do with genes, those strands of DNA on the chromosomes in the cell nucleus which are the basis of heredity. Genes determine why living creatures are what they are and why each species is different from every other species on Earth.

Life, as we know it on Earth today, is the culmination of many millions of years of evolutionary adaption by species to the environments in which they live. These environments, however, are not static and are subject to change over time. Climates may become warmer or cooler, wetter or drier. Habitats may suffer in the short term from floods, fire and drought. New species of plants and animals may invade and become established, competing with species that are already a part of the ecosystem. Species which cannot adapt to these sorts of environmental changes become extinct, replaced by species which are better adapted to the newer conditions. This is an entirely natural process which has been going on since life first appeared on Earth. What is unnatural is the current rate of extinction which is a direct consequence of man's activities. These include the direct effects of overhunting and the introduction of exotic plants and animals, combined with the indirect effects of habitat changes brought about by the clearing of natural vegetation for agriculture, logging of forests for timber and paper pulp, damming of waterways for irrigation and power generation, and pollution by the waste products of our industrial society.

Biologists have long been concerned with the alarming trend towards extinction of more and more species but the general community has only recently become aware of the priceless heritage we have in the biological diversity, represented by wildlife and the natural environment. This concern is firstly, and predominantly, with the biological diversity represented by all the various forms of life, which biologists classify into different species, genera, families, orders, classes and phyla. But to successfully conserve this biological diversity at the various taxonomic levels we also must concern ourselves with the genetic diversity within individual species.

Charles Darwin's theory of evolution by natural selection, published in 1859, provided an explanation for the mechanism for evolutionary change in wild populations, but the genetic basis for this was not understood until well into the twentieth century.

Genetic Diversity

In sexually-reproducing organisms, the chromosomes which carry the genes occur in pairs. One of each pair of chromosomes, with the genes contained on them, is passed on to each offspring so that a son or daughter inherits one set of genes from its mother and another from its father. There are many thousands of genes in each species, 10,000 is the estimate for humans, and every individual has two copies of each gene. These copies may be the same (homozygous) or they may be different (heterozygous). Within a population a particular gene may be present in several different forms, called alleles, but an individual can carry no more than two of these, one on each of the pair of chromosomes that carry that gene. Geneticists have found that the percentage of genes which occur in a heterozygous condition varies but is commonly up to 15 per cent. The amount of genetic diversity within individuals and species is of critical importance in captive-breeding programs, as allelic diversity is highly advantageous to both individuals and populations.

Firstly, an individual which carries different alleles for a particular gene, or series of genes, seems to have superior 'fitness', that is, it seems to grow faster, survive longer and has higher reproductive success. This superior fitness is demonstrated in several ways. When related animals are bred together (inbreeding) the probability of an offspring inheriting the same allele for a particular gene from each parent is increased. Such inbred animals are more likely to have reduced genetic variability as a consequence (they are more homozygous). As levels of inbreeding, and hence homozygosity, increase, there is often a noticeable, even marked, decline in fertility, hatchability of eggs and viability of newborn, an increased susceptibility to disease and reduced longevity. This phenomenon is called 'inbreeding depression' and is widely seen in small captive-breeding populations where relatives are often paired up for breeding. The most extreme consequence of inbreeding is the appearance of genetic deformities in inbred stock. The wise breeder of aviary birds and livestock often seeks to introduce 'new blood' to overcome these genetically-based problems.

Successful captive breeding of the Numbat is proving difficult on a regular basis. Babs & Bert Wells/NPIAW

On the other hand, when two different inbred lines of animals or plants are mated to each other there is often a marked increase in fitness which is known as 'hybrid vigour'. Plant and animal breeders take advantage of this.

On this sort of evidence, it seems likely that individuals of wild animal and plant species will have a better chance of surviving and reproducing if a significant number of their genes occur in a heterozygous state. Indeed, biologists have discovered many diverse strategies, which have evolved to enable cross-pollination and cross-fertilisation in wild populations, which enable genetic variation to be maintained in individuals. There is negative evidence from the wild to support this view. There is cause for concern at the status of the Cheetah in the wild and it has proven to be difficult to breed in captivity. Genetic studies on wild Cheetahs in southern Africa have revealed very low levels of genetic variability and it seems likely that this is a major cause of the difficulties encountered with this species. In Australia, no significant genetic variability has yet been found in the declining population of the Eastern Barred Bandicoot in western Victoria. It is assumed that wild populations like these have lost their genetic diversity through inbreeding in the past, perhaps associated with periodical population crashes, followed by recovery from small remnant populations of related animals.

The second important advantage for a species with a diversity of alleles in its population, is the ability to adapt to environmental changes. Individuals which carry a set of genes suited to a particular environment may be at a disadvantage if faced with a climatic change, a new predator or disease organism, or a new competitor for resources such as food or shelter. In these circumstances, a genetically diverse population will usually contain some individuals which do better under the new conditions than under the old ones. These are more likely to survive and reproduce. When this happens the frequency of the beneficial alleles in the population increases and the genetic composition of the descendent population begins to differ from the ancestral one. This can happen over very short time spans as a consequence of a major challenge such as a disease outbreak or a drought, or more gradually such as when vegetation changes occur due to long-term changes to weather patterns. The end result is an evolutionary change in the genetic make-up of the species.

The Bustard is one of several Australian bird species being bred in captivity for the purpose of replenishing wild populations.   Frithfoto/Olympus

Alleles may occur in wild populations at low frequencies where there is no selection pressure favouring their survival. Common alleles may also not be expressed very often if they are recessive to a dominant form of the gene. However, it is the extent of this genetic diversity that determines the likelihood of a species continuing to evolve and thus surviving into the future. Preserving this evolutionary potential is central to modern Conservation Biology theory and is one of the major tasks of any captive-breeding program. This can only be achieved with very careful genetic management of the captive population.

Regrettably, because captive breeding has usually been seen as a last resort, many programs are not started until the wild population is down to its last few individuals. By this stage the population has usually lost the major portion of its genetic variability and may have already been subjected to a degree of inbreeding as the population has declined and the choice of unrelated breeding partners has become more restricted. The International Union for Conservation of Nature and Natural Resources (IUCN) recommends much earlier use of captive breeding as a conservation tool and urges that captive-breeding programs be commenced when declining populations are still in their thousands, not when the species is about to go extinct. Such early commencement allows a much wider sampling of the gene pool to ensure genetic diversity in the

captive population, and, of course, a greatly increased probability of conserving the species in the longer term.

Australian Experience

In Australia, most State wildlife authorities have established captive stocks of threatened species as an aid to their conservation. The former Victorian Department of Fisheries and Wildlife, now the National Parks and Wildlife Division of the Department of Conservation, Forests and Lands, has been systematically breeding several species at the Serendip Wildlife Research Station. At Serendip, breeding colonies of the Magpie Goose, Cape Barren Goose, Brolga and Australian Bustard have been maintained for the purpose of re-establishing these species in those parts of Victoria where they once occurred. The facilities have also housed research colonies of the Eastern Barred Bandicoot and the Long-nosed Potoroo.

Since the mid-1970s the Department has worked closely with the Zoological Board of Victoria in establishing breeding colonies of threatened Victorian species at the Board's zoos. Three Long-footed Potoroos were established in outdoor breeding pens at the Healesville Sanctuary, north-east of Melbourne, in 1980. This resulted in the first captive birth of this newly-discovered and very rare species within a year. A program to breed Leadbeater's Possum was commenced at Melbourne Zoo in 1982. The program was later extended to include the Healesville

Sanctuary and Taronga Zoo in Sydney. Progeny from this successful exercise have been returned to the wild in a trial release program and selected animals have been sent to several major overseas zoos to expand the size of the captive population. The first breeding of Leadbeater's Possum in an overseas zoo was achieved at London Zoo in March 1989. In 1986, a pair of Mountain Pygmy-possums from Mount Hotham in the Victorian Alps were lodged at the Healesville Sanctuary for captive breeding.

These efforts were undertaken primarily to utilise the accommodation and captive-husbandry expertise at the Board's zoos and to provide a back-up captive population in case of deterioration of those species in the wild. In 1989, the Victorian Department and the Zoological Board joined forces in a much more urgent captive-breeding program. The continued decline of the remaining known wild population of the Helmeted Honey-eater, at Yellingbo in the Yarra Valley, required the immediate establishment of a captive colony as part of a recovery program. To achieve this, nestlings are being hand-reared at the Healesville Sanctuary to start a captive-breeding colony, with the aim of providing progeny for return to the wild when other measures have been taken to improve the habitat available to the birds. The remaining birds will be studied genetically, using the latest molecular techniques, to determine the amount of genetic variation still present so that the breeding program can be designed to maximise retention of the variation available.

The Department of Conservation and Land Management, and its predecessors in Western Australia, have been supporting captive breeding for many years. The Brush-tailed Bettong, now restricted to parts of the south-west of Western Australia, is well established in captivity. Much of the captive population is descended from Perth Zoo's prolific colony which was established during the 1960s. The zoo's colony grew after it received stock from the University of Western Australia in 1971. Dr Andrew Burbidge, Director of Wildlife Research in Western Australia, was later instrumental in the deposition of additional specimens in zoos in Australia and overseas to expand the genetic base of the captive population. An international studbook for the bettong was established in 1983, the first international studbook for any Australian species. Captive breeding is not always so easy and efforts to breed the critically endangered Western Swamp Turtle in Western Australia have had only limited success to date. More recent efforts to breed the Numbat and the Chuditch (Western Quoll) were initially successful, but these species are proving difficult to breed on a regular basis. The Perth Zoo has been involved with both these species and works closely with biologists at the Western Australian Wildlife Research Centre at Woodvale.

The South Australian National Parks and Wildlife Service, in 1975, set out to breed up the Brush-tailed Bettong for release onto islands off the South Australian coast. The Service started with a few animals derived from the Perth Zoo colony and in a few years had a population explosion on their hands. These small kangaroos can produce three young a year with high potential for rapid population growth; a feature of their reproductive biology that would be very useful to a species likely to suffer population crashes in the wild during a series of bad seasons. Though the captive-breeding project was spectacularly successful, subsequent attempts to establish the captive-bred stock on islands, safe from predators like the fox, have had mixed success, and efforts are continuing. The Service has also been breeding the Greater Stick-nest Rat, now extinct on the mainland, in case the remaining island populations suffer some catastrophe. Captive-breeding facilities for these and other threatened species have been established at Monarto in association with the Adelaide Zoo's Breeding and Agistment Area.

In the early 1980s, the New South Wales National Parks and Wildlife Service embarked on a program to save the Lord Howe Island Woodhen from extinction. This relict island bird was facing severe competition from feral pigs and rats. Successful breeding in enclosures on the Island, using the avicultural skills of Glen Fraser, provided numbers of birds for release back into the wild after the feral animals had been removed. A conservation program for the Malleefowl has also recently commenced in New South Wales. Under this extensive program, eggs taken from wild mounds are being incubated at Taronga Zoo. Chicks are being raised at the Western Plains Zoo at

A Bilby from the captive-breeding program at Alice Springs, Northern Territory.

Open Space

Dubbo where a captive-breeding program will be started to provide chicks for release back to the wild. Other Australian zoos and the National Parks and Wildlife Service of South Australia are co-operating in this program.

The Queensland National Parks and Wildlife Service have captive-breeding and research facilities at Pallarenda, Townsville and at Warwick in southern Queensland, and public display facilities at Fleay's Fauna Centre at Burleigh Heads. Captive breeding in Queensland, however, is currently focused on providing biological data rather than the establishment of viable captive populations for conservation purposes.

Tasmania, despite having lost the Thylacine, is in better shape than other States from a conservation point of view because of its physical isolation from the mainland of Australia. The Tasmanian Devil survives in Tasmania because the Dingo probably arrived in Australia after Bass Strait was flooded by rising sea levels. The fox fortunately was not introduced by European colonisers during the misguided acclimatisation frenzy last century. The survival of the Tasmanian (or Eastern) Bettong and the Tasmanian (or Red-bellied) Pademelon in Tasmania is no doubt due to the absence of the Fox, and the Eastern Quoll may be in a similar situation. All three are extinct on the mainland. The National Parks Service in Tasmania is, however, breeding the Orange-bellied Parrot in captivity as part of a three-State recovery plan for this migratory species that breeds in the heathlands of the south-west coast.

Perhaps the most concerted captive-breeding programs have been undertaken by the Conservation Commission of the Northern Territory at the Arid Zone Research Station near Alice Springs. Two conservation programs there, managed by Dr Ken Johnson, have received a great deal of publicity. Both are centred on remnant populations of two marsupials from the Tanami Desert. The only known surviving mainland population of the Rufous Hare-wallaby (or Mala) occurs there as does the Greater Bilby, which has disappeared from most of its former extensive range over nearly all of inland Australia. Animals captured in the Tanami, with the help of the local Aboriginal owners of the reserve, have been used to establish captive-breeding colonies, expressly to be used for re-introduction to suitable habitats in other parts of the Northern Territory where the species is known to have previously occurred. The

Helmeted Honeyeater fledglings taken from the wild for handraising at Healesville Sanctuary.

Healesville Sanctuary/Mark Griffin

breeding program has been extended through provision of some captive-bred animals to the Western Plains Zoo at Dubbo and to the Territory Wildlife Park at Berry Springs near Darwin, to establish subsidiary colonies.

Inbreeding Depression

Sustainable captive reproduction was not a high priority in zoos around the world a generation or two ago. Replacements for exhibit animals were readily obtainable by direct import from the wild, or through purchase or trade with a zoo that had surplus stock. There were exceptions, of course, where zoos held stocks of species that were extremely rare or even extinct in the wild. Successful captive breeding of such species was more often due to good luck than good management, however. As concern developed for the plight of wildlife around the globe, zoos began to reassess their role and set out to become nett producers of wildlife rather than nett consumers. They soon found out that successful breeding programs required more than simply putting males and females together. Initial breeding successes were often followed by poor performances in the second and third generations. We now know that this was primarily due to the phenomenon of inbreeding depression, brought about by the mating of close rela-

tives. It was common practice to mate brothers and sisters and often littermates were sent to another zoo as a breeding pair. This was easier than swapping animals between several institutions. In many cases, particularly favoured herd sires were often left as the breeder for several generations, mating in turn with their daughters and grand-daughters. Breeding programs in zoos today are often still compromised by the legacy of these past inappropriate breeding practices.

Inbreeding does not always hinder successful captive breeding. There are many examples, in the zoo world and in private aviculture, of captive populations originating from a prolific breeding pair or small number of founding individuals. However, captive populations which originate from such a small founder base are unlikely to contain anything like the full range of the genetic variation that is present in the wild population from which they are derived. They are likely, in fact, to have gone through a process of selection for genes which suit the environmental conditions of captivity. This is the first step in the domestication of a wild species. Continued selection of the best breeders in captivity, along with selection for other characteristics such as docility, size, colour or conformation, eventually leads to domestic breeds which may bear little resemblance to their wild ancestors.

157

Captive breeding of wild species for the purposes of conservation must, of necessity, take stringent efforts to preserve, not modify, the gene pool, so that the stock is genetically suitable to be returned to the wild at some time in the future. Any trend towards domestication has to be avoided at all costs.

Genetic Variability

Genetic variability is easily lost in small populations. At each generation, only a proportion of the variability present in the parents is passed on to the offspring. The more offspring that two parents produce the more genetic variation is passed on. In a large population, alleles which are not passed on by one breeding pair are likely to be passed on by others in the population. As the population gets smaller, the chances of losing alleles becomes greater. This phenomenon is not restricted to captive-breeding populations. Relict populations in isolated habitats are often too small for the lost genetic variation to be replaced by random mutations which normally produce new genetic variation in wild populations. When this begins to happen, the extinction process is speeded up. The smaller a population gets, the faster it loses genetic variation and the less it is able to cope with the environmental factors that initiated its decline in the first place. This downward spiral has been dubbed the 'extinction vortex'. In many sedentary species, which once formed more or less continous populations, maintenance of genetic variability was dependent on gene flow, brought about by interbreeding between neighbouring communities. For many species, opportunities for individuals to disperse into neighbouring communities no longer exist. In the absence of gene flow by natural means, intervention by man is the only hope of preventing continued deterioration of the gene pool and inevitable extinction of the isolated populations. Continued extinction of these small isolated populations eventually results in extinction of the species as the last isolated population dies out.

Relocation of animals into suitable habitat, where the environmental pressures are less severe, and transfer of individuals between isolated populations are labour-intensive and costly ways to overcome these problems, and there is always the risk of initial failure and further loss of precious genetic variability. At this point captive breeding provides

Co-operation between the States and the Government has helped save the Orange-bellied Parrot from extinction.

D Watts/NPIAW

a very useful technique to prevent further loss of genetic variation and to build up numbers for re-introduction.

Establishing Captive-breeding Programs

When establishing a threatened species in captivity or relocating a population in vacant habitat, it is important that the genetic variability present in the wild population is adequately sampled in founding the new population. Geneticists recommend a minimum of 20 founders, unrelated to each other, to statistically ensure that 98 per cent of the variation present in the wild population is available at the start of the breeding program. It is then necessary to ensure that each of these founders breeds and passes on a high percentage of its genes to the next generation. Ideally 12 offspring should be bred from each founder to ensure that 98 per cent of each founder's genes are passed on. This is a critical step as alleles may be lost if some animals fail to breed or do not produce an adequate number of offspring. If there are problems in getting the stock to breed or if the reproductive rate of the species is low, it may be necessary to start with a higher number of founders to counteract this. Unfortunately, most captive-breeding exercises start with far too few founding animals brought in from the wild.

Once the population is established in captivity it is then necessary to ensure that, in each generation, an equal number of males and females are allowed to breed and that each breeding pair contributes an equal number of offspring to the next generation. This requires careful management and often some hard decisions, without which the more prolific breeders would soon dominate the population and the genes of the less prolific breeders would gradually die out.

Keeping track of pedigrees and the genetic representation of founders is a time-consuming task, particularly as the population, and the amount of data on it, grows. Computers have become an indispensable tool for handling both the data and the calculations necessary for adequate population analysis. Computer programs are now available to store pedigree data in the form of studbooks and to analyse this data to determine the genetic contributions of founders, the degree of inbreeding, the life expectancy of individuals, fertility rates and projected population growth.

The international zoo community began to organise breeding programs for rare and endangered species on a global scale with the

Despite recent successful captive breeding, the Western Swamp Turtle remains one of Australia's most endangered species.

Robert W G Jenkins

adoption of international studbooks by the International Union of Directors of Zoological Gardens in 1966. In 1972, the first international conference devoted to the breeding of endangered species in captivity was held at the Jersey Wildlife Preservation Trust in the Channel Isles. Papers presented at this conference dealt mainly with case studies. At the second international conference held at London Zoo in 1976, key papers illustrated how population biology theory could be applied to the genetic and demographic management of zoo populations and how computerised databases could be used to assist with the application of those techniques. Several subsequent conferences and specialist workshops have brought zoo biologists together with population geneticists and demographers from the academic community, to advance the theory and to formulate practical recommendations for its application to conservation of threatened species. At the same time the relevance of these population management techniques to small populations in isolated, fragmented habitat patches in the wild has received increasing attention.

Regional zoo organisations in North America, Australasia, the British Isles, Europe and the Netherlands have taken on the responsibility of co-ordinating breeding programs on a geographical basis. Regional databases have been developed with links to the international database, the International Species Information System, established at the Minnesota Zoo in the United States of America in 1976. At the international level,

captive breeding of threatened species is co-ordinated globally by the Captive Breeding, Specialist Group (CBSG) of the IUCN's Species Survival Commission. The CBSG meets annually in conjunction with other international zoo meetings. Its workload is growing rapidly in response to the continuing decline in the status of many species worldwide.

Conservation has become the top priority of most major zoos, which have a dual role in this area. They are uniquely placed to influence public opinion through their educational programs and high public profile. Zoos have considerable accumulated expertise in areas such as animal husbandry, behaviour in captivity, reproduction, enclosure design, handling and transportation techniques, diets and nutrition of wild species and disease prevention and control. Many zoos are also developing collaborative programs with universities and wildlife authorities and appointing specialist research staff to work, both in-house and on-field studies, with threatened species. The capacity of zoos to house viable populations of threatened species, is however, very limited. Zoos will no doubt continue to give priority to those high-profile species with which the zoo-going public identifies, but there is plenty of scope for involvement of the zoo community in collaborative captive-breeding projects covering a wide range of species.

An effort in this regard is being made with IUCN's *Action Plan for Australasian Marsupials and Monotremes,* and may set an example for future co-operative programs.

Wildlife Trade
and Exploitation

FRANK ANTRAM

Ivory, rhinoceros horn, cat skins, parrots, crocodile and snake skins, aquarium fish, butterflies, corals and shells, orchids and tropical timber: the world market for wildlife, and wildlife products, is absolutely enormous. It has been estimated to be worth at least US$5 billion annually (excluding the value of the tropical timber trade), and one year's international trade would be likely to include about 40,000 apes and monkeys, ivory tusks from at least 90,000 elephants, at least 1 million orchids, 4 million live birds, 10 million reptile skins, 15 million furskins, 350 million tropical fish, and a miscellaneous assortment of other 'souvenirs'.

It is the natural reaction of most people to be appalled at this dramatic destruction of wildlife, but how bad is it from a conservation viewpoint? The answer, however, is not straightforward. The first point that must be emphasised is that habitat destruction is a far more serious threat, in most cases, than any direct exploitation of the wildlife. There are some notable exceptions where hunting of a species has been directly responsible for its extinction; for example, Steller's Sea Cow, the Great Auk, or the Passenger Pigeon. Today, we can see that some rhinoceros species, for example, have been hunted to the brink of extinction, while other species, such as the African Elephant, have been severely decimated over much of their range. However, if the 'harvest' of a wildlife species is sustainable, that is, if the cull is not so consistently excessive as to cause a long-term decline in the populations of that species, then the exploitation of that species is not going to affect its conservation. Whether it is morally right to exploit wildlife is another, and I would suggest, entirely subjective, matter.

The Major Mitchell Cockatoo is highly valued by illegal international markets.

Leo Meier/Courtesy Weldon Trannies

Control Measures

Public concern about wildlife trade began in the late 1800s and was focused on the trade in bird feathers for the fashion industry. One of the first treaties which placed restrictions on importation of certain birds was a European Convention for the Protection of Birds Useful to Agriculture, signed in 1902. In 1916, the United Kingdom and the United States signed the Convention for the Protection of Migratory Birds, which prohibited international trade in certain birds or their eggs during closed seasons. At about the same time, the first treaty to control the harvest of fur seals was concluded, its main provision being to curtail pelagic sealing. In 1933, the London Convention Relative to the Preservation of Fauna and Flora in their Natural State was designed to regulate domestic and international trade in hunting trophies of a number of African species, the principal purpose being to preserve supplies of species popular with trophy hunters. It was superseded in 1968 by the African Convention on the Conservation of Nature and Natural Resources.

One of the first international agreements to go beyond the notion of simply conserving commercially-valuable wildlife, to advocate protection of all species from man-induced extinction, was the Convention on Nature Protection and Wildlife Preservation in the Western Hemisphere, concluded in 1940. Known as the Western Hemisphere Convention, it was a visionary instrument which covered many elements of wildlife conservation for the first time in an international treaty. However, the Western Hemisphere Convention's greatest weakness was, and still is, its failure to establish an administrative structure to encourage enforcement of its terms. Article IX of the Convention, which seeks to regulate international trade in wildlife, has now been largely superseded by the Convention on International Trade in Endangered Species of Wild Fauna and Flora.

The massive scale of the world trade in wild animals and plants continued unabated. Increasing public concern about this led to the drafting of the Convention on International Trade in Endangered Species of Wild Fauna and Flora, which was concluded in Washington, D.C. on 3 March 1973. Better known as CITES (usually pronounced sy-tees) or the Washington Convention, it seeks to prohibit commercial trade in a list (Appendix I) of endangered species, and to control and monitor trade, via a system based on the issuance of export or re-export permits, of a list (Appendix II) of threatened species. Appendix I of CITES includes all apes, lemurs, the Giant Panda, many South American monkeys, great whales, cheetahs, leopards, tigers, elephants, rhinoceros, many birds of prey and parrots, all sea turtles, some crocodiles and lizards, giant salamanders, and some mussels, orchids and cacti.

Appendix II of CITES consists of species which might become endangered if trade in them is not controlled and monitored. It also includes species which may not necessarily be threatened but which *look* like species which are threatened or endangered; these species are listed to prevent threatened species from being traded under the guise of non-threatened species. Appendix II includes all primates, cats, otters, whales, dolphins and porpoises, birds of prey, parrots, tortoises, crocodiles and orchids which are not already listed on Appendix I. It also includes many other species such as several butterflies and many corals.

CITES covers international trade only, and has no jurisdiction over domestic trade and utilisation of wildlife. As of January 1990, the total number of countries which are a Party to the Convention is 105.

Australia's Role

In world terms, Australia's wildlife trade is relatively insignificant. However, that doesn't mean that there are not many highly sought-after and valuable Australian native species. It simply means that, due largely to our long-term restrictive policy on wildlife exports, that we do not engage in the large-scale exports of live birds for the pet trade, or reptile skins for the exotic leather industry that so many African, Asian and South American countries rely on, to a degree, for foreign currency earnings. Neither is Australia a major consumer of wildlife on the scale of Japan and the European and North American countries; this is probably largely due to Australia's relatively small human population.

Australia does, however, maintain commercial export industries in a number of relatively abundant species, including kangaroos and wallabies, possums, muttonbirds, shells and wildflowers. These will be discussed in more detail later. There is also a substantial overseas demand for live Australian native birds and reptiles for the collector trade. This trade is illegal but, nevertheless, continues.

In September 1976, a House of Representatives Standing Committee on Environment and Conservation reported on its investigations into fauna trafficking in Australia. The Committee's report found that 'international smuggling of Australian native birds is a highly capitalised and organised activity involving land, sea and air operations and a network of contacts throughout Australia and overseas'. The Committee reported that the illegal export trade in Australian native birds was variously estimated to be worth $1 million a year, or up to several times that figure. The total illegal trade in Australian wildlife has been calculated to be worth $40 million annually. Although the basis for this estimate is unclear, it has since been widely quoted, so much so that it is now more or less regarded as fact. However, I would suggest that, by its very undercover nature, it is not possible to make anything more than a wild guess at the value of illegal trade.

The Australian Law

Each State and Territory of Australia has its own legislation covering the protection of fauna and flora. The regulations regarding the taking, keeping, and trading in native species vary considerably from State to State. However, all international trade, that is, import to and export from Australia, is subject to the provisions of the federal law known as the Wildlife Protection (Regulation of Exports and Imports) Act 1982. This Act, which is administered by the Australian National Parks and Wildlife Service, came into force in 1984. Amongst other things, the Act enables implementation of CITES in Australia and places controls on the export of most Australian native fauna and flora. Australia ratified CITES on 29 July 1976 and, prior to the introduction of the Wildlife Protection Act, the provisions of CITES were enforced in Australia via Endangered Species Regulations under the Customs Act 1901.

Mammals

Many of Australia's native mammals have a long history of exploitation. Before European settlement, Aborigines exploited, in particular, the macropodids (kangaroos and wallabies) and possums, for food and clothing.

With European settlement and the clearing of land for agriculture, kangaroos came to be regarded as pests and were destroyed as such, or hunted for sport. A commercial export industry in kangaroo skins soon developed. These days only the largest and most abundant species are exported, principally the Red Kangaroo, Eastern Grey Kangaroo, Western Grey Kangaroo and, to a lesser extent, the Euro or Wallaroo. The skins, which produce a strong but soft leather are used mainly to make sports shoes and other sporting accessories. The skins are also used to make rugs and furry toys (often fashioned into toy koalas for the tourist souvenir industry). Since about the 1950s, the meat has been used commercially for human food, but mainly for pet food. The current value of the export trade in skins and products is about $10 million a year, but domestic sales probably raise the industry's value to as much as twice that figure. Management plans were introduced for kangaroos in all States during the 1970s and, today, these plans are subject to approval by the Federal Government before exports can be licensed. The quotas for each State are also federally-approved.

Several other native mammal species were exploited for their fur, especially the Australian Fur Seal, Koala, and the Common Brushtail Possum. All three of these species were exploited commercially on a scale sufficient to bring them close to extinction.

Koalas were trapped in huge numbers in the early 1900s, the numbers increasing until in 1924 approximately two million skins were exported. Koala numbers declined dramatically (also due to disease) and, by 1927, most trapping had ceased, except in Queensland. Today, with protection, Koala numbers have built up again in many areas and, although habitat fragmentation and disease continue

Drugged birds are taped and stuffed into plastic tubing for illegal transportation. Many die in transit.

Courtesy Australian Customs

Peregrine Falcon and dove. Unscrupulous traders often supply live food for predatory wildlife in transit.
Courtesy World Wildlife Fund – US

to cause severe problems, the species is unlikely to become extinct.

Possums have been heavily exploited for their skins since European settlement. The Common Brushtail, Mountain Brushtail and Ringtail Possum were all taken. In 1906, over four million Brushtail Possum skins were marketed in London and New York. Today only the Brushtail is still exploited, and only in Tasmania where it is classified as 'partly protected wildlife' under that State's wildlife regulations. An annual quota is set on the number of skins which may enter trade, and this has stood at 250,000 for several years. Since 1984, under the federal Wildlife Protection Act, there is a requirement for an approved management program before any commercial export of wild-taken fauna or flora can be permitted. Each year, the Tasmanian Government submits a management program to the Federal Government for approval, and the numbers exported in the four-year period, 1984-87, have totalled 458,617. Tasmanian Government statistics show that the total number of possums shot in this period were 592,353, with 417,946 skins entering trade. The reasons for discrepancies in the figures are unclear, but possibly due to errors in the statistics, stockpiling of skins from year to year prior to export, and/or illegal skins entering the trade.

The Platypus was formerly hunted for its fur, prior to legal protection in all States in which it occurred by the early twentieth century. There was some overseas export and reputedly a considerable domestic trade. Platypus are occasionally drowned in fishermen's nets and, although there is little evidence of any exploitation today, it is worth noting that a fisherman was convicted in New South Wales, in 1988, for possession of six Platypus skins.

Birds

In the 1950s and 1960s the demand for cagebirds was astronomical. Many Australian species of parrots, lorikeets, cockatoos and finches were trapped for the overseas market. However, legal export was prohibited by the Federal Government in 1960. Illegal trafficking continues to this day, although it is difficult to judge the exact extent of this trade. The 1976 Parliamentary Committee's report, referred to above, recommended that export controls should be relaxed to reduce the incentive for smuggling. The same argument that the total ban on importation of birds encouraged smuggling was used by the Department of Primary Industries and Energy in its recent plans to build quarantine facilities and allow limited imports of birds and eggs. However, I dispute whether limited trade in certain species will reduce smuggling by any appreciable extent. Illegal trade in anything certainly occurs when the desired item is not legally available, however it also occurs when that item is not available in sufficient quantity through a legal source, or when it is available more cheaply through an illegal source. In the case of a limited trade in birds, there will always be a great number of 'desirable' threatened or endangered species that will continue to be unavailable legally. The existence of a limited legal trade also provides easier avenues for the laundering of illegally acquired specimens.

Rumours abound of light aircraft visiting remote airstrips in northern Australia, under cover of darkness, to collect consignments of birds, or of yachts putting into small fishing ports, picking up birds and island-hopping back to Indonesia and Singapore. It is certainly true that Australia has a vast and remote coastline which is more or less impossible to control, but there has been little evidence in recent years to support these claims. During the late 1970s, the owner of a bird park near Cairns was convicted, together with another man, on charges of illegally importing and exporting birds by boat. In 1984, a former Mafia boss, Vincent 'Fat Vinnie' Teresa, was indicted in the United States of America on charges of conspiring to import birds from Australia in what was alleged to be a million-dollar operation in the late 1970s.

Since then, there have been a number of cases involving persons, usually foreigners, attempting to smuggle birds, both into and out of Australia. However, all these recent attempts have been through the major airports where persons, usually later identified as couriers, have attempted to smuggle birds concealed in their baggage. The most common method is to drug the birds using phenobarbitol or valium, and stuff them into short lengths of plastic tubing; the tubes are then put into a suitcase which has been modified to allow air to circulate inside. The birds are usually taken to Singapore or Thailand, from whence they are often exported to Europe and the United States of America as 'captive-bred' specimens with legal documentation.

The birds most commonly smuggled out of Australia these days are the cockatoos, probably because they are more difficult to breed in captivity than many of the other parrots (indeed, many Australian parrot species are bred overseas in large numbers). The Major Mitchell (or Pink) Cockatoo is perhaps the species most frequently subjected to the smuggler's devious and cruel methods; not surprisingly as it currently sells on the American market for about US$17,000 a pair. The Gang-gang Cockatoo is another highly sought after species. It is rarely available on overseas markets, so it is difficult to know what its value might be, but enquiries to American aviculturists suggest that the birds could be worth US$20,000-25,000 a pair.

The following is an example of a typical consignment: a German national was arrested at Sydney airport in October 1989 attempting to smuggle out a consignment of 26 birds, valued at US$298,500 on the American market, in two suitcases; the birds involved were 11 Major Mitchell Cockatoos, 8 Gang-gang cockatoos, 1 Yellow-tailed Black Cockatoo and 6 Long-billed Corellas. The penalties imposed for this type of offence vary considerably depending on the particular judge that handles the case. Under the Wildlife Protection Act, the maximum penalty that may be imposed on an individual is $100,000 or five years' imprisonment. In many cases, the sentence that has been handed down has been woefully inadequate when one takes into account the profits that the successful smuggler stands to make. There seems, however, to be an increasing tendency for jail terms of about two years to be imposed for offences like the one above.

Whilst all the trade in live native birds is illegal, Australia does permit export of the products of the Muttonbird industry in Tasmania. The Muttonbird or Short-tailed Shearwater is the only Australian bird, harvested directly from the wild, to form the basis of a commercial industry. There is also a substantial non-commercial harvest of Muttonbirds. The chicks are taken for their feathers, oil and meat. The harvesting of Muttonbirds dates back to the early 1800s. In the early 1900s, approximately one million birds were harvested annually, but harvest levels declined slowly to less than 500,000 by the 1940s, to around 300,000 at present. The birds, fresh, salted or frozen, are either exported to New Zealand or interstate, or sold locally in delicatessens and 'fast-food' shops. Feathers are sold to mills in Melbourne, and oil is sold locally in Tasmania. The commercial industry appears to be declining due to social and economic factors and the controversial non-commercial harvesting, which is opposed by animal welfare groups on the grounds of cruelty, has been shut down except on the Bass Strait islands and on the west coast of Tasmania.

The only other Australian bird to form the basis of a commercial industry is the Emu; however, unlike the Muttonbirds, the Emus are captive bred in farming operations. Recently (1989), the Australian National Parks and Wildlife Service approved eleven Western Australian farms and one South Australian farm as captive-breeding operations for Emus in accordance with the conditions laid down under the Wildlife Protection Act. There is every indication that commercial farming of Emus will expand over the next few years as the demand increases for Emu 'steaks', leather, oil, feathers and eggs.

Much of the illegal trade in Australian reptiles is conducted through the post. Courtesy Australian Customs

Reptiles

All marine turtles are listed on Appendix I of CITES, thereby banning commercial trade. However, in many countries, such as Indonesia, turtle exploitation continues on a large scale. In Australia, turtles were exploited by the early settlers but are now fully protected except for the right of the Aborigines to take them for food. It may therefore be surprising to know that turtle shells are one of the most commonly seized tourist souvenirs in Australia: Customs' warehouses are full of these, and other thoughtless purchases! Australians returning from holidays in places like Bali or Fiji often bring back local 'handicrafts' in the form of turtle shells and other 'tortoiseshell' products.

The two Australian species of crocodile, the Saltwater Crocodile and the Freshwater Crocodile, were both ruthlessly hunted for the skin trade during the 1950s and 1960s. Both species became severely depleted in numbers, and it was not until an import/export ban was imposed by the Federal Government in 1972 that the period of intensive exploitation ended. Numbers of crocodiles have built up again with protection and there are now federally-approved management programs for the ranching of both species in the Northern Territory. (Ranching is a term used to describe a farming operation where there is still some

input of wild stock, that is, it includes at least a percentage of animals or eggs which are taken from the wild and reared in captivity, rather than actually bred in captivity.) The numbers exported by the ranches are still quite low, for example, 1,240 Freshwater Crocodile skins and 1,047 Saltwater Crocodile skins were exported, mainly to Japan, during 1988. There is also one approved crocodile farm, that is, captive-breeding operation, situated in Queensland.

The only other Australian reptiles which are presently exploited for their skins are the sea snakes Hydrophiidae and sea kraits Laticaudidae. No export is currently permitted under the federal Wildlife Protection Act as no management programs for sea snakes have been approved. The snakes are caught accidentally by prawn trawling operations along the coasts of Queensland, Northern Territory and Western Australia, but mainly in the Gulf of Carpentaria. Queensland is the only State which issues licences to tanneries for obtaining sea-snakes taken as a by-catch, but both the Northern Territory and Western Australia are examining the feasibility of commercial exploitation of this by-catch which is currently 'wasted'. The incidental catch of sea snakes in the Gulf is about 100,000 per year and mortality is approximately 40 per cent. The Queensland Government licenses the use of 40,000 snakes per year, and the products (wallets, belts, handbags, etc) are marketed in the eastern States of Australia.

As with birds, there is an extensive overseas demand for Australian native reptiles for the collector trade. Unlike birds, however, reptiles are fairly easy to smuggle and much of the illegal trade is conducted by post. Small lizards and skinks, such as Shinglebacks and Bluetongues, are taped up, so they cannot move around, and placed in boxes or tins, which are then mailed in padded bags, perhaps labelled as 'books' or 'shoes'. In 1987, a Western Australian couple were convicted on charges of mailing 41 Shinglebacks, 1 Western Bluetongue Skink, 8 other skinks, 2 Western Bearded Dragons and 5 geckoes to dealers in West Germany and Denmark. The animals were estimated to be worth $20,000 on the European market. The defendants were given nine-month prison sentences, to be suspended if they entered into bonds to be of good behaviour, and one of them was fined $2,000.

Fish and Invertebrates

The worldwide trade in tropical fish for the aquarium trade is known to be massive, but there has been no quantitative study performed on Australia's role in this trade. Schedule 4 of the Wildlife Protection Act exempts marine fish from export control, and Schedule 6 lists those species of marine and freshwater fish which are not subject to import control.

According to an unpublished report by the Malacological Society of Australia, the Australian export trade in marine shells is estimated to be worth about $2½ million a year, approximately $2 million of this being derived from the specimen shell trade (that is, the collector trade). Although there is a requirement, under the Wildlife Protection Act, for there to be an approved management program before exports of wild-taken specimens of native fauna and flora can be licensed, the Federal Minister has consistently authorised exports of shells under Section 44 of the Act (which allows for permits to be issued in exceptional circumstances). The report referred to above recommended that certain species be prohibited from commercial trade, that temporary bans should be placed on others until the resilience of stocks to collection has been established, whilst there was little conservation value in trying to control the trade in others.

The international trade in corals, like the shell trade, is substantial. Although there is no evidence that commercial collection has yet caused the extinction of any coral or marine mollusc species, the current heavy demand and the considerable number of reports of depleted populations give cause for concern. In Australia, coral collection is permitted to licensed collectors on the Great Barrier Reef. Although this collection is well managed, there is no federally-approved management program and, consequently, no legal exports of corals. However, there is evidence to show that native corals are exported in small quantities by tourists, who purchase them as souvenirs.

The other main group of invertebrates which are subject to international trade are the insects. This trade is partly in dead specimens for the specialist collector, and partly a mass trade in usually common, often-farmed, specimens for decorative purposes (butterflies embedded in perspex, framed insects to hang on the wall, table mats, etc). Although there is some importation from countries like Taiwan for the decorative trade, Australia does not represent a significant market in world terms. Export of native insects is controlled under the Wildlife Protection Act, and currently only captive-bred birdwing butterflies are being exported legally.

There is, however, some indication of illegal trade (which, like much of the live reptile trade and the specimen shell trade, is conducted by post, and therefore difficult to detect). A recent report prepared by TRAFFIC Oceania indicates that there is a demand for some of the Australian native beetles, such as the striking stag beetle *Phalacrognathus muelleri*, and the colourful jewel beetles, and that these insects fetch high prices on overseas markets.

Plants

It will come as no surprise to anybody to learn that the international trade in plants is a multi-billion dollar business but, what is not quite so obvious is that, amongst all the many artificially propagated specimens, there is still a very large number of wild-collected plants in trade, for example, cyclamen bulbs from Turkey. A great many plants are listed on CITES; all the orchids and cacti, for example. The trade in wild-collected specimens of slipper orchids is of particular concern and, in 1989, all the slipper orchids were transferred to Appendix I of CITES, in an effort to prohibit the trade in wild-collected specimens. Australia imports *Paphiopedilum* (slipper) orchids, all declared as artificially propagated, but there is evidence to suggest that many of them are in fact collected from the wild.

Australia is a significant exporter of cut wildflowers. The main centre of this trade is Western Australia where the collection and export of wildflowers is closely managed by the State Government. Many of the species involved were, until 1985, listed in Appendix II of CITES, but were taken off CITES at the request of the Australian Government on the grounds that the local management program (approved under the Wildlife Protection Act) was sufficient to ensure the conservation of the species.

USEFUL ADDRESSES

Australian Customs Service
COASTWATCH Free Phone:
(062) 47 6666

Australian National Parks and Wildlife Service, GPO Box 636, Canberra, ACT 2601 Tel: (062) 46 6211

This federal agency is the body responsible for administration of the Wildlife Protection Act. N.B. There are also State and Territory wildlife services in all capital cities, responsible for wildlife matters.

TRAFFIC Oceania Inc., PO Box 799, Manly, NSW 2095 Tel: (02) 977 4786

A non-governmental wildlife trade research and 'watch-dog' organisation.

CITES Secretariat, Case postale 78, 1000 Lausanne 9, Switzerland
Tel: 0011 41 21 20 00 81

The Secretariat of the Convention on International Trade in Endangered Species of Wild Fauna and Flora.

World Wildlife Fund Australia, GPO Box 528, Sydney, NSW 2001 Tel: (02) 261 5572

WHAT CAN I DO?

1 Report all suspicious activities to your local police and wildlife service (see your local telephone directory), and/or to Customs Coastwatch or TRAFFIC (see above for addresses and phone numbers).

2 Think before you buy any wildlife or wildlife product – do you really need it, is it legal, etc?

3 Lobby your local Member of Parliament for increased financial resources for wildlife conservation.

4 Support the World Wildlife Fund (address above) which provides the finances for TRAFFIC's work.

APPENDIX I

The Threatened Vertebrates

PE Probably Extinct   **E** Endangered   **V** Vulnerable   **PV** Potentially Vulnerable

The Mammals

Family name	Scientific name	Common name	Conservation Status
Balaenidae	Eubalaena australis	Southern Right Whale	E
Balaenopteridae	Balaenoptera acutorostrata	Minke Whale	V
Balaenopteridae	Balaenoptera borealis	Sei Whale	E
Balaenopteridae	Balaenoptera edeni	Bryde's Whale	V
Balaenopteridae	Balaenoptera musculus	Blue Whale	E
Balaenopteridae	Balaenoptera physalus	Fin Whale	E
Balaenopteridae	Megaptera novaeangliae	Humpback Whale	E
Burramyidae	Burramys parvus	Mountain Pygmy-possum	E
Dasyuridae	Antechinomys laniger	Kultarr	PV
Dasyuridae	Antechinus godmani	Atherton Antechinus	E
Dasyuridae	Antechinus leo	Cinnamon Antechinus	PV
Dasyuridae	Dasyuroides byrnei	Kowari	E
Dasyuridae	Dasycercus cristicauda	Mulgara	E
Dasyuridae	Dasyurus geoffroii	Chuditch	E
Dasyuridae	Dasyurus maculatus	Tiger Quoll	PV
Dasyuridae	Dasyurus viverrinus	Eastern Quoll	PV
Dasyuridae	Parantechinus apicalis	Dibbler	E
Dasyuridae	Pseudantechinus rosamondae	Little Red Antechinus	PV
Dasyuridae	Phascogale calura	Red-tailed Phascogale	E
Dasyuridae	Phascogale tapoatafa	Brush-tailed Phascogale	PV
Dasyuridae	Sminthopsis aitkeni	Kangaroo Island Dunnart	PV
Dasyuridae	Sminthopsis butleri	Carpentarian Dunnart	PV
Dasyuridae	Sminthopsis douglasi	Julia Creek Dunnart	E
Dasyuridae	Sminthopsis psammophila	Sandhill Dunnart	V
Dasyuridae	Sminthopsis virginiae	Red-cheeked Dunnart	PV
Delphinidae	Sousa chinensis	Indopacific Hump-backed Dolphin	PV
Dugongidae	Dugong dugon	Dugong	V
Emballonuridae	Taphozous australis	North-eastern Sheathtail-bat	PV
Emballonuridae	Taphozous mixtus	Papuan Sheathtail-bat	PV
Macropodidae	Dendrolagus bennettianus	Bennett's Tree-kangaroo	PV
Macropodidae	Dendrolagus lumholtzi	Lumholtz's Tree-kangaroo	PV
Macropodidae	Lagorchestes asomatus	Central Hare-wallaby	PE
Macropodidae	Lagorchestes conspicillatus	Spectacled Hare-wallaby	PV
Macropodidae	Lagorchestes hirsutus	Rufous Hare-wallaby	E
Macropodidae	Lagorchestes leporides	Eastern Hare-wallaby	PE
Macropodidae	Lagostrophus fasciatus	Banded Hare-wallaby	E
Macropodidae	Macropus eugenii	Tammar Wallaby	V
Macropodidae	Macropus greyi	Toolache Wallaby	PE
Macropodidae	Macropus irma	Western Brush Wallaby	PV
Macropodidae	Macropus parma	Parma Wallaby	PV
Macropodidae	Onychogalea fraenata	Bridled Nailtail Wallaby	E
Macropodidae	Onychogalea lunata	Crescent Nailtail Wallaby	PE
Macropodidae	Petrogale concinna	Nabarlek	PV
Macropodidae	Petrogale godmani	Godman's Rock-wallaby	PV
Macropodidae	Petrogale lateralis	Black-footed Rock-wallaby	V
Macropodidae	Petrogale penicillata	Brush-tailed Rock-wallaby	V
Macropodidae	Petrogale persephone	Proserpine Rock-wallaby	E
Macropodidae	Petrogale xanthopus	Yellow-footed Rock-wallaby	PV
Macropodidae	Setonix brachyurus	Quokka	PV
Megadermatidae	Macroderma gigas	Ghost Bat	V
Monodontidae	Orcaella brevirostris	Irrawaddy Dolphin	PV
Muridae	Conilurus albipes	White-footed Rabbit-rat	PE
Muridae	Leggadina lakedownensis	Lakelands Downs Mouse	PV
Muridae	Leporillus apicalis	Lesser Stick-nest Rat	PE
Muridae	Leporillus conditor	Greater Stick-nest Rat	E
Muridae	Maslacomys fuscous	Broad-toothed Rat	PV
Muridae	Melomys cervinipes	Fawn-footed Melomys	PV
Muridae	Melomys hadrourus	Thornton Peak Melomys	V
Muridae	Mesembriomys gouldii	Black-footed Tree-rat	PV
Muridae	Mesembriomys macrurus	Golden-backed Tree-rat	PV
Muridae	Notomys amplus	Short-tailed Hopping-mouse	PE
Muridae	Notomys aquilo	Northern Hopping-mouse	V
Muridae	Notomys fuscus	Dusky Hopping-mouse	V
Muridae	Notomys longicaudatus	Long-tailed Hopping-mouse	PE
Muridae	Notomys macrotis	Big-eared Hopping-mouse	PE
Muridae	Notomys mitchelli	Mitchell's Hopping-mouse	PV
Muridae	Notomys mordax	Darling Downs Hopping-mouse	PE
Muridae	Pogonomys mollipilosus	Prehensile-tailed Rat	PV
Muridae	Pseudomys albocinereous	Ash-grey Mouse	PV
Muridae	Pseudomys australis	Plains Rat	PV
Muridae	Pseudomys chapmani	Pebble-mound Mouse	PV
Muridae	Pseudomys desertor	Desert Mouse	PV
Muridae	Pseudomys fieldi	Alice Springs Mouse	PE
Muridae	Pseudomys fumeus	Smoky Mouse	E
Muridae	Pseudomys gouldii	Gould's Mouse	PE
Muridae	Pseudomys nanus	Western Chestnut Mouse	PV
Muridae	Pseudomys occidentalis	Western Mouse	V
Muridae	Pseudomys oralis	Hastings River Mouse	V
Muridae	Pseudomys pilligaensis	Pilliga Mouse	V
Muridae	Pseudomys praeconis	Shark Bay Mouse	V
Muridae	Pseudomys shortridgei	Heath Rat	V
Muridae	Rattus tunneyi	Pale Field Rat	PV
Muridae	Xeromys myoides	False Water-rat	V
Muridae	Zyzomys pedunculatus	Central Rock-rat	E
Myrmecobiidae	Myrmecobius fasciatus	Numbat	E
Notoryctidae	Notoryctes typhlops	Marsupial Mole	PV
Ornithorhynchidae	Ornithorhynchus anatinus	Platypus	PV
Otariidae	Neophoca cinerea	Australian Sea-lion	E
Peramelidae	Chaeropus ecaudatus	Pig-footed Bandicoot	PE
Peramelidae	Echymipera rufescens	Rufous Spiny Bandicoot	PV
Peramelidae	Isoodon auratus	Golden Bandicoot	E
Peramelidae	Isoodon obesulus	Southern Brown Bandicoot	PV
Peramelidae	Perameles bougainville	Western Barred Bandicoot	E
Peramelidae	Perameles eremiana	Desert Bandicoot	PE
Peramelidae	Perameles gunnii	Eastern Barred Bandicoot	E
Petauridae	Gymnobelideus leadbeateri	Leadbeater's Possum	E
Petauridae	Hemibelideus lemuroides	Lemuroid Ringtail Possum	PV
Petauridae	Petaurus australis	Yellow-bellied Glider	PV
Petauridae	Petauroides volans	Greater Glider	PV
Petauridae	Petaurus norfolcensis	Squirrel Glider	PV
Petauridae	Pseudocheirus archeri	Green Ringtail Possum	PV
Petauridae	Pseudocheirus herbertensis	Herbert River Ringtail Possum	PV
Petauridae	Pseudocheirus herbertensis cinereus	Daintree River Ringtail Possum	PV
Petauridae	Pseudocheirus occidentalis	Western Ringtail Possum	E
Phalangeridae	Trichosurus arnhemensis	Northern Brushtail Possum	PV
Phalangeridae	Trichosurus caninus	Mountain Brushtail Possum	PV
Phalangeridae	Trichosurus vulpecula	Central Australian Brushtail Possum	E
Phascolarctidae	Phascolarctos cinereus	Koala	PV
Physeteridae	Kogia breviceps	Pygmy Sperm Whale	PV
Physeteridae	Kogia simus	Dwarf Sperm Whale	PV
Physeteridae	Physeter macrocephalus	Sperm Whale	E
Potoroidae	Bettongia gaimardi	Tasmanian Bettong	PV
Potoroidae	Bettongia lesueur	Burrowing Bettong	E
Potoroidae	Bettongia penicillata	Brush-tailed Bettong	E
Potoroidae	Bettongia tropica	Northern Brush-tailed Bettong	E
Potoroidae	Caloprymnus campestris	Desert Rat-kangaroo	PE
Potoroidae	Hypsiprymnodon moschatus	Musky Rat-kangaroo	PV
Potoroidae	Potorous longipes	Long-footed Potoroo	E
Potoroidae	Potorous platyops	Broad-faced Potoroo	PE
Potoroidae	Potorous tridactylus	Long-nosed Potoroo	PV
Pteropodidae	Dobsonia moluccense	Bare-backed Fruit-bat	PV
Rhinolophidae	Hipposideros cervinus	Fawn Horseshoe-bat	PV
Rhinolophidae	Hipposideros semoni	Greater Wart-nosed Horseshoe-bat	PV
Rhinolophidae	Hipposideros stenotis	Lesser Wart-nosed Horseshoe-bat	PV
Rhinolophidae	Rhinolophus philippinensis	Large-eared Horseshoe-bat	PV
Rhinolophidae	Rhinonicteris aurantius	Orange Horseshoe-bat	V
Tarsipedidae	Tarsipes rostratus	Honey-possum	PV
Thylacinidae	Thylacinus cynocephalus	Thylacine	PE
Thylacomyidae	Macrotis lagotis	Bilby	E
Thylacomyidae	Macrotis leucura	Lesser Bilby	PE
Vespertilionidae	Eptesicus douglasorum	Yellow-Tipped Eptesicus	PV
Vespertilionidae	Eptesicus sagittula	Large Forest Eptesicus	PV
Vespertilionidae	Miniopterus australis	Little Bent-wing Bat	PV
Vespertilionidae	Miniopterus schreibersii	Common Bent-wing Bat	PV
Vespertilionidae	Murina florium	Tube-nosed Insectivorous Bat	PV
Vespertilionidae	Nycticeius influatas	Hughenden Broad-nosed Bat	PV
Vespertilionidae	Nyctophilus walkeri	Pygmy Long-eared Bat	PV
Vespertilionidae	Phoniscus papuensis	Golden-tipped Bat	PV
Vespertilionidae	Pipistrellus tasmaniensis	Great Pipistrelle	PV
Vombatidae	Lasiorhinus krefftii	Northern Hairy-nosed Wombat	E
Vombatidae	Lasiorhinus latifrons	Southern Hairy-nosed Wombat	PV

The Birds

Family name	Scientific name	Common name	Conservation Status
Acanthizidae	Aphelocephala pectoralis	Chestnut-breasted Whiteface	PV
Acanthizidae	Dasyornis brachypterus	Eastern Bristlebird	V
Acanthizidae	Dasyornis broadbenti broadbenti	Rufous Bristlebird (Eastern)	PV
Acanthizidae	Dasyornis broadbenti litoralis	Rufous Bristlebird (South-west)	PE
Acanthizidae	Dasyornis broadbenti whitei	Rufous Bristlebird (Western)	PV
Acanthizidae	Dasyornis longirostris	Western Bristlebird	E
Acanthizidae	Sericornis keri	Atherton Scrubwren	PV
Accipitridae	Erythrotriorchis radiatus	Red Goshawk	V
Anatidae	Stictonetta naevosa	Freckled Duck	V
Anatidae	Tadorna radjah	Radjah Shelduck	PV
Atrichornithidae	Atrichornis clamosus	Noisy Scrub-bird	E
Atrichornithidae	Atrichornis rufescens	Rufous Scrub-bird	V
Burhinidae	Burhinus magnirostris	Bush Thick-knee	PV
Cacatuidae	Cacatua leadbeateri	Pink Cockatoo	PV
Cacatuidae	Cacatua tenuirostris	Long-billed Corella	PV
Cacatuidae	Calyptorhynchus baudinii	Baudin's Cockatoo	V

Family name	Scientific name	Common name	Conservation Status
Cacatuidae	*Calyptorhynchus lathami*	Glossy Black Cockatoo	PV
Cacatuidae	*Probosciger aterrimus*	Palm Cockatoo	PV
Casuariidae	*Casuarius casuarius*	Cassowary	V
Charadriidae	*Charadrius rubricallis*	Hooded Plover	V
Columbidae	*Ducula whartonii*	Christmas Island Imperial Pigeon	V
Columbidae	*Petrophassa scripta*	Squatter Pigeon	PV
Columbidae	*Petrophassa smithii*	Partridge Pigeon	V
Columbidae	*Ptilinopus cinctus*	Banded Fruit-dove	V
Columbidae	*Ptilinopus magnificus*	Wompoo Fruit-dove	PV
Cracticidae	*Strepera graculina crissalis*	Lord Howe Island Currawong	E
Diomedeidae	*Pterodroma leucoptera*	Gould's Petrel	PV
Diomedeidae	*Pterodroma solandri*	Providence Petrel	PV
Dromaiidae	*Drommaius minor*	Dwarf Emu	PE
Ephthianuridae	*Ephthianura crocea*	Yellow Chat	PV
Falconidae	*Falco hypoleucos*	Grey Falcon	PV
Falconidae	*Falco peregrinus*	Peregrine Falcon	V
Fregatidae	*Fregata andrewsi*	Christmas Island Frigatebird	E
Laridae	*Anous tenuirostris*	Lesser Noddy	V
Laridae	*Larus pacificus*	Pacific Gull	PV
Laridae	*Sterna albifrons sinensis*	(Australian) Little Tern	V
Laridae	*Sterna douglii*	Roseate Tern	PV
Laridae	*Sterna nereis*	Fairy Tern	PV
Maluridae	*Amytornis barbatus*	Grey Grasswren	PV
Maluridae	*Amytornis dorotheae*	Carpentarian Grasswren	PV
Maluridae	*Amytornis goyderi*	Eyrean Grasswren	PV
Maluridae	*Amytornis housei*	Black Grasswren	PV
Maluridae	*Amytornis textilis*	Thick-billed Grasswren	V
Maluridae	*Amytornis woodwardi*	White-throated Grasswren	PV
Maluridae	*Malurus coronatus coronatus*	Purple-crowned Fairy-wren	PV
Maluridae	*Malurus coronatus macgillivrayi*	Purple-winged Fairy-wren	PV
Maluridae	*Malurus leucopterus edouardii*	White-winged Fairy-wren	PV
Maluridae	*Malurus leucopterus leucopterus*	White-winged Fairy-wren	PV
Maluridae	*Stipiturus ruficeps mallee*	Rufous Crowned Emu-wren	PV
Megapodiidae	*Leipoa ocellata*	Malleefowl	V
Megapodiidae	*Megapodius reinwardt*	Orange-footed Scrubfowl	PV
Meliphagidae	*Glycichaera fallax*	Green-backed Honeyeater	PV
Meliphagidae	*Lichenostomus hindwoodi*	Eungella Honeyeater	PV
Meliphagidae	*Lichenostomus melanops cassidix*	Helmeted Honeyeater	E
Meliphagidae	*Manorina melanotis*	Black-eared Miner	E
Meliphagidae	*Xanthomyza phrygia*	Regent Honeyeater	E
Menuridae	*Menura alberti*	Albert's Lyrebird	V
Muscicapidae	*Falcunculus frontatus leucogaster*	Crested Shrike-tit	PV
Muscicapidae	*Falcunculus frontatus whitei*	Crested Shrike-tit	PV
Muscicapidae	*Microca (flavigaster) tormenti*	Kimberley Flycatcher	PV
Muscicapidae	*Microeca griseoceps*	Yellow-legged Flycatcher	PV
Muscicapidae	*Pachycephala rufogularis*	Red-lored Whistler	V
Muscicapidae	*Turdus poliocephalus poliocephalus*	Grey-headed Thrush	E
Opopsittidae	*Psittaculirostris diophthalma coxeni*	Double-eyed Fig-parrot	E
Orthonychidae	*Cinclosma alisteri*	Nullabor Quail-thrush	PV
Orthonychidae	*Psophodes nigrogularis*	Western Whipbird	V
Otididae	*Ardeotis australis*	Australian Bustard	PV
Paradisaeidae	*Prionodura newtoniana*	Golden Bowerbird	PV
Paradisaeidae	*Ptiloris paradiseus*	Paradise Riflebird	PV
Pardalotidae	*Pardalotus quadragintus*	Forty-spotted Pardalote	E
Pedionomidae	*Pedionomus torquatus*	Plains Wanderer	E
Platycercidae	*Geopsittacus occidentalis*	Night Parrot	E
Platycercidae	*Neophema chrysogaster*	Orange-bellied Parrot	E
Platycercidae	*Neophema pulchella*	Turquoise Parrot	PV
Platycercidae	*Neophema splendida*	Scarlet-chested Parrot	V
Platycercidae	*Pezoporus wallicus*	Ground Parrot	E
Platycercidae	*Psephotus chrysopterygius*	Golden-shouldered Parrot	E
Platycercidae	*Psephotus dissimilis*	Hooded Parrot	V
Platycercidae	*Psephotus pulcherrimus*	Paradise Parrot	PE
Ploceidae	*Emblema oculata*	Red-eared Firetail	PV
Ploceidae	*Erythrura gouldiae*	Gouldian Finch	E
Ploceidae	*Lonchura flaviprymna*	Yellow-rumped Mannakin	PV
Ploceidae	*Peophila cincta*	Black-throated Finch	PV
Podargidae	*Podargus ocellatus marmoratus*	Marbled Frogmouth	V
Podargidae	*Podargus ocellatus plumiferus*	Marbled Frogmouth	V
Polytelitidae	*Polytelis alexandrae*	Alexandra's Parrot	PV
Polytelitidae	*Polytelis swainsonii*	Superb Parrot	PV
Psittacidae	*Cyanoramphus novaezelandiae cookii*	Norfolk Island Parrot	E
Psittacidae	*Eclectus roratus macgillivrayi*	Eclectus Parrot	PV
Rallidae	*Eulabeornis castaneouertris*	Chestnut Rail	PV
Rallidae	*Rallus philippensis andrewsi*	Cocos Buff-banded Rail	E
Rallidae	*Tricholimnas sylvestris*	Lord Howe Island Woodhen	E
Strigidae	*Ninox rufa*	Rufous Owl	PV
Strigidae	*Ninox squamipila natalis*	Christmas Island Owl	V
Strigidae	*Ninox novaeseelandiae undulata*	Norfolk Island Boobook Owl	E
Sulidae	*Sula abbotti*	Abbott's Booby	E
Turnicidae	*Turnix castanota*	Chestnut-backed Button-quail	PV
Turnicidae	*Turnix melanogaster*	Black-breasted Button-quail	E
Turnicidae	*Turnix olivei*	Buff-breasted Button-quail	PV
Tytonidae	*Tyto longimembris*	Eastern Grass Owl	PV
Tytonidae	*Tyto multipunctata*	Lesser Sooty Owl	PV
Tytonidae	*Tyto tenebricosa*	Sooty Owl	PV
Zosteropidae	*Zosterops albogularis*	Norfolk Island Silvereye	E

The Reptiles

Family name	Scientific name	Common name	Conservation Status
Agamidae	*Amphibolurus gibba*		PV
Agamidae	*Amphibolurus maculosus*	Lake Eyre Dragon	PV
Agamidae	*Amphibolurus femoralis*		PV
Agamidae	*Amphibolurus fionni*		PV
Agamidae	*Amphibolurus microlepidotus*		PV
Agamidae	*Amphibolurus rufescens*		PV
Agamidae	*Amphibolurus vadnappa*		PV
Agamidae	*Diporiphora albilabris*		PV
Agamidae	*Diporiphora convergens*		PV
Agamidae	*Diporiphora superba*		PV
Agamidae	*Gonocephalus boydii*	Boyd's Forest Dragon	PV
Agamidae	*Gonocephalus spinipes*	Southern Angle-headed Dragon	PV
Agamidae	*Tympanocryptis parviceps*		PV
Boidae	*Chondrophython viridis*	Green Python	PV
Boidae	*Liasis albertisii*		PV
Boidae	*Liasis amethystinus*		PV
Boidae	*Morelia carinata*		PV
Boidae	*Morelia oenpelliensis*	Oenpelli Python	PV
Boidae	*Morelia spilota spilota*	Diamond Python	V
Carettochelydidae	*Carettochelys insculpta*	Pig-nosed Turtle	PV
Chelidae	*Emydura signata*		PV
Chelidae	*Emydura subglobosa*		PV
Chelidae	*Pseudemydura umbrina*	Western Swamp Turtle	E
Cheloniidae	*Caretta caretta*	Loggerhead Turtle	PV
Cheloniidae	*Chelonia depressa*	Flatback Turtle	PV
Cheloniidae	*Chelonia mydas*	Green Turtle	PV
Cheloniidae	*Lepidochelys olivacea*	Pacific Ridley Turtle	PV
Cheloniidae	*Eretmochelys imbricata*	Hawksbill Turtle	PV
Crocodylidae	*Crocodylus johnstoni*	Freshwater Crocodile	PV
Crocodylidae	*Crocodylus porosus*	Saltwater Crocodile	V
Dermochelyidae	*Dermochelys coriacea*	Leathery Turtle	E
Elapidae	*Cacophis krefftii*	Dwarf Crowned Snake	PV
Elapidae	*Denisonia maculata*	Ornamental Snake	PV
Elapidae	*Echiopsis atriceps*		PV
Elapidae	*Elapognathus minor*	Little Brown Snake	PV
Elapidae	*Glyphodon dunmalli*	Dunmall's Snake	PV
Elapidae	*Hoplocephalus bungaroides*	Broad-headed Snake	E
Elapidae	*Hoplocephalus stephensi*	Stephen's Banded Snake	V
Elapidae	*Simoselaps minima*		PV
Elapidae	*Simoselaps warro*		PV
Elapidae	*Simoselaps woodjonesi*		PV
Elapidae	*Neelaps calonotus*	Western Black-striped Snake	E
Gekkonidae	*Carphodactylus laevis*	Chameleon Gecko	PV
Gekkonidae	*Cyrtodactylus galgajuga*		PV
Gekkonidae	*Cyrtodactylus louisiadensis*	Ring-tailed Gecko	PV
Gekkonidae	*Diplodactylus alboguttatus*		PV
Gekkonidae	*Diplodactylus michaelseni*		PV
Gekkonidae	*Diplodactylus mitchelli*		PV
Gekkonidae	*Diplodactylus occultus*		PV
Gekkonidae	*Diplodactylus savagei*		PV
Gekkonidae	*Diplodactylus taenicauda*	Golden-tailed Gecko	PV
Gekkonidae	*Diplodactylus wilsoni*		PV
Gekkonidae	*Gehyra baliola*		PV
Gekkonidae	*Gehyra booroloola*		PV
Gekkonidae	*Gehyra fenestra*		PV
Gekkonidae	*Lepidodactylus pumilus*		PV
Gekkonidae	*Nephrurus deleani*		PV
Gekkonidae	*Oedura coggeri*	Northern Spotted Velvet Gecko	PV
Gekkonidae	*Oedura gemmata*		PV
Gekkonidae	*Phyllodactylus guentheri*		V
Gekkonidae	*Phyllurus caudiannulatus*		PV
Gekkonidae	*Phyllurus platurus*	Southern Leaf-tailed Gecko	PV
Gekkonidae	*Pseudothecadactylus australis*		PV
Gekkonidae	*Underwoodisaurus sphyrurus*		PV
Pygopodidae	*Aclys concinna*		PV
Pygopodidae	*Aprasia aurita*		PV
Pygopodidae	*Aprasia parapulchella*		V
Pygopodidae	*Aprasia pseudopulchella*		PV
Pygopodidae	*Aprasia rostrata*		PV
Pygopodidae	*Aprasia smithi*		PV
Pygopodidae	*Delma elegans*		PV
Pygopodidae	*Delma molleri*		PV
Pygopodidae	*Delma torquata*		PV
Pygopodidae	*Ophidiocephalus taeniatus*	Bronze-backed Legless Lizard	V
Pygopodidae	*Paradelma orientalis*		PV
Scincidae	*Anomalopus frontalis*		PV
Scincidae	*Anomalopus pluto*		PV
Scincidae	*Anomalopus reticulatus*		PV
Scincidae	*Anomalopus truncatus*		PV
Scincidae	*Calyptotis ruficauda*		PV
Scincidae	*Calyptotis temporalis*		PV
Scincidae	*Calyptotis thorntonensis*		PV
Scincidae	*Carlia coensis*		PV
Scincidae	*Carlia dogare*		PV
Scincidae	*Carlia johnstonei*		PV
Scincidae	*Carlia rhomboidalis*		PV
Scincidae	*Carlia rimula*		PV
Scincidae	*Carlia scirtetis*		PV
Scincidae	*Cryptoblepharus fuhni*		PV
Scincidae	*Ctenotus alleni*		PV
Scincidae	*Ctenotus arcanus*		PV
Scincidae	*Ctenotus brachyonyx*		PV
Scincidae	*Ctenotus catenifer*		PV
Scincidae	*Ctenotus coggeri*		PV
Scincidae	*Ctenotus delli*		PV
Scincidae	*Ctenotus lancelini*	Lancelin Island Striped Skink	E
Scincidae	*Ctenotus mastigura*		PV
Scincidae	*Ctenotus militaris*		PV
Scincidae	*Ctenotus quinkan*		PV

Family name	Scientific name	Common name	Conservation Status
Scincidae	*Ctenotus rawlinsoni*		PV
Scincidae	*Ctenotus youngsoni*		PV
Scincidae	*Ctenotus zastictus*		PV
Scincidae	*Emoia atrocostata irrorata*		PV
Scincidae	*Emoia cyanogaster*		PV
Scincidae	*Eulamprus kosciusko*		PV
Scincidae	*Eulamprus leurgensis*		PV
Scincidae	*Eulamprus murrayi*		PV
Scincidae	*Eulamprus tigrinus*		PV
Scincidae	*Glaphyromorphus brongersamai*		PV
Scincidae	*Glaphyromorphus gracilipes*		PV
Scincidae	*Glaphyromorphus mjobergi*		PV
Scincidae	*Glaphyromorphus pumilis*		PV
Scincidae	*Gnypetoscincus queenslandiae*		PV
Scincidae	*Hemiergis graciloides*		PV
Scincidae	*Hemiergis peronii*		PV
Scincidae	*Leiolopisma baudini*		PV
Scincidae	*Leiolopisma greeni*		PV
Scincidae	*Leiolopisma jigurru*		PV
Scincidae	*Leiolopisma lichenigera*	Lord Howe Island Skink	V
Scincidae	*Lerista ameles*		PV
Scincidae	*Lerista apoda*		PV
Scincidae	*Lerista borealis*		PV
Scincidae	*Lerista carpentariae*		PV
Scincidae	*Lerista cinerea*		PV
Scincidae	*Lerista griffini*		PV
Scincidae	*Lerista haroldi*		PV
Scincidae	*Lerista humphriesi*		PV
Scincidae	*Lerista kalumburu*		PV
Scincidae	*Lerista lineata*	Lined Burrowing Skink	V
Scincidae	*Lerista neander*		PV
Scincidae	*Lerista onsloviana*		PV
Scincidae	*Lerista separanda*		PV
Scincidae	*Lerista simillima*		PV
Scincidae	*Lerista storri*		PV
Scincidae	*Lerista stylis*		PV
Scincidae	*Lerista vittata*		PV
Scincidae	*Menetia concinna*		PV
Scincidae	*Menetia maini*		PV
Scincidae	*Menetia zynja*		PV
Scincidae	*Notoscincus davisi*		PV
Scincidae	*Notoscincus wotjulum*		PV
Scincidae	*Ophioscincus cooloolensis*		PV
Scincidae	*Pseudemoia palfreymani*	Pedra Branca Skink	PV
Scincidae	*Tiliqua adelaidensis*	Adelaide Pygmy Bluetongue Skink	PE
Scincidae	*Tiliqua maxima*		PV
Typhlopidae	*Ramphotyphlops centralis*		PV
Typhlopidae	*Ramphotyphlops howi*		PV
Typhlopidae	*Typhlina leptosoma*		PV
Typhlopidae	*Typhlina leucoprocta*		PV
Typhlopidae	*Typhlina minima*		PV
Typhlopidae	*Typhlina tovelli*		PV
Typhlopidae	*Typhlina yirrikalae*		PV
Varanidae	*Varanus indicus*	Mangrove Monitor	PV
Varanidae	*Varanus kingorom*		PV
Varanidae	*Varanus prasinus*	Emerald Monitor	PV

The Amphibians

Family name	Scientific name	Common name	Conservation Status
Hylidae	*Cyclorana cryptotis*		PV
Hylidae	*Litoria aurea*	Green and Gold Bell Frog	PV
Hylidae	*Litoria brevipalmata*	Green-thighed Frog	PV
Hylidae	*Litoria cooloolensis*		PV
Hylidae	*Litoria flavipunctata*		PV
Hylidae	*Litoria longirostris*	Long-nosed Tree Frog	V
Hylidae	*Litoria lorica*		PV
Hylidae	*Litoria nyakalensis*		PV
Hylidae	*Litoria piperata*		PV
Hylidae	*Litoria revelata*		PV
Hylidae	*Litoria rheocolus*		PV
Hylidae	*Nyctimystes hosmeri*		PV
Hylidae	*Nyctimystes tympanocryptis*		PV
Hylidae	*Nyctimystes vestigia*		PV
Microhylidae	*Cophixalus concinnus*	Elegant Microhylid	V
Microhylidae	*Cophixalus exiguus*		PV
Microhylidae	*Cophixalus neglectus*		PV
Microhylidae	*Cophixalus ornatus*		PV
Microhylidae	*Cophixalus saxatilis*	Rock-dwelling Elegant Microhylid	V
Microhylidae	*Sphenophryne fryi*		PV
Microhylidae	*Sphenophryne pluvialis*		PV
Myobatrachidae	*Arenophryne rotunda*	Round Frog	V
Myobatrachidae	*Assa darlingtoni*	Pouched Frog	V
Myobatrachidae	*Crinia tinnula*	Wallum Froglet	PV
Myobatrachidae	*Geocrinis laevis*		PV
Myobatrachidae	*Heleioporus barycragus*		PV
Myobatrachidae	*Kyrannus loveridgei*	Loveridge's Frog	PV
Myobatrachidae	*Limnodynastes depressus*		E
Myobatrachidae	*Philoria frosti*	Baw Baw Frog	E
Myobatrachidae	*Philoria kundagungan*		PV
Myobatrachidae	*Philoria sphagnicolus*	Sphagnum Frog	PV
Myobatrachidae	*Pseudophryne corroboree*	Corroboree Frog	PV
Myobatrachidae	*Pseudophryne dendyi*	Southern Toadlet	PV
Myobatrachidae	*Rheobatrachus silus*	Platypus Frog	E
Myobatrachidae	*Rheobatrachus vitellinus*		E
Myobatrachidae	*Taudactylus acutirostris*	Sharp-snouted Torrent Frog	PV
Myobatrachidae	*Taudactylus diurnis*	Mount Glorious Torrent Frog	E

Family name	Scientific name	Common name	Conservation Status
Myobatrachidae	*Taudactylus eungellensis*	Eungella Torrent Frog	PV
Myobatrachidae	*Taudactylus rheophilus*		PV
Myobatrachidae	*Uperoleia crassa*		PV
Myobatrachidae	*Uperoleia minima*		PV

The Fish

Family name	Scientific name	Common name	Conservation Status
Ambassidae	*Ambassis castelnaui*	Chanda Perch	PV
Ambassidae	*Ambassis elongatus*	Yellowfin Perchlet	PV
Aplochitonidae	*Lovettia sealii*	Tasmanian Whitebait	PV
Ariidae	*Cinedotus froggati*	Frogatt's Catfish	PV
Atherinidae	*Craterocephalus dalhousiensis*	Dalhousie Hardyhead	PV
Atherinidae	*Craterocephalus marianae*	Alligator R. Hardyhead	PV
Atherinidae	*Craterocephalus n. sp.*	Drysdale Hardyhead	PV
Atherinidae	*Craterocephalus n. sp.*	Prince Regent Hardyhead	PV
Centropomidae	*Lates calcarifer*	Giant Perch	PV
Ceratodidae	*Neoceratodus forsteri*	Queensland Lungfish	PV
Eleotridae	*Gen. & sp. nov.*	Drysdale Gudgeon	PV
Eleotridae	*Gen. & sp. nov.*	Mitchell Gudgeon	PV
Eleotridae	*Hypseleotris aurea*	Golden Gudgeon	PV
Eleotridae	*Hypseleotris ejuncida*	Slender Gudgeon	PV
Eleotridae	*Hypseleotris kimberleyensis*	Barnett River Gudgeon	PV
Eleotridae	*Hypseleotris regalis*	Prince Regent Gudgeon	PV
Eleotridae	*Milyeringa veritas*	Blind Gudgeon	PV
Eleotridae	*Mogurnda adspersa*	Purple-spotted Gudgeon	PV
Eleotridae	*Mogurnda n. sp.*	False-spotted Gudgeon	PV
Eleotridae	*Mogurnda n. sp.*	Flinders Gudgeon	PV
Eleotridae	*Mogurnda n. sp.*	Flinders Ranges Gudgeon	PV
Engraulidae	*Thryssa scratchleyi*	Freshwater Anchovy	PV
Gadopsidae	*Gadopsis marmoratus*	River Blackfish	PV
Galaxiidae	*Galaxias fontanus*	Swan Galaxias	E
Galaxiidae	*Galaxias fuscus*	Brown Galaxias	E
Galaxiidae	*Galaxias johnstoni*	Clarence Galaxias	E
Galaxiidae	*Galaxias parvus*	Swamp Galaxias	PV
Galaxiidae	*Galaxias pedderensis*	Lake Pedder Galaxias	V
Galaxiidae	*Galaxias tanycephalus*	Saddled Galaxias	V
Galaxiidae	*Galaxiella munda*	Western Mud Minnow	PV
Galaxiidae	*Galaxiella nigrostriata*	Black Stripe Minnow	PV
Galaxiidae	*Paragalaxias mesotes*	Arthur's Paragalaxias	PV
Gobiidae	*Chlamydogobius eremius*	Desert Goby	PV
Gobiidae	*Chlamydogobius n. sp.*	Dalhousie Goby	PV
Gobiidae	*Chlamydogobius n. sp.*	Elizabeth Springs Goby	V
Gobiidae	*Glossogobius n. sp.*	Mulgrave Goby	V
Kuhliidae	*Kuhlia marginata*	Flagtail	PV
Kuhliidae	*Kuhlia rupestris*	Jungle Perch	PV
Kuhliidae	*Nannoperca n. sp.*	Ewens Pygmy Perch	PV
Kuhliidae	*Nannoperca oxleyana*	Oxleyan Pygmy Perch	PV
Lepidogalaxiidae	*Lepidogalaxias salamandroides*	Salamanderfish	PV
Melanotaemiidae	*Cairnsichthys rhombosomoides*	Cairns Rainbowfish	PV
Melanotaemiidae	*Melanotaenia eachamensis*	Lake Eacham Rainbowfish	E
Melanotaemiidae	*Melanotaenia exquisita*	Exquisite Rainbowfish	PV
Melanotaemiidae	*Melanotaenia gracilis*	Slender Rainbowfish	PV
Melanotaemiidae	*Melanotaenia pygmaea*	Pygmy Rainbowfish	PV
Melanotaemiidae	*Pseudomugil mellis*	Honey Blue-eye	V
Osteoglossidae	*Scleropages jardini*	Gulf Saratoga	PV
Osteoglossidae	*Scleropages leichardti*	Saratoga or Spotted Barramundi	V
Percichthyidae	*Maccullochella ikei*	Eastern Freshwater Cod	E
Percichthyidae	*Maccullochella macquariensis*	Trout Cod	E
Percichthyidae	*Maccullochella n. sp.*	Mary River Cod	PV
Percichthyidae	*Maccullochella peeli*	Murray Cod	PV
Percichthyidae	*Macquaria ambigua*	Yellowbelly	PV
Percichthyidae	*Macquaria australasica*	Macquarie Perch	V
Percichthyidae	*Macquaria australasica*	Estuary Perch	PV
Percichthyidae	*Macquaria colonorum*	Australian Bass	PV
Petromyzonidae	*Macquaria novemaculeata*	Non-parasitic Lamprey	PV
Plotosidae	*Neosilurus n. sp.*	Bulloo Tandan	PV
Plotosidae	*Neosilurus n. sp.*	Coopers Creek Tandan	PV
Plotosidae	*Neosilurus n. sp.*	Coopers Creek Silver Tandan	PV
Plotosidae	*Neosilurus n. sp.*	Dalhousie Catfish	PV
Plotosidae	*Neosilurus n. spp.*	Undescribed Tandans	PV
Plotosidae	*Porochilus obbesi*	Eeltailed Catfish	V
Plotosidae	*Tandanus tandanus*	Tandan	PV
Prototroctidae	*Prototroctes maraena*	Australian Grayling	PV
Synbranchidae	*Ophisternon candidum*	Blind Cave Eel	V
Teraponidae	*Hannia greenwayi*	Greenway's Grunter	PV
Teraponidae	*Hephaestus epirrhinos*	Long-nose Sooty Grunter	PV
Teraponidae	*Leiopotherapon aheneus*	Fortesque Grunter	PV
Teraponidae	*Leiopotherapon macrolepis*	Large-scale Grunter	PV
Teraponidae	*Pingalla gilberti*	Gilbert's Grunter	PV
Teraponidae	*Pingalla midgleyi*	Midgley's Grunter	PV
Teraponidae	*Scortum hillii*	Leathery Grunter	PV
Teraponidae	*Scortum neilli*	Angalari R. Grunter	PV
Teraponidae	*Scortum parviceps*	Small-headed Grunter	PV
Teraponidae	*Syncomistes kimberleyensis*	Kimberley Grunter	PV
Teraponidae	*Syncomistes rastellus*	Drysdale Grunter	PV
Toxotidae	*Toxotes oligolepis*	Big-scale Archerfish	PV

The Marine Fish

Family name	Scientific name	Common name	Conservation Status
Lamnidae	*Carcharodon carcharias*	Great White Shark	PV
Odontaspididae	*Eugomphodus taurus*	Grey Nurse Shark	PV
Odontaspididae	*Ondotapsis herbsti*	Herbst's Shark	PV
Scombridae	*Thunnus maccoyii*	Southern Bluefin Tuna	V
Serranidae	*Epinephelus damelii*	Black Cod	V

The Threatened Invertebrates

The following lists of threatened invertebrates are taken from three sources. The list of freshwater crustaceans is that referred to by Geoff Williams in Chapter VIII. The selected list of threatened arthropods and selected list of threatened insects are reproduced from the 'Conservation of insects and related wildlife', by L. Hill and F. B. Michaelis, Occasional Paper No. 13, and published by the Australian National Parks and Wildlife Service (1988). The 'Threatened Invertebrate Species' list was developed by I. Fry and M. Robinson, and published in Ecofund's *A Threatened Species Conservation Strategy for Australia*' (1986).

Geoff Williams' chapter explains the difficulties of assigning conservation status to individual invertebrate species, but the compilations that follow will help the reader begin to comprehend the immensity of the task. Many other invertebrate species under threat are referred to throughout the text in Chapter VIII, and many other lists are in existence. For example, the latest *IUCN Invertebrate Red Data Book* contains over 80 Australian species. Clearly, a national Action Plan for the conservation of invertebrate species is urgently needed.

Invertebrate Species, Ecofund (1986)

International Union for Conservation of Nature and Natural Resources Status Guide

Ex Extinct
E Endangered

V Vulnerable
R Rare
I Indeterminate
K Insufficiently known
M This category is a type of 'catch all'

for species which would appear to need some form of monitoring due to a 'general vulnerability' but which cannot be slotted into existing IUCN categories.

Family name	Scientific name	Common name	Conservation Status
Annelids			
Megascolecidae	*Megascolides australis*	Giant Gippsland Earthworm	V
Arthropods			
Aculagnathidae	*Aculagnathus mirabilis*	Beetle	M
Agonoxenidae	*Agonoxena phoenicia*	Moth	M
Anaspididae	*Allanaspides helonomus*	Tasmanian Anaspid Crustacean	V
Anaspididae	*Allanaspides hickmani*	Tasmanian Anaspid Crustacean	V
Anaspididae	*Anaspides spinulae*	Tasmanian Anaspid Crustacean	V
Anaspididae	*Aanaspides tasmaniae*	Tasmanian Anaspid Crustacean	V
Anaspididae	*Paranaspides lacustris*		V
Aniosopodidae	*Olbiogaster n. sp.*	Fly	R
Austroperlidae	*Tasmanoperla n. sp.*	Stonefly	M
Blepharoceridae	*Edwardsina gigantea*	Giant Torrent Midge	E
Blepharoceridae	*Edwardsina tasmaniensis*	Tasmanian Torrent Midge	E
Calopterygidae	*Neurobasis australis*	Dragonfly	R
Carthaeidae	*Carathaea saturnioides*	Moth	M
Chlorocyphidae	*Rhinocypha tincta*	Dragonfly	R
Corduliidae	*Austrocordulia n. sp.*	Arnhem Land Dragonfly	V
Ephemerellidae	*Telagonodinae n. sp.*	Mayfly	M
Eriocraniidae	*Agathiphaga queenslandensis*		M
Eumastacidae	*Achurimima n. sp.*	Taemas Bridge Grasshopper	V
Eumastacidae	*Achurimima n. sp.*	Marsden-Rankin Springs Grasshopper	V
Eumastacidae	*Keyacris scurra*		R
Eustheniidae	*Eusthenia nothofagi*	Otway Stonefly	E
Formicidae	*Nothomyrmecia macrops*	Australian Nothomyrmecia Ant	K
Gomphidae	*Hemigomphus n. sp.*	Arnhem Land Dragonfly	V
Gomphidae	*Ictinogomphus dobsoni*	Western Australian Dragonfly	V
Gripopterygidae	*Leptoperla cacuminis*	Mt Kosciusko Wingless Stonefly	R
Gripopterygidae	*Riekoperla darlingtoni*	Mt Donna Buang Wingless Stonefly	R
Haliomococcidae	*Colobopyga kewensis*	Scale Insect	K
Hemiphlebiidae	*Hemiphlebia mirabilis*	Small Hemiphlebia Damselfly	E
Hyblaeida	*Hyblaea n. sp.*	Moth	M
Hygrobiidae	*Hygrobia australasiae*	Water Beetle	M
Hygrobiidae	*Hygrobia niger*	Water Beetle	M
Lestidae	*Austrolestes n. sp.*	Eastern Dune Lake Dragonfly	V
Lestoideidae	*Lestoidea barbarae*	Dragonfly	M
Libellulidae	*Orthetrum n. sp.*	Eastern Dune Lake Dragonfly	V
Libytheidae	*Libythea geoffroyi*	Moth	M
Limnephilidae	*Archaeophylax n. sp.*	Victorian	M
Limnephilidae	*Archaeophylax n. sp.*	Tasmanian	M
Lucanidae	*Phalacrognathus muelleri*	Muellers Stag Beetle	E
Melittidae	*Ctenoplecta n. sp.*	Bee	M
Meropeidae	*Austromerope poultoni*	Scorpion Fly	M
Mycetophilidae	*Arachnocampa richardsae*	Richard's Glow Worm	V
Papilionidae	*Argynnis hyperbius inconstans*	Australian Fritillary Butterfly	V
Papilionidae	*Euschamon rafflesia*	Regent Skipper Butterfly	V
Papilionidae	*Ornithoptera richmondia*	Richmond Birdwing Butterfly	V
Papilionidae	*Tisiphone abeona*	Sword-grass Brown Butterfly	V
Parastacidae	*Astacopsis gouldi*	Giant Tasmanian Freshwater Crayfish	V
Parastacidae	*Astacopsis spp.*	Tasmanian Freshwater Crayfish	V
Parastacidae	*Euastacus armatus*	Murray Crayfish	R

Family name	Scientific name	Common name	Conservation Status
Parastacidae	*Euastacus n. sp.*	Spiny Crayfish	V
Perissommatidae	*Perissomma n. sp.*	Fly	M
Phasmatidae	*Dryococelus australis*	Lord Howe Island Phasmid	E
Phycosecidae	*Phycosecis ammophilus*		M
Phycosecidae	*Phycosecis hilli*		M
Phycosecidae	*Phycosecis litoralis*		M
Phylliidae	*Phyllium n. sp.*	Leaf Insect	M
Polyctenidae	*Adroctenes magnus*		M
Polyctenidae	*Eoctenes intermedius*		M
Polyphagidae	*Tivia australica*	Cockroach	M
Protoneuridae	*Nososticta pilbara*	Pilbara Dragonfly	V
Prototheoridae	*Anomoses hylecoetes*	Moth	M
Scarabaeidae	*Anoplagnathus viridiaeneus*	Green-bronze Christmas Beetle	R
Scarabaeidae	*Trioplagnathus griseopilosus*	Grey Christmas Beetle	R
Sialidae	*Austrosialis n. sp.*	Alderfly	M
Sialidae	*Austrosialis n. sp.*	Alderfly	M
Siphlonuridae	*Tasmanophlebia lacus-coerulei*	Large Blue Lake Mayfly	R
Tettigarctidae	*Tettigarcta crinita*	Hairy Cicada	E
Tettigarctidae	*Tettigarcta tomentosa*	Hairy Cicada	M
Nemertines			
Prosorhochmidae	*Argonemertes australiensis*	Nemertine Worm	R
Prosorhochmidae	*Argonemertes hillii*	Nemertine Worm	R
Prosorhochmidae	*Argonemertes stocki*	Nemertine Worm	R
Molluscs			
Bursidae	*Bursa rosa*	Frog Shell	M
Bursidae	*Tutufa tenuigranosa*	Frog Shell	M
Cancellaridae	*Cancellaria elegans*	Nutmeg Shell	M
Cancellaridae	*Cancellaria granosa*	Nutmeg Shell	M
Cancellaridae	*Cancellaria melanostoma westralis*	Nutmeg Shell	M
Cancellaridae	*Fusiaphera dampierensis*	Nutmeg Shell	M
Cancellaridae	*Trigonostoma lamellosa*	Nutmeg Shell	M
Cancellaridae	*Trigonostoma textilis*	Nutmeg Shell	M
Caryodidae	*Anoglypta launcestonensis*	Granulated Tasmanian Snail	E
Cassidae	*Phalium adcocki*	Helmet Shell	V
Cassidae	*Phalium whitworthi*	Helmet Shell	M
Colubrariidae	*Colubraria tortuosa*	Dwarf Tritons	M
Columbariidae	*Columbarium spinicinctum*	Pagoda Shell	M
Columbellidae	*Mitrella intexta*	Dove Shell	M
Conidae	*Conus advertex*	Cone Shell	M
Conidae	*Conus ammiralis*	Cone Shell	M
Conidae	*Conus angasi*	Cone Shell	M
Conidae	*Conus aulicus*	Cone Shell	M
Conidae	*Conus cocceus*	Cone Shell	M
Conidae	*Conus compressus*	Cone Shell	M
Conidae	*Conus distans*	Cone Shell	M
Conidae	*Conus episcopus*	Cone Shell	M
Conidae	*Conus frigidus*	Cone Shell	M
Conidae	*Conus geographus*	Cone Shell	M
Conidae	*Conus glans*	Cone Shell	M
Conidae	*Conus klemae*	Cone Shell	M
Conidae	*Conus nielsenae*	Cone Shell	M
Conidae	*Conus nussatella*	Cone Shell	M
Conidae	*Conus obscurus*	Cone Shell	M
Conidae	*Conus omaria*	Cone Shell	M

Family name	Scientific name	Common name	Conservation Status	Family name	Scientific name	Common name	Conservation Status
Conidae	Conus mitratus	Cone Shell	M	Muricidae	Homalocantha anatomica	Murex Shell	M
Conidae	Conus parvulus	Cone Shell	M	Muricidae	Homalocantha secunda	Murex Shell	M
Conidae	Conus scabriusculus	Cone Shell	M	Muricidae	Murex coppingeri	Murex Shell	M
Conidae	Conus sculetti	Cone Shell	M	Muricidae	Murex macgillivrayi	Murex Shell	M
Conidae	Conus segravei	Cone Shell	M	Muricidae	Murex nigrospinosus	Murex Shell	M
Conidae	Conus tenellus	Cone Shell	M	Muricidae	Murex pecten	Murex Shell	M
Conidae	Conus tulipa	Cone Shell	M	Muricidae	Pterynotus bednalli	Murex Shell	M
Cymatiidae	Charonia tritonis	Giant Triton	R	Muricidae	Pterynotus duffusi	Murex Shell	M
Cymatiidae	Cymatium lotorium	Triton	M	Muricidae	Pterynotus patagiatus	Murex Shell	M
Cymatiidae	Distorsio anus	Triton	M	Muricidae	Pterynotus tripterus	Murex Shell	M
Cymatiidae	Fusitriton retiolus	Triton	M	Muricidae	Pterynotus triqueter	Murex Shell	M
Cymatiidae	Ranularia pyrum	Triton	M	Muricidae	Typhis philippensis	Murex Shell	M
Cymatiidae	Septa hepatica	Triton	M	Muricidae	Vitularia miliaris	Murex Shell	M
Cypraeidae	Cypraea argus	Cowry	M	Olividae	Oliva tessellata	Olive Shell	M
Cypraeidae	Cypraea armeniaca	Cowry	R	Olividae	Zemira australis	Olive Shell	M
Cypraeidae	Cypraea asellus	Cowry	M	Ovulidae	Volva philippinarum	Spindle Cowry	M
Cypraeidae	Cypraea bistrinotata	Cowry	M	Planorbidae	Ancylastrum cumingianus	Tasmanian Freshwater Limpet	E
Cypraeidae	Cypraea brevidentata	Cowry	M				
Cypraeidae	Cypraea cernica	Cowry	M	Strombidae	Rimella cancellata	Stromb	M
Cypraeidae	Cypraea chinensis	Cowry	M	Strombidae	Strombus dilatatus	Stromb	M
Cypraeidae	Cypraea cribraria	Cowry	M	Strombidae	Strombus plicatus	Stromb	M
Cypraeidae	Cypraea felina	Cowry	M	Terebridae	Hastula brazieri	Auger Shell	M
Cypraeidae	Cypraea fimbriata	Cowry	M	Terebridae	Hastula lanceata	Auger Shell	M
Cypraeidae	Cypraea friendii	Cowry	M	Terebridae	Terebra albida	Auger Shell	M
Cypraeidae	Cypraea globulus	Cowry	M	Terebridae	Terebra albomarginata	Auger Shell	M
Cypraeidae	Cypraea hammondae	Cowry	M	Terebridae	Terebra commaculata	Auger Shell	M
Cypraeidae	Cypraea hirundo	Cowry	M	Terebridae	Terebra felina	Auger Shell	M
Cypraeidae	Cypraea hungerfordi coucomi	Cowry	M	Terebridae	Terebra guttata	Auger Shell	M
Cypraeidae	Cypraea kieneri	Cowry	M	Terebridae	Terebra hectica	Auger Shell	M
Cypraeidae	Cypraea langfordi moretonensis	Cowry	M	Terebridae	Terebra nebulosa	Auger Shell	M
Cypraeidae	Cypraea lutea	Cowry	M	Terebridae	Terebra pertusa	Auger Shell	M
Cypraeidae	Cypraea mappa	Cowry	M	Terebridae	Terebra triseriata	Auger Shell	M
Cypraeidae	Cypraea marginata	Cowry	R	Terebridae	Terebra undulata	Auger Shell	M
Cypraeidae	Cypraea microdon	Cowry	M	Thaidinae	Dicathais baileyana		M
Cypraeidae	Cypraea miliaris	Cowry	M	Thaidinae	Drupina lobata	Drupe Shell	M
Cypraeidae	Cypraea molleri	Cowry	M	Thaidinae	Vexilla vexillum	Drupe Shell	M
Cypraeidae	Cypraea nucleus	Cowry	M	Tonnidae	Tonna canaliculata	Ton Shell	M
Cypraeidae	Cypraea pallidula	Cowry	M	Tridacnidae	Hippopus hippopus	Horse's Hoof Clam	V
Cypraeidae	Cypraea poraria	Cowry	M	Tridacnidae	Tridacna crocea	Crocus Clam	V
Cypraeidae	Cypraea punctata	Cowry	M	Tridacnidae	Tridacna derasa	Southern Giant Clam	V
Cypraeidae	Cypraea pyriformis	Cowry	M	Tridacnidae	Tridacna maxima	Small Giant Clam	V
Cypraeidae	Cypraea quadrimaculata	Cowry	M	Tridacnidae	Tridacna squamosa	Fluted Clam	V
Cypraeidae	Cypraea queenslandica	Cowry	E	Trochidae	Calliostoma australe	Top Shell	M
Cypraeidae	Cypraea reevei	Cowry	R	Trochidae	Calliostoma ciliaris	Top Shell	M
Cypraeidae	Cypraea rosselli	Cowry	V	Trochidae	Clanculus personatus	Top Shell	M
Cypraeidae	Cypraea saulae	Cowry	R	Trochidae	Clanculus undatus	Top Shell	M
Cypraeidae	Cypraea scurra	Cowry	M	Trochidae	Phasianotrochus eximus	Top Shell	M
Cypraeidae	Cypraea staphylaea	Cowry	M	Turbinidae	Turbo jourdani	Turban Shell	M
Cypraeidae	Cypraea stolida	Cowry	M	Turridae	Daphnella botanica	Turrid	M
Cypraeidae	Cypraea talpa	Cowry	M	Turridae	Inquisitor formidabilis	Turrid	M
Cypraeidae	Cypraea teres	Cowry	M	Vasidae	Altivasum flindersi	Vase Shell	M
Cypraeidae	Cypraea testudinaria	Cowry	M	Vasidae	Tudicula armigera	Vase Shell	M
Cypraeidae	Cypraea ursellus	Cowry	M	Vasidae	Tudicula inermis	Vase Shell	M
Cypraeidae	Cypraea venusta	Cowry	M	Vasidae	Tudicula rasilistoma	Vase Shell	M
Cypraeidae	Cypraea walkeri	Cowry	M	Vasidae	Tudicula spinosa	Vase Shell	M
Cypraeidae	Cypraea ziczac	Cowry	M	Volutidae	Amorena benthalis	Volute	M
Cypraeidae	Cypraea humphreysii	Cowry	M	Volutidae	Amorena sclateri	Volute	M
Diastomidae	Diastoma melanoides	Diastomid Shell	M	Volutidae	Amoria dampieria	Volute	M
Epitoniidae	Cirsotrema kieneri	Wentletrap	M	Volutidae	Amoria ellioti	Volute	M
Epitoniidae	Cirsotrema varicosum	Wentletrap	M	Volutidae	Amoria exoptanda	Volute	M
Epitoniidae	Epitonium perplexa	Wentletrap	M	Volutidae	Amoria jamrachi	Volute	M
Fasciolariidae	Fusinus salisburyi		M	Volutidae	Amoria praetexta	Volute	M
Fasciolariidae	Fusinus tessellatus		M	Volutidae	Amoria turneri	Volute	M
Fasciolariidae	Latirus pictus		M	Volutidae	Aulica rutila	Volute	M
Fissurellidae	Amblychilepas javanicensis	Keyhole Limpet	M	Volutidae	Aulicina sophiae	Volute	M
Haliotidae	Haliotis conicopora	Abalone	M	Volutidae	Aulinina irvinae	Volute	M
Haliotidae	Haliotis elegans	Abalone	M	Volutidae	Cottonia nodiplicata	Volute	M
Haliotidae	Haliotis scalaris	Abalone	M	Volutidae	Cymbiolacca cracenta	Volute	M
Haliotidae	Haliotis semiplicata	Abalone	M	Volutidae	Cymbiolacca wisemani	Volute	M
Harpidae	Austroharpa exquisita	Harp Shell	V	Volutidae	Cymbiolena magnifica	Volute	M
Harpidae	Austroharpa loisae	Harp Shell	R	Volutidae	Ericusa fulgetrum	Volute	M
Harpidae	Austroharpa punctata	Harp Shell	V	Volutidae	Ericusa papillosa	Volute	M
Magilidae	Coralliophila costularis	Coral Shell	M	Volutidae	Livonia mammilla	Volute	M
Magilidae	Rapa rapa	Coral Shell	M	Volutidae	Livonia roadnightae	Volute	M
Magilidae	Tolema australis	Coral Shell	M	Volutidae	Lyreneta laseroni	Volute	V
Marginellidae	Epiginella deburghi	Margin Shell	M	Volutidae	Lyria deliciosa	Volute	M
Mitridae	Cancilla interlirata	Mitre	M	Volutidae	Lyria mitraeformis	Volute	M
Mitridae	Cancilla nodostaminea	Mitre	M	Volutidae	Lyria nucleus	Volute	M
Mitridae	Eumitra cookii	Mitre	M	Volutidae	Melo georginae	Baler Shell	M
Mitridae	Mitra ferruginea	Mitre	M	Volutidae	Melo miltonis	Baler Shell	M
Mitridae	Mitra papalis	Mitre	M	Volutidae	Melo umbilicatus	Baler Shell	M
Mitridae	Pterygia nucea	Mitre	M	Volutidae	Mesericusa sowerbyi	Baler Shell	M
Mitridae	Pterygia solida	Mitre	M	Volutidae	Nannamoria parabola	Volute	M
Mitridae	Pusia patriarchalis	Mitre	M	Volutidae	Notovoluta kreuslerae	Volute	M
Mitridae	Swainsonia casta	Mitre	M	Volutidae	Notovoluta perplicata	Volute	R
Mitridae	Vexillum caffrum	Mitre	M	Volutidae	Notovoluta verconis	Volute	M
Mitridae	Vexillum gruneri	Mitre	M	Volutidae	Paramoria guntheri	Volute	M
Mitridae	Vexillum rugosum	Mitre	M	Volutidae	Pseudocymbiola provocationis	Volute	M
Mitridae	Vexillum taeniatum	Mitre	M	Volutidae	Relegamoria molleri	Volute	M
Muricidae	Chicoreus banksii	Murex Shell	M	Volutidae	Volutoconus bednalli	Volute	M
Muricidae	Chicoreus cerricornis	Murex Shell	M	Volutidae	Volutoconus coniformis	Volute	R
Muricidae	Chicoreus damicornis	Murex Shell	M	Volutidae	Volutoconus grossi grossi	Volute	M
Muricidae	Chicoreus huttoniae	Murex Shell	M	Volutidae	Volutoconus grossi mcmichaeli	Volute	M
Muricidae	Chicoreus recticornis	Murex Shell	M	Volutidae	Volutoconus hargreavesi daisyae	Volute	R
Muricidae	Chicoreus territus	Murex Shell	M	Volutidae	Volutoconus hargreavesi hargreavesi	Volute	R
Muricidae	Haustellum multiplicatum	Murex Shell	M				

Species of freshwater Crayfish with limited distribution

Crustacea: Decapoda: Parastacida – after Riek 1969. In reality, the distribution is far more restricted than the general geographic area indicated. Many spp. are only known from single streams and river sections.

Genus	Species	General Distribution
Engaewa	(all spp)	SW tip of WA
Tenuibranchiurus	glypticus	extreme SE corner Qld
Engaeus	strictifrons	SW Vic
E.	sericatus	SW Vic
E.	fultoni	SW Vic
E.	urostrictus	S. Vic
E.	laevis	SE Vic
E.	sternalis	SE Vic
E.	phyllocerus	SE Vic
E.	australis	SE Vic
E.	marmoratus	E. Vic
E.	orientalis	E. Vic – SE NSW
E.	parvulus	SE NSW
E.	cymus	NE Vic
E.	affinis	Cent. E. Vic
E.	victoriensis	SE Vic
E.	tuberculatus	SE Vic

Genus	Species	General Distribution
E.	connectus	SE Vic
E.	hemicirratulus	SE Vic
E.	jumbunna	SE Vic
E.	fossor	NW Tas
E.	cunicularius	N. Tas
E.	leptorhynchus	NE Tasmania
Geocharax	(3ssp) (all spp)	Kangaroo Is., King Is. Sw Vic, NW Tas
Parastacoides	(6spp) (all spp)	SW Tas
Astacopsis	franklini	N. Cent. Tas
A.	gouldi	NW Tas
A.	tricornis	Cent. Tas
A.	fluviatilis	S. Tas
Euastacus	fleckeri	Cape York Pen.
E.	hystricosus	SE Qld
E.	cunninghami	SE Qld
E.	suttoni	SE Qld
E.	sulcatus	SE Qld, NE NSW
E.	valentulus	SE Qld, NE NSW
E.	simplex	NE NSW
E.	aquilus	NE NSW
E.	neohirsutus	NE NSW
E.	spinosus	NE NSW
E.	polysetosus	E. NSW
E.	reductus	E. NSW
E.	alienus	E. NSW

Genus	Species	General Distribution
E.	australiensis	E. NSW
E.	nobilis	E. NSW
E.	spinifer	E. NSW
E.	kierensis	SE NSW
E.	hirsutus	SE NSW
E.	clydensis	SE NSW
E.	claytoni	SE NSW
E.	brachythorax	SE NSW
E.	diversus	E. NSW
E.	neodiversus	SE Vic
E.	bispinosus	SW Vic
E.	kershawi	SE Vic
Euastacoides	urospinosus	SE Qld
E.	setosus	SE Qld
E.	maidae	SE Qld, NE NSW
Cherax	barretti	Wessell Is. NT
C.	rhyncotus	Cape York Pen.
C.	cairnensis	NE Qld
C.	glastonensis	Cent. E. Qld
C.	robustus	Fraser Is.
C.	dispar	SE Qld
C.	depressus	SE Qld
C.	punctatus	SE Qld
C.	urospinosus	SE Qld
C.	neopunctatus	NE NSW
C.	esculus	Nth T/lands of NSW

A selected list of threatened insects.

(An asterisk denotes species listed in the *IUCN Invertebrate Red Data Book*.) (Hill and Michaelis, 1988)

Species	Sites	State or Territory	Habitat; Locality	Threats
COLLEMBOLA				
Australotomurus n.sp. Springtail	1	WA	Sedges and grasses; Guildford cemetery	Clearing of remnant native vegetation
Corynephoria n.sp.1 Springtail	1	Qld	Woodland over native grass; Cooloola	Off road vehicles, sandmining
THYSANURA				
Trinemura russendenensis Smith & Shipp Troglophilic silverfish	1	Qld	Russenden Cave (limestone) possibly other cryptic sites	Site flooded
Trinemura anemone Smith Cave silverfish	1	NSW	3 Bungonia Caves	Tourist ventilation, trampling
EPHEMEROPTERA				
*Tasmanophlebia lacus-coerulei Tillyard Large Blue Lake mayfly	5	NSW	Alpine lakes; Kosciusko National Park	Two lakes subject to pollution
ODONATA				
Archipetalia auriculata Tillyard Dragonfly	9	Tas	Montane streams from boulder fields	Water pollution, fire
*Hemiphlebia mirabilis Selys Small Hemiphlebia damselfly	2	Vic	Freshwater	One site degraded, agricultural dams and clearing
PLECOPTERA				
*Eusthenia nothofagi Zwick Otway stonefly	?	Vic	Streams; Otway Ranges	Forest clearing
*Leptoperla cacuminis Hynes Mount Kosciusko wingless stonefly	1	NSW	Alpine stream; Mt Kosciusko	Local disturbance
*Riekoperla darlingtoni Illies Mt Donna Buang wingless stonefly	1	Vic	Alpine stream; Mt Donna Buang	Carpark construction
ORTHOPTERA				
Coryphistes n.sp. Grasshopper	1	Qld	Acacia shirleyi; Croydon stoney ridge	Site cleared
Genurellia cylindrica Sjostedt Grasshopper	1	NSW	Shrubs or trees; Pilliga	Agricultural clearing
New genus 3 sp.1 Grasshopper	3	Qld, NSW	Black soil depression vegetation	Overgrazing
New genus 23 sp.1 Grasshopper	3	NSW	Saltbush; Riverina	Agricultural clearing
New genus 45 sp.1 Grasshopper	2	NSW	Mulga; Louth, Cobar	Agricultural clearing, mulga decline
'Calliptamus' baiulus Grasshopper	1	Tas	Heath, Woolnorth	Pastoralism
New genus 49 sp.1 Grasshopper	1	WA	Saltbush on sand	Loss of host plants
New genus 96 sp.1 Grasshopper	3	WA	?Scaevola crassifolia; Monte Bello	Loss of host plants
New genus 103 sp.1 Grasshopper	2	WA	? thamnicolous; Shark Bay and Meekatharra	Loss of host plants
Testudinella unicolor Sjostedt Grasshopper	2	SA	Gibber plain; Oodnadatta, Coober Pedy	Overgrazing, drought
PHASMATODEA				
Tropiderus childreni Gray Stick insect	1(SA)	SA, Vic, NSW	Savannah, mallee, grass; Adelaide Hills	Urbanisation in SA
HEMIPTERA				
Glycaspis inusitata Moore Lerp insect	–	Qld, NSW	Eucalyptus bakeri, host specific feeder	Host plant endangered

Species	Sites	State or Territory	Habitat; Locality	Threats
Glycaspis paludis Moore Lerp insect	2	Qld, NSW	Melaleuca quinquenervia; Palm Beach, Qld, Tweed Heads	Urbanisation
Glycaspis wallumaris Moore Lerp insect	6	Qld	Eucalyptus conglomerata host specific feeder	Host plant endangered
Glycaspis surculina Moore Lerp insect	6	Qld	Eucalyptus conglomerata host specific feeder	Host plant endangered
Lestonia haustorifera China Bug	5	SA, Vic, NSW	Callitris preissi	Urban and agricultural clearing
Neophyllaphis gingerensis Carver Aphid	1	ACT	Podocarpus lawrencei; Mt Gingera	Habitat modification, fire
Taiwanaphis furcifera Carver & Hales Aphid	??	NSW	Nothofagus moorei	Host plant restricted
COLEOPTERA				
Aptenocanthon rossi Matthews Scarab beetle	2	NSW	Wet forest; Blue Mountains	Urbanisation
Chrysophtharta philomela Blackburn Tortoise-shell beetle	1(Tas)	Tas, ACT	Eucalyptus amygdalina (Tas) Eucalyptus blakelyi (ACT)	Woodchipping (Tas)
Stigmodera armata Thomson Jewel beetle	1	NSW	Heath-woodland; Sydney Basin	Urbanisation
Stigmodera goryi Laporte & Gory Jewel beetle	4	NSW	Eucalyptus woodland-forest; Sydney Basin	Urbanisation, last sighting 50 years
MECOPTERA				
Apteropanorpa tasmanica Carpenter Alpine scorpion-fly	4	Tas	Alpine shrubland, active on snow	Fire, pastoral trampling
DIPTERA				
*Edwardsina gigantea Zwick Giant torrent midge	2	NSW	Fast streams; Spencers Ck. Thredbo R.	Pollution
*Edwardsina tasmaniensis Tonnoir Tasmanian torrent midge	2	Tas	Fast streams	One site flooded
TRICHOPTERA				
Taskiria lacustris Neboiss Caddis-fly	1	Tas	Freshwater; old L. Pedder	Only site flooded
Taskiropsyche maccubbini Neboiss Caddis-fly	1	Tas	Freshwater; old L. Pedder	Only site flooded
LEPIDOPTERA				
Acalyphes philorites Turner Alpine moth	2	Tas	Athrotaxis alpine woodland	Fire, pastoral trampling
Dirce oriplancta Turner Alpine moth	6	Tas	Alpine shrubland	Fire, pastoral trampling
Acrodipsas arcana Lycaenid butterfly	2	Qld, NSW	Associated with ants; Grafton, Isla Gorge	Fire, clearing
Acrodipsas illidgei Waterhouse and Lyell Lycaenid butterfly	2	Qld	Mangroves with ants; Gold Coast, Moreton Bay	Urbanisation mosquito insecticides
Acrodipsas n.sp. Lycaenid butterfly	1	WA	Associated with ants; Yanchep	Agricultural clearing
Anisynta albovenata Waterhouse White veined skipper	2(SA)	SA, WA, NSW	Stipa grass	Roadworks, clearing, overgrazing
Antipodia atralba dactyliota Meyrick Skipper butterfly	1	WA	Gahnia filum; Geraldton	Urbanisation
Dirce aesiodora Turner Alpine moth	2	Tas	Alpine shrubland	Fire, pastoral trampling
Hesperilla chaostola leucophaeae Couchman Skipper butterfly	5	Tas	Gahnia radula	Urbanisation

Species	Sites	State or Territory	Habitat; Locality	Threats
Hesperilla donnysa galena Waterhouse Skipper butterfly	6	WA	Gahnia trifida, Geraldton	Sandmining, agricultural clearing
Hesperilla flavescens flavescens Waterhouse Skipper butterfly	4	Vic	Gahnia filum saline flats	Urbanisation
Hesperilla flavescens flavia Waterhouse Skipper butterfly	1	SA	Gahnia filum saline flats	Urbanisation
Hesperilla mastersi marakupa Couchman Skipper butterfly	1	Tas	Gahnia sp., Bridport	Urbanisation, agriculture
Hypochrysops epicurus Miskin Lycaenid butterfly	6	Qld, NSW	Associated with ants in mangroves	Urbanisation, mosquito control
Hypochrysops ignitus ignitus Leach Lycaenid butterfly	1(SA)	SA, Vic, NSW	Choretrum glomeratum – Acacia pycnantha scrub	Fire, drought
Hypochrysops piceatus Macqueen & Sands Lycaenid butterfly	1	Qld	Casuarina leuhmannii; Leyburn	Roadworks, agricultural clearing
Leptosia nina Pierid butterfly	4	WA	Rainforest; Mitchell Plateau	Bauxite mining
Motasingha dirphia trimaculata Tepper Skipper butterfly	9	SA	Lepidosperma in heath	Fire
Ogyris idmo halmaturia Tepper Lycaenid butterfly	6	SA, Vic	With sugar ants in mallee heath	Fire, agricultural clearing
Ogyris otanes Felder Lycaenid butterfly	10	SA, WA NSW	With sugar ants on Choretrum glomeratum	Fire, agricultural clearing
Oreisplanus munionga larana Couchman Skipper butterfly	1	Tas	Carex swamp; N.W.	Pastoral, agricultural drainage, clearing
Oreixenica kershawi kanunda Tindale Nymphalid butterfly	1(SA)	SA, Vic	Open grass; Canunda National Park	Fire
Paralucia spinefera Edwards & Common Lycaenid butterfly	1	NSW	Bursaria spinosa; Bathurst	Roadwork, agricultural clearing
Tisiphone abeona antoni Tindale Swordgrass brown butterfly	2(SA)	SA, Vic	Gahnia swamp	Roadworks
Tisiphone abeona joanna Butler Swordgrass brown butterfly		NSW	Gahnia swamp	Urban and agricultural clearing
Trapezites luteus luteus Tepper Rare white spot skipper	1(SA)	SA, Vic	Lomandra dura	Fire, drought
HYMENOPTERA				
*Nothomyrmecia macrops Clark Primitive ant	5	SA, WA	Mallee	Fire, telecommunication constructions
Parephedrus relictus Stary & Carver Parasitic wasp		NSW	parasite of Taiwanaphis furcifera (q.v.)	Host aphid and its host plant restricted

A selected list of threatened arthropods, excluding insects.

(The following abbreviation is used: NI – Norfolk Island Territory. An asterisk denotes species listed in the *IUCN Invertebrate Red Data Book*.) (Hill and Michaelis, 1988)

Species	Sites	State or Territory	Habitat; Locality	Threats
ISOPODA				
Abebaioscia troglodytes Vandel Cavernicolous isopod	1 or 2	WA	Pannikin Plain Cave [49], Nullarbor Plain	Tourism – recreation
Armadillo cavernae Wahrberg Isopod	1	Qld	4 Chillagoe Caves	Tourism – recreation
Echinodillo cavaticus Green Isopod	1	Tas	Ranga Cave, Flinders Island	Tourism – recreation
Styloniscus n. sp. Cavernicolous isopod	1	Tas	Cave PB3 Precipitous Bluff	Tourism – recreation
SYNCARIDA				
*Allanaspides helonomus Swain et al. Syncarid	2	Tas	Freshwater; old L. Pedder, McPartlan Pass	One site flooded
*Allanaspides hickmani Swain et al. Syncarid	1	Tas	Freshwater, McPartlan Pass	Vulnerable to local disturbance
*Anaspides spinulae Williams Syncarid	1	Tas	Alpine lake, L. St. Clair	Exotic Brown Trout predation
*Paranaspides lacustris Smith Syncarid	5	Tas	Alpine lakes	Exotic Brown Trout predation, flooding
*Anaspides tasmaniae Thompson Syncarid	many	Tas	Alpine, subalpine waters, widespread	Exotic Brown Trout, flooding
DECAPODA				
*Astacopsis gouldi Clark Giant freshwater crayfish	many	Tas	Pools in running waters, widespread in N and NW	Streamside clearing, overfishing
ARANEAE				
Aganippe raphiduca Rainbow & Pulleine Rottnest trapdoor spider	1	WA	Swamp; Rottnest Is. race is distinctive	Tourist trampling and constructions
Idiosoma nigrum Main Trapdoor spider	2+	WA	York gum/jam association; several endangered populations	Pastoral clearing and grazing
Kwonkan wonganensis (Main) Trapdoor spider	1	WA	Wandoo belt; Wongan Hills	Pastoral and wheat agriculture
Kwonkan moriartii Main Trapdoor spider	1	WA	Wandoo belt; Kathleen Valley	Pastoral and wheat agriculture
Kwonkan anatolian Main Trapdoor spider	1	SA	Penong	Pastoral and wheat agriculture
Kwonkan eboracum Main Trapdoor spider	2	WA	Yorkrakine Rock fauna sanctuary	One site cleared for agriculture
Troglodiplura lowryi Main Trapdoor spider	2	WA	Two Caves; Nullarbor Plain	Tourist lighting ventilation, trampling
PSEUDOSCORPIONIDA				
Austrochthonius n.sp. False scorpion	1	NI	Lion Rock off Norfolk Is.	Exotic plants and animals
Cryptocheridium n.sp. False scorpion	1	NI	Lion Rock off Norfolk Is.	Exotic plants and animals

APPENDIX III

Technical Note

This review of Australia's threatened species follows on from others in which the general editor has been integrally involved. The first was published in 1983 by Reed Australia, entitled *Our Wildlife in Peril*, written by the Total Environment Centre's Endangered Species Group. The second was published by Ecofund Australia in 1986, called *A Threatened Species Conservation Strategy for Australia – Policies for the Future*, while the third was *An Action Plan for Australasian Marsupials and Monotremes* published by the World Conservation Union, World Wildlife Fund Australia and the Federal Endangered Species Advisory Committee.

The conservation status assignment system used in developing the Marsupial Action Plan has also been utilised in this book. In the process of this review, the complete Ecofund list of threatened vertebrate species has been re-assessed for status and taxonomy, and 8 deletions and 144 additions were made comprising the following: marsupials – 8 deletions, 28 additions; rodents – 9 additions; bats – 3 additions; marine mammals – 2 additions; birds – 17 additions; reptiles – 32 additions; amphibians – 4 additions; fish – 44 additions (+ 5 marine species).

The vertebrate taxonomy employed adheres generally to Strahan (1983) for mammals, Royal Australasian Ornithologists Union (1984) for birds, Cogger (1988) for reptiles and amphibians, and Merrick and Schmida (1984) for fish, with some small departures for more recent taxonomic changes and new descriptions. The maps have also been developed based on the latter publications and the Reader's Digest *Complete Book of Australian Birds* (1988), with reference to more recent data where necessary. Information on distribution for the fish is taken from Michaelis (ANPWS, 1985), and for whales from the CITES Identification Manual (1987).

The conservation assessment of Australia's wildlife in this publication must be followed up with a comprehensive national review by the Federal Endangered Species Advisory Committee. Such a review must be published in the interest of public participation and concern, and should be updated on a regular basis.

APPENDIX IV
The Threatened Plants

Explanation of Threat Codes

Distribution Category Codes
1 only known from the type collection

2 maximum geographic range of 100 km

3 a range extending 100km but with small populations generally restricted to highly specific habitats

Conservation Status Codes
X PRESUMED EXTINCT – species not found for at least 50 years despite searching

E ENDANGERED – species in serious risk of extinction in the wild within one or two decades

V VULNERABLE – species at risk of disappearing from the wild over two to five decades if depletion continues

R RARE – while not endangered or vulnerable, may have a large population over a restricted area or small populations over a wider area, or intermediate distribution pattern

K POORLY KNOWN – suspected, but not definitely known, to belong to any of the above categories. At present field distribution information is inadequate

[k] Species considered too poorly known by the Western Australian Department of Conservation and Land Management (CALM) to belong to the other categories. This is related to CALM's requirements for addition or deletion to the Schedule of Declared Rare Flora in that State

Conservation Adequacy and Reservation Codes
C known to occur in a conservation reserve

a considered adequately conserved with at least 1000 individuals in reserves

i species is considered inadequately conserved with less than 1000 individuals in reserves

- while a species is known to occur in a reserve its population size in the reserve is unknown

t total known population is conserved in reserves

State(s) in which species occur
(Upper case) State(s) in which species still occurs

(Lower case) State(s) where species once occurred but is now Presumed Extinct

W Western Australia
Y Northern Territory
S South Australia
Q Queensland
N New South Wales
V Victoria
T Tasmania

(Reproduced from *Rare or Threatened Australian Plants* by J D Briggs and J H Leigh, 1988, Australian National Parks and Wildlife Service)

Family	Species	Threat Code	States
Acanthaceae	*Acanthus ebracteatus*	3K+	WYQ
Acanthaceae	*Asystasia* sp.1	1K	Q
Acanthaceae	*Brunoniella spiciflora*	3E	Q
Acanthaceae	*Graptophyllum excelsum*	2E	Q
Acanthaceae	*Graptophyllum ilicifolium*	3VC-	Q
Acanthaceae	*Graptophyllum thorogoodii*	3K	Q
Acanthaceae	*Hemigraphis royenii*	2K+	Q
Acanthaceae	*Isoglossa eranthemoides*	3VC-	QN
Acanthaceae	*Lepidagathis* sp.1	2K	Q
Acanthaceae	*Peristrophe brassii*	3KC-	Q
Acanthaceae	*Rhaphidospora bonneyana*	3VCi	Qn
Acanthaceae	*Rhaphidospora cavernarum*	3K	Q
Acanthaceae	*Sarojusticia kempeana*	3RC-	WY
Acanthaceae	*Xerothamnella herbacea*	2E	Q
Acanthaceae	*Xerothamnella parvifolia*	3V	QN
Agavaceae	*Cordyline congesta*	2RC-	QN
Agavaceae	*Cordyline fruticosa*	2K+	Q
Aizoaceae	*Glinus orygioides*	3K	YSQN
Aizoaceae	*Gunniopsis divisa*	2K	W
Aizoaceae	*Gunniopsis kochii*	3R	S
Aizoaceae	*Macarthuria complanata*	2RC-	Q
Aizoaceae	*Macarthuria ephedroides*	3VC-	Q
Aizoaceae	*? Sarcozona bicarinata*	3KC-	S
Aizoaceae	*Trianthema cussackiana*	1K	W
Aizoaceae	*Trianthema cypseloides*	1X	N
Alismataceae	*Limnophyton australiense*	2RC-	Q
Amaranthaceae	*Dipteranthemum crosslandii*	2KC-	W
Amaranthaceae	*Gomphrena conferta*	3R	Q
Amaranthaceae	*Hemichroa mesembryanthema*	3K	SQ
Amaranthaceae	*Ptilotus alexandri*	3K	W
Amaranthaceae	*Ptilotus aphyllus*	3K	W
Amaranthaceae	*Ptilotus aristatus*	3V	YS
Amaranthaceae	*Ptilotus beardii*	1K	W
Amaranthaceae	*Ptilotus beckerianus*	3ECi	S
Amaranthaceae	*Ptilotus blakeanus*	1K	Q
Amaranthaceae	*Ptilotus caespitulosus*	1X	W
Amaranthaceae	*Ptilotus chortophytus*	3K	W
Amaranthaceae	*Ptilotus extenuatus*	2X	N
Amaranthaceae	*Ptilotus fasciculatus*	1X	W
Amaranthaceae	*Ptilotus lazaridis*	3K	W
Amaranthaceae	*Ptilotus maconochiei*	3V	Q
Amaranthaceae	*Ptilotus marduguru*	1K	W
Amaranthaceae	*Ptilotus procumbens*	1K	W
Amaranthaceae	*Ptilotus pseudohelipteroid*	3R	Q
Amaranthaceae	*Ptilotus pyramidatus*	1X	W
Amaranthaceae	*Ptilotus remotiflorus*	2K	Q
Amaranthaceae	*Ptilotus robynsianus*	3K	YS
Amaranthaceae	*Ptilotus royceanus*	2R	WY
Amaranthaceae	*Ptilotus symonii*	3R	WS
Amaranthaceae	*Ptilotus tetrandrus*	1K	W

Family	Species	Threat Code	States
Amaranthaceae	*Pupalia lappacea*	3K+	Y
Amaryllidaceae	*Proiphys alba*	3K+	WQ
Anacardiaceae	*Buchanania mangoides*	3V	Q
Angiopteridaceae	*Angiopteris evecta*	3RC-	Q
Annonaceae	*Acana* sp.1	3RC-	Q
Annonaceae	*Artabotrys* sp.1	2R	Q
Annonaceae	*Desmos goezeanus*	3RC-	Q
Annonaceae	*Haplostichanthus johnsonii*	3RC-	Q
Annonaceae	*Haplostichanthus* sp.1	2RC-	Q
Annonaceae	*Haplostichanthus* sp.2	2R	Q
Annonaceae	*Haplostichanthus* sp.3	2RC-	Q
Annonaceae	*Polyalthia michaelii*	2RC-	Q
Annonaceae	*Polyalthia* sp.1	2R	Q
Annonaceae	*Polyaulax* sp.1	2K	Q
Annonaceae	*Pseuduvaria froggattii*	2RC-	Q
Annonaceae	*Pseuduvaria hylandii*	2RC-	Q
Annonaceae	*Pseuduvaria mulgraveana*	2RC-	Q
Annonaceae	*Pseuduvaria villosa*	2RC-	Q
Annonaceae	*Rauwenhoffia* sp.1	1K	Q
Annonaceae	*Uvaria* sp.1	3KC-	Q
Annonaceae	*Uvaria* sp.2	3KC-	Q
Apiaceae	*Actinotus rhomboideus*	3KC-	W
Apiaceae	*Actinotus schwarzii*	3VC-	Y
Apiaceae	*Gingidia algens*	2RCa	N
Apiaceae	*Gingidia montana*	2RC-t+	N
Apiaceae	*Hydrocotyle comocarpa*	3RCi	ST
Apiaceae	*Hydrocotyle crassiuscula*	3KC-	WS
Apiaceae	*Hydrocotyle hispidula*	3K	W
Apiaceae	*Hydrocotyle lemnoides*	2VCa	W
Apiaceae	*Hydrocotyle muriculata*	2VC-	W
Apiaceae	*Hydrocotyle scutellifera*	3KC-	W
Apiaceae	*Hydrocotyle* sp.1	2K	N
Apiaceae	*Hydrocotyle* sp.2	3V	W
Apiaceae	*Hydrocotyle* sp.3	3E	W
Apiaceae	*Hydrocotyle* sp.4	2R	Y
Apiaceae	*Hydrocotyle* sp.5	2RC-	W
Apiaceae	*Hydrocotyle* sp.6	2R	Y
Apiaceae	*Hydrocotyle* sp.7	3V	W
Apiaceae	*Neosciadium glochidiatum*	3K	WS
Apiaceae	*Oenanthe javanica*	2R+	Q
Apiaceae	*Oreomyrrhis brevipes*	3RC-	NV
Apiaceae	*Oreomyrrhis gunnii*	2VCi	T
Apiaceae	*Oschatzia cuneifolia*	3RC-	NV
Apiaceae	*Platysace cirrosa*	2K	W
Apiaceae	*Platysace clelandii*	2RCa	N
Apiaceae	*Platysace commutata*	2K	W
Apiaceae	*Platysace deflexa*	2RCa	W
Apiaceae	*? Platysace dissecta*	1X	W
Apiaceae	*Platysace eatoniae*	1X	W
Apiaceae	*Platysace filiformis*	2KC-	W

Family	Species	Threat Code	States
Apiaceae	*Platysace haplosciadia*	2K	W
Apiaceae	*Platysace pendula*	3K	W
Apiaceae	*Platysace stephensonii*	3RC-	N
Apiaceae	*Platysace tenuissima*	3K	W
Apiaceae	*Platysace teres*	2K	W
Apiaceae	*Schoenolaena tenuior*	2K	W
Apiaceae	*Trachymene croniniana*	3V	W
Apiaceae	*Trachymene geraniifolia*	2RC-	Q
Apiaceae	*Trachymene glandulosa*	3RC-	YQ
Apiaceae	*Trachymene inflata*	3R	Y
Apiaceae	*Trachymene lacerata*	3K	W
Apiaceae	*Trachymene longipedunculata*	1K	Y
Apiaceae	*Xanthosia hederifolia*	3KC-	W
Apiaceae	*Xanthosia peduncularis*	2KCi	W
Apiaceae	*Xanthosia singuliflora*	2KC-	W
Apiaceae	*Xanthosia tomentosa*	2R	W
Apocynaceae	*Alyxia orophila*	3RC-	Q
Apocynaceae	*Cerbera inflata*	2RC-	Q
Apocynaceae	*Melodinus bacellianus*	3RC-	Q
Apocynaceae	*Neisosperma kilneri*	2V	Q
Apocynaceae	*Ochrosia moorei*	2RC-	QN
Apocynaceae	*Parsonsia densivestita*	2R	Q
Apocynaceae	*Parsonsia diaphanophlebia*	2R	W
Apocynaceae	*Parsonsia lilacina*	3RC-	QN
Apocynaceae	*Parsonsia tenuis*	2RC-	QN
Apocynaceae	*Wrightia versicolor*	2V	Q
Aponogetonaceae	*Aponogeton hexatepalus*	3V	W
Aquifoliaceae	*Ilex* sp.1	2R	Q
Araceae	*Pothos brassii*	3RC-	Q
Araceae	*Pothos brownii*	2R	Q
Araceae	*Raphidophora pachyphylla*	3R	Q
Araceae	*Scindapsus altissimus*	3R+	Q
Araceae	*Typhonium eliosurum*	3EC-	N
Araliaceae	*Aralia macdowalliana*	2RC-	Q
Araliaceae	*Astrotricha parvifolia*	2RCi	V
Araliaceae	*Polyscias bellendenkerensis*	2VC-	Q
Araliaceae	*Polyscias mollis*	2R	Q
Araliaceae	*Polyscias willmottii*	3RC-	Q
Araliaceae	*Pseudopanax gunnii*	3RCa	T
Araliaceae	*Schefflera versteegii*	2RC-+	Q
Araucariaceae	*Agathis atropurpurea*	3RC-	Q
Araucariaceae	*Agathis microstachya*	2RC-	Q
Arecaceae	*Arenga australasica*	3RC-	Q
Arecaceae	*Arenga microcarpa*	2K+	Q
Arecaceae	*Calamus aruensis*	2RC-+	Q
Arecaceae	*Calamus warburgii*	2VC-+	Q
Arecaceae	*Corypha elata*	3RC-+	YQ
Arecaceae	*Gulubia costata*	3RC-	Q
Arecaceae	*Linospadix microcarya*	2RC-	Q
Arecaceae	*Linospadix palmeriana*	2RC-	Q

Family	Species	Threat Code	States
Arecaceae	Linospadix sp.1	2K	Q
Arecaceae	Livistona alfredii	3VC-	W
Arecaceae	Livistona drudei	3VC-	Q
Arecaceae	Livistona eastonii	2R	W
Arecaceae	Livistona loriphylla	3RC-	W
Arecaceae	Livistona mariae	2VCa	Y
Arecaceae	Livistona sp.1	2RC-	Q
Arecaceae	Livistona sp.2	2R	Q
Arecaceae	Livistona sp.3	2RC-	Q
Arecaceae	Livistona sp.4	2R	Q
Arecaceae	Livistona sp.5	3RC-	Q
Arecaceae	Normanbya normanbyi	2RC-	Q
Arecaceae	Nypa fruticans	3RC-+	YQ
Arecaceae	Oraniopsis appendiculata	3RC-	Q
Arecaceae	Ptychosperma bleeseri	2E	Y
Arecaceae	Wodyetia bifurcata	2RC-	Q
Asclepiadaceae	Cynanchum elegans	2EC-	N
Asclepiadaceae	Cynanchum erubescens	2K	Q
Asclepiadaceae	Cynanchum leptolepis	3R	Q
Asclepiadaceae	Gymnema brevifolium	3V	Q
Asclepiadaceae	Gymnema micradenium	3V	Q
Asclepiadaceae	Gymnema muelleri	3RC-	Y
Asclepiadaceae	Hoya gracilipes	2RC-+	Q
Asclepiadaceae	Hoya macgillivrayi	3RC-	Q
Asclepiadaceae	? Marsdenia coronata	2X	Q
Asclepiadaceae	Marsdenia longiloba	3EC-	QN
Asclepiadaceae	Thozetia racemosa	3VC-	QN
Asclepiadaceae	Thozetia sp.1	1K	Q
Asclepiadaceae	Tylophora calcarata	1K	Q
Asclepiadaceae	Tylophora colorata	3RC-	Q
Asclepiadaceae	Tylophora woollsii	2E	N
Aspidiaceae	Dryopteris sparsa	3RC-	Q
Aspidiaceae	Lastreopsis grayi	2R	Q
Aspidiaceae	Lastreopsis silvestris	2RCa	QN
Aspidiaceae	Lastreopsis sp.1	2R	Q
Aspidiaceae	Polystichum fragile	3R	Q
Aspidiaceae	Tectaria devexa	3V	Q
Aspidiaceae	Tectaria siifolia	2RC-	Q
Aspleniaceae	Asplenium excisum	2RC-	Q
Aspleniaceae	Asplenium hookerianum	3VC-+	VT
Aspleniaceae	Asplenium normale	3K+	Q
Aspleniaceae	Asplenium pellucidum	2VC-+	Q
Aspleniaceae	Asplenium sp.1	3RC-	Q
Aspleniaceae	Asplenium sp.2	2K	Q
Aspleniaceae	Asplenium unilaterale	2R+	Q
Aspleniaceae	Asplenium wildii	2V	Q
Asteraceae	Abrotanella nivigena	3RCa	NV
Asteraceae	Acanthocladium dockeri	3X	SN
Asteraceae	Achnophora tatei	2RCa	S
Asteraceae	Acomis acoma	3RC-	QN
Asteraceae	Acomis sp.1	2K	Q
Asteraceae	Ammobium craspedioides	2V	N
Asteraceae	Angianthus axiliflorus	3VC-	W
Asteraceae	Angianthus brachycarpus	3R	Q
Asteraceae	Angianthus microcephalus	2R	W
Asteraceae	Angianthus micropodioides	3R	W
Asteraceae	Asteridea gracilis	2K	W
Asteraceae	Athrixia croniniana	2K	W
Asteraceae	Athrixia gracilis	3K	W
Asteraceae	Basedowia tenerrima	2V	S
Asteraceae	Blennospora phegmatocarpa	2K	W
Asteraceae	Blumea prostrata	1K	W
Asteraceae	Blumea pungens	1K	W
Asteraceae	Brachycome ascendens	2VC-	Q
Asteraceae	Brachycome billardieri	2K	W
Asteraceae	Brachycome eriogona	3RC-	SQ
Asteraceae	Brachycome eyrensis	1KC-t	W
Asteraceae	Brachycome gracilis	3RCa	NV
Asteraceae	Brachycome muelleri	2E	S
Asteraceae	Brachycome muelleroides	3VCa	NV
Asteraceae	Brachycome papillosa	3V	N
Asteraceae	Brachycome petrophila	2RC-	V
Asteraceae	Brachycome radicata	2K+	T
Asteraceae	Brachycome rara	1K	Q
Asteraceae	Brachycome riparia	3RC-	V
Asteraceae	Brachycome stolonifera	3RCat	N
Asteraceae	Brachycome tatei	3K	WS
Asteraceae	Brachycome xanthocarpa	2RC-t	S
Asteraceae	Brachyglottis brunonis	2RCa	T
Asteraceae	Calocephalus aervoides	2K	W
Asteraceae	Calocephalus globosus	1X	W
Asteraceae	Calocephalus phlegmatocarpus	2R	W
Asteraceae	? Calocephalus stowardii	2K	W
Asteraceae	Calotis glabrescens	1K	Q
Asteraceae	Calotis glandulosa	3VC-	N
Asteraceae	Calotis suffruticosa	3R	Q
Asteraceae	Cassinia collina	2RC-	Q
Asteraceae	Celmisia sericophylla	2RCa	V
Asteraceae	? Chthonocephalus multiceps	2K	W
Asteraceae	Chthonocephalus tomentellus	2R	W
Asteraceae	Cotula drummondii	2KC-	W
Asteraceae	Craspedia leucantha	2RCat	N
Asteraceae	Elachanthus glaber	3RC-	SV
Asteraceae	Elachanthus pusillus	3K	W
Asteraceae	Epaltes tatei	3KCa	WSV
Asteraceae	Erigeron setosus	3RC-t	N
Asteraceae	Ethulia conyzoides	2R+	Q
Asteraceae	Glossogyne orthochaeta	3R	Q
Asteraceae	Gnaphalium nitidulum	3VCa+	V
Asteraceae	Gnephosis acicularis	3K	W
Asteraceae	? Gnephosis arachnoidea	3K	W
Asteraceae	Gnephosis baracchiana	2V	V
Asteraceae	Gnephosis exilis	3R	W
Asteraceae	Gnephosis intonsa	3KC-	W
Asteraceae	Gnephosis tenuissima	3KC-	W
Asteraceae	Haeckeria cassiniiformis	2RC-	S
Asteraceae	Helichrysum cassiope	3K	W
Asteraceae	Helichrysum costatifructum	3RC-	T
Asteraceae	Helichrysum eriocephalum	2VC-	Q
Asteraceae	Helichrysum expansifolium	3RC-	T
Asteraceae	Helichrysum lindsayanum	2RCa	Q
Asteraceae	Helichrysum lycopodioides	2R	T
Asteraceae	Helichrysum monochaetum	3R	S
Asteraceae	Helichrysum oligochaetum	2X	W
Asteraceae	Helichrysum puteale	3K	W
Asteraceae	Helichrysum sp.1	2X	T
Asteraceae	Helichrysum sp.1	2RC-	QN
Asteraceae	Helichrysum spiceri	2X	T
Asteraceae	Helichrysum tesselatum	2VC-	N
Asteraceae	Helichrysum thomsonii	3RCa	Y
Asteraceae	Helichrysum vagans	2RCa	QN
Asteraceae	Helichrysum whitei	3RC-	QN
Asteraceae	? Helipterum chlorocephalum	2K	W
Asteraceae	Helipterum gracile	3V	W
Asteraceae	? Helipterum guilfoylei	1X	W
Asteraceae	Helipterum pyrethrum	2RC-	W
Asteraceae	Helipterum zacchaeus	3KC-	W
Asteraceae	Ixiochlamys integerrima	3R	YQ
Asteraceae	Ixiolaena pluriseta	3R	S
Asteraceae	Ixiolaena websteri	1K	W
Asteraceae	Leptorhynchos gatesii	2VCa	V
Asteraceae	Minuria tridens	2VCit	Y
Asteraceae	Myriocephalus appendiculatus	3K	W
Asteraceae	Myriocephalus suffruticosus	2K	W
Asteraceae	Odixia achlaena	2RCi	T
Asteraceae	Odixia angusta	3RCa	T
Asteraceae	Olearia adenophora	2KC-	V
Asteraceae	Olearia allenderae	3RC-	V
Asteraceae	? Olearia arida	3X	WS
Asteraceae	Olearia aspera	2K	W
Asteraceae	Olearia astroloba	2V	V
Asteraceae	Olearia brachyphylla	2RC-	W
Asteraceae	Olearia cassiniae	3VC-	W
Asteraceae	Olearia cordata	2RCa	N
Asteraceae	Olearia ericoides	3RC-	T
Asteraceae	Olearia flocktoniae	2E	N
Asteraceae	Olearia frostii	2RCa	V
Asteraceae	Olearia heterocarpa	2RCa	QN
Asteraceae	Olearia hookeri	2RC-	T
Asteraceae	Olearia hygrophila	2E	Q
Asteraceae	Olearia lanceolata	3RCa	T
Asteraceae	Olearia macdonnellensis	2VCit	Y
Asteraceae	Olearia microdisca	2ECa	S
Asteraceae	Olearia oliganthema	2X	N
Asteraceae	Olearia quercifolia	3RC-	N
Asteraceae	Olearia sp.1	3V	W
Asteraceae	Olearia sp.2	2RCit	N
Asteraceae	Olearia stilwelliae	3RCa	N
Asteraceae	Parantennaria uniceps	3RC-t	NV
Asteraceae	Picris evae	3V	Q
Asteraceae	Pithocarpa achilleoides	2K	W
Asteraceae	Pithocarpa melanostigma	2K	W
Asteraceae	Pleuropappus phyllocalymmeus	3VCa	S
Asteraceae	Podolepis microcephala	3K	W
Asteraceae	Podolepis monticola	2RCa	QN
Asteraceae	? Podolepis nutans	3K	W
Asteraceae	Rhaponticum australis	3V	Qnv
Asteraceae	Rutidosis acutiglumis	2K	Q
Asteraceae	Rutidosis heterogama	2VCa	N
Asteraceae	Rutidosis leiolepis	2VC-	N
Asteraceae	Rutidosis leptorhynchoides	3ECa	NV
Asteraceae	Senecio behrianus	3X	SNV
Asteraceae	Senecio capillifolius	3RCa	T
Asteraceae	Senecio georgianus	3X	WSNV
Asteraceae	Senecio gilbertii	2K	W
Asteraceae	? Senecio laticostatus	2V	V
Asteraceae	Senecio leucoglossus	2K	W
Asteraceae	Senecio macranthus	3RC-	N
Asteraceae	Senecio macrocarpus	3VCa	SVt
Asteraceae	Senecio megaglossus	3E	S
Asteraceae	Senecio papillosus	2RCa	T
Asteraceae	Senecio primulifolius	2RCa	T
Asteraceae	Taraxacum aristum	3RC-	NVT
Asteraceae	Taraxacum cygnorum	3KC-	WVT
Asteraceae	Taraxacum magellanicum	1K+	N
Asteraceae	Vittadinia constricta	3K	Q
Asteraceae	Vittadinia decora	3K	Q
Asteraceae	Vittadinia scabra	3KC-	Q
Asteraceae	Vittadinia sericea	2V	Q
Atherospermaceae	Daphnandra dielsii	3VC-	Q
Athyriaceae	Cystopteris filix-fragilis	3RCa+	NVT
Athyriaceae	Diplazium cordifolium	2R+	Q
Balanopaceae	Balanops montana	2RC-	Q
Bignoniaceae	Dolichandrone spathacea	3R+	Q
Bignoniaceae	Neosepicaea viticoides	2KC-+	Q
Bignoniaceae	Pandorea nervosa	2RC-	Q
Bignoniaceae	Tecomanthe hillii	3RC-	Q
Blechnaceae	Blechnum gregsonii	2RC-	N
Blechnaceae	Doodia maxima	2K	Q
Blechnaceae	Steenisioblechnu acuminatum	2R	Q
Boraginaceae	Embadium johnstonii	2V	S
Boraginaceae	Embadium stagnense	2K	S
Boraginaceae	Halgania corymbosa	2VC-	W
Boraginaceae	Halgania tomentosa	3KC-	W
Boraginaceae	Heliotropium muticum	1X	W
Boraginaceae	Heliotropium sp.1	2K	Q
Boraginaceae	Heliotropium sp.2	2K	Q
Brassicaceae	Ballantinia antipoda	2V	Vt
Brassicaceae	Barbarea australis	2EC-	T
Brassicaceae	Cheesemania radicata	3RCa	T
Brassicaceae	Drabastrum alpestre	3RC-	NV
Brassicaceae	Hutchinsia tasmanica	1X	T
Brassicaceae	Irenepharsus magicus	2RC-	NV
Brassicaceae	Irenepharsus trypherus	2RC-	N
Brassicaceae	Lepidium aschersonii	3ECi	WnV
Brassicaceae	Lepidium catapycnon	2V	W
Brassicaceae	Lepidium drummondii	2X	W
Brassicaceae	Lepidium flexicaule	3RC-+	T
Brassicaceae	Lepidium genistoides	2VC-	W
Brassicaceae	Lepidium hyssopifolium	3ECa+	NVT
Brassicaceae	Lepidium linifolium	3K	W
Brassicaceae	Lepidium merrallii	2E	W
Brassicaceae	Lepidium monoplocoides	3ECi	NV
Brassicaceae	Lepidium peregrinum	3X	N
Brassicaceae	Lepidium pseudo-papillosum	2VCa	snV
Brassicaceae	Lepidium pseudo-ruderale	3R	WS
Brassicaceae	Lepidium puberulum	3K	W
Brassicaceae	Menkea draboides	2X	W
Brassicaceae	Menkea lutea	3R	WS
Brassicaceae	Microlepidium alatum	2V	S
Brassicaceae	Microlepidium pilosulum	3RCa	WSV
Brassicaceae	Phlegmatospermum drummondii	3X	W
Brassicaceae	Phlegmatospermum eremaeum	3KCi	WSnV
Brassicaceae	Phlegmatospermum richardsii	2E	wS
Burmanniaceae	Thismia rodwayi	3KC-+	QNVT
Cabombaceae	Brasenia schreberi	3V+	qNV
Caesalpiniaceae	Caesalpinia major	3K+	Q
Caesalpiniaceae	Caesalpinia robusta	2R	Q
Caesalpiniaceae	Cassia marksiana	3VCi	QN
Caesalpiniaceae	Cassia queenslandica	3RC-	Q
Caesalpiniaceae	Crudia papuana	2R+	Q
Caesalpiniaceae	Labichea brassii	3R	Q
Caesalpiniaceae	Labichea buettneriana	2R	Q
Caesalpiniaceae	Labichea eremaea	2K	W
Caesalpiniaceae	Labichea obtrullata	2K	W
Caesalpiniaceae	Storckiella australiensis	3RC-	Q
Callitrichaceae	Callitriche brachycarpa	3KCa	VT
Campunulaceae	Wahlenbergia cyclocarpa	3V	NV
Campanulaceae	Wahlenbergia densifolia	3RCa	NV
Campanulaceae	Wahlenbergia sp.1	3RC-	Q
Campanulaceae	Wahlenbergia sp.2	2RC-	Q
Campanulaceae	Wahlenbergia sp.3	2RC-	QN
Capparidaceae	Capparis humistrata	2K	Q
Capparidaceae	Capparis thozetiana	3K	Q
Capparidaceae	Cleome kenneallyi	2K	W
Capparidaceae	Crateva religiosa	3R+	Q
Cartonemataceae	Cartonema baileyi	3R	Q
Cartonemataceae	Cartonema brachyantherum	2R	Q
Cartonemataceae	Cartonema philydroides	3K	W
Caryophyllaceae	Colobanthus nivicola	2RC-t	N
Caryophyllaceae	Colobanthus pulvinatus	2RC-t	N
Caryophyllaceae	Colobanthus strictus	2E+	T
Casuarinaceae	Allocasuarina acuaria	3RC-	W
Casuarinaceae	Allocasuarina fibrosa	2VCit	W
Casuarinaceae	Allocasuarina ramosissima	2V	W
Casuarinaceae	Allocasuarina sp.1	2V	N
Casuarinaceae	Allocasuarina sp.2	2ECit	N
Casuarinaceae	Allocasuarina sp.3	2RC-	Q
Casuarinaceae	Allocasuarina sp.4	2E	Q
Casuarinaceae	Allocasuarina sp.5	2E	Q
Casuarinaceae	Allocasuarina sp.6	2RC-	W
Casuarinaceae	Gymnostoma sp.	2RC-	Q
Celastraceae	Apatophyllum constablei	2E	N
Celastraceae	Apatophyllum olsenii	2VC-	Q
Celastraceae	Apatophyllum sp.1	2K	Q
Celastraceae	? Cassine glauca	1K+	W
Celastraceae	Denhamia parvifolia	3V	Q
Celastraceae	Denhamia viridissima	3RC-	Q
Celastraceae	Euonymus globularis	2RC-	Q
Celastraceae	Hexaspora pubescens	2V	Q
Celastraceae	Hypsophila halleyana	2RC-	Q
Celastraceae	Perrottetia arborescens	3RC-	Q
Centrolepidaceae	Centrolepis caespitosa	1X	W
Centrolepidaceae	Centrolepis inconspicua	3K	W
Centrolepidaceae	Centrolepis muscoides	2RC-	T
Centrolepidaceae	Centrolepis mutica	3K	W
Centrolepidaceae	Centrolepis paludicola	2RC-	T

Family	Species	Threat Code	States
Centrolepidaceae	*Centrolepis pedderensis*	2EC-	T
Centrolepidaceae	*Centrolepis pulvinata*	2RC-	T
Centrolepidaceae	*Gaimardia amblyphylla*	2RC-	T
Chenopodiaceae	*Atriplex eichleri*	3R	S
Chenopodiaceae	*Atriplex kochiana*	2E	S
Chenopodiaceae	*Atriplex morrisii*	3V	N
Chenopodiaceae	*Halosarcia bulbosa*	2V	W
Chenopodiaceae	*Halosarcia entrichoma*	2RCat	W
Chenopodiaceae	*Halosarcia flabelliformis*	3V	SV
Chenopodiaceae	*Maireana cheelii*	3V	NV
Chenopodiaceae	*Maireana melanocarpa*	3V	S
Chenopodiaceae	*Maireana murrayana*	3V	W
Chenopodiaceae	*Malacocera gracilis*	3V	S
Chenopodiaceae	*Rhagodia acicularis*	2V	W
Chenopodiaceae	*Roycea pycnophylloides*	3VC-	W
Chenopodiaceae	*Sclerolaena beaugleholei*	1K	W
Chenopodiaceae	*Sclerolaena bicuspis*	3R	WS
Chenopodiaceae	*Sclerolaena blakei*	2K	Q
Chenopodiaceae	*Sclerolaena deserticola*	1K	Y
Chenopodiaceae	*Sclerolaena everistiana*	3R	Q
Chenopodiaceae	*Sclerolaena holtiana*	3K	YS
Chenopodiaceae	*Sclerolaena medicaginoides*	2K	W
Chenopodiaceae	*Sclerolaena microcarpa*	3K	W
Chenopodiaceae	*Sclerolaena napiformis*	3E	nV
Chenopodiaceae	*Sclerolaena stylosa*	1K	W
Chenopodiaceae	*Sclerolaena symoniana*	3R	WY
Chenopodiaceae	*Sclerolaena walkeri*	2K	Q
Chenopodiaceae	*Tegicornia uniflora*	3RCa	W
Cloanthaceae	*Dicrastylis glauca*	3K	W
Cloanthaceae	*Dicrastylis incana*	1K	W
Cloanthaceae	*Dicrastylis linearifolia*	2K	W
Cloanthaceae	*Dicrastylis morrisonii*	1X	W
Cloanthaceae	*Dicrastylis obovata*	2KC-	W
Cloanthaceae	*Dicrastylis petermannensis*	1K	Y
Cloanthaceae	*Lachnostachys albicans*	3KC-	W
Cloanthaceae	*Newcastelia velutina*	2V	Q
Cloanthaceae	*Pityrodia augustensis*	2V	W
Cloanthaceae	*Pityrodia byrnesii*	2R	Y
Cloanthaceae	*Pityrodia canaliculata*	2K	W
Cloanthaceae	*Pityrodia chorisepala*	3K	WY
Cloanthaceae	*Pityrodia chrysocalyx*	3K	W
Cloanthaceae	*Pityrodia exserta*	2RC-t	W
Cloanthaceae	*Pityrodia gilruthiana*	3RC-	Y
Cloanthaceae	*Pityrodia glabra*	2R	W
Cloanthaceae	*Pityrodia lanceolata*	2R	Y
Cloanthaceae	*Pityrodia loricata*	3K	WY
Cloanthaceae	*Pityrodia megalophylla*	2R	Y
Cloanthaceae	*Pityrodia obliqua*	3K	W
Cloanthaceae	*Pityrodia ovata*	3K	W
Cloanthaceae	*Pityrodia puberula*	2RCa	Y
Cloanthaceae	*Pityrodia scabra*	2V	W
Cloanthaceae	*Pityrodia serrata*	2R	Y
Cloanthaceae	*Pityrodia spenceri*	3RC-	Y
Cloanthaceae	*Pityrodia viscida*	2K	W
Combretaceae	*Combretum trifoliatum*	2R+	Q
Combretaceae	*Dansiea elliptica*	3R	Q
Combretaceae	? *Lumnitzera rosea*	2RCit	Q
Combretaceae	*Macropteranthes fitzalanii*	3R	Q
Combretaceae	*Macropteranthes montana*	2V	Q
Combretaceae	*Terminalia supranitifolia*	2K	W
Commelinaceae	*Floscopa scandens*	2K+	Q
Connaraceae	*Rourea brachyandra*	3R	Q
Convolvulaceae	*Argyreia queenslandica*	2R	Q
Convolvulaceae	*Argyreia soutteri*	1K	Q
Convolvulaceae	*Bonamia dietrichiana*	2RC-	Q
Convolvulaceae	*Ipomoea antonschmidii*	2R	Q
Convolvulaceae	*Ipomoea saintronanensis*	2RC-	Q
Convolvulaceae	*Ipomoea stolonifera*	3R+	YQ
Convolvulaceae	*Operculina brownii*	3K	YQ
Corsiaceae	*Corsia* sp.1	2K	Q
Crassulaceae	*Crassula moschata*	2RC-+	T
Cucurbitaceae	*Benincasa hispida*	2X+	Q
Cucurbitaceae	*Coccinia grandis*	2K+	Y
Cucurbitaceae	*Lagenaria siceraria*	2E+	Q
Cucurbitaceae	*Momordica cochinchinensis*	2KC-+	Q
Cucurbitaceae	*Muellerargia timorensis*	2K+	Q
Cucurbitaceae	*Mukia* sp.1	3V	Q
Cucurbitaceae	*Mukia* sp.2	2K	Q
Cucurbitaceae	*Mukia* sp.3	1K	W
Cucurbitaceae	*Nothoalsomitra suberosa*	2VCi	Q
Cucurbitaceae	*Trichosanthes subvelutina*	3RC-	QN
Cunoniaceae	*Acrophyllum australe*	2VCi	N
Cunoniaceae	*Ceratopetalum corymbosum*	2RC-	Q
Cunoniaceae	*Ceratopetalum macrophyllum*	2RC-	Q
Cunoniaceae	*Ceratopetalum* sp.1	2K	Q
Cunoniaceae	*Ceratopetalum* sp.2	2KC-	Q
Cunoniaceae	*Ceratopetalum virchowii*	2RC-	Q
Cunoniaceae	*Schizomeria whitei*	2RC-	Q
Cupressaceae	*Callitris oblonga*	3VCi	N
Cupressaceae	*Callitris* sp.1 (*aff. oblonga*)	2CCi	T
Cyathaceae	*Cyathea baileyana*	3RC-	Q
Cyathaceae	*Cyathea celebica*	3R+	Q
Cyathaceae	*Cyathea cunninghamii*	3RCa+	QVT
Cyathaceae	*Cyathea felina*	3R+	Q
Cycadaceae	*Cycas angulata*	3K	YQ
Cycadaceae	*Cycas cairnsiana*	3R	Q
Cyperaceae	*Bulbostylis burbidgeae*	3R	W
Cyperaceae	*Carex breviscapa*	3RC-+	Q
Cyperaceae	*Carex capillacea*	3RC-+	NV
Cyperaceae	*Carex cephalotes*	3RCa+	NV
Cyperaceae	*Carex paupera*	2RCi	V
Cyperaceae	*Carex rafflesiana*	3RC-+	Q
Cyperaceae	*Carex raleighii*	3RCa	NVT
Cyperaceae	*Carex tasmanica*	3E+	VT
Cyperaceae	*Carpha gracilepes*	2K	W
Cyperaceae	*Chorizandra multiarticulata*	3KC-	W
Cyperaceae	? *Cladium drummondii*	1X	W
Cyperaceae	*Cyperus malaccensis*	3K+	Y
Cyperaceae	*Cyperus ohwii*	2E+	Q
Cyperaceae	*Cyperus rupicola*	2RC-	QN
Cyperaceae	*Cyperus semifertilis*	3VC-	Q
Cyperaceae	*Cyperus serotinus*	2K+	Q
Cyperaceae	*Eleocharis blakeana*	3V	QN
Cyperaceae	*Eleocharis obicis*	3V	N
Cyperaceae	*Eleocharis papillosa*	3K	Y
Cyperaceae	*Eleocharis retroflexa*	2VC-+	Q
Cyperaceae	*Evandra aristata*	3K	W
Cyperaceae	*Evandra pauciflora*	2K	W
Cyperaceae	*Fimbristylis adjuncta*	1EC-t	Q
Cyperaceae	*Fimbristylis clavata*	3K	YQ
Cyperaceae	*Fimbristylis compacta*	3V	Y
Cyperaceae	*Fimbristylis corynocarya*	3K	WYQ
Cyperaceae	*Fimbristylis distincta*	1K	Q
Cyperaceae	*Fimbristylis dolera*	3K	YQ
Cyperaceae	*Fimbristylis elegans*	1K	Q
Cyperaceae	*Fimbristylis micans*	1K	Q
Cyperaceae	*Fimbristylis pilifera*	3KC-	WY
Cyperaceae	*Fimbristylis spiralis*	3K	Y
Cyperaceae	*Fimbristylis vagans*	2RC-	Q
Cyperaceae	*Gahnia drummondii*	3RC-	W
Cyperaceae	*Gahnia graminifolia*	3RC-	T
Cyperaceae	*Gahnia hystrix*	2RCa	S
Cyperaceae	*Gahnia insignis*	3RCa	QN
Cyperaceae	*Gymnoschoenus anceps*	3K	W
Cyperaceae	*Hypolytrum compactum*	3K+	Q
Cyperaceae	*Isolepis limbata*	2RC-	T
Cyperaceae	*Isolepis* sp.1	3K	W
Cyperaceae	*Lepidosperma aphyllum*	3RC-	W
Cyperaceae	*Lepidosperma leptophyllum*	3KCa	W
Cyperaceae	*Lepidosperma rostratum*	1K	W
Cyperaceae	*Lepidosperma rupestre*	2RC-	W
Cyperaceae	*Lepidosperma ustulatum*	3RC-	W
Cyperaceae	*Mesomelaena* sp.1	3K	W
Cyperaceae	*Paramapania parvibractea*	2R+	Q
Cyperaceae	*Reedia spathacea*	3R	W
Cyperaceae	*Schoenus absconditus*	2V	T
Cyperaceae	? *Schoenus acuminatus*	1X	W
Cyperaceae	*Schoenus andrewsii*	3K	W
Cyperaceae	*Schoenus benthamii*	3V	W
Cyperaceae	*Schoenus biglumis*	3RC-	T
Cyperaceae	*Schoenus brevisetus*	2K	W
Cyperaceae	*Schoenus centralis*	3R	WY
Cyperaceae	*Schoenus clandestinus*	2KC-	W
Cyperaceae	*Schoenus discifer*	3RCa	S
Cyperaceae	*Schoenus efoliatus*	2K	W
Cyperaceae	*Schoenus indutus*	2K	W
Cyperaceae	*Schoenus latitans*	1K	W
Cyperaceae	*Schoenus multiglumis*	3K	W
Cyperaceae	*Schoenus natans*	2X	W
Cyperaceae	*Schoenus obtusifolius*	3KC-	W
Cyperaceae	*Schoenus pennisetis*	2K	W
Cyperaceae	*Schoenus pygmaeus*	2RC-	T
Cyperaceae	*Schoenus rigens*	3K	W
Cyperaceae	*Schoenus rodwayanus*	3K	W
Cyperaceae	*Schoenus subfascicularis*	3RCa	W
Cyperaceae	*Schoenus submicrostachyus*	3KC-	W
Cyperaceae	*Scirpus oldfieldianus*	2K	W
Cyperaceae	*Scirpus tasmanicus*	3RC-	T
Cyperaceae	*Scleria carphiformis*	2KC-+	Q
Cyperaceae	*Scleria pergracilis*	2K+	Q
Cyperaceae	*Tetraria australiensis*	2X	W
Cyperaceae	*Tetraria microcarpa*	3K	W
Davidsoniaceae	*Davidsonia* sp.	2E	QN
Dennstaedtiaceae	*Oenotrichia dissecta*	2K	Q
Dicksoniaceae	*Culcita villosa*	3K+	Q
Dilleniaceae	*Hibbertia andrewsiana*	3KC-	W
Dilleniaceae	*Hibbertia argentea*	2KC-	W
Dilleniaceae	*Hibbertia bracteosa*	2VCa	W
Dilleniaceae	*Hibbertia crispula*	3V	S
Dilleniaceae	*Hibbertia elata*	3RC-	QN
Dilleniaceae	*Hibbertia glaberrima*	3RCa	YS
Dilleniaceae	*Hibbertia hermanniifolia*	3RCa	NV
Dilleniaceae	*Hibbertia hexandra*	3RC-	QN
Dilleniaceae	*Hibbertia humifusa*	2RC-t	V
Dilleniaceae	? *Hibbertia inclusa*	3KC-	W
Dilleniaceae	? *Hibbertia leptopus*	1K	W
Dilleniaceae	*Hibbertia miniata*	2RC-	W
Dilleniaceae	*Hibbertia monticola*	2RC-	Q
Dilleniaceae	*Hibbertia muelleri*	3K	Y
Dilleniaceae	*Hibbertia nitida*	2RC-	N
Dilleniaceae	*Hibbertia paeninsularis*	2E	S
Dilleniaceae	*Hibbertia porongurup*	2KC-	W
Dilleniaceae	*Hibbertia rostellata*	3K	W
Dilleniaceae	*Hibbertia scabra*	2KC-	Y
Dilleniaceae	*Hibbertia silvestris*	2K	W
Dilleniaceae	*Hibbertia sp.1*	2R	Y
Dilleniaceae	*Hibbertia sp.2*	2RCat	N
Dilleniaceae	*Hibbertia sp.3*	2KC-	Q
Dilleniaceae	*Hibbertia spathulata*	2RC-	V
Dioscoreaceae	*Discorea pentaphylla*	2X+	Q
Dipteridaceae	*Dipteris conjugata*	3RC-+	Q
Droseraceae	*Aldrovanda vesiculosa*	3RC-+	WYqN
Droseraceae	*Drosera adelae*	2RC-	Q
Droseraceae	*Drosera fimbriata*	2VCa	W
Droseraceae	*Drosera graniticola*	2RC-	W
Droseraceae	*Drosera marchantii*	2K	W
Droseraceae	*Drosera occidentalis*	2V	W
Droseraceae	? *Drosera omissa*	3K	W
Droseraceae	*Drosera prolifera*	2RC-	Q
Droseraceae	*Drosera schizandra*	2R	Q
Droseraceae	*Drosera* sp.1	2KC-	W
Ebenaceae	*Diospyros mabacea*	2ECi	N
Ebenaceae	*Diospyros* sp.1	2RC-	Q
Ebenaceae	*Diospyros* sp.2	2R	Q
Ehretiaceae	*Ehretia microphylla*	2K+	Q
Ehretiaceae	*Ehretia* sp.1	3K	Q
Elaeocarpaceae	*Aceratium ferrugineum*	2R	Q
Elaeocarpaceae	*Aceratium sericoleopsis*	2R	Q
Elaeocarpaceae	*Elaeocarpus carolinae*	3R	Q
Elaeocarpaceae	*Elaeocarpus coorangooloo*	3R	Q
Elaeocarpaceae	*Elaeocarpus linsmithii*	2RC-	Q
Elaeocarpaceae	*Elaeocarpus* sp.1	2RC-	Q
Elaeocarpaceae	*Elaeocarpus thelmae*	2E	Q
Elaeocarpaceae	*Elaeocarpus williamsonianus*	2E	N
Elaeocarpaceae	*Peripentadenia mearsii*	2R	Q
Elaeocarpaceae	*Peripentadenia phelpsii*	2RC-	Q
Epacridaceae	*Acrotriche baileyana*	2RC-	Q
Epacridaceae	*Acrotriche halmaturina*	2RCa	S
Epacridaceae	*Acrotriche plurilocularis*	3RC-	W
Epacridaceae	*Andersonia auriculata*	2K	W
Epacridaceae	*Andersonia axilliflora*	2RC-t	W
Epacridaceae	*Andersonia barbata*	3K	W
Epacridaceae	*Andersonia bifida*	2X	W
Epacridaceae	*Andersonia carinata*	3K	W
Epacridaceae	*Andersonia echinocephala*	3RC-	W
Epacridaceae	*Andersonia grandiflora*	2RC-	W
Epacridaceae	*Andersonia longifolia*	1X	W
Epacridaceae	*Andersonia macranthera*	3VC-	W
Epacridaceae	*Andersonia micrantha*	3KC-	W
Epacridaceae	*Andersonia setifolia*	3K	W
Epacridaceae	*Astroloma foliosum*	2K	W
Epacridaceae	? *Choristemon humilis*	1X	V
Epacridaceae	*Coleanthera coelophylla*	3X	W
Epacridaceae	*Coleanthera virgata*	3X	W
Epacridaceae	? *Conostephium minus*	2K	W
Epacridaceae	*Conostephium sp.1*	2V	W
Epacridaceae	*Cyathodes nitida*	2VCa	T
Epacridaceae	*Cyathodes pendulosa*	3RCi	T
Epacridaceae	*Dracophyllum sayeri*	2RC-	Q
Epacridaceae	*Epacris acuminata*	3KCi	T
Epacridaceae	*Epacris apiculata*	2RCa	N
Epacridaceae	*Epacris apsleyensis*	2R	T
Epacridaceae	*Epacris barbata*	2VCa	T
Epacridaceae	*Epacris coriaceae*	3RC-	N
Epacridaceae	*Epacris exserta*	3RCa	T
Epacridaceae	*Epacris grandis*	2V	T
Epacridaceae	*Epacris hamiltonii*	2E	N
Epacridaceae	*Epacris marginata*	2RCa	T
Epacridaceae	*Epacris mucronulata*	3RCa	T
Epacridaceae	*Epacris muelleri*	3RC-	N
Epacridaceae	*Epacris navicularis*	3RCa	T
Epacridaceae	*Epacris stuartii*	2VCit	T
Epacridaceae	*Epacris virgata*	2V	T
Epacridaceae	*Leucopogon alternifolius*	3K	W
Epacridaceae	*Leucopogon amplectens*	3K	W
Epacridaceae	*Leucopogon apiculatus*	3RC-	W
Epacridaceae	*Leucopogon blepharolepis*	3KC-	W
Epacridaceae	*Leucopogon bracteolaris*	3K	W
Epacridaceae	*Leucopogon brevicuspis*	2KC-	W
Epacridaceae	*Leucopogon breviflorus*	3KC-	W
Epacridaceae	*Leucopogon compactus*	3KC-	W
Epacridaceae	? *Leucopogon confertus*	2V	N
Epacridaceae	*Leucopogon cordatus*	3K	W
Epacridaceae	*Leucopogon crassiflorus*	2RC-	W
Epacridaceae	*Leucopogon cryptanthus*	1X	W
Epacridaceae	*Leucopogon decussatus*	2RC-	W
Epacridaceae	*Leucopogon denticulatus*	3KC-	W
Epacridaceae	*Leucopogon durus*	2K	W
Epacridaceae	*Leucopogon exolasius*	2VC-	N
Epacridaceae	*Leucopogon fletcheri*	3RC-	N
Epacridaceae	*Leucopogon florulentus*	2K	W
Epacridaceae	*Leucopogon glaucifolius*	3K	W
Epacridaceae	*Leucopogon interruptus*	2RC-	W
Epacridaceae	*Leucopogon lasiophyllus*	1K	W
Epacridaceae	*Leucopogon malayanus*	3RC-+	Q
Epacridaceae	*Leucopogon mollis*	2RC-t	W
Epacridaceae	*Leucopogon multiflorus*	3RC-	W

Family	Species	Threat Code	States
Epacridaceae	*Leucopogon neurophyllus*	2VCa	V
Epacridaceae	*? Leucopogon nutans*	3KC-	W
Epacridaceae	*Leucopogon obtectus*	2VCi	W
Epacridaceae	*Leucopogon opponens*	3KC-	W
Epacridaceae	*? Leucopogon ozothamnoides*	3K	W
Epacridaceae	*Leucopogon planifolius*	3K	W
Epacridaceae	*Leucopogon pleurandroides*	1KC-	W
Epacridaceae	*Leucopogon plumuliflorus*	2V	W
Epacridaceae	*Leucopogon pogonocalyx*	2RC-	W
Epacridaceae	*Leucopogon polystachyus*	2K	W
Epacridaceae	*Leucopogon pubescens*	3KC-	W
Epacridaceae	*Leucopogon recurvisepalus*	3RC-	QN
Epacridaceae	*Leucopogon riparius*	2RCa	V
Epacridaceae	*Leucopogon rotundifolius*	3RC-	W
Epacridaceae	*Leucopogon rupicolus*	2RC-	Q
Epacridaceae	*Leucopogon sonderensis*	3R	Y
Epacridaceae	*Leucopogon* sp.1	1V	W
Epacridaceae	*Leucopogon* sp.2	1V	W
Epacridaceae	*Leucopogon* sp.3	2V	W
Epacridaceae	*Leucopogon* sp.4	3VC-	Q
Epacridaceae	*Leucopogon* sp.5	2RC-	Q
Epacridaceae	*Leucopogon* sp.6	3RC-	Q
Epacridaceae	*Leucopogon* sp.7	2K	Q
Epacridaceae	*Leucopogon strongylophyllus*	2KC-	W
Epacridaceae	*Leucopogon tamariscinus*	3KC-	W
Epacridaceae	*Lissanthe sapida*	3RCa	N
Epacridaceae	*Lysinema elegans*	2E	W
Epacridaceae	*Lysinema fimbriatum*	2K	W
Epacridaceae	*Lysinema lasianthum*	2K	W
Epacridaceae	*Monotoca ledifolia*	3RC-	N
Epacridaceae	*Monotoca leucantha*	2K	W
Epacridaceae	*Monotoca linifolia*	2RCa	T
Epacridaceae	*Monotoca rotundifolia*	3RCi	NV
Epacridaceae	*Monotoca* sp.1	3RCa	T
Epacridaceae	*Monotoca* sp.2	2RCat	W
Epacridaceae	*Pentachondra ericifolia*	3R	T
Epacridaceae	*Rupicola gnidioides*	2VC-t	N
Epacridaceae	*Rupicola* sp.1	2R	N
Epacridaceae	*Rupicola sprengelioides*	2RC-t	N
Epacridaceae	*Sphenotoma drummondii*	2RC-t	W
Epacridaceae	*Sprengelia distichophylla*	2RCa	T
Epacridaceae	*Sprengelia monticola*	2RC-t	N
Epacridaceae	*Styphelia pulchella*	3KC-	W
Epacridaceae	*Styphelia* sp. 1	3RC-	N
Epacridaceae	*Trochocarpa bellendenkerensis*	3RC-	Q
Epacridaceae	*Trochocarpa disticha*	2RC-	T
Epacridaceae	*Trochocarpa parviflora*	2KC-	W
Ericaceae	*Agapetes meiniana*	3RC-	Q
Ericaceae	*Pernettya lanceolata*	3RCi	T
Ericaceae	*Rhododendron lochae*	3RC-	Q
Eriocaulaceae	*Eriocaulon australasicum*	2VCa	nV
Eriocaulaceae	*Eriocaulon bifistulosum*	2K	Q
Eriocaulaceae	*Eriocaulon carsonii*	3E	SN
Eriocaulaceae	*Eriocaulon fistulosum*	2R	Q
Eriocaulaceae	*? Eriocaulon graphitinum*	1K	Y
Eriocaulaceae	*Eriocaulon pusillum*	2V	Q
Erythroxylaceae	*Erythroxylum ecarinatum*	2RC-+	Q
Escalloniaceae	*Argophyllum cryptophlebum*	3RC-	Q
Escalloniaceae	*Argophyllum nullumense*	3RCa	QN
Escalloniaceae	*Corokia whiteana*	2VCi	N
Escalloniaceae	*Polyosma rigidiuscula*	3RC-	Q
Escalloniaceae	*Polyosma* sp.1	2KC-	Q
Escalloniaceae	*Polyosma* sp.2	2K	Q
Escalloniaceae	*Quintinia quatrefagesii*	3RC-	Q
Eucryphiaceae	*Eucryphia* sp.1	2KC-	Q
Euphorbiaceae	*Actephila foetida*	2RC-	Q
Euphorbiaceae	*Actephila sessilifolia*	3R	Q
Euphorbiaceae	*Amperea protensa*	2X	W
Euphorbiaceae	*Amperea spicata*	2RCa	Y
Euphorbiaceae	*Amperea volubilis*	2VC-	W
Euphorbiaceae	*Austrobuxus nitidus*	2R+	Q
Euphorbiaceae	*Austrobuxus swainii*	3RCa	QN
Euphorbiaceae	*Baloghia marmorata*	3VC-	QN
Euphorbiaceae	*Bertya astrotricha*	2RC-	N
Euphorbiaceae	*Bertya findlayi*	3RCa	NV
Euphorbiaceae	*Bertya opponens*	3VC-	Q
Euphorbiaceae	*Bertya pedicellata*	3RC-	Q
Euphorbiaceae	*Bertya pinifolia*	3RC-	Q
Euphorbiaceae	*Bertya polystigma*	2RC-	Q
Euphorbiaceae	*Bertya* sp.1	2VCit	N
Euphorbiaceae	*Bertya* sp.2	2E	Q
Euphorbiaceae	*Beyeria bickertonensis*	3K	Y
Euphorbiaceae	*Beyeria cinerea*	2K	W
Euphorbiaceae	*Beyeria cygnorum*	1X	W
Euphorbiaceae	*Beyeria gardneri*	2K	W
Euphorbiaceae	*Beyeria latifolia*	3RCa	W
Euphorbiaceae	*Beyeria lepidopetala*	1X	W
Euphorbiaceae	*Beyeria subtecta*	2VCa	S
Euphorbiaceae	*Calycopeplus marginatus*	2RC-t	W
Euphorbiaceae	*Choriceras majus*	2R	Q
Euphorbiaceae	*Cleistanthus discolor*	2R	Q
Euphorbiaceae	*Croton byrnesii*	3RC-	Y
Euphorbiaceae	*Croton densivestitus*	2RC-	Q
Euphorbiaceae	*Croton magneticus*	2VC-	Q
Euphorbiaceae	*Croton* sp.	1K	Y

Family	Species	Threat Code	States
Euphorbiaceae	*Croton* sp.	1KC-t	W
Euphorbiaceae	*Croton stockeri*	2R	Q
Euphorbiaceae	*Croton storckii*	2R	Q
Euphorbiaceae	*Croton tomentellus*	3R	YQ
Euphorbiaceae	*Euphorbia carissoides*	2X	Q
Euphorbiaceae	*Euphorbia clementii*	1K	W
Euphorbiaceae	*Euphorbia inappendiculata*	1K	W
Euphorbiaceae	*Euphorbia petala*	3K	Y
Euphorbiaceae	*Euphorbia plumerioides*	3K	Q
Euphorbiaceae	*? Euphorbia pubicaulis*	3K	Y
Euphorbiaceae	*Euphorbia sarcostemmoides*	3RCa	WYQn
Euphorbiaceae	*Fontainea australis*	2E	N
Euphorbiaceae	*Fontainea oraria*	2E	N
Euphorbiaceae	*Fontainea picrosperma*	2RC-	Q
Euphorbiaceae	*Fontainea rostrata*	2E	Q
Euphorbiaceae	*Fontainea venosa*	3V	Q
Euphorbiaceae	*Glochidion pungens*	2R	Q
Euphorbiaceae	*Macaranga dallachyanus*	2K	Q
Euphorbiaceae	*Macaranga polyadenia*	3KC-+	Q
Euphorbiaceae	*Margaritaria indica*	3RC-+	Q
Euphorbiaceae	*Neoroepera buxifolia*	2V	Q
Euphorbiaceae	*Phyllanthus aridus*	1K	W
Euphorbiaceae	*Phyllanthus brassii*	3RC-	Q
Euphorbiaceae	*Phyllanthus distichus*	2R	Q
Euphorbiaceae	*Phyllanthus eboracens*	2K	Q
Euphorbiaceae	*Phyllanthus indigoferoides*	3K	W
Euphorbiaceae	*Phyllanthus sauropodoides*	2R	Q
Euphorbiaceae	*Pimelodendron amboinicum*	2R+	Q
Euphorbiaceae	*Pseudanthus divaricatissimus*	3RCa	NV
Euphorbiaceae	*Pseudanthus micranthus*	2RCa	S
Euphorbiaceae	*Pseudanthus nematophorus*	1X	W
Euphorbiaceae	*Ricinocarpos gloria-medii*	2VCat	Y
Euphorbiaceae	*Ricinocarpos marginatus*	2K	W
Euphorbiaceae	*Ricinocarpos trichophorus*	3VCi	W
Euphorbiaceae	*Rockinghamia brevipes*	2RC-	Q
Euphorbiaceae	*Sauropus huntii*	3R	Y
Euphorbiaceae	*Sauropus macranthus*	2V	Q
Euphorbiaceae	*Sauropus ramosissimus*	3RC-	YSQN
Euphorbiaceae	*Sauropus rigidulus*	1K	Y
Euphorbiaceae	*Stachystemon axillaris*	3VC-	W
Euphorbiaceae	*Trigonostemon inopinatus*	2V	Q
Euphorbiaceae	*Whyanbeelia terrae-reginae*	3R	Q
Fabaceae	*Aotus carinata*	2V	W
Fabaceae	*Aotus cordifolia*	2KC-	W
Fabaceae	*Aotus passerinoides*	2K	W
Fabaceae	*Aotus phylicoides*	2RC-	W
Fabaceae	*Bossiaea disticha*	2V	W
Fabaceae	*Bossiaea divaricata*	3E	W
Fabaceae	*Bossiaea oligosperma*	2V	N
Fabaceae	*Bossiaea* sp.	2K	Q
Fabaceae	*Bossiaea strigillosa*	2K	W
Fabaceae	*Brachysema bracteolosum*	3RC-	W
Fabaceae	*Brachysema* sp.1	3KC-	W
Fabaceae	*Brachysema subcordatum*	2RC-	W
Fabaceae	*Brachysema tomentosum*	3RC-	W
Fabaceae	*Brachysema uniflorum*	3RC-	Y
Fabaceae	*Burtonia asperula*	2V	W
Fabaceae	*Cajanus mareebensis*	2E	Q
Fabaceae	*Chorizema* sp.1	3V	W
Fabaceae	*Chorizema varium*	2X	W
Fabaceae	*Daviesia anceps*	2RCa	W
Fabaceae	*Daviesia arthropoda*	3RCa	WYSQ
Fabaceae	*Daviesia crenulata*	2RC-	W
Fabaceae	*Daviesia debilior*	3V	W
Fabaceae	*Daviesia dielsii*	2E	W
Fabaceae	*Daviesia discolor*	3VC-	Q
Fabaceae	*Daviesia elongata*	3V	W
Fabaceae	*Daviesia epiphyllum*	2V	W
Fabaceae	*Daviesia eremaea*	3K	Y
Fabaceae	*Daviesia euphorbioides*	2V	W
Fabaceae	*Daviesia mesophylla*	2RC-t	W
Fabaceae	*Daviesia microphylla*	2VC-	W
Fabaceae	*Daviesia mollis*	3RC-	W
Fabaceae	*Daviesia obovata*	2VC-t	W
Fabaceae	*Daviesia oppositifolia*	2RC-	W
Fabaceae	*Daviesia ovata*	2VCi	W
Fabaceae	*Daviesia pachyloma*	3RC-	W
Fabaceae	*Daviesia pectinata*	3RC-	SV
Fabaceae	*Daviesia polyphylla*	3RC-	W
Fabaceae	*Daviesia purpurascens*	3E	W
Fabaceae	*Daviesia quadrilatera*	3RC-	W
Fabaceae	*Daviesia* sp.	3RCa	N
Fabaceae	*Daviesia* sp.1	1KC-t	W
Fabaceae	*Daviesia* sp.10	3K	W
Fabaceae	*Daviesia* sp.11	3RC-	W
Fabaceae	*Daviesia* sp.12	2RC-t	W
Fabaceae	*Daviesia* sp.13	3V	W
Fabaceae	*Daviesia* sp.14	3RC-	W
Fabaceae	*Daviesia* sp.15	2E	W
Fabaceae	*Daviesia* sp.16	2V	W
Fabaceae	*Daviesia* sp.17	2VC-	W
Fabaceae	*Daviesia* sp.18	2V	W
Fabaceae	*Daviesia* sp.19	2VCit	W
Fabaceae	*Daviesia* sp.2	2E	W
Fabaceae	*Daviesia* sp.20	2VCit	W

Family	Species	Threat Code	States
Fabaceae	*Daviesia* sp.21	3VC-	W
Fabaceae	*Daviesia* sp.22	2VCi	W
Fabaceae	*Daviesia* sp.23	2E	W
Fabaceae	*Daviesia* sp.24	2VCi	W
Fabaceae	*Daviesia* sp.3	2VC-	W
Fabaceae	*Daviesia* sp.4	3VCat	W
Fabaceae	*Daviesia* sp.5	2E	W
Fabaceae	*Daviesia* sp.6	3KC-	W
Fabaceae	*Daviesia* sp.7	3KC-	W
Fabaceae	*Daviesia* sp.8	3RC-	W
Fabaceae	*Daviesia* sp.9	2VC-	W
Fabaceae	*Daviesia spinosissima*	3RC-	W
Fabaceae	*Daviesia spiralis*	2VCi	W
Fabaceae	*Daviesia striata*	2RCa	W
Facaeae	*Daviesia stricta*	3RC-	S
Fabaceae	*Daviesia trigonophylla*	2RC-	W
Fabaceae	*Derris koolgibberah*	2K+	Q
Fabaceae	*Desmodium acanthocladum*	2V	N
Fabaceae	*Desmodium macrocarpum*	3K	Q
Fabaceae	*Dillwynia acerosa*	3K	W
Fabaceae	*? Dillwynia capitata*	2RC-	V
Fabaceae	*Dillwynia divaricata*	3KC-	W
Fabaceae	*Dillwynia* sp.	2RC-	N
Fabaceae	*Dillwynia* sp.	2RC-t	N
Fabaceae	*Dillwynia stipulifera*	3RCi	N
Fabaceae	*Dillwynia tenuifolia*	2VCi	N
Fabaceae	*Dioclea reflexa*	3V	Q
Fabaceae	*Erichsenia uncinata*	2RC-	W
Fabaceae	*Gastrolobium appressum*	2V	W
Fabaceae	*Gastrolobium brownii*	2K	W
Fabaceae	*Gastrolobium crenulatum*	2KC-	W
Fabaceae	*Gastrolobium epacridioides*	2KC-	W
Fabaceae	*Gastrolobium glaucum*	2V	W
Fabaceae	*Gastrolobium hamulosum*	2E	W
Fabaceae	*Gastrolobium ilicifolium*	2K	W
Fabaceae	*Gastrolobium lehmannii*	2X	W
Fabaceae	*Gastrolobium ovalifolium*	2E	W
Fabaceae	*Gastrolobium propinquum*	3E	W
Fabaceae	*Gastrolobium pyramidale*	2RC-	W
Fabaceae	*Gastrolobium rotundifolium*	3E	W
Fabaceae	*Gastrolobium stenophyllum*	2RC-	W
Fabaceae	*Gastrolobium stipulare*	2VCi	W
Fabaceae	*Gastrolobium tomentosum*	2V	W
Fabaceae	*Glycine argyrea*	2RCa	Q
Fabaceae	*Glycine latrobeana*	3RCa	SVT
Fabaceae	*Glycine* sp.1	2K	W
Fabaceae	*Glycine* sp.2	2K	Y
Fabaceae	*Glycine* sp.3	2K	W
Fabaceae	*Glycine* sp.4	2K	W
Fabaceae	*Gompholobium burtonioides*	3KC-	W
Fabaceae	*Gompholobium eatoniae*	2K	W
Fabaceae	*Hardenbergia* sp.1	2K	Q
Fabaceae	*Hovea acanthoclada*	3RCa	W
Fabaceae	*Indigofera efoliata*	2V	N
Fabaceae	*Isotropis canescens*	3K	W
Fabaceae	*Isotropis foliosa*	2V	Q
Fabaceae	*Isotropis forrestii*	3K	W
Fabaceae	*Isotropis winneckei*	3K	Y
Fabaceae	*Jacksonia calycina*	2RC-	W
Fabaceae	*Jacksonia carduacea*	2KC-	W
Fabaceae	*Jacksonia mollissima*	3K	W
Fabaceae	*Jacksonia* sp.1	3KC-	W
Fabaceae	*Jacksonia stricta*	1K	W
Fabaceae	*Jacksonia velutina*	2K	W
Fabaceae	*Jansonia formosa*	3RC-	W
Fabaceae	*Kennedia beckxiana*	2VCi	W
Fabaceae	*Kennedia exaltata*	1K	Q
Fabaceae	*Kennedia glabrata*	2V	W
Fabaceae	*Kennedia macrophylla*	2VCi	W
Fabaceae	*Kennedia retrorsa*	2VCa	N
Fabaceae	*Latrobea brunonis*	2K	W
Fabaceae	*Latrobea diosmifolia*	2K	W
Fabaceae	*Leptosema* sp.1	3K	Q
Fabaceae	*Millettia australis*	3VC-+	QN
Fabaceae	*Millettia pilipes*	3RC-+	Q
Fabaceae	*Millettia* sp.1	2K	Q
Fabaceae	*Mirbelia confertiflora*	3RC-	Q
Fabaceae	*Mirbelia densiflora*	1X	W
Fabaceae	*Mirbelia stipitata*	1K	W
Fabaceae	*Muelleranthus crenulatus*	1K	W
Fabaceae	*Nemcia* sp.1	2RC-t	W
Fabaceae	*Nemcia* sp.2	2RC-	W
Fabaceae	*Nemcia vestita*	2RC-t	W
Fabaceae	*Ormocarpum cochinchinense*	3K+	Q
Fabaceae	*Oxylobium acutum*	2X	W
Fabaceae	*Oxylobium heterophyllum*	3KC-	W
Fabaceae	*Oxylobium racemosum*	2RCa	W
Fabaceae	*Oxylobium rigidum*	2RCi	W
Fabaceae	*Oxylobium* sp.	3RC-	N
Fabaceae	*Phyllodium pulchellum*	3R+	Q
Fabaceae	*Phyllota gracilis*	3KC-	W
Fabaceae	*Phyllota humifusa*	2ECa	N
Fabaceae	*Plagiocarpus axillaris*	3K	WY
Fabaceae	*Platylobium alternifolium*	2RC-	V
Fabaceae	*Psoralea archeri*	3E	WY

Family	Species	Threat Code	States
Fabaceae	*Psoralea parva*	3ECi	SnV
Fabaceae	*Psoralea walkingtonii*	3V	WY
Fabaceae	*Pterocarpus* sp.1	2KC-	Q
Fabaceae	*Ptychosema pusillum*	2E	W
Fabaceae	*Pultenaea aristata*	2VC-	N
Fabaceae	*Pultenaea baeuerlenii*	2VCit	N
Fabaceae	*Pultenaea calycina*	3RC-	W
Fabaceae	*Pultenaea cambagei*	3RC-	QN
Fabaceae	*Pultenaea campbellii*	3V	N
Fabaceae	*Pultenaea costata*	2RCa	V
Fabaceae	*Pultenaea glabra*	3VCa	N
Fabaceae	*Pultenaea incurvata*	2RC-t	N
Fabaceae	*Pultenaea maidenii*	2RC-	V
Fabaceae	*Pultenaea parviflora*	2V	N
Fabaceae	*Pultenaea patellifolia*	2RC-t	V
Fabaceae	*Pultenaea pauciflora*	2V	W
Fabaceae	*Pultenaea pinifolia*	2K	W
Fabaceae	*Pultenaea pycnophylla*	3RCa	QN
Fabaceae	*Pultenaea radiata*	2K	W
Fabaceae	*Pultenaea selaginoides*	2V	T
Fabaceae	*Pultenaea setulosa*	2V	Q
Fabaceae	*Pultenaea skinneri*	2V	W
Fabaceae	*Pultenaea* sp.1	2VCit	N
Fabaceae	*Pultenaea* sp.2	2E	Q
Fabaceae	*Pultenaea* sp.3	2K	Q
Fabaceae	*Pultenaea* sp.4	2RC-	N
Fabaceae	*Pultenaea spinulosa*	3KCi	W
Fabaceae	*Pultenaea stuartiana*	3VC-	QN
Fabaceae	*Pultenaea subalpina*	2RC-t	V
Fabaceae	*Pultenaea trichophylla*	2E	S
Fabaceae	*Pultenaea trifida*	2RCa	S
Fabaceae	*Pultenaea villifera*	3RC-	N
Fabaceae	*Pultenaea viscidula*	3RC-	S
Fabaceae	*Pultenaea weindorferi*	3RCa	V
Fabaceae	*Pultenaea whiteana*	2RC-t	Q
Fabaceae	*Pultenaea williamsoniana*	2VC-t	V
Fabaceae	*Rhynchosia rostrata*	1K	W
Fabaceae	*Sesbania erubescens*	3R+	WYQ
Fabaceae	*Sophora fraseri*	3VC-	QN
Fabaceae	*Sphaerolobium alatum*	3RC-	W
Fabaceae	*Sphaerolobium nudiflorum*	3RC-	W
Fabaceae	*Strongylodon ruber*	2R+	Q
Fabaceae	*Swainsona dictyocarpa*	1K	S
Fabaceae	*Swainsona drummondii*	2K	W
Fabaceae	*Swainsona laxa*	3VCa	SNV
Fabaceae	*Swainsona leeana*	3K	WS
Fabaceae	*Swainsona microcalyx*	3K	YSNV
Fabaceae	*Swainsona minutiflora*	3V	S
Fabaceae	*Swainsona murrayana*	3V	SNV
Fabaceae	*Swainsona pedunculata*	3K	W
Fabaceae	*Swainsona plagiotropis*	3ECi	NV
Fabaceae	*Swainsona recta*	3ECi	Nv
Fabaceae	*Swainsona tephrotricha*	3KC-	S
Fabaceae	*Swainsona viridis*	3K	SN
Fabaceae	*Templetonia battii*	3K	W
Fabaceae	*Templetonia drummondii*	3KC-	W
Fabaceae	*Templetonia neglecta*	3KC-	W
Fabaceae	*Tephrosia baueri*	3KC-	Qn
Fabaceae	*Tephrosia crocea*	3KC-	WY
Fabaceae	*Tephrosia debilis*	3K	Q
Fabaceae	*Tephrosia leveillei*	3V	Q
Fabaceae	*Tephrosia oligophylla*	2K	Q
Fabaceae	*Tephrosia savannicola*	3V	Q
Fabeceae	*Tephrosia subpectinata*	3KC-	YQ
Fabaceae	*Zornia pallida*	2V	Q
Flacourtiaceae	*Baileyoxylon lanceolatum*	2RC-	Q
Flacourtiaceae	*Casearia grayi*	2R	Q
Flacourtiaceae	*Ryparosa javanica*	2VC-+	Q
Flacourtiaceae	*Xylosma ovatum*	3R	Q
Flacourtiaceae	*Xylosma* sp.1	2K	Q
Flacourtiaceae	*Xylosma terrae-reginae*	3RC-	Q
Flindersiaceae	*Flindersia brassii*	2R	Q
Flindersiaceae	*Flindersia oppositifolia*	3RC-	Q
Frankeniaceae	*Frankenia bracteata*	2K	W
Frankeniaceae	*Frankenia cinerea*	3RCa	WS
Frankeniaceae	*Frankenia conferta*	1X	W
Frankeniaceae	*Frankenia confusa*	2K	W
Frankeniaceae	*Frankenia cupularis*	3K	S
Frankeniaceae	*Frankenia decurrens*	1X	W
Frankeniaceae	*Frankenia drummondii*	2K	W
Frankeniaceae	? *Frankenia flabellata*	3E	SQ
Frankeniaceae	*Frankenia georgii*	2K	W
Frankeniaceae	*Frankenia glomerata*	2K	W
Frankeniaceae	*Frankenia granulata*	2E	S
Frankeniaceae	*Frankenia muscosa*	3K	YS
Frankeniaceae	? *Frankenia orthotricha*	3K	SQ
Frankeniaceae	*Frankenia parvula*	1X	W
Frankeniaceae	*Frankenia plicata*	3E	S
Frankeniaceae	? *Frankenia pseudo-flabellata*	3K	S
Frankeniaceae	*Frankenia stuartii*	1K	Y
Frankeniaceae	*Frankenia subteres*	2K	S
Gentianaceae	*Gentiana baeuerlenii*	1X	N
Gentianaceae	*Gentiana bredboensis*	2V	N
Gentianaceae	*Gentiana wingecarribiensis*	2E	N
Gentianaceae	*Gentiana wissmannii*	2RC-	N
Geraniaceae	*Geranium graniticola*	3RC-	N
Geraniaceae	*Geranium obtusisepalum*	3RC-	N
Gesneriaceae	*Lenbrassia australiana*	2RC-	Q
Gleicheniaceae	*Diplopterygium longissimum*	3RC-+	Q
Gleicheniaceae	*Gleichenia abscida*	3RCa	T
Gleicheniaceae	*Gleichenia milnei*	2R+	Q
Goodeniaceae	*Calogyne quadrifida*	2V	Y
Goodeniaceae	*Coopernookia georgei*	2VCit	W
Goodeniaceae	*Coopernookia scabridiuscula*	3RC-	Q
Goodeniaceae	*Dampiera carinata*	3KC-	W
Goodeniaceae	*Dampiera conospermoides*	3K	W
Goodeniaceae	? *Dampiera dielsii*	2K	W
Goodeniaceae	*Dampiera diversifolia*	3RC-	W
Goodeniaceae	*Dampiera eriantha*	1K	W
Goodeniaceae	*Dampiera glabrescens*	2K	W
Goodeniaceae	? *Dampiera helmsii*	1X	W
Goodeniaceae	? *Dampiera humilis*	1X	W
Goodeniaceae	? *Dampiera prostrata*	2K	W
Goodeniaceae	? *Dampiera restiacea*	2K	W
Goodeniaceae	? *Dampiera rupicola*	1X	W
Goodeniaceae	*Goodenia anfracta*	2K	Ws
Goodeniaceae	*Goodenia angustifolia*	3R	Q
Goodeniaceae	*Goodenia arthrotricha*	2K	W
Goodeniaceae	? *Goodenia bariletii*	2K	W
Goodeniaceae	? *Goodenia calogynoides*	3K	W
Goodeniaceae	*Goodenia chambersii*	3R	S
Goodeniaceae	? *Goodenia clementii*	1X	W
Goodeniaceae	*Goodenia faucium*	2R	Y
Goodeniaceae	*Goodenia glomerata*	2RCa	N
Goodeniaceae	*Goodenia lobata*	3K	S
Goodeniaceae	*Goodenia megasepala*	2V	Q
Goodeniaceae	*Goodenia nuda*	3K	W
Goodeniaceae	? *Goodenia propinqua*	2K	W
Goodeniaceae	*Goodenia quadrilocularis*	2KC-	W
Goodeniaceae	*Goodenia rostrivalvis*	2RCa	N
Goodeniaceae	*Goodenia rupestris*	2R	Y
Goodeniaceae	*Goodenia schwerinensis*	3K	WY
Goodeniaceae	*Goodenia sericostachya*	2K	W
Goodeniaceae	*Goodenia* sp.1	2R	Q
Goodeniaceae	*Goodenia* sp.2	2KC-	Q
Goodeniaceae	*Goodenia* sp.3	3R	Q
Goodeniaceae	*Goodenia* sp.4	1K	W
Goodeniaceae	*Goodenia stenophylla*	2KC-	W
Goodeniaceae	*Goodenia trichophylla*	3K	W
Goodeniaceae	*Goodenia xanthotricha*	2KC-	W
Goodeniaceae	*Isotoma luticola*	3R	Y
Goodeniaceae	*Lechenaultia acutiloba*	2RC-	W
Goodeniaceae	*Lechenaultia chlorantha*	2VCi	W
Goodeniaceae	*Lechenaultia juncea*	2V	W
Goodeniaceae	*Lechenaultia laricina*	2V	W
Goodeniaceae	*Lechenaultia longiloba*	2VC-	W
Goodeniaceae	*Lechenaultia pulvinaris*	3VCa	W
Goodeniaceae	*Lechenaultia* sp.1	1K	Y
Goodeniaceae	*Lechenaultia superba*	2RCat	W
Goodeniaceae	*Neogoodenia minutiflora*	3V	W
Goodeniaceae	*Nigromnia globosa*	3E	W
Goodeniaceae	*Scaevola attenuata*	2X	W
Goodeniaceae	*Scaevola brookeana*	2RC-	W
Goodeniaceae	*Scaevola cunninghamii*	1K	W
Goodeniaceae	*Scaevola hamiltonii*	2K	W
Goodeniaceae	*Scaevola linearis*	3K	W
Goodeniaceae	*Scaevola macrophylla*	2X	W
Goodeniaceae	*Scaevola myrtifolia*	3KC-	W
Goodeniaceae	*Scaevola oldfieldii*	2X	W
Goodeniaceae	*Scaevola stenostachya*	1K	W
Goodeniaceae	? *Scaevola tortuosa*	3K	W
Goodeniaceae	*Selliera exigua*	2K	W
Goodeniaceae	*Velleia foliosa*	2RC-t	W
Goodeniaceae	*Velleia perfoliata*	2RC-	N
Goodeniaceae	*Verreauxia verreauxii*	2K	W
Goodeniaceae	*Verreauxia villosa*	3K	W
Grammitidaceae	*Ctenopteris blechnoides*	2V+	Q
Grammitidaceae	*Ctenopteris repandula*	2K+	Q
Grammitidaceae	*Grammitis albosetosa*	2RC-	Q
Grammitidaceae	*Grammitis pseudociliata*	2RCi+	T
Grammitidaceae	*Grammitis reinwardtii*	2VC-+	Q
Guttiferеae	*Calophyllum bicolor*	3VC-+	Q
Guttiferеae	*Garcinia brassii*	2RC-	Q
Guttiferеae	*Garcinia gibbsiae*	2RC-	Q
Guttiferеae	*Garcinia mestonii*	2RC-	Q
Guttiferеae	*Garcinia* sp.1	3K	Q
Guttiferеae	*Mammea touriga*	2RC-	Q
Guttiferеae	*Mesua larnachiana*	2RC-	Q
Guttiferеae	*Mesua* sp.1	2V	Q
Gyrostemonaceae	*Codonocarpus pyramidalis*	3RC-	Sn
Gyrostemonaceae	*Cypselocarpus haloragoides*	3KC-	W
Gyrostemonaceae	*Gyrostemon brownii*	3K	W
Gyrostemonaceae	*Gyrostemon ditrigynus*	2V	W
Gyrostemonaceae	*Gyrostemon prostratus*	3ECi	W
Gyrostemonaceae	*Gyrostemon reticulatus*	3V	W
Gyrostemonaceae	*Gyrostemon sessilis*	2RC-t	W
Gyrostemonaceae	*Walteranthus erectus*	2KC-	W
Haemodoraceae	*Anigozanthos gabrielae*	2RC-	W
Haemodoraceae	*Anigozanthos kalbarriensis*	2RC-	W
Haemodoraceae	*Anigozanthos onycis*	2RC-	W
Haemodoraceae	*Conostylis deplexa*	2KC-	W
Haemodoraceae	*Conostylis dielsii*	2V	W
Haemodoraceae	*Conostylis drummondii*	2VCi	W
Haemodoraceae	*Conostylis lepidospermoides*	2VC-	W
Haemodoraceae	*Conostylis micrantha*	2V	W
Haemodoraceae	*Conostylis misera*	2VCi	W
Haemodoraceae	*Conostylis rogeri*	2VCi	W
Haemodoraceae	*Conostylis wonganensis*	2VCi	W
Haemodoraceae	*Haemodorum brevisepalum*	3VC-	W
Haemodoraceae	*Haemodorum distichophyllum*	2RCa	T
Haemodoraceae	*Phlebocarya pilosissima*	2K	W
Haemodoraceae	*Tribonanthes purpurea*	2VCi	W
Haloragaceae	*Gonocarpus cordiger*	3V	W
Haloragaceae	? *Gonocarpus diffusus*	3K	W
Haloragaceae	*Gonocarpus effusus*	2RC-t	Q
Haloragaceae	*Gonocarpus ephemerus*	1K	W
Haloragaceae	*Gonocarpus ericifolius*	1K	W
Haloragaceae	*Gonocarpus hexandrus*	2K	W
Haloragaceae	*Gonocarpus hispidus*	1KC-t	W
Haloragaceae	*Gonocarpus implexus*	3RC-	WY
Haloragaceae	*Gonocarpus intricatus*	3X	W
Haloragaceae	*Gonocarpus longifolius*	3RC-	QN
Haloragaceae	*Gonocarpus pithyoides*	3K	W
Haloragaceae	*Gonocarpus pusillus*	2K	W
Haloragaceae	*Gonocarpus pycnostachyus*	1K	W
Haloragaceae	*Gonocarpus rudis*	2VC-	W
Haloragaceae	*Gonocarpus salsoloides*	3RCa	N
Haloragaceae	*Gonocarpus scordioides*	2RC-	W
Haloragaceae	*Gonocarpus simplex*	2V	W
Haloragaceae	*Gonocarpus trichostachyus*	3KCa	W
Haloragaceae	*Gonocarpus urceolatus*	2V	Q
Haloragaceae	*Haloragis aculeolata*	3K	W
Haloragaceae	*Haloragis digyna*	3V	W
Haloragaceae	*Haloragis eichleri*	3RCa	S
Haloragaceae	*Haloragis exalata*	3VCa	QNV
Haloragaceae	*Haloragis eyreana*	2E	S
Haloragaceae	*Haloragis foliosa*	2K	W
Haloragaceae	*Haloragis hamata*	3K	W
Haloragaceae	*Haloragis platycarpa*	2K	W
Haloragaceae	*Haloragis scoparia*	2K	W
Haloragaceae	*Haloragis* sp.1	1K	W
Haloragaceae	*Haloragis stricta*	3VC-	Qn
Haloragaceae	*Haloragis tenuifolia*	2X	W
Haloragaceae	*Haloragodendron baeuerlenii*	3RCa	NV
Haloragaceae	*Haloragodendron glandulosum*	3K	W
Haloragaceae	*Haloragodendron lucasii*	2ECi	N
Haloragaceae	*Haloragodendron* sp. 1	2KC-	N
Haloragaceae	*Meziella trifida*	1X	W
Haloragaceae	*Myriophyllum callitrichoides*	3KC-	WY
Haloragaceae	*Myriophyllum coronatum*	2V+	Q
Haloragaceae	*Myriophyllum costatum*	1KC-t	W
Haloragaceae	*Myriophyllum echinatum*	2K	W
Haloragaceae	*Myriophyllum implicatum*	2E	Qn
Haloragaceae	*Myriophyllum patraeum*	3KC-	W
Haloragaceae	*Myriophyllum porcatum*	2VCi	V
Hamamelidaceae	*Neostrearia fleckeri*	3R	Q
Hamamelidaceae	*Noahdendron nicholasii*	2RC-	Q
Hamamelidaceae	*Ostrearia australiana*	2RC-	Q
Hernandiaceae	*Hernandia bivalvis*	3VC-	Q
Hernandiaceae	*Valvanthera albiflora*	2RC-+	Q
Himantandraceae	*Galbulimima belgraveana*	3RC-+	Q
Hydatellaceae	*Hydatella australis*	3VC-	W
Hydatellaceae	*Hydatella dioicia*	2VC-	W
Hydatellaceae	*Hydatella filamentosa*	3RCa	T
Hydatellaceae	? *Hydatella leptogyne*	1X	W
Hydatellaceae	*Trithuria bibracteata*	3K	W
Hydrocharitaceae	*Hydrocharis dubia*	2V	Q
Hydrocharitaceae	*Vallisneria caulescens*	3V	Q
Hymenophyllaceae	*Crepidomanes majorae*	3RC-	Q
Hymenophyllaceae	*Didymoglossum exiguum*	1KC-+	Q
Hymenophyllaceae	*Hymenophyllum eboracense*	2RC-	Q
Hymenophyllaceae	*Hymenophyllum gracilescens*	2RC-	Q
Hymenophyllaceae	*Hymenophyllum kerianum*	3RC-	Q
Hymenophyllaceae	*Hymenophyllum lobbii*	1KC-+	Q
Hymenophyllaceae	*Hymenophyllum pumilum*	3RC-	N
Hymenophyllaceae	*Hymenophyllum whitei*	2RC-	Q
Hymenophyllaceae	*Microgonium mindorense*	2RC-+	Q
Hymenophyllaceae	*Microtrichomanes digitatum*	3RC-+	Q
Hymenophyllaceae	*Pleuromanes pallidum*	3RC-+	Q
Hymenophyllaceae	*Reediella endlicheriana*	2R	Q
Hymenophyllaceae	*Sphaerocionium lyallii*	3RC-+	N
Hymenophyllaceae	*Trichomanes aphlebioides*	2KC-+	Q
Icacinaceae	*Rhyticaryum longifolia*	3R+	Q
Idiospermaceae	*Idiospermum australiense*	3VC-	Q
Iridaceae	*Orthrosanthus muelleri*	2KC-	W
Iridaceae	*Patersonia argyrea*	2R	W
Iridaceae	*Patersonia inaequalis*	3RC-	W
Iridaceae	*Patersonia maxwellii*	3KC-	W
Isoetaceae	*Isoetes brevicula*	1K	W
Juncaginaceae	*Triglochin muelleri*	3K	W
Juncaginaceae	*Triglochin stowardii*	3K	W
Lamiaceae	? *Ajuga sinuata*	2KC-	S
Lamiaceae	*Eichlerago tysoniana*	2K	W
Lamiaceae	*Hemiandra gardneri*	2V	W
Lamiaceae	*Hemiandra linearis*	2K	W

Family	Species	Threat Code	States
Lamiaceae	*Hemiandra rutilans*	2V	W
Lamiaceae	*Hemigenia brachyphylla*	2K	W
Lamiaceae	*Hemigenia clotteniana*	1K	Q
Lamiaceae	*Hemigenia coccinea*	2K	W
Lamiaceae	*Hemigenia conferta*	2V	W
Lamiaceae	*Hemigenia curvifolia*	2K	W
Lamiaceae	*Hemigenia exilis*	1X	W
Lamiaceae	*Hemigenia glabrescens*	2K	W
Lamiaceae	*Hemigenia macrantha*	2KC-	W
Lamiaceae	*Hemigenia obtusa*	2X	W
Lamiaceae	*Hemigenia pimelifolia*	3X	W
Lamiaceae	*Hemigenia platyphylla*	2V	W
Lamiaceae	*Hemigenia podalyrina*	3RC-t	W
Lamiaceae	*Hemigenia ramosissima*	1X	W
Lamiaceae	*Hemigenia saligna*	3K	W
Lamiaceae	*Hemigenia tysonii*	1X	W
Lamiaceae	*Hemigenia viscida*	3VCi	W
Lamiaceae	*Microcorys cephalantha*	2V	W
Lamiaceae	*Microcorys elliptica*	1RC-t	Y
Lamiaceae	*Microcorys eremophiloides*	2VCi	W
Lamiaceae	*Microcorys longiflora*	2RC-	W
Lamiaceae	*Microcorys macrediana*	3K	WY
Lamiaceae	*Microcorys pimeleoides*	2K	W
Lamiaceae	*Microcorys tenuifolia*	2KC-	W
Lamiaceae	*Microcorys virgata*	3K	W
Lamiaceae	*Microcorys wilsoniana*	2V	W
Lamiaceae	*Plectranthus argentatus*	3RC-	Q
Lamiaceae	*Plectranthus spectablis*	2R	Q
Lamiaceae	*Prostanthera albo-hirta*	1K	Q
Lamiaceae	*Prostanthera atroviolaceae*	2R	Q
Lamiaceae	*Prostanthera calycina*	2VCi	S
Lamiaceae	*Prostanthera carrickiana*	2E	W
Lamiaceae	*Prostanthera cineolifera*	3V	N
Lamiaceae	*Prostanthera cruciflora*	2RC-t	N
Lamiaceae	*Prostanthera cryptandroides*	2VC-t	N
Lamiaceae	*Prostanthera densa*	3VC-	N
Lamiaceae	*Prostanthera discolor*	2VC-	N
Lamiaceae	*Prostanthera eurybioides*	3ECi	S
Lamiaceae	*Prostanthera magnifica*	3V	W
Lamiaceae	*Prostanthera monticola*	3RC-	NV
Lamiaceae	*Prostanthera nudula*	2K	S
Lamiaceae	*Prostanthera pedicellata*	2E	W
Lamiaceae	*Prostanthera porcata*	3RC-t	N
Lamiaceae	*Prostanthera scutata*	3E	W
Lamiaceae	*Prostanthera* sp.1	2K	Q
Lamiaceae	*Prostanthera* sp.2	2V	Q
Lamiaceae	*Prostanthera* sp.3	2V	Q
Lamiaceae	*Prostanthera* sp.4	2V	W
Lamiaceae	*Prostanthera stricta*	2V	N
Lamiaceae	*Prostanthera teretifolia*	2V	N
Lamiaceae	*Prostanthera walteri*	3RCa	NV
Lamiaceae	*Teucrium ajugaceum*	2K	Q
Lamiaceae	*Teucrium grandiusculum*	3RC-	WYS
Lamiaceae	*Teucrium hyriocladum*	3KC-	W
Lamiaceae	*Westringia blakeana*	2RCa	QN
Lamiaceae	*Westringia crassifolia*	3E	V
Lamiaceae	*Westringia cremnophila*	2RCa	V
Lamiaceae	*Westringia davidii*	2V	N
Lamiaceae	*Westringia grandifolia*	2RC-	Q
Lamiaceae	*Westringia lucida*	2RC-	N
Lamiaceae	*Westringia parvifolia*	2V	Q
Lamiaceae	? *Westringia raleighii*	3KC-	T
Lamiaceae	*Westringia rupicola*	2RCa	Q
Lamiaceae	*Westringia saxatilis*	2RC-t	N
Lamiaceae	*Wrixonia schultzii*	2VC-	Y
Lauraceae	*Beilschmiedia* sp.1	2RC-	Q
Lauraceae	*Beilschmiedia* sp.2	2RC-	Q
Lauraceae	*Beilschmiedia* sp.3	3RC-	Q
Lauraceae	*Cassytha flava*	3KC-	W
Lauraceae	*Cassytha micrantha*	3RC-	W
Lauraceae	*Cassytha nodiflora*	2K	W
Lauraceae	*Cassytha pedicellosa*	1X	T
Lauraceae	*Cassytha racemosa*	3KC-	W
Lauraceae	*Cinnamomum baileyanum*	3RC-	Q
Lauraceae	*Cinnamomum propinquum*	3RC-	Q
Lauraceae	*Cryptocarya burckiana*	2RC-+	Q
Lauraceae	*Cryptocarya floydii*	3RCi	QN
Lauraceae	*Cryptocarya foetida*	3VCi	QN
Lauraceae	*Cryptocarya* sp.1	2RCa	N
Lauraceae	*Cryptocarya* sp.2	3RCa	N
Lauraceae	*Cryptocarya* sp.3	2RCi	N
Lauraceae	*Cryptocarya* sp.4	3K	Q
Lauraceae	*Cryptocarya* sp.5	3RC-	Q
Lauraceae	*Cryptocarya* sp.6	2R	Q
Lauraceae	*Cryptocarya* sp.7	3RC-	Q
Lauraceae	*Endiandra anthropophagorum*	2RC-	Q
Lauraceae	*Endiandra globosa*	2RC-	QN
Lauraceae	*Endiandra hayesii*	3VC-	QN
Lauraceae	*Endiandra microneura*	2RC-	Q
Lauraceae	*Endiandra palmerstonii*	2RC-	Q
Lauraceae	*Endiandra* sp.1	2E	N
Lauraceae	*Endiandra* sp.2	2RC-	Q
Lauraceae	*Endiandra* sp.3	2RC-	Q
Lauraceae	*Endiandra* sp.4	2R	Q
Lauraceae	*Endiandra* sp.5	2RC-	Q
Lauraceae	*Endiandra* sp.6	3RC-	Q
Lauraceae	*Endiandra* sp.7	2R+	Q
Lauraceae	*Litsea macrophylla*	3R+	Q
Lauraceae	*Litsea* sp.1	3RC-	Q
Lauraceae	*Litsea* sp.2	2RC-	Q
Lentibulariaceae	*Utricularia albiflora*	2K	Q
Lentibulariaceae	*Utricularia cheiranthos*	2K	Y
Lentibulariaceae	*Utricularia helix*	2RCat	W
Lentibulariaceae	*Utricularia holtzei*	2K	Y
Lentibulariaceae	*Utricularia kenneallyi*	1K	W
Lentibulariaceae	*Utricularia rhododactylos*	2RC-t	Y
Lentibulariaceae	*Utricularia singerana*	3K	Wy
Lentibulariaceae	*Utricularia tridactyla*	2K	W
Lentibulariaceae	*Utricularia triflora*	2K	Y
Lentibulariaceae	*Utricularia westonii*	2RCit	W
Liliaceae	*Alania endlicheri*	3RCa	N
Liliaceae	*Arnocrinum drummondii*	2RC-	W
Liliaceae	*Arnocrinum* sp.1	2K	W
Liliaceae	*Arthropodium dianellaceum*	2V	Q
Liliaceae	*Astelia australiana*	2V	V
Liliaceae	*Astelia psychrocharis*	2RCa	N
Liliaceae	*Blandfordia cunninghamii*	3RC-	N
Liliaceae	*Borya jabirabella*	3KC-	WY
Liliaceae	*Borya mirabilis*	2VCit	V
Liliaceae	*Borya scirpoidea*	3R	W
Liliaceae	*Borya subulata*	2V	W
Liliaceae	*Burchardia monantha*	2K	W
Liliaceae	*Dianella* sp.1	2K	Q
Liliaceae	*Hensmania chapmanii*	2V	W
Liliaceae	*Hensmania turbinata*	3K	W
Liliaceae	*Hodgsoniola junciformis*	2K	W
Liliaceae	*Johnsonia inconspicua*	1K	W
Liliaceae	*Laxmannia* sp.1	2V	W
Liliaceae	*Milligania johnstonii*	2RCa	T
Liliaceae	*Milligania longifolia*	2VCi	T
Liliaceae	*Murchisonia fragrans*	2V	W
Liliaceae	*Neoastelia* sp.1	2RC-t	N
Liliaceae	*Sowerbaea multicaulis*	2K	W
Liliaceae	*Sowerbaea subtilis*	2R	Q
Liliaceae	*Stawellia dimorphantha*	2V	W
Liliaceae	*Stawellia gymnocephala*	3KC-	W
Liliaceae	*Thelionema grande*	3RC-	QN
Liliaceae	*Thysanotus acerosifolius*	2EC-	W
Liliaceae	*Thysanotus anceps*	2VC-	W
Liliaceae	*Thysanotus arbuscula*	3K	W
Liliaceae	*Thysanotus brachyantherus*	2RC-	W
Liliaceae	*Thysanotus brevifolius*	2K	W
Liliaceae	*Thysanotus cymosus*	3K	W
Liliaceae	*Thysanotus fastigatus*	2VC-	W
Liliaceae	*Thysanotus formosus*	2V	W
Liliaceae	*Thysanotus fractiflexus*	2RCa	S
Liliaceae	*Thysanotus gageoides*	3VC-	W
Liliaceae	*Thysanotus glaucus*	3E	W
Liliaceae	*Thysanotus gracilis*	3K	W
Liliaceae	*Thysanotus isantherus*	2K	W
Liliaceae	*Thysanotus lavanduliflora*	2K	W
Liliaceae	*Wurmbea drummondii*	3VCi	W
Liliaceae	*Wurmbea murchisoniana*	2V	W
Liliaceae	*Wurmbea tubulosa*	2VCi	W
Lindsaeaceae	*Lindsaea pulchella*	2V+	Q
Lindsaeaceae	*Lindsaea walkerae*	3RC-+	Q
Lobeliaceae	*Hypsela sessiliflora*	2X	N
Lobeliaceae	*Lobelia douglasiana*	1K	Q
Lobeliaceae	*Pratia gelida*	2RC-	V
Lobeliaceae	*Pratia irrigua*	2VC-	T
Lobeliaceae	*Pratia podenzanea*	3R	Q
Loganiaceae	*Logania callosa*	3KC-	W
Loganiaceae	*Logania cordifolia*	3RC-	Q
Loganiaceae	*Logania diffusa*	2VC-	Q
Loganiaceae	*Logania insularis*	2VCa	S
Loganiaceae	*Logania recurva*	3RC-	S
Loganiaceae	*Logania* sp.1	2K	W
Loganiaceae	*Mitrasacme nummularia*	1K	W
Loganiaceae	*Mitrasacme palustris*	2V	W
Lomariopsidaceae	*Elaphoglossum callifolium*	3RC-	Q
Loranthaceae	*Amyema haematodes*	2K	Y
Loranthaceae	*Atkinsonia ligustrina*	2RCa	N
Loranthaceae	*Dactyliophora novae-guineae*	2RC-+	Q
Loranthaceae	*Lysiana filifolia*	3RC-	Q
Loranthaceae	*Muellerina myrtifolia*	3RC-	QN
Lycopodiaceae	*Lycopodium carinatum*	3VC-	Q
Lycopodiaceae	*Lycopodium dalhousieanum*	3E+	Q
Lycopodiaceae	*Lycopodium lockyeri*	3V	Q
Lycopodiaceae	*Lycopodium marsupiiforme*	3R	Q
Lycopodiaceae	*Lycopodium phlegmaria*	3RC-+	QN
Lycopodiaceae	*Lycopodium phlegmarioides*	3RC-+	Q
Lycopodiaceae	*Lycopodium polytrichioides*	3VC-	Q
Lycopodiaceae	*Lycopodium proliferum*	3RC-+	Q
Lycopodiaceae	*Lycopodium serpentinum*	3KC-	Q
Lycopodiaceae	*Lycopodium serratum*	2KC-	Q
Lycopodiaceae	*Lycopodium squarrosum*	3VC-	Q
Lythraceae	*Lagerstroemia subsessiliflora*	1K	Q
Lythraceae	*Nesaea robertsii*	2K	Q
Malpighiaceae	*Tristellateia australasiae*	2R+	Q
Malvaceae	? *Abutilon longilobum*	1K	W
Malvaceae	*Althaea australis*	1K	S
Malvaceae	*Decaschistia byrnesii*	3R	WY
Malvaceae	*Gossypium cunninghamii*	2RCa	Y
Malvaceae	*Gossypium pulchellum*	2R	W
Malvaceae	*Hibiscus menzeliae*	2RCat	Y
Malvaceae	*Lawrencia buchananensis*	2V	Q
Malvaceae	*Lawrencia diffusa*	3RC-	W
Malvaceae	*Macrostelia grandiflora*	3RC-	Q
Malvaceae	*Selenothamnus helmsii*	3K	W
Malvaceae	? *Sida pritzellii*	1X	W
Marsilaceae	? *Marsilea paradoxa*	1X	W
Meliaceae	*Aglaia argentea*	2R+	Q
Meliaceae	*Amoora cucullata*	3R+	Q
Meliaceae	*Dysoxylum setasum*	3R+	Q
Meliaceae	*Dysoxylum* sp.1	2K	Q
Meliaceae	*Owenia cepiodora*	2ECi	QN
Menispermaceae	*Carronia pedicellata*	2V	Q
Menispermaceae	*Cissampelos pareira*	3K+	Q
Menispermaceae	*Hypserpa reticulata*	2R	Q
Menispermaceae	*Tinospora tinosporoides*	3VC-	QN
Menyanthaceae	*Nymphoides elliptica*	2K	Q
Menyanthaceae	*Nymphoides planosperma*	2RC-	Y
Menyanthaceae	*Nymphoides triangularis*	2K	Q
Menyanthaceae	*Villarsia calthifolia*	2VCa	W
Menyanthaceae	*Villarsia congestiflora*	2K	W
Menyanthaceae	*Villarsia lasiosperma*	3V	W
Menyanthaceae	*Villarsia submersa*	3VC-	W
Mimosaceae	*Acacia abbreviata*	2K	Y
Mimosaceae	*Acacia aciphylla*	3R	W
Mimosaceae	*Acacia adunca*	3RC-	QN
Mimosaceae	*Acacia albizioides*	3R	Q
Mimosaceae	*Acacia amblyophylla*	3K	W
Mimosaceae	*Acacia amentifera*	1K	Y
Mimosaceae	*Acacia ammophila*	3V	Q
Mimosaceae	*Acacia anarthros*	2E	W
Mimosaceae	*Acacia anomala*	2V	W
Mimosaceae	*Acacia aphylla*	2VCi	W
Mimosaceae	*Acacia araneosa*	2VC-	S
Mimosaceae	*Acacia argutifolia*	2RCat	W
Mimosaceae	*Acacia armitii*	3VC-	Q
Mimosaceae	*Acacia asparagoides*	2R	N
Mimosaceae	*Acacia attenuata*	3VC-	Q
Mimosaceae	*Acacia auricoma*	3K	WY
Mimosaceae	*Acacia ausfeldii*	3RCa	NV
Mimosaceae	*Acacia axillaris*	3V	T
Mimosaceae	*Acacia bakeri*	3VC-	QN
Mimosaceae	*Acacia barattensis*	2V	S
Mimosaceae	*Acacia barbinervis*	2K	W
Mimosaceae	*Acacia botrydion*	2RC-	W
Mimosaceae	*Acacia bynoeana*	3VC-	N
Mimosaceae	*Acacia calantha*	2V	Q
Mimosaceae	*Acacia campylophylla*	2KC-	W
Mimosaceae	*Acacia carnei*	3RC-	SN
Mimosaceae	*Acacia chalkeri*	2RC-	N
Mimosaceae	*Acacia chinchillensis*	2V	Q
Mimosaceae	*Acacia chrysotricha*	2R	N
Mimosaceae	*Acacia clunies-rossiae*	2VC-t	N
Mimosaceae	*Acacia cochlocarpa*	2K	W
Mimosaceae	*Acacia confluens*	2R	S
Mimosaceae	*Acacia constablei*	2V	N
Mimosaceae	*Acacia costiniana*	3RCa	N
Mimosaceae	*Acacia covenyi*	2RCa	N
Mimosaceae	*Acacia crassuloides*	3RCa	W
Mimosaceae	*Acacia crombiei*	3V	Q
Mimosaceae	*Acacia curranii*	3V	QN
Mimosaceae	*Acacia daweana*	3KC-	W
Mimosaceae	*Acacia deflexa*	2KC-	W
Mimosaceae	*Acacia dempsteri*	3V	W
Mimosaceae	*Acacia denticulosa*	3VCi	W
Mimosaceae	*Acacia depressa*	2VCi	W
Mimosaceae	*Acacia deuteroneura*	2V	Q
Mimosaceae	*Acacia dodonaeifolia*	3RC-	S
Mimosaceae	*Acacia dolichophylla*	2R	Y
Mimosaceae	*Acacia dubia*	2K	W
Mimosaceae	*Acacia dura*	2V	W
Mimosaceae	*Acacia empelioclada*	2RC-	W
Mimosaceae	*Acacia enterocarpa*	3EC-	SV
Mimosaceae	*Acacia eremophiloides*	2V	Q
Mimosaceae	*Acacia flabellifolia*	3KC-	W
Mimosaceae	*Acacia flagelliformis*	2R	W
Mimosaceae	*Acacia fleckeri*	3V	Q
Mimosaceae	*Acacia flocktoniae*	2VC-	N
Mimosaceae	*Acacia floydii*	2RC-	QN
Mimosaceae	? *Acacia forrestiana*	2K	W
Mimosaceae	*Acacia forsythii*	2RC-t	N
Mimosaceae	*Acacia fulva*	2RC-	N
Mimosaceae	*Acacia georgensis*	2VCi	N
Mimosaceae	*Acacia gillii*	2VCi	S
Mimosaceae	*Acacia gittinsii*	2RC-	Q
Mimosaceae	*Acacia glandulicarpa*	3VCa	SV
Mimosaceae	*Acacia gnidium*	3V	Q
Mimosaceae	*Acacia gracilifolia*	3RCa	S
Mimosaceae	*Acacia grandifolia*	2V	Q
Mimosaceae	*Acacia grisea*	3V	W
Mimosaceae	*Acacia guinetii*	2VC-	W
Mimosaceae	*Acacia guymeri*	2V	Q
Mimosaceae	*Acacia handonis*	2V	Q
Mimosaceae	*Acacia helicophylla*	3RCa	Y

Family	Species	Threat Code	States
Mimosaceae	*Acacia hockingsii*	2RCa	Q
Mimosaceae	*Acacia holotricha*	3R	Q
Mimosaceae	*Acacia homaloclada*	2RC-	Q
Mimosaceae	*Acacia horridula*	2K	W
Mimosaceae	*Acacia howittii*	2R	V
Mimosaceae	*Acacia hylonoma*	2R	Q
Mimosaceae	*Acacia imbricata*	2V	S
Mimosaceae	*Acacia incrassata*	3K	W
Mimosaceae	*Acacia ingramii*	2RCa	N
Mimosaceae	*Acacia ingrata*	2KC-	W
Mimosaceae	*Acacia inops*	2K	W
Mimosaceae	*Acacia islana*	2RCa	Q
Mimosaceae	*Acacia iteaphylla*	3RCa	S
Mimosaceae	*Acacia jackesiana*	3RC-	Q
Mimosaceae	*Acacia jasperensis*	3RC-	Y
Mimosaceae	*Acacia jonesii*	2RCa	N
Mimosaceae	*Acacia kerryana*	3KC-	W
Mimosaceae	*Acacia kydrensis*	2RCa	N
Mimosaceae	*Acacia lachnophylla*	3K	W
Mimosaceae	*Acacia lanuginosa*	3K	W
Mimosaceae	*Acacia latisepala*	2RC-	QN
Mimosaceae	*Acacia latzii*	3V	Y
Mimosaceae	*Acacia lauta*	2V	Q
Mimosaceae	*Acacia longipedunculata*	3R	Q
Mimosaceae	*Acacia lucasii*	3RCa	NV
Mimosaceae	*Acacia megacephala*	2K	W
Mimosaceae	*Acacia meisneri*	2R	W
Mimosaceae	*? Acacia menzelii*	3VC-	S
Mimosaceae	*Acacia merrickae*	2V	W
Mimosaceae	*Acacia microneura*	2V	W
Mimosaceae	*Acacia multilineata*	3K	W
Mimosaceae	*? Acacia murruboensis*	1X	N
Mimosaceae	*Acacia newbeyi*	3KC-	W
Mimosaceae	*Acacia nigricans*	3RC-	W
Mimosaceae	*Acacia oldfieldii*	2RC-	W
Mimosaceae	*Acacia olsenii*	2RCat	N
Mimosaceae	*Acacia oxyclada*	3R	W
Mimosaceae	*Acacia pataczekii*	2R	T
Mimosaceae	*Acacia perangusta*	3V	Q
Mimosaceae	*Acacia peuce*	3VCi	YQ
Mimosaceae	*Acacia pharangites*	2V	W
Mimosaceae	*Acacia phasmoides*	2VC-	NV
Mimosaceae	*Acacia phlebopetala*	2RC-	W
Mimosaceae	*Acacia phlebophylla*	2RCa	V
Mimosaceae	*Acacia pickardii*	3V	YS
Mimosaceae	*Acacia pinguifolia*	3E	S
Mimosaceae	*Acacia plicata*	2V	W
Mimosaceae	*Acacia prismifolia*	2X	W
Mimosaceae	*Acacia pritzeliana*	3KC-	W
Mimosaceae	*Acacia prominens*	2RCa	N
Mimosaceae	*Acacia pubescens*	2VCa	N
Mimosaceae	*Acacia pubicosta*	3VC-	Q
Mimosaceae	*Acacia pubifolia*	2VC-	Q
Mimosaceae	*Acacia purpureopetala*	2V	Q
Mimosaceae	*Acacia quornensis*	2VC-	S
Mimosaceae	*Acacia ramiflora*	3V	Q
Mimosaceae	*Acacia rendlei*	3R	W
Mimosaceae	*Acacia retrorsa*	2K	W
Mimosaceae	*Acacia rhetinocarpa*	3VC-	S
Mimosaceae	*Acacia rhigiophylla*	3RCa	SN
Mimosaceae	*Acacia ridleyana*	3K	W
Mimosaceae	*Acacia robinae*	2R	W
Mimosaceae	*Acacia ruppii*	3VC-	QN
Mimosaceae	*Acacia saxicola*	2RC-	Q
Mimosaceae	*Acacia scapelliformis*	3KC-	W
Mimosaceae	*Acacia sciophanes*	2R	W
Mimosaceae	*Acacia sedifolia*	3V	W
Mimosaceae	*Acacia semicircinalis*	2VCi	W
Mimosaceae	*Acacia semitrullata*	2RC-	W
Mimosaceae	*Acacia simulans*	2VCit	W
Mimosaceae	*Acacia sorophylla*	3KC-	W
Mimosaceae	*Acacia* sp.1	2RC-	N
Mimosaceae	*Acacia* sp.10	2K	W
Mimosaceae	*Acacia* sp.11	2V	W
Mimosaceae	*Acacia* sp.12	2VCi	W
Mimosaceae	*Acacia* sp.2	2E	S
Mimosaceae	*Acacia* sp.3	2RCa	S
Mimosaceae	*Acacia* sp.4	2RC-	N
Mimosaceae	*Acacia* sp.5	3R	Q
Mimosaceae	*Acacia* sp.6	2R	Q
Mimosaceae	*Acacia* sp.7	2R	Q
Mimosaceae	*Acacia* sp.8	3RC-	Q
Mimosaceae	*Acacia* sp.9	3KC-	W
Mimosaceae	*Acacia spania*	3R	Q
Mimosaceae	*Acacia storyi*	2RC-	Q
Mimosaceae	*Acacia subflexuosa*	2K	W
Mimosaceae	*Acacia subracemosa*	2R	W
Mimosaceae	*Acacia subtilinervis*	3RCa	NV
Mimosaceae	*Acacia symonii*	3R	WS
Mimosaceae	*Acacia tayloriana*	2V	W
Mimosaceae	*Acacia tenuinervis*	3V	Q
Mimosaceae	*Acacia tenuior*	1K	S
Mimosaceae	*Acacia tetanophylla*	3KC-	W
Mimosaceae	*Acacia undoolyana*	2VCi	Y
Mimosaceae	*Acacia vassalii*	2V	W
Mimosaceae	*Acacia wardellii*	3V	Q

Family	Species	Threat Code	States
Mimosaceae	*Acacia williamsonii*	2RCa	V
Mimosaceae	*Albizia retusa*	2RC-+	Q
Mimosaceae	*Albizia* sp.1	2RC-	Q
Mimosaceae	*Archidendron hirsutum*	3K	Q
Mimosaceae	*Archidendron lovelliae*	3VC-	Q
Mimosaceae	*Archidendron lucyi*	3VC-+	Q
Mimosaceae	*Archidendron muellerianum*	3RCa	QN
Mimosaceae	*Archidendron ramiflorum*	3RC-	Q
Mimosaceae	*Archidendron whitei*	3RC-	Q
Mimosaceae	*Archidendropsis xanthoxyla*	2RC-	Q
Monimiaceae	*Dryadodaphne* sp.1	2R	Q
Monimiaceae	*Palmeria hypotephra*	2RC-	Q
Monimiaceae	*Tetrasynandra* sp.1	2R	Q
Monimiaceae	*Wilkiea wardellii*	3R	Q
Moraceae	*Fatoua pilosa*	3KC-+	WYQ
Moraceae	*Ficus melinocarpa*	3K+	Q
Moraceae	*Ficus triradiata*	2K	Q
Musaceae	*Musa fitzalanii*	1K	Q
Musaceae	*Musa jackeyi*	3RC-	Q
Myoporaceae	*Eremophila adenotricha*	2X	W
Myoporaceae	*Eremophila barbata*	2VCi	S
Myoporaceae	*Eremophila biserrata*	3VC-	W
Myoporaceae	*Eremophila brevifolia*	3K	W
Myoporaceae	*Eremophila chamaephila*	2V	W
Myoporaceae	*Eremophila compressa*	2V	W
Myoporaceae	*Eremophila denticulata*	2VCit	W
Myoporaceae	*Eremophila dicroantha*	3KCa	W
Myoporaceae	*Eremophila hillii*	3R	WS
Myoporaceae	*Eremophila inflata*	2V	W
Myoporaceae	*Eremophila lactea*	2V	W
Myoporaceae	*Eremophila merrallii*	2E	W
Myoporaceae	*Eremophila microtheca*	3VCi	W
Myoporaceae	*Eremophila nivea*	2E	W
Myoporaceae	*Eremophila parvifolia*	3R	WS
Myoporaceae	*Eremophila pentaptera*	3R	S
Myoporaceae	*Eremophila phillipsii*	2KC-	W
Myoporaceae	*Eremophila purpurascens*	2K	W
Myoporaceae	*Eremophila racemosa*	2V	W
Myoporaceae	*Eremophila resinosa*	2V	W
Myoporaceae	*Eremophila sargentii*	2V	W
Myoporaceae	*Eremophila scaberula*	1X	W
Myoporaceae	*Eremophila serpens*	3VC-	W
Myoporaceae	*Eremophila* sp.1	1K	W
Myoporaceae	*Eremophila* sp.2	2KC-	W
Myoporaceae	*Eremophila ternifolia*	2V	W
Myoporaceae	*Eremophila tetraptera*	3V	Q
Myoporaceae	*Eremophila undulata*	2R	W
Myoporaceae	*Eremophila veronica*	2K	W
Myoporaceae	*Eremophila verticillata*	2E	W
Myoporaceae	*Eremophila virens*	2V	W
Myoporaceae	*Eremophila viscida*	3V	W
Myoporaceae	*Myoporum beckeri*	3RC-	W
Myoporaceae	*Myoporum floribundum*	3RCi	NV
Myoporaceae	*Myoporum latisepalum*	3V	Q
Myoporaceae	*Myoporum salsoloides*	3VCi	W
Myoporaceae	*Myoporum turbinatum*	2E	W
Myrsinaceae	*Ardisia bakeri*	2RC-	QN
Myrsinaceae	*Ardisia bifaria*	2RC-	Q
Myrsinaceae	*Rapanea* sp.1	2X	N
Myrsinaceae	*Tapeinosperma fleuckigeri*	2K	Q
Myrtaceae	*Acmena mackinnoniana*	3R	Q
Myrtaceae	*Acmenosperma pringlei*	2RC-	Q
Myrtaceae	*Agonis undulata*	2RCat	W
Myrtaceae	*Angasomyrtus salina*	2VC-	W
Myrtaceae	*Astartea clavifolia*	2V	W
Myrtaceae	*Astartea clavulata*	2K	W
Myrtaceae	*Astartea intratropica*	2R	Y
Myrtaceae	*Austromyrtus fragrantissima*	3EC-	QN
Myrtaceae	*Austromyrtus gonoclada*	2V	Q
Myrtaceae	*Austromyrtus inophloia*	3RC-	Q
Myrtaceae	*Austromyrtus lucida*	2RC-	Q
Myrtaceae	*Austromyrtus pubiflora*	2RC-	Q
Myrtaceae	*Austromyrtus* sp.1	2R	Q
Myrtaceae	*Austromyrtus* sp.2	2V	Q
Myrtaceae	*Austromyrtus* sp.3	2R	Q
Myrtaceae	*Austromyrtus* sp.4	2K	Q
Myrtaceae	*Austromyrtus* sp.5	2RC-	Q
Myrtaceae	*Austromyrtus* sp.6	2R	Q
Myrtaceae	*Backhousia anisata*	2RCa	N
Myrtaceae	*Baeckea arbuscula*	2VCi	W
Myrtaceae	*Baeckea blacketti*	2K	W
Myrtaceae	*Baeckea clavifolia*	3K	W
Myrtaceae	*Baeckea crenatifolia*	2VC-t	V
Myrtaceae	*Baeckea decipiens*	3K	W
Myrtaceae	*Baeckea denticulata*	3RCa	N
Myrtaceae	*Baeckea gracilis*	3K	W
Myrtaceae	*Baeckea polystemona*	3RCa	WY
Myrtaceae	*Baeckea subcuneata*	2K	W
Myrtaceae	*Balaustion microphyllum*	2V	W
Myrtaceae	*Beaufortia eriocephala*	2RC-	W
Myrtaceae	*Beaufortia* sp.1	2K	W
Myrtaceae	*? Callistemon acuminatus*	3RC-	N
Myrtaceae	*Callistemon formosus*	3VCi	Q
Myrtaceae	*Callistemon pearsonii*	2RC-	Q
Myrtaceae	*Callistemon shiressii*	3RC-	N
Myrtaceae	*Callistemon* sp.1	2K	Q

Family	Species	Threat Code	States
Myrtaceae	*Calothamnus accedens*	2E	W
Myrtaceae	*Calothamnus affinis*	3VC-	W
Myrtaceae	*Calothamnus asper*	2RC-	W
Myrtaceae	*? Calothamnus blepharantherus*	2X	W
Myrtaceae	*Calothamnus brevifolius*	3K	W
Myrtaceae	*Calothamnus lateralis*	3VC-	W
Myrtaceae	*Calothamnus lehmannii*	3ECi	W
Myrtaceae	*Calothamnus longissimus*	2E	W
Myrtaceae	*Calothamnus macrocarpus*	2RCat	W
Myrtaceae	*? Calothamnus microcarpus*	2KC-	W
Myrtaceae	*Calothamnus pinifolius*	2RCa	W
Myrtaceae	*Calothamnus planifolius*	2RC-	W
Myrtaceae	*Calothamnus preissii*	3ECi	W
Myrtaceae	*Calothamnus robustus*	2E	W
Myrtaceae	*Calothamnus rupestris*	2RCi	W
Myrtaceae	*Calothamnus schaueri*	2ECi	W
Myrtaceae	*Calothamnus validus*	2RCat	W
Myrtaceae	*Calytrix chrysantha*	2V	W
Myrtaceae	*Calytrix creswellii*	2K	W
Myrtaceae	*Calytrix divergens*	3K	W
Myrtaceae	*Calytrix drummondii*	3V	W
Myrtaceae	*Calytrix eneabbensis*	2V	W
Myrtaceae	*Calytrix erosipetala*	3K	W
Myrtaceae	*Calytrix faucicola*	2RCa	Y
Myrtaceae	*Calytrix formosa*	2RC-	W
Myrtaceae	*Calytrix gurulmundensis*	2K	Q
Myrtaceae	*Calytrix habrantha*	3KC-	W
Myrtaceae	*Calytrix islensis*	2RCa	Q
Myrtaceae	*Calytrix micrairoides*	2RC-	Y
Myrtaceae	*Calytrix mimiana*	2R	Y
Myrtaceae	*Calytrix parvivallis*	2V	W
Myrtaceae	*Calytrix paucicostata*	2R	W
Myrtaceae	*Calytrix platycheiridia*	2KC-	W
Myrtaceae	*Calytrix plumulosa*	3V	W
Myrtaceae	*Calytrix praecipua*	2V	W
Myrtaceae	*Calytrix pulchella*	3V	W
Myrtaceae	*Calytrix rupestris*	2RCa	Y
Myrtaceae	*Calytrix similis*	2KC-	W
Myrtaceae	*Calytrix simplex*	3RC-	W
Myrtaceae	*Calytrix* sp.1	3K	W
Myrtaceae	*Calytrix superba*	2EC-	W
Myrtaceae	*Calytrix surdiviperana*	1RC-	Y
Myrtaceae	*Calytrix tenuiramea*	3K	W
Myrtaceae	*Calytrix variabilis*	3KC-	W
Myrtaceae	*Calytrix verruculosa*	3K	W
Myrtaceae	*Calytrix verticillata*	2RCa	Y
Myrtaceae	*Calytrix warburtonensis*	2K	W
Myrtaceae	*Chamaelaucium* sp.1	2K	W
Myrtaceae	*Chamaelaucium* sp.2	2V	W
Myrtaceae	*Chamaelaucium* sp.3	2V	W
Myrtaceae	*Choricarpia subargentea*	3VC-	Q
Myrtaceae	*Corynanthera flava*	2VC-	W
Myrtaceae	*Darwinia acerosa*	2V	W
Myrtaceae	*Darwinia apiculata*	2V	W
Myrtaceae	*Darwinia biflora*	2VCa	N
Myrtaceae	*Darwinia carnea*	2E	W
Myrtaceae	*Darwinia collina*	2VCit	W
Myrtaceae	*Darwinia decumbens*	2V	Q
Myrtaceae	*Darwinia diminuta*	3RCi	N
Myrtaceae	*Darwinia glaucophylla*	2RCa	N
Myrtaceae	*Darwinia grandiflora*	2RC-	N
Myrtaceae	*Darwinia macrostegia*	2RCat	W
Myrtaceae	*Darwinia masonii*	2V	W
Myrtaceae	*Darwinia meeboldii*	2VCit	W
Myrtaceae	*Darwinia oxylepis*	2RCat	W
Myrtaceae	*Darwinia peduncularis*	3RCi	N
Myrtaceae	*Darwinia pimelioides*	2VC-	W
Myrtaceae	*Darwinia porteri*	2V	Q
Myrtaceae	*Darwinia procera*	2RCa	N
Myrtaceae	*Darwinia repens*	1V	W
Myrtaceae	*Darwinia rhadinophylla*	2R	W
Myrtaceae	*Darwinia* sp.1	2VCit	W
Myrtaceae	*Darwinia* sp.2	2K	Q
Myrtaceae	*Darwinia* sp.3	1K	W
Myrtaceae	*Darwinia* sp.4	1K	W
Myrtaceae	*Darwinia* sp.5	2KC-	W
Myrtaceae	*Darwinia* sp.6	2E	W
Myrtaceae	*Darwinia squarrosa*	2RCat	W
Myrtaceae	*Darwinia thomasii*	3RC-	Q
Myrtaceae	*Darwinia wittwerorum*	2RCat	W
Myrtaceae	*Decaspermum* sp.1	2K	Q
Myrtaceae	*Eremaea acutifolia*	2K	W
Myrtaceae	*Eremaea purpurea*	2RC-	W
Myrtaceae	*Eucalyptus abergiana*	3K	Q
Myrtaceae	*Eucalyptus acies*	3RC-	W
Myrtaceae	*Eucalyptus angustissima*	3RC-	W
Myrtaceae	*Eucalyptus apiculata*	2R	N
Myrtaceae	*Eucalyptus approximans*	3RCa	QN
Myrtaceae	*Eucalyptus aquilina*	2RCat	W
Myrtaceae	*Eucalyptus archeri*	2RCa	T
Myrtaceae	*Eucalyptus argillacea*	2R	W
Myrtaceae	*Eucalyptus argophloia*	2V	Q
Myrtaceae	*Eucalyptus badjensis*	2RCi	N
Myrtaceae	*Eucalyptus baeuerlenii*	3RCa	N
Myrtaceae	*Eucalyptus barberi*	2R	T
Myrtaceae	*Eucalyptus beardiana*	2V	W

Family	Species	Threat Code	States
Myrtaceae	? *Eucalyptus bennettiae*	2V	W
Myrtaceae	*Eucalyptus benthamii*	2VCi	N
Myrtaceae	? *Eucalyptus brachyphylla*	3V	W
Myrtaceae	*Eucalyptus brevipes*	2V	W
Myrtaceae	*Eucalyptus brevistylis*	2RC-	W
Myrtaceae	*Eucalyptus brockwayi*	2R	W
Myrtaceae	*Eucalyptus burdettiana*	2RCit	W
Myrtaceae	*Eucalyptus burgessiana*	2RCa	N
Myrtaceae	*Eucalyptus caesia*	3RCa	W
Myrtaceae	*Eucalyptus calcicola*	2RCa	W
Myrtaceae	*Eucalyptus camfieldii*	2VCi	N
Myrtaceae	*Eucalyptus cannonii*	2V	N
Myrtaceae	*Eucalyptus carnabyi*	2V	W
Myrtaceae	*Eucalyptus ceracea*	2V	W
Myrtaceae	*Eucalyptus cerasiformis*	2VC-	W
Myrtaceae	*Eucalyptus codonocarpa*	3RCa	QN
Myrtaceae	*Eucalyptus confluens*	3K	W
Myrtaceae	*Eucalyptus conglomerata*	2VC-	Q
Myrtaceae	*Eucalyptus cordata*	3RCi	T
Myrtaceae	*Eucalyptus coronata*	2VCit	W
Myrtaceae	*Eucalyptus corrugata*	3K	W
Myrtaceae	*Eucalyptus crenulata*	2VC-	V
Myrtaceae	*Eucalyptus crucis*	2VC-	W
Myrtaceae	*Eucalyptus curtisii*	3RC-	Q
Myrtaceae	*Eucalyptus deflexa*	3VC-	W
Myrtaceae	*Eucalyptus desmondensis*	2V	W
Myrtaceae	*Eucalyptus deuaensis*	2RCit	N
Myrtaceae	*Eucalyptus distans*	2K	Y
Myrtaceae	*Eucalyptus dunnii*	3RCa	QN
Myrtaceae	*Eucalyptus effusa*	3K	W
Myrtaceae	*Eucalyptus erectifolia*	2VCit	W
Myrtaceae	*Eucalyptus exilipes*	2K	Q
Myrtaceae	*Eucalyptus exilis*	3RC-	W
Myrtaceae	*Eucalyptus ficifolia*	2RC-	W
Myrtaceae	*Eucalyptus fitzgeraldii*	2R	W
Myrtaceae	*Eucalyptus formanii*	2R	W
Myrtaceae	*Eucalyptus fraseri*	3RCa	W
Myrtaceae	*Eucalyptus froggattii*	3RCa	V
Myrtaceae	*Eucalyptus fusiformis*	2R	N
Myrtaceae	*Eucalyptus georgei*	2R	W
Myrtaceae	*Eucalyptus glaucina*	3VCa	N
Myrtaceae	*Eucalyptus gonianthe*	2K	W
Myrtaceae	*Eucalyptus gregsoniana*	3RCa	N
Myrtaceae	*Eucalyptus guilfoylei*	2RC-	W
Myrtaceae	*Eucalyptus hallii*	2VC-	Q
Myrtaceae	*Eucalyptus halophila*	2VC-	W
Myrtaceae	*Eucalyptus howittiana*	2R	Q
Myrtaceae	*Eucalyptus imlayensis*	2VCit	N
Myrtaceae	*Eucalyptus insularis*	2RCat	W
Myrtaceae	*Eucalyptus jacksonii*	2RC-	W
Myrtaceae	*Eucalyptus johnsoniana*	2V	W
Myrtaceae	*Eucalyptus jutsonii*	3R	W
Myrtaceae	*Eucalyptus kartzoffiana*	2VCi	N
Myrtaceae	*Eucalyptus kitsoniana*	3VCa	V
Myrtaceae	*Eucalyptus koolpinensis*	2R	Y
Myrtaceae	*Eucalyptus kruseana*	2RC-	W
Myrtaceae	*Eucalyptus lansdowneana*	2V	S
Myrtaceae	*Eucalyptus largeana*	3R	N
Myrtaceae	*Eucalyptus lateritica*	2V	W
Myrtaceae	*Eucalyptus ligulata*	3RC-	W
Myrtaceae	*Eucalyptus lucens*	3RC-	Y
Myrtaceae	*Eucalyptus luehmanniana*	2RCa	N
Myrtaceae	*Eucalyptus macarthurii*	2RCi	N
Myrtaceae	*Eucalyptus macrandra*	2RCa	W
Myrtaceae	*Eucalyptus mckieana*	2V	N
Myrtaceae	*Eucalyptus megacornuta*	2RCi	W
Myrtaceae	*Eucalyptus melanoleuca*	3RC-	Q
Myrtaceae	*Eucalyptus merrickiae*	3V	W
Myrtaceae	*Eucalyptus michaeliana*	3RCa	QN
Myrtaceae	*Eucalyptus mitchelliana*	2RC-t	V
Myrtaceae	*Eucalyptus mooreana*	3V	W
Myrtaceae	*Eucalyptus morrisbyi*	2ECi	T
Myrtaceae	*Eucalyptus neglecta*	3R	V
Myrtaceae	*Eucalyptus newbeyi*	3RC-	W
Myrtaceae	*Eucalyptus nicholii*	3V	N
Myrtaceae	*Eucalyptus nutans*	2RC-	W
Myrtaceae	*Eucalyptus olsenii*	2RC-t	N
Myrtaceae	*Eucalyptus ornata*	3RC-	W
Myrtaceae	*Eucalyptus ovularis*	2RCi	W
Myrtaceae	*Eucalyptus pachycalyx*	3R	Q
Myrtaceae	*Eucalyptus paliformis*	2RCat	N
Myrtaceae	*Eucalyptus parvifolia*	2VCi	N
Myrtaceae	*Eucalyptus pendens*	2RCi	W
Myrtaceae	*Eucalyptus pilbarensis*	3R	W
Myrtaceae	*Eucalyptus pimpineana*	3R	WS
Myrtaceae	*Eucalyptus pulverulenta*	3V	N
Myrtaceae	*Eucalyptus pumila*	2VCi	N
Myrtaceae	*Eucalyptus quadricostata*	2R	Q
Myrtaceae	? *Eucalyptus rameliana*	1K	W
Myrtaceae	*Eucalyptus raveretiana*	3VC-	Q
Myrtaceae	*Eucalyptus rhodantha*	2V	W
Myrtaceae	*Eucalyptus risdonii*	2RCa	T
Myrtaceae	*Eucalyptus rubiginosa*	3RCi	Q
Myrtaceae	*Eucalyptus rudderi*	3RC-	N
Myrtaceae	*Eucalyptus rummeryi*	3RC-	N
Myrtaceae	*Eucalyptus rupicola*	2RCa	N
Myrtaceae	*Eucalyptus saxatilis*	3RC-	V
Myrtaceae	*Eucalyptus scoparia*	2VCi	Q
Myrtaceae	*Eucalyptus sepulcralis*	3RCat	W
Myrtaceae	*Eucalyptus* sp.1	2E	N
Myrtaceae	*Eucalyptus* sp.10	2RCa	N
Myrtaceae	*Eucalyptus* sp.11	2RC-	Q
Myrtaceae	*Eucalyptus* sp.12	2R	W
Myrtaceae	*Eucalyptus* sp.13	2R	W
Myrtaceae	*Eucalyptus* sp.14	2RC-	W
Myrtaceae	*Eucalyptus* sp.15	2R	W
Myrtaceae	*Eucalyptus* sp.16	2RC-	W
Myrtaceae	*Eucalyptus* sp.17	2RC-	W
Myrtaceae	*Eucalyptus* sp.18	2KC-	W
Myrtaceae	*Eucalyptus* sp.19	2K	W
Myrtaceae	*Eucalyptus* sp.2	2E	V
Myrtaceae	*Eucalyptus* sp.20	2V	W
Myrtaceae	*Eucalyptus* sp.21	2VCi	W
Myrtaceae	*Eucalyptus* sp.22	2E	W
Myrtaceae	*Eucalyptus* sp.23	2VCi	W
Myrtaceae	*Eucalyptus* sp.24	2VCi	W
Myrtaceae	*Eucalyptus* sp.25	2V	W
Myrtaceae	*Eucalyptus* sp.26	2V	W
Myrtaceae	*Eucalyptus* sp.27	2VCi	W
Myrtaceae	*Eucalyptus* sp.28	2VCi	W
Myrtaceae	*Eucalyptus* sp.29	2VCi	W
Myrtaceae	*Eucalyptus* sp.3	2RC-t	N
Myrtaceae	*Eucalyptus* sp.30	2K	W
Myrtaceae	*Eucalyptus* sp.31	1KC-	W
Myrtaceae	*Eucalyptus* sp.32	2V	W
Myrtaceae	*Eucalyptus* sp.33	2VCi	W
Myrtaceae	*Eucalyptus* sp.4	2V	N
Myrtaceae	*Eucalyptus* sp.5	2RCa	N
Myrtaceae	*Eucalyptus* sp.6	2RC-	Q
Myrtaceae	*Eucalyptus* sp.7	2V	Q
Myrtaceae	*Eucalyptus* sp.8	2RC-	Q
Myrtaceae	*Eucalyptus* sp.9	3RC-	Q
Myrtaceae	*Eucalyptus sparsa*	3R	WYS
Myrtaceae	*Eucalyptus sphaerocarpa*	2RCa	Q
Myrtaceae	*Eucalyptus steedmanii*	2V	W
Myrtaceae	*Eucalyptus stoatei*	2VCi	W
Myrtaceae	*Eucalyptus sturgissiana*	2VC-	N
Myrtaceae	*Eucalyptus suberea*	2V	W
Myrtaceae	*Eucalyptus tetrapleura*	2VCi	N
Myrtaceae	*Eucalyptus triflora*	2RCa	N
Myrtaceae	*Eucalyptus virens*	3RC-	Q
Myrtaceae	*Eucalyptus wilcoxii*	2RCat	N
Myrtaceae	*Eucalyptus woodwardii*	2R	W
Myrtaceae	*Eucalyptus yarraensis*	3RCa	V
Myrtaceae	*Homalocalyx chapmanii*	3V	W
Myrtaceae	*Homalocalyx grandiflorus*	2K	W
Myrtaceae	*Homalocalyx inerrabundus*	2VC-	W
Myrtaceae	*Homoranthus darwinioides*	3VCa	N
Myrtaceae	*Homoranthus decasetus*	2RC-	Q
Myrtaceae	*Homoranthus papillatus*	2RCa	Q
Myrtaceae	*Homoranthus tropicus*	2R	Q
Myrtaceae	*Hypocalymma ericifolium*	2K	W
Myrtaceae	*Hypocalymma longifolium*	2X	W
Myrtaceae	*Hypocalymma phillipsii*	2RC-	W
Myrtaceae	*Hypocalymma tetrapterum*	2K	W
Myrtaceae	*Kunzea baxteri*	3RC-	W
Myrtaceae	*Kunzea bracteolata*	3RC-	QN
Myrtaceae	*Kunzea calida*	1K	Q
Myrtaceae	*Kunzea cambagei*	2VCa	N
Myrtaceae	*Kunzea eriocalyx*	2KCa	W
Myrtaceae	*Kunzea flavescens*	3RC-	Q
Myrtaceae	*Kunzea graniticola*	2RC-	Q
Myrtaceae	*Kunzea jucunda*	3RCa	W
Myrtaceae	*Kunzea pauciflora*	2V	W
Myrtaceae	*Kunzea rupestris*	2ECi	N
Myrtaceae	*Kunzea spicata*	2K	W
Myrtaceae	*Leptospermum epacridoideum*	2RC-	N
Myrtaceae	*Leptospermum glabrescens*	2K	V
Myrtaceae	*Leptospermum luehmannii*	2RC-	Q
Myrtaceae	*Leptospermum maxwellii*	2KCa	W
Myrtaceae	*Leptospermum sericeum*	2RC-	W
Myrtaceae	*Leptospermum* sp.1	2RC-	N
Myrtaceae	*Leptospermum* sp.10	2RC-	Q
Myrtaceae	*Leptospermum* sp.11	2RC-	N
Myrtaceae	*Leptospermum* sp.12	2R	N
Myrtaceae	*Leptospermum* sp.13	3K	W
Myrtaceae	*Leptospermum* sp.14	2K	N
Myrtaceae	*Leptospermum* sp.15	2V	N
Myrtaceae	*Leptospermum* sp.16	2RC-	Q
Myrtaceae	*Leptospermum* sp.2	3RC-	N
Myrtaceae	*Leptospermum* sp.3	2RC-	N
Myrtaceae	*Leptospermum* sp.4	2V	N
Myrtaceae	*Leptospermum* sp.5	2RC-	N
Myrtaceae	*Leptospermum* sp.6	2RCa	N
Myrtaceae	*Leptospermum* sp.8	2K	W
Myrtaceae	*Leptospermum* sp.9	2RC-t	W
Myrtaceae	*Leptospermum wooroonooran*	3RC-	Q
Myrtaceae	*Lhotskya brevifolia*	2V	W
Myrtaceae	*Lhotskya ciliata*	3VC-	W
Myrtaceae	*Lhotskya harvestiana*	3RC-	W
Myrtaceae	*Lhotskya purpurea*	2RC-	W
Myrtaceae	*Lhotskya smeatoniana*	2RC-	S
Myrtaceae	*Melaleuca agathosmoides*	2V	W
Myrtaceae	*Melaleuca arenaria*	1X	W
Myrtaceae	*Melaleuca arenicola*	1X	W
Myrtaceae	*Melaleuca arnhemica*	2RC-	Y
Myrtaceae	*Melaleuca basicephala*	2K	W
Myrtaceae	*Melaleuca cheelii*	2RC-	Q
Myrtaceae	*Melaleuca ciliosa*	3RC-	W
Myrtaceae	*Melaleuca citrina*	2RCat	W
Myrtaceae	*Melaleuca cliffortioides*	3KC-	W
Myrtaceae	*Melaleuca coccinea*	3RCi	W
Myrtaceae	? *Melaleuca concinna*	1K	W
Myrtaceae	*Melaleuca corrugata*	3R	YS
Myrtaceae	*Melaleuca deanei*	3RC-	N
Myrtaceae	*Melaleuca diosmifolia*	2K	W
Myrtaceae	? *Melaleuca graminea*	1K	W
Myrtaceae	*Melaleuca groveana*	3VC-	QN
Myrtaceae	*Melaleuca kunzeoides*	2V	Q
Myrtaceae	*Melaleuca micromera*	3VC-	W
Myrtaceae	*Melaleuca nanophylla*	3K	WS
Myrtaceae	*Melaleuca nesophila*	3RCa	W
Myrtaceae	*Melaleuca polycephala*	2V	W
Myrtaceae	*Melaleuca pustulata*	2RCi	T
Myrtaceae	*Melaleuca sciotostyla*	2VCi	W
Myrtaceae	*Melaleuca sclerophylla*	3KCa	W
Myrtaceae	*Melaleuca sericea*	2K	W
Myrtaceae	*Melaleuca* sp.1	3K	W
Myrtaceae	*Melaleuca* sp.2	3K	W
Myrtaceae	*Melaleuca* sp.3	1V	W
Myrtaceae	*Melaleuca* sp.4	2E	W
Myrtaceae	*Melaleuca* sp.6	2K	W
Myrtaceae	*Melaleuca steedmanii*	3E	W
Myrtaceae	*Melaleuca tortifolia*	2RC-t	N
Myrtaceae	*Micromyrtus blakelyi*	2VC-	N
Myrtaceae	*Micromyrtus helmsii*	1K	W
Myrtaceae	*Micromyrtus minutiflora*	2V	N
Myrtaceae	*Micromyrtus serrulata*	1K	W
Myrtaceae	*Micromyrtus stenocalyx*	3R	W
Myrtaceae	*Neofabricia mjoebergii*	2R	Q
Myrtaceae	*Phymatocarpus sparsiflorus*	3KC-	W
Myrtaceae	*Pilidiostigma* sp.1	2K	Q
Myrtaceae	*Regelia cymbifolia*	2E	W
Myrtaceae	*Regelia megacephala*	2V	W
Myrtaceae	*Regelia velutina*	2RCat	W
Myrtaceae	*Rhodamnia glabrescens*	3R	Q
Myrtaceae	*Rhodamnia maideniana*	2RC-	QN
Myrtaceae	*Rhodamnia* sp.1	3R	Q
Myrtaceae	*Rhodomyrtus* sp.1	2RC-	Q
Myrtaceae	*Rhodomyrtus* sp.2	2R	Q
Myrtaceae	*Rinzia affinis*	3K	W
Myrtaceae	*Rinzia crassifolia*	3K	W
Myrtaceae	*Rinzia longifolia*	2KC-	W
Myrtaceae	*Rinzia oxycoccoides*	2RCat	W
Myrtaceae	*Rinzia rubra*	3KCi	W
Myrtaceae	*Ristantia pachysperma*	3VC-	Q
Myrtaceae	*Ristantia* sp.1	2V	Q
Myrtaceae	*Ristantia* sp.2	2R	Q
Myrtaceae	*Scholtzia eatoniana*	2K	W
Myrtaceae	*Scholtzia uberiflora*	2KC-	W
Myrtaceae	*Syncarpia hillii*	3RC-	Q
Myrtaceae	*Syzygium alatoramulum*	3R	Q
Myrtaceae	*Syzygium alliiligneum*	3RC-	Q
Myrtaceae	*Syzygium amplum*	2K	Q
Myrtaceae	*Syzygium aqueum*	3R+	Q
Myrtaceae	*Syzygium argyropedicum*	2R	Q
Myrtaceae	*Syzygium boonjee*	2RC-	Q
Myrtaceae	*Syzygium buettnerianum*	3RC-+	Q
Myrtaceae	*Syzygium dansiei*	2R	Q
Myrtaceae	*Syzygium hodgkinsoniae*	3VC-	QN
Myrtaceae	*Syzygium macilwraithianum*	3R	Q
Myrtaceae	*Syzygium malaccense*	3R+	Q
Myrtaceae	*Syzygium moorei*	2VCi	QN
Myrtaceae	*Syzygium paniculatum*	3ECi	N
Myrtaceae	*Syzygium pseudofastigiatum*	3R	Q
Myrtaceae	*Syzygium puberulum*	3R+	Q
Myrtaceae	*Syzygium rubrimolle*	2R	Q
Myrtaceae	*Syzygium sharonae*	2RC-	Q
Myrtaceae	*Syzygium velae*	2V	Q
Myrtaceae	*Syzygium xerampelinum*	3RC-	Q
Myrtaceae	*Thryptomene dielsiana*	3K	W
Myrtaceae	*Thryptomene stenophylla*	2E	W
Myrtaceae	*Thryptomene wittweri*	3RC-	WY
Myrtaceae	*Uromyrtus australis*	2ECi	N
Myrtaceae	*Uromyrtus metrosideros*	3RC-	Q
Myrtaceae	*Uromyrtus* sp.1	2RC-	Q
Myrtaceae	*Verticordia carinata*	1X	W
Myrtaceae	*Verticordia etheliana*	2RC-	W
Myrtaceae	*Verticordia fastigiata*	3RCa	W
Myrtaceae	*Verticordia fimbrilepis*	3E	W
Myrtaceae	*Verticordia helichrysantha*	2RCa	W
Myrtaceae	*Verticordia hughanii*	2E	W
Myrtaceae	*Verticordia lehmannii*	2V	W
Myrtaceae	*Verticordia lindleyi*	2RC-	W
Myrtaceae	*Verticordia penicillaris*	2R	W
Myrtaceae	*Verticordia* sp.13	2V	W
Myrtaceae	*Verticordia* sp.14	2R	W
Myrtaceae	*Verticordia* sp.19	2V	W

Family	Species	Threat Code	States
Myrtaceae	Verticordia sp.2	2VC-	W
Myrtaceae	Verticordia sp.22	2VCi	W
Myrtaceae	Verticordia sp.28	2RC-	W
Myrtaceae	Verticordia sp.29	2E	W
Myrtaceae	Verticordia sp.3	2V	W
Myrtaceae	Verticordia sp.30	2E	W
Myrtaceae	Verticordia sp.31	2E	W
Myrtaceae	Verticordia sp.32	2E	W
Myrtaceae	Verticordia sp.33	2RC-	W
Myrtaceae	Verticordia sp.38	2VCi	W
Myrtaceae	Verticordia sp.39	2V	W
Myrtaceae	Verticordia sp.4	2E	W
Myrtaceae	Verticordia sp.40	2RC-	W
Myrtaceae	Verticordia sp.48	2V	W
Myrtaceae	Verticordia sp.50	2V	W
Myrtaceae	Verticordia sp.51	2V	W
Myrtaceae	Verticordia sp.53	2V	W
Myrtaceae	Verticordia sp.54	2V	W
Myrtaceae	Verticordia sp.9	2RC-	W
Myrtaceae	Verticordia staminosa	3V	W
Myrtaceae	Verticordia stenopetala	3K	W
Myrtaceae	Waterhousea mulgraveana	3RC-	Q
Myrtaceae	Xanthostemon oppositifolius	3VC-	Q
Myrtaceae	Xanthostemon sp.1	2R	Q
Myrtaceae	Xanthostemon sp.2	2RC-	Q
Myrtaceae	Xanthostemon verticillatus	2R	Q
Myrtaceae	Xanthostemon youngii	3R	Q
Myrtaceae	ZGenus nov.1 sp.1	2V	Q
Myrtaceae	ZGenus nov.2 sp.1	2R	Q
Myrtaceae	ZGenus nov.3 sp.1	2RC-	Q
Myrtaceae	ZGenus nov.3 sp.2	2R	Q
Myrtaceae	ZGenus nov.4 sp.1	2R	Q
Naucleaceae	Uncaria cordata	2RC-+	Q
Nephrolepidaceae	Nephrolepis obliterata	3K	WY
Nymphaeaceae	Ondinea purpurea	3R	W
Olacaceae	Anacolosa sp.1	2K	Q
Olacaceae	Olax angulata	2RCa	N
Olacaceae	Olax spartea	1K	W
Oleaceae	Notelaea lloydii	2V	Q
Oleaceae	Notelaea pungens	2V	Q
Onagraceae	Epilobium brunnescens	2VCit+	V
Onagraceae	Epilobium perpusillum	3VCa	T
Onagraceae	Epilobium willisii	3RCa	vT
Orchidaceae	Acianthus amplexicaulis	3RC-	QN
Orchidaceae	? Acianthus ledwardii	3V	QN
Orchidaceae	Acianthus sublestus	2RC-	Q
Orchidaceae	Adenochilus nortonii	3RC-	N
Orchidaceae	? Aphyllorchis anomala	2K+	Q
Orchidaceae	Aphyllorchis queenslandica	2K	Q
Orchidaceae	Arthrochilus byrnesii	2ECi	Y
Orchidaceae	Bulbophyllum argyropus	3RCi+	QN
Orchidaceae	Bulbophyllum boonjee	2V	Q
Orchidaceae	Bulbophyllum evasum	2RC-	Q
Orchidaceae	Bulbophyllum globuliforme	3RC-	QN
Orchidaceae	Bulbophyllum gracillimum	2RC-+	Q
Orchidaceae	Bulbophyllum longiflorum	3RC-+	Q
Orchidaceae	Bulbophyllum masdevalliaceum	3RC-+	Q
Orchidaceae	Bulbophyllum weinthalii	3RCi	QN
Orchidaceae	Burnettia cuneata	3RC-	NVT
Orchidaceae	Cadetia collinsii	3RC-	Q
Orchidaceae	Cadetia wariana	2RC-	Q
Orchidaceae	Caladenia alata	3R	QNT
Orchidaceae	? Caladenia atkinsoniana	1X	T
Orchidaceae	Caladenia bryceana	3VCi	W
Orchidaceae	Caladenia caudata	3VC-	T
Orchidaceae	Caladenia cristata	3V	W
Orchidaceae	Caladenia dorrienii	2V	W
Orchidaceae	Caladenia echidnachila	3VC-	T
Orchidaceae	Caladenia gladiolata	3VCa	S
Orchidaceae	Caladenia hastata	2ECi	V
Orchidaceae	Caladenia infundibularis	3RC-	W
Orchidaceae	Caladenia integra	3VCi	W
Orchidaceae	? Caladenia lavandulacea	3K	W
Orchidaceae	? Caladenia longii	2V	T
Orchidaceae	Caladenia ovata	3VCa	S
Orchidaceae	Caladenia plicata	3VCi	W
Orchidaceae	Caladenia pumila	2X	V
Orchidaceae	Caladenia rigida	2V	S
Orchidaceae	Caladenia sp.1	2R	W
Orchidaceae	Caladenia sp.10	3VCi	W
Orchidaceae	Caladenia sp.11	2V	W
Orchidaceae	Caladenia sp.12	2VCi	W
Orchidaceae	Caladenia sp.13	2V	W
Orchidaceae	Caladenia sp.14	2RC-	W
Orchidaceae	Caladenia sp.15	2RC-	W
Orchidaceae	Caladenia sp.2	2V	W
Orchidaceae	Caladenia sp.3	2V	W
Orchidaceae	Caladenia sp.4	3V	W
Orchidaceae	Caladenia sp.5	3VCi	W
Orchidaceae	Caladenia sp.6	3VCi	W
Orchidaceae	Caladenia sp.7	3VCi	W
Orchidaceae	Caladenia sp.8	2VCi	W
Orchidaceae	Caladenia sp.9	2E	W
Orchidaceae	Caladenia tesselata	3V	NV
Orchidaceae	? Caladenia triangularis	3VC-	W
Orchidaceae	Caladenia wanosa	2VCi	W

Family	Species	Threat Code	States
Orchidaceae	Calochilus richae	2E	V
Orchidaceae	Corybas abellianus	2RC-	Q
Orchidaceae	Corybas neocaledonicus	3K+	Q
Orchidaceae	Corybas sp.1	2V	W
Orchidaceae	Corybas undulatus	3KC-	QN
Orchidaceae	Cryptostylis hunteriana	3VC-	NV
Orchidaceae	Dendrobium antennatum	2R+	Q
Orchidaceae	Dendrobium carronii	3RC-+	Q
Orchidaceae	Dendrobium johannis	3RCa	Q
Orchidaceae	Dendrobium lobbii	3RC-+	YQ
Orchidaceae	Dendrobium malbrownii	2R	Q
Orchidaceae	Dendrobium mirbelianum	3EC-+	Q
Orchidaceae	Dendrobium nindii	3VC-+	Q
Orchidaceae	Dendrobium schneiderae	3RC-	QN
Orchidaceae	Dendrobium toressae	3RC-	Q
Orchidaceae	Dendrobium tozerensis	3VC-	Q
Orchidaceae	Dendrobium wassellii	2V	Q
Orchidaceae	Didymoplexis pallens	3K+	YQ
Orchidaceae	Diplocaulobium masonii	2K+	Q
Orchidaceae	Dipodium pandanum	3RC-+	Q
Orchidaceae	Dipodium sp.1	3RC-	Q
Orchidaceae	Diuris aequalis	3VC-	N
Orchidaceae	Diuris brevifolia	3RCa	S
Orchidaceae	Diuris pallens	2E	N
Orchidaceae	Diuris purdiei	2VCi	W
Orchidaceae	Diuris sheaffiana	3V	N
Orchidaceae	Diuris sp.1	3K	Q
Orchidaceae	Diuris sp.2	2KC-	W
Orchidaceae	Diuris sp.3	3E	W
Orchidaceae	Diuris sp.4	2E	W
Orchidaceae	Diuris venosa	2VC-	N
Orchidaceae	Drakaea jeanensis	2E	W
Orchidaceae	Drakaea sp.1	3VCi	W
Orchidaceae	Drakaea sp.2	3VC-	W
Orchidaceae	Drakaea sp.3	2VCi	W
Orchidaceae	Eria dischorensis	3R+	Q
Orchidaceae	Eria irukandjiana	3RC-	Q
Orchidaceae	Eulophia fitzalanii	3R+	Q
Orchidaceae	Eulophia pulchra	3RC-+	Q
Orchidaceae	Eulophia zollingeri	3R+	Q
Orchidaceae	Flickingeria convexa	3RC-+	Q
Orchidaceae	Gastrodia queenslandica	3RC-	Q
Orchidaceae	Genoplesium baueri	3RC-	N
Orchidaceae	Goodyera grandis	3RC-+	Q
Orchidaceae	Goodyera viridiflora	3RC-	Q
Orchidaceae	? Habenaria divaricata	2RC-	Q
Orchidaceae	Habenaria hymenophylla	3RC-	YQ
Orchidaceae	Habenaria macraithii	1V	Q
Orchidaceae	? Habenaria propinquior	2V	Q
Orchidaceae	Habenaria xanthantha	3V	Q
Orchidaceae	Hetaeria polygonoides	3R+	Q
Orchidaceae	Liparis condylobulbon	3RC-	Q
Orchidaceae	Liparis simmondsii	3K	Q
Orchidaceae	Malaxis acuminata	3R	Y
Orchidaceae	Malaxis fimbriata	2R	Q
Orchidaceae	Malaxis lawleri	2E	Q
Orchidaceae	Malaxis xanthochila	3RC-+	Q
Orchidaceae	Microtis globula	3RC-t	W
Orchidaceae	Microtis pulchella	3RC-	W
Orchidaceae	Nervillea crociformis	2RC-+	Q
Orchidaceae	? Oberonia attenuata	2EC-	Q
Orchidaceae	Oberonia carnosa	3RC-	Q
Orchidaceae	Pachystoma holtzei	3RC-+	yQ
Orchidaceae	Papillilabium beckleri	3RC-	QN
Orchidaceae	Peristylis banfieldii	3RC-	Q
Orchidaceae	Phaius australis	3VCa	QN
Orchidaceae	Phaius bernaysii	2E	Q
Orchidaceae	Phaius pictus	3KC-+	Q
Orchidaceae	Phaius tancarvilliae	3VC-+	QN
Orchidaceae	Phalaenopsis amabilis	3VC-+	Q
Orchidaceae	Podochilus australiensis	3RC-	Q
Orchidaceae	Pomatocalpa marsupiale	3RC-+	Q
Orchidaceae	Prasophyllum buftonianum	3RCa	T
Orchidaceae	Prasophyllum concinnum	2KCi	T
Orchidaceae	Prasophyllum diversiflorum	2E	V
Orchidaceae	? Prasophyllum exiguum	2K	N
Orchidaceae	Prasophyllum firthii	3RC-	T
Orchidaceae	Prasophyllum laminatum	3R	N
Orchidaceae	Prasophyllum morganii	2VCit	Nv
Orchidaceae	Prasophyllum nublingii	2KC-	N
Orchidaceae	? Prasophyllum obovatum	2KC-	N
Orchidaceae	Prasophyllum pallidum	3VCa	S
Orchidaceae	Prasophyllum subbisectum	1X	V
Orchidaceae	Prasophyllum triangulare	3VCi	W
Orchidaceae	Prasophyllum truncatum	3VCi	SVT
Orchidaceae	? Prasophyllum validum	2VC-	S
Orchidaceae	Pteroceras hirticalcar	2V	Q
Orchidaceae	Pterostylis angusta	3RC-	W
Orchidaceae	Pterostylis aphylla	3RC-	SVT
Orchidaceae	Pterostylis cucullata	3VCa	SVT
Orchidaceae	Pterostylis depauperata	3RC-	Q
Orchidaceae	Pterostylis gibbosa	2E	N
Orchidaceae	Pterostylis longicurva	3RC-	QN
Orchidaceae	Pterostylis pulchella	2VC-	N
Orchidaceae	Pterostylis pusilla	3VCi	W
Orchidaceae	Pterostylis sp.1	2ECi	V

Family	Species	Threat Code	States
Orchidaceae	Pterostylis sp.2	3E	SV
Orchidaceae	Pterostylis sp.3	3ECi	SV
Orchidaceae	Pterostylis sp.4	3V	N
Orchidaceae	Pterostylis sp.5	3K	Q
Orchidaceae	Pterostylis sp.6	1K	Q
Orchidaceae	Pterostylis sp.7	2VC-	Q
Orchidaceae	Pterostylis sp.8	2E	W
Orchidaceae	Pterostylis tenuissima	3VC-	SV
Orchidaceae	Pterostylis woollsii	3RCi	QNV
Orchidaceae	Rhizanthella gardneri	3VCi	W
Orchidaceae	Rhizanthella slateri	3KC-	QN
Orchidaceae	Robiquetia wassellii	2RC-	Q
Orchidaceae	Saccolabiopsis rectifolia	2RC-	Q
Orchidaceae	Sarcochilus dilatatus	3RC-	Qn
Orchidaceae	Sarcochilus fitzgeraldii	3VC-	QN
Orchidaceae	Sarcochilus hartmannii	3VC-	QN
Orchidaceae	Sarcochilus serrulatus	3RC-	Q
Orchidaceae	Sarcochilus weinthalii	3EC-	QN
Orchidaceae	Schistotylus purpuratus	3RCi	N
Orchidaceae	Schoenorchis sarcophylla	3VC-+	Q
Orchidaceae	Spathoglottis plicata	3RC-+	Q
Orchidaceae	Taeniophyllum confertum	2K	Q
Orchidaceae	Taeniophyllum lobatum	3KC-	Q
Orchidaceae	Tainia parviflora	3RC-+	Q
Orchidaceae	Thelasis carinata	3KC-	Q
Orchidaceae	Thelymitra cucullata	3RC-	W
Orchidaceae	Thelymitra epipactoides	3ECa	SnV
Orchidaceae	? Thelymitra matthewsii	3VCi+	SV
Orchidaceae	? Thelymitra psammophila	2VCi	W
Orchidaceae	Thelymitra stellata	3V	W
Orchidaceae	Thelymitra tigrina	3RC-	W
Orchidaceae	Trachoma subluteum	2RC-+	Q
Orchidaceae	Trichoglottis australiensis	3RC-	Q
Orchidaceae	Tropidia curculigoides	2E+	Y
Orchidaceae	Vanda hindsii	3VC-+	Q
Orchidaceae	Vrydagzinia sp.1	2V	Q
Pandanaceae	Freycinetia marginata	3RC-	Q
Pandanaceae	Freycinetia percostata	3V+	Q
Pandanaceae	Pandanus gemmifer	3RC-	Q
Pandanaceae	Pandanus oblatus	2VCi	Q
Pandanaceae	Pandanus sp.1	2RC-t	Q
Petermanniaceae	Smilax aculeatissima	2K	Q
Petermanniaceae	Smilax blumei	3K+	Q
Petermanniaceae	Smilax kaniensis	2K+	Q
Philydraceae	Helmholtzia glaberrima	2RCa	QN
Piperaceae	Piper mestonii	2RC-	Q
Pittosporaceae	Bentleya spinescens	2E	W
Pittosporaceae	Billardiera granulata	2KC-	W
Pittosporaceae	Billardiera mollis	2V	W
Pittosporaceae	Billardiera villosa	3KC-	W
Pittosporaceae	Cheiranthera volubilis	2VCa	S
Pittosporaceae	Pittosporum oreillyanum	2RCat	QN
Pittosporaceae	Pittosporum resinosum	3K	W
Pittosporaceae	Pittosporum sp.1	2KC-	Q
Pittosporaceae	Sollya drummondii	2K	W
Plantaginaceae	Plantago cladarophylla	2RC-	N
Plantaginaceae	Plantago multiscapa	3K	Y
Plantaginaceae	Plantago palustris	2RC-	N
Poaceae	Agrostis adamsonii	1X	V
Poaceae	Agrostis drummondiana	3K	W
Poaceae	? Agrostis limitanea	1X	S
Poaceae	Agrostis meionectes	3KC-	NV
Poaceae	Amphibromus fluitans	3V+	NVT
Poaceae	Amphibromus pithogastrus	3K	NV
Poaceae	Amphibromus vickeryae	2KC-	W
Poaceae	Amphibromus whitei	1V	Q
Poaceae	Amphipogon avenaceus	1K	W
Poaceae	Ancistrachne maidenii	2KC-	N
Poaceae	Apluda mutica	2R+	Q
Poaceae	Aristida annua	2V	Q
Poaceae	Aristida burraensis	1K	Q
Poaceae	Aristida cumingiana	3K+	Q
Poaceae	Aristida granitica	1K	Q
Poaceae	Arthraxon hispidus	3EC-+	QN
Poaceae	Arundinella grevillensis	2RC-t	Q
Poaceae	Arundinella montana	3RC-	Q
Poaceae	Bambusa forbesii	3RC-+	Q
Poaceae	Bambusa moreheadiana	3RC-	Q
Poaceae	Bothriochloa biloba	3V	QN
Poaceae	Bothriochloa bunyensis	3VC-	Q
Poaceae	Centosteca philippensis	3V+	Q
Poaceae	Chionochloa frigida	2RCat	N
Poaceae	Danthonia occidentalis	3K	W
Poaceae	Danthonia popinensis	3E	T
Poaceae	Danthonia sp.1	2KC-	T
Poaceae	Danthonia sp.2	2R	T
Poaceae	Deyeuxia accedens	3RC-	NVT
Poaceae	Deyeuxia affinis	3RC-	NV
Poaceae	Deyeuxia appressa	2E	N
Poaceae	Deyeuxia benthamiana	3RC-	VT
Poaceae	Deyeuxia drummondii	1X	W
Poaceae	Deyeuxia inaequalis	2K	W
Poaceae	? Deyeuxia lawrencei	1X	T
Poaceae	Deyeuxia microseta	3KC-	NV
Poaceae	Dichanthium setosum	3VC-	QN
Poaceae	Digitaria porrecta	3E	QN

Family	Species	Threat Code	States
Poaceae	*Echinochloa inundata*	3KC-	SQN
Poaceae	*Echinochloa lacunaria*	3K	Nv
Poaceae	*Ectrosia anomala*	3K	Q
Poaceae	*Ectrosia blakei*	2V	Q
Poaceae	*Enteropogon dolichostachyus*	3K+	Q
Poaceae	*Eragrostiella bifaria*	2K+	Q
Poaceae	*Eragrostis infecunda*	3VC-	SV
Poaceae	*Eragrostis subsecunda*	2K+	Q
Poaceae	*Eremochloa ciliaris*	2R+	Q
Poaceae	*Eremochloa muricata*	2V+	Q
Poaceae	*Eriachne bleeseri*	3KC-	Y
Poaceae	*Eriachne scleranthoides*	2RCa	Y
Poaceae	*Eriachne tenuiculmis*	2K	W
Poaceae	*Erythranthera pumila*	2VC-t+	N
Poaceae	*Festuca benthamiana*	3X	S
Poaceae	? *Festuca plebeia*	3RC-	T
Poaceae	*Garnotia stricta*	3R+	Q
Poaceae	*Germainia capitata*	3V+	Q
Poaceae	*Glyceria drummondii*	2X	W
Poaceae	*Heterachne baileyi*	2E	Q
Poaceae	*Hierochloe submutica*	3RC-	NV
Poaceae	*Homopholis belsonii*	2K	qN
Poaceae	*Ichnanthus vicinus*	3KC-+	Q
Poaceae	? *Koeleria australiensis*	3KC-	NV
Poaceae	*Lepturus geminatus*	3R	Q
Poaceae	*Lepturus xerophilus*	3R	Q
Poaceae	*Lophatherum gracile*	3KC-+	Q
Poaceae	*Micraira compacta*	2RCa	Y
Poaceae	*Micraira dentata*	2RCa	Y
Poaceae	*Micraira pungens*	3RC-	Y
Poaceae	*Micraira spinifera*	2RC-	Y
Poaceae	*Micraira subspicata*	2RC-	Y
Poaceae	*Neurachne lanigera*	3K	WS
Poaceae	*Neurachne tenuifolia*	3RCa	Y
Poaceae	*Notochloe microdon*	2RC-	N
Poaceae	*Paspalidium grandispiculatum*	3V	Q
Poaceae	*Paspalidium scabrifolium*	1V	Q
Poaceae	*Paspalum* sp.1	1K	Q
Poaceae	*Plectrachne bromoides*	3X	W
Poaceae	*Plinthanthesis rodwayi*	2VC-t	N
Poaceae	*Poa halmaturina*	3RC-	S
Poaceae	*Poa umbricola*	3RC-	S
Poaceae	*Scrotochloa tararaensis*	2K+	Q
Poaceae	*Scrotochloa urceolata*	2K+	Q
Poaceae	*Stipa aphylla*	3RCa	T
Poaceae	*Stipa aquarii*	2K	Y
Poaceae	*Stipa breviglumis*	3RC-	SV
Poaceae	*Stipa centralis*	3R	Y
Poaceae	*Stipa feresetaceae*	2R	Y
Poaceae	*Stipa metatoris*	3V	SN
Poaceae	*Stipa multispiculis*	3KC-	S
Poaceae	*Stipa mundula*	3KC-	SV
Poaceae	*Stipa nullaborensis*	3K	W
Poaceae	*Stipa nullanulla*	3R	SNV
Poaceae	*Stipa plumigera*	3K	S
Poaceae	*Stipa vickeryana*	3K	wS
Poaceae	*Stipa wakoolica*	2K	N
Poaceae	*Triodia cunninghamii*	2K	W
Poaceae	*Triodia inaequiloba*	1K	W
Poaceae	*Triodia lanata*	3RCa	S
Poaceae	*Triodia plurinervata*	3KC-	W
Poaceae	*Urochloa argentea*	3K	Y
Poaceae	*Whiteochloa multiciliata*	3R	Y
Podocarpaceae	*Microstrobos fitzgeraldii*	2VCit	N
Podocarpaceae	*Prumnopitys ladei*	2R	Q
Podostemaceae	*Torrenticola queenslandica*	2RC-	Q
Podostemaceae	*Tristicha trifaria*	3RCi+	WY
Polygalaceae	*Comesperma acerosum*	3V	W
Polygalaceae	*Comesperma breviflorum*	2RC-	Q
Polygalaceae	*Comesperma lanceolatum*	3VCi	W
Polygalaceae	*Comesperma oblongatum*	2V	Q
Polygalaceae	*Comesperma praecelsum*	2RC-t	Q
Polygalaceae	*Comesperma rhadinocarpum*	1X	W
Polygalaceae	*Comesperma viscidulum*	3K	WY
Polygalaceae	*Muehlenbeckia coccoloboides*	3KC-	SN
Polygalaceae	*Polygala pycnophylla*	3R	Q
Polygalaceae	*Xanthophyllum fragrans*	2RC-	Q
Polygonaceae	*Polygonum elatius*	3V	Q
Polypodiaceae	*Lemmaphyllum accedens*	1K+	Q
Polypodiaceae	*Microsorium membranifolium*	3RC-	Q
Portulacaceae	? *Calandrinia composita*	3X	W
Portulacaceae	? *Calandrinia cylindrica*	1K	W
Portulacaceae	? *Calandrinia dielsii*	1X	W
Portulacaceae	? *Calandrinia monogyna*	1K	W
Portulacaceae	*Calandrinia polypetala*	2RC-	W
Portulacaceae	*Calandrinia porifera*	3KC-	W
Portulacaceae	*Calandrinia* sp.	2K	Q
Portulacaceae	? *Calandrinia sphaerophylla*	1K	S
Portulacaceae	? *Portulaca napiformis*	1K	Y
Portulacaceae	*Rumicastrum chamaecladum*	2RC-t	W
Portulacaceae	*Sedopsis filsonii*	3RC-	Y
Primulaceae	*Samolus eremaeus*	3R	WYS
Proteaceae	*Adenanthos acanthophylla*	2RC-	W
Proteaceae	*Adenanthos cacomorpha*	2RCi	W
Proteaceae	? *Adenanthos cunninghamii*	2VCi	W
Proteaceae	*Adenanthos detmoldii*	2VCi	W

Family	Species	Threat Code	States
Proteaceae	*Adenanthos dobagii*	2VC-t	W
Proteaceae	*Adenanthos elliptica*	2RCat	W
Proteaceae	*Adenanthos eyrei*	2VC-t	W
Proteaceae	*Adenanthos filifolia*	2RCat	W
Proteaceae	*Adenanthos gracilipes*	3VCi	W
Proteaceae	*Adenanthos ileticos*	3V	W
Proteaceae	*Adenanthos labillardierei*	2RCat	W
Proteaceae	*Adenanthos linearis*	2RCa	W
Proteaceae	*Adenanthos oreophila*	3RCa	W
Proteaceae	*Adenanthos pungens*	3VCa	W
Proteaceae	*Adenanthos velutina*	2VCit	W
Proteaceae	*Adenanthos venosa*	2RCat	W
Proteaceae	*Austromuellera* sp.	2R	Q
Proteaceae	*Austromuellera trinervia*	3RC-	Q
Proteaceae	*Banksia aculeata*	2RC-t	W
Proteaceae	*Banksia brownii*	2VCi	W
Proteaceae	*Banksia burdettii*	2RC-	W
Proteaceae	*Banksia chamaephyton*	3RCi	W
Proteaceae	*Banksia conferta*	3RC-	QN
Proteaceae	*Banksia cuneata*	2VCi	W
Proteaceae	*Banksia elegans*	3RCi	W
Proteaceae	*Banksia epica*	2RCit	W
Proteaceae	*Banksia goodii*	2VCa	W
Proteaceae	*Banksia lanata*	2RC-	W
Proteaceae	*Banksia laricina*	2RC-	W
Proteaceae	*Banksia lullfitzii*	3KCi	W
Proteaceae	*Banksia micrantha*	2RC-	W
Proteaceae	*Banksia oligantha*	2VCit	W
Proteaceae	*Banksia plagiocarpa*	2RC-	Q
Proteaceae	*Banksia scabrella*	2RC-	W
Proteaceae	*Banksia solandri*	2RC-t	W
Proteaceae	*Banksia tricuspis*	2V	W
Proteaceae	*Banksia verticillata*	3VCi	W
Proteaceae	*Banksia victoriae*	2RC-	W
Proteaceae	*Buckinghamia sp.*	2RC-	Q
Proteaceae	*Conospermum burgessiorum*	3RCa	QN
Proteaceae	*Conospermum debile*	2K	W
Proteaceae	*Conospermum densiflorum*	2K	W
Proteaceae	*Conospermum dorrienii*	2RC-t	W
Proteaceae	*Conospermum eatoniae*	2K	W
Proteaceae	*Conospermum huegelii*	3KC-	W
Proteaceae	*Conospermum scaposum*	2E	W
Proteaceae	*Conospermum toddii*	3VCi	W
Proteaceae	*Darlingia ferruginea*	2RC-	Q
Proteaceae	*Dryandra comosa*	2RC-	W
Proteaceae	*Dryandra concinna*	2RCat	W
Proteaceae	*Dryandra foliolata*	2RC-t	W
Proteaceae	*Dryandra foliosissima*	3VC-	W
Proteaceae	*Dryandra horrida*	2RC-	W
Proteaceae	*Dryandra longifolia*	3RC-	W
Proteaceae	*Dryandra mimica*	3E	W
Proteaceae	*Dryandra polycephala*	2VC-	W
Proteaceae	*Dryandra preissii*	2R	W
Proteaceae	*Dryandra proteoides*	2RC-	W
Proteaceae	*Dryandra pulchella*	2RC-	W
Proteaceae	*Dryandra sclerophylla*	3KC-	W
Proteaceae	*Dryandra seneciifolia*	2KC-	W
Proteaceae	*Dryandra serra*	3K	W
Proteaceae	*Dryandra serrataloides*	2V	W
Proteaceae	*Dryandra* sp.1	2VC-	W
Proteaceae	*Dryandra* sp.12	2EC-	W
Proteaceae	*Dryandra* sp.16	2R	W
Proteaceae	*Dryandra* sp.18	3K	W
Proteaceae	*Dryandra* sp.20	2E	W
Proteaceae	*Dryandra* sp.22	2RC-	W
Proteaceae	*Dryandra* sp.23	2E	W
Proteaceae	*Dryandra* sp.3	2RC-	W
Proteaceae	*Dryandra* sp.31	2E	W
Proteaceae	*Dryandra* sp.36	2V	W
Proteaceae	*Dryandra* sp.37	2ECit	W
Proteaceae	*Dryandra* sp.38	2E	W
Proteaceae	*Dryandra* sp.41	2E	W
Proteaceae	*Dryandra* sp.42	2E	W
Proteaceae	*Dryandra* sp.44	2K	W
Proteaceae	*Dryandra* sp.45	3K	W
Proteaceae	*Dryandra* sp.46	2E	W
Proteaceae	*Dryandra* sp.48	2VCi	W
Proteaceae	*Dryandra* sp.50	2KC-	W
Proteaceae	*Dryandra* sp.7	2K	W
Proteaceae	*Dryandra subulata*	2KC-	W
Proteaceae	*Dryandra tridentata*	2KC-	W
Proteaceae	*Floydia praealta*	3VC-	QN
Proteaceae	*Franklandia triaristata*	2RC-	W
Proteaceae	*Grevillea acerata*	2RC-t	N
Proteaceae	*Grevillea adenotricha*	2RC-	W
Proteaceae	*Grevillea annulifera*	2RC-	W
Proteaceae	*Grevillea barklyana*	3RCa	NV
Proteaceae	*Grevillea batrachioides*	1X	W
Proteaceae	*Grevillea baxteri*	2VCa	W
Proteaceae	*Grevillea beadleana*	3ECi	N
Proteaceae	*Grevillea bedggoodiana*	2RC-	V
Proteaceae	*Grevillea benthamiana*	2V	Y
Proteaceae	*Grevillea brachystachya*	3VC-	W
Proteaceae	*Grevillea brachystylis*	2R	W
Proteaceae	*Grevillea byrnesii*	3K	WY
Proteaceae	*Grevillea calcicola*	2K	W

Family	Species	Threat Code	States
Proteaceae	*Grevillea caleyi*	2VCi	N
Proteaceae	*Grevillea candelabroides*	3KC-	W
Proteaceae	*Grevillea candolleana*	2V	W
Proteaceae	*Grevillea christiniae*	3V	W
Proteaceae	*Grevillea cirsiifolia*	3VC-	W
Proteaceae	*Grevillea confertifolia*	2RC-t	V
Proteaceae	*Grevillea costata*	2RC-	W
Proteaceae	*Grevillea curviloba*	2V	W
Proteaceae	*Grevillea cyranostigma*	3RC-	Q
Proteaceae	*Grevillea decipiens*	3RC-	W
Proteaceae	*Grevillea divaricata*	1X	N
Proteaceae	*Grevillea drummondii*	3RC-	W
Proteaceae	*Grevillea dryandroides*	3VCi	W
Proteaceae	*Grevillea erectiloba*	2K	W
Proteaceae	*Grevillea eriobotrya*	3E	W
Proteaceae	*Grevillea evansiana*	2VC-	N
Proteaceae	*Grevillea fistulosa*	2RC-	W
Proteaceae	? *Grevillea flexuosa*	1X	W
Proteaceae	*Grevillea floripendula*	2RCa	V
Proteaceae	*Grevillea fulgens*	2V	W
Proteaceae	*Grevillea globosa*	3R	W
Proteaceae	*Grevillea glossadenia*	2V	Q
Proteaceae	*Grevillea iaspicula*	2E	N
Proteaceae	*Grevillea inconspicua*	3V	W
Proteaceae	*Grevillea infecunda*	2VCi	V
Proteaceae	*Grevillea infundibularis*	2VCi	W
Proteaceae	*Grevillea intricata*	2K	W
Proteaceae	*Grevillea involucrata*	2VCa	W
Proteaceae	? *Grevillea jamesoniana*	3K	W
Proteaceae	*Grevillea jephcottii*	2RC-t	V
Proteaceae	*Grevillea johnsonii*	2RCi	N
Proteaceae	*Grevillea kenneallyi*	2V	W
Proteaceae	*Grevillea kennedyana*	2VCi	N
Proteaceae	*Grevillea latifolia*	3K	W
Proteaceae	*Grevillea leptopoda*	2V	W
Proteaceae	*Grevillea leucoclada*	2RC-	W
Proteaceae	*Grevillea linsmithii*	3RCa	QN
Proteaceae	*Grevillea lissopleura*	1K	W
Proteaceae	*Grevillea longicuspis*	3K	Y
Proteaceae	*Grevillea longifolia*	2RC-	N
Proteaceae	*Grevillea lullfitzii*	1K	W
Proteaceae	*Grevillea makinsonii*	2E	W
Proteaceae	*Grevillea maxwellii*	2V	W
Proteaceae	*Grevillea microstegia*	2RC-t	V
Proteaceae	*Grevillea miniata*	3K	W
Proteaceae	*Grevillea minutiflora*	2V	W
Proteaceae	*Grevillea molyneuxii*	2R	N
Proteaceae	*Grevillea montis-cole*	2RC-	V
Proteaceae	*Grevillea murex*	2V	W
Proteaceae	*Grevillea muricata*	2RCa	S
Proteaceae	*Grevillea mysodes*	2K	W
Proteaceae	*Grevillea nana*	3K	W
Proteaceae	*Grevillea newbeyi*	3VC-	W
Proteaceae	*Grevillea obtecta*	2R	V
Proteaceae	*Grevillea obtusiflora*	3RCa	N
Proteaceae	*Grevillea oldei*	2RC-	N
Proteaceae	*Grevillea olivacea*	2RC-	W
Proteaceae	*Grevillea phanerophlebia*	2E	W
Proteaceae	*Grevillea pinifolia*	2E	W
Proteaceae	*Grevillea polyacida*	3RC-	Y
Proteaceae	*Grevillea polybotrya*	3K	W
Proteaceae	*Grevillea prostrata*	3RCa	W
Proteaceae	*Grevillea psilantha*	2K	W
Proteaceae	*Grevillea quinquenervis*	2RCa	S
Proteaceae	*Grevillea renwickiana*	2RCa	N
Proteaceae	*Grevillea repens*	3RCa	V
Proteaceae	*Grevillea ripicola*	3R	W
Proteaceae	*Grevillea rivularis*	2VCi	N
Proteaceae	*Grevillea rogersii*	2KC-	S
Proteaceae	*Grevillea rogersoniana*	2K	W
Proteaceae	*Grevillea rosieri*	2V	W
Proteaceae	*Grevillea roycei*	3V	W
Proteaceae	*Grevillea rudis*	2KC-	W
Proteaceae	*Grevillea saccata*	3V	W
Proteaceae	*Grevillea scabra*	2VCi	W
Proteaceae	*Grevillea scabrida*	2V	W
Proteaceae	*Grevillea scapigera*	2E	W
Proteaceae	*Grevillea scortechinii*	3VC-	QN
Proteaceae	*Grevillea secunda*	3KC-	W
Proteaceae	*Grevillea shiressii*	2VCit	N
Proteaceae	*Grevillea singuliflora*	3RC-	Q
Proteaceae	*Grevillea* sp.	3K	Q
Proteaceae	*Grevillea spinosa*	3K	W
Proteaceae	*Grevillea spinosissima*	3V	W
Proteaceae	*Grevillea steiglitziana*	2RCa	V
Proteaceae	*Grevillea stenomera*	3KC-	W
Proteaceae	*Grevillea subtiliflora*	2K	W
Proteaceae	*Grevillea tenuiloba*	3V	W
Proteaceae	*Grevillea tetrapleura*	2R	W
Proteaceae	*Grevillea thyrsoides*	2K	W
Proteaceae	*Grevillea trachytheca*	2RC-	W
Proteaceae	*Grevillea treueriana*	2V	S
Proteaceae	*Grevillea triloba*	2K	W
Proteaceae	*Grevillea variifolia*	2RC-	W
Proteaceae	*Grevillea venusta*	3VC-	Q
Proteaceae	*Grevillea versicolor*	2R	Y

Family	Species	Threat Code	States
Proteaceae	*Grevillea willisii*	2R	V
Proteaceae	*Grevillea wittweri*	3KC-	W
Proteaceae	*Hakea aculeata*	2E	W
Proteaceae	*Hakea aenigma*	2RCa	S
Proteaceae	*Hakea baxteri*	3RC-	W
Proteaceae	*Hakea constablei*	2RCa	N
Proteaceae	? *Hakea crassinervia*	2X	W
Proteaceae	*Hakea cristata*	2RC-	W
Proteaceae	*Hakea dolichostyla*	3R	W
Proteaceae	*Hakea grammatophylla*	3RC-	Y
Proteaceae	*Hakea hookeriana*	2RCat	W
Proteaceae	*Hakea megalosperma*	2V	W
Proteaceae	*Hakea myrtoides*	3RC-	W
Proteaceae	*Hakea neurophylla*	2R	W
Proteaceae	*Hakea obtusa*	2RCa	W
Proteaceae	*Hakea pulvinifera*	2V	N
Proteaceae	*Hakea* sp.1	2VCi	Q
Proteaceae	*Hakea* sp.2	2RCit	N
Proteaceae	*Hakea* sp.3	1K	W
Proteaceae	*Hakea* sp.4	2V	W
Proteaceae	*Hakea* sp.5	2V	W
Proteaceae	*Hakea* sp.6	2VC-	W
Proteaceae	*Hakea standleyensis*	2RC-	Y
Proteaceae	? *Hakea tamminensis*	1X	W
Proteaceae	*Hakea trineura*	3KC-	QN
Proteaceae	*Hakea victoria*	2RCa	W
Proteaceae	*Helicia blakei*	2RC-	Q
Proteaceae	*Helicia grayi*	2R	Q
Proteaceae	*Helicia lewisensis*	2R	Q
Proteaceae	*Helicia recurva*	2R	Q
Proteaceae	*Hollandaea sayeriana*	2RC-	Q
Proteaceae	*Hollandaea* sp.1	2R	Q
Proteaceae	*Isopogon adenanthoides*	2K	W
Proteaceae	*Isopogon alcicornis*	2V	W
Proteaceae	*Isopogon axillaris*	2VC-	W
Proteaceae	*Isopogon baxteri*	2RC-	W
Proteaceae	*Isopogon cuneatus*	2RC-	W
Proteaceae	*Isopogon drummondii*	3K	W
Proteaceae	*Isopogon fletcheri*	2VCat	N
Proteaceae	*Isopogon heterophyllus*	3K	W
Proteaceae	*Isopogon inconspicuus*	2K	W
Proteaceae	*Isopogon latifolius*	2RC-	W
Proteaceae	*Isopogon longifolius*	3RC-	W
Proteaceae	*Isopogon uncinatus*	3VCi	W
Proteaceae	*Lambertia echinata*	2VCi	W
Proteaceae	*Lambertia ericifolia*	2RC-	W
Proteaceae	*Lambertia fairallii*	2VCi	W
Proteaceae	*Lambertia orbifolia*	3V	W
Proteaceae	*Lambertia propinqua*	2K	W
Proteaceae	*Lambertia rariflora*	2VCi	W
Proteaceae	*Lambertia uniflora*	2RC-	W
Proteaceae	*Lomatia tasmanica*	2VCit	T
Proteaceae	*Macadamia integrifolia*	3VC-	Q
Proteaceae	*Macadamia* sp.1	2KC-	Q
Proteaceae	*Macadamia* sp.2	2E	Q
Proteaceae	*Macadamia ternifolia*	3V	Q
Proteaceae	*Macadamia tetraphylla*	2VC-	QN
Proteaceae	*Oreocallis pinnata*	3RCa	QN
Proteaceae	*Oreocallis sp.*	2R	Q
Proteaceae	*Orites milliganii*	3RCa	T
Proteaceae	*Orites* sp.1	2RC-	Q
Proteaceae	*Orites* sp.2	3RC-	Q
Proteaceae	*Persoonia acerosa*	2VC-	N
Proteaceae	? *Persoonia amaliae*	2V	Q
Proteaceae	? *Persoonia articulata*	3R	W
Proteaceae	*Persoonia brachystylis*	2VC-	W
Proteaceae	*Persoonia dillwynioides*	2RCi	W
Proteaceae	*Persoonia flexifolia*	2KC-	W
Proteaceae	*Persoonia glaucescens*	2V	N
Proteaceae	*Persoonia hakeiformis*	3VCi	W
Proteaceae	*Persoonia hirsuta*	3KCi	N
Proteaceae	*Persoonia leucopogon*	1X	W
Proteaceae	*Persoonia marginata*	2V	N
Proteaceae	*Persoonia microcarpa*	3RC-	W
Proteaceae	*Persoonia moscalii*	2RCa	T
Proteaceae	*Persoonia nutans*	2E	N
Proteaceae	*Persoonia pungens*	3V	W
Proteaceae	*Persoonia rudis*	3E	W
Proteaceae	*Persoonia scabra*	3RC-	W
Proteaceae	*Persoonia* sp.1	2EC-t	W
Proteaceae	*Persoonia* sp.10	2RCa	NV
Proteaceae	*Persoonia* sp.11	2K	W
Proteaceae	*Persoonia* sp.12	2KC-	W
Proteaceae	*Persoonia* sp.13	3V	W
Proteaceae	*Persoonia* sp.14	2K	W
Proteaceae	*Persoonia* sp.15	2K	Q
Proteaceae	*Persoonia* sp.16	2K	Q
Proteaceae	*Persoonia* sp.2	3RC-	N
Proteaceae	*Persoonia* sp.3	2ECi	N
Proteaceae	*Persoonia* sp.4	2VCi	W
Proteaceae	*Persoonia* sp.6	2RC-	W
Proteaceae	*Persoonia* sp.7	2K	W
Proteaceae	*Persoonia* sp.8	3K	W
Proteaceae	*Persoonia* sp.9	2E	W
Proteaceae	*Persoonia sulcata*	2VCi	W
Proteaceae	*Petrophile anceps*	2KC-	W
Proteaceae	*Petrophile biloba*	2V	W
Proteaceae	*Petrophile carduacea*	2KC-	W
Proteaceae	*Petrophile crispata*	3K	W
Proteaceae	*Petrophile plumosa*	2VC-	W
Proteaceae	*Sphalmium racemosum*	2R	Q
Proteaceae	*Stenocarpus* sp.1	3RC-	Q
Proteaceae	*Stenocarpus* sp.2	2RC-	Q
Proteaceae	*Stirlingia simplex*	3K	W
Proteaceae	*Synaphea acutiloba*	2K	W
Proteaceae	*Synaphea brachystachya*	2K	W
Proteaceae	*Synaphea favosa*	3K	W
Proteaceae	*Synaphea pinnata*	2RC-	W
Proteaceae	*Triunia montana*	2RC-	Q
Proteaceae	*Triunia robusta*	2X	Q
Proteaceae	*ZGenus* nov.1 sp.1	2K	Q
Ranunculaceae	*Clematis fawcettii*	3VC-	QN
Ranunculaceae	*Ranunculus anemoneus*	2VCat	N
Ranunculaceae	*Ranunculus clivicola*	2RCat	N
Ranunculaceae	*Ranunculus collicolus*	2RCit	T
Ranunculaceae	*Ranunculus dissectifolius*	2RCat	N
Ranunculaceae	*Ranunculus eichleranus*	2RC-	V
Ranunculaceae	*Ranunculus jugosus*	2RCi	T
Ranunculaceae	*Ranunculus niphophilus*	2RCat	N
Ranunculaceae	*Ranunculus prasinus*	2E	T
Ranunculaceae	*Ranunculus productus*	3RC-t	N
Restionaceae	*Alexgeorgia* sp.1	2E	W
Restionaceae	*Hopkinsia* sp.1	3K	W
Restionaceae	*Lepidobolus deserti*	3R	W
Restionaceae	*Lepidobolus* sp.1	2K	W
Restionaceae	*Lepidobolus* sp.2	2RCa	W
Restionaceae	*Lepyrodia heleocharoides*	1X	W
Restionaceae	*Lepyrodia* sp.1	2RC-	W
Restionaceae	*Lepyrodia valliculae*	2RCa	S
Restionaceae	*Loxocarya* sp.1	2ECit	W
Restionaceae	*Onchyosepalum laxiflorum*	3VC-	W
Restionaceae	*Restio chaunocoleus*	1X	W
Restionaceae	*Restio confertospicatus*	3VC-	W
Restionaceae	*Restio glaber*	3RC-	T
Restionaceae	*Restio gracilior*	3K	W
Restionaceae	*Restio leucoblepharus*	2V	W
Restionaceae	*Restio longipes*	2VC-	N
Restionaceae	*Restio ornatus*	3KC-	W
Restionaceae	*Restio* sp.1	2RCa	W
Restionaceae	*Restio* sp.2	2V	W
Restionaceae	*Restio stenostachyus*	3V	W
Restionaceae	*Restio ustulatus*	3K	W
Restionaceae	*Winifredia sola*	2RCa	T
Rhamnaceae	*Cryptandra alpina*	3RCa	T
Rhamnaceae	*Cryptandra gracilipes*	2K	W
Rhamnaceae	*Cryptandra hispidula*	2RC-	S
Rhamnaceae	*Cryptandra humilis*	2K	W
Rhamnaceae	*Cryptandra intratropica*	2RC-	W
Rhamnaceae	*Cryptandra leucopogon*	2KC-	W
Rhamnaceae	*Cryptandra miliaris*	3K	W
Rhamnaceae	*Cryptandra nudiflora*	2X	W
Rhamnaceae	*Cryptandra petraea*	1K	W
Rhamnaceae	*Cryptandra polyclada*	2RC-	W
Rhamnaceae	*Cryptandra pumila*	2K	W
Rhamnaceae	*Cryptandra scoparia*	3K	W
Rhamnaceae	*Cryptandra* sp.1	3K	Q
Rhamnaceae	*Cryptandra* sp.2	2K	Q
Rhamnaceae	*Cryptandra* sp.3	2KC-	Q
Rhamnaceae	*Cryptandra tubulosa*	2X	W
Rhamnaceae	*Cryptandra waterhousei*	2RC-	S
Rhamnaceae	*Discaria nitida*	3RC-	NV
Rhamnaceae	*Discaria pubescens*	3RCa	QNVT
Rhamnaceae	*Gouania australiana*	2R	Q
Rhamnaceae	*Gouania hillii*	3R	Q
Rhamnaceae	*Pomaderris bilocularis*	2RCat	W
Rhamnaceae	*Pomaderris brogoensis*	3RC-	N
Rhamnaceae	*Pomaderris brunnea*	2V	N
Rhamnaceae	*Pomaderris costata*	3VC-	NV
Rhamnaceae	? *Pomaderris cotoneaster*	3VC-	nV
Rhamnaceae	*Pomaderris gilmourii*	2RC-t	N
Rhamnaceae	*Pomaderris grandis*	2RCa	W
Rhamnaceae	? *Pomaderris halmaturina*	2E	S
Rhamnaceae	*Pomaderris humilis*	2RCat	V
Rhamnaceae	*Pomaderris intangenda*	3VCi	W
Rhamnaceae	*Pomaderris myrtilloides*	2RC-	W
Rhamnaceae	*Pomaderris notata*	2RC-t	QN
Rhamnaceae	*Pomaderris pallida*	2V	N
Rhamnaceae	*Pomaderris pauciflora*	3RC-	NV
Rhamnaceae	? *Pomaderris sericea*	3VCi	nV
Rhamnaceae	*Pomaderris* sp.3	2VC-	N
Rhamnaceae	*Pomaderris virgata*	2RC-	N
Rhamnaceae	*Sageretia hamosa*	3K	Q
Rhamnaceae	*Siegfriedia darwinioides*	3RC-	W
Rhamnaceae	*Spyridium cinereum*	3RCa	NV
Rhamnaceae	*Spyridium coactilifolium*	2VCa	S
Rhamnaceae	*Spyridium divaricatum*	2K	W
Rhamnaceae	*Spyridium gunnii*	3RCa	T
Rhamnaceae	*Spyridium halmaturinum*	2RC-	S
Rhamnaceae	*Spyridium kalganense*	1X	W
Rhamnaceae	*Spyridium leucopogon*	2VC-	S
Rhamnaceae	*Spyridium microcephalum*	1X	W
Rhamnaceae	*Spyridium microphyllum*	2VC-	T
Rhamnaceae	*Spyridium obcordatum*	2VCi	T
Rhamnaceae	*Spyridium spathulatum*	3RCa	SV
Rhamnaceae	*Spyridium westringiifolium*	2K	W
Rhamnaceae	*Stenanthemum pimeleoides*	2VCa	T
Rhamnaceae	*Trymalium albicans*	2X	W
Rhamnaceae	*Trymalium angustifolium*	2RC-	W
Rhamnaceae	*Trymalium minutiflorum*	1V	Q
Rhamnaceae	? *Trymalium ramosissimum*	2RCa	V
Rhamnaceae	*Trymalium urceolare*	2E	W
Rosaceae	*Aphanes pentamera*	2V	nV
Rosaceae	? *Aphanes pumila*	1K	N
Rosaceae	*Geum talbotianum*	3RCa	T
Rubiaceae	*Aidia* sp.1	2K	Q
Rubiaceae	*Asperula asthenes*	3VC-	N
Rubiaceae	*Asperula charophyton*	3RCa	QNVT
Rubiaceae	*Asperula syrticola*	3K	S
Rubiaceae	*Bobea myrtoides*	2RC-	Q
Rubiaceae	*Canthium costatum*	2V	Q
Rubiaceae	*Canthium* sp.1	3RC-	Q
Rubiaceae	*Canthium* sp.2	2K	Q
Rubiaceae	*Diplospora cameronii*	3VC-	Q
Rubiaceae	*Durringtonia paludosa*	3RC-	QN
Rubiaceae	*Galium terrae-reginae*	3K	Q
Rubiaceae	*Gardenia jardinei*	3RC-	Q
Rubiaceae	*Gardenia merikin*	3RC-	Q
Rubiaceae	*Gardenia* sp.1	2K	Q
Rubiaceae	*Gardenia* sp.2	2R	Q
Rubiaceae	*Gardenia* sp.3	2KC-	Q
Rubiaceae	*Hedyotis novoguineensis*	2R+	Q
Rubiaceae	*Hedyotis polyclada*	2E	Q
Rubiaceae	*Lasianthus cyanocarpus*	2K+	Q
Rubiaceae	*Lasianthus graciliflorus*	2RC-	Q
Rubiaceae	*Opercularia apiciflora*	3KC-	W
Rubiaceae	*Opercularia hirsuta*	3X	W
Rubiaceae	*Opercularia liberifolia*	2KC-	W
Rubiaceae	*Opercularia ocolytantha*	1X	W
Rubiaceae	*Opercularia rubioides*	3KC-	W
Rubiaceae	*Psychotria lorentzii*	2KC-+	Q
Rubiaceae	*Psychotria submontana*	2RC-	Q
Rubiaceae	*Randia audasii*	2R	Q
Rubiaceae	*Randia moorei*	3ECi	QN
Rubiaceae	*Spermacoce suffruticosa*	1K	Y
Rubiaceae	*Tarenna foliosa*	1K	Y
Rubiaceae	*Wendlandia basistaminea*	2RC-	Q
Rubiaceae	*Wendlandia connata*	2RC-	Q
Rubiaceae	*Wendlandia psychotrioides*	1K	Q
Rubiaceae	*Wendlandia urceolata*	3KC-	Q
Rutaceae	*Acradenia frankliniae*	3RCa	T
Rutaceae	*Acronychia aberrans*	3R	Q
Rutaceae	*Acronychia acuminata*	2RC-	Q
Rutaceae	*Acronychia baeuerlenii*	3RC-	QN
Rutaceae	*Acronychia chooreechillum*	3RC-	Q
Rutaceae	*Acronychia crassipetala*	2VC-	Q
Rutaceae	*Acronychia eungellensis*	1V	Q
Rutaceae	*Acronychia littoralis*	3ECi	N
Rutaceae	*Asterolasia grandiflora*	2VCi	W
Rutaceae	*Asterolasia hexapetala*	2RC-	N
Rutaceae	*Asterolasia muricata*	2RCa	S
Rutaceae	*Asterolasia phebalioides*	3VC-	SV
Rutaceae	*Asterolasia* sp.1	2V	W
Rutaceae	*Boronia adamsiana*	2V	W
Rutaceae	*Boronia amabilis*	2RC-	Q
Rutaceae	*Boronia busselliana*	3K	W
Rutaceae	*Boronia clavata*	2RC-	W
Rutaceae	*Boronia coriacea*	2K	W
Rutaceae	*Boronia crassipes*	2K	W
Rutaceae	*Boronia deanei*	3VCa	N
Rutaceae	*Boronia defoliata*	2K	W
Rutaceae	*Boronia edwardsii*	3RCa	S
Rutaceae	*Boronia eriantha*	2RC-	Q
Rutaceae	*Boronia ericifolia*	2K	W
Rutaceae	*Boronia fabianoides*	3K	W
Rutaceae	*Boronia filicifolia*	1K	W
Rutaceae	*Boronia fraseri*	2RCa	N
Rutaceae	*Boronia keysii*	2VCi	Q
Rutaceae	*Boronia latipinna*	2RC-t	V
Rutaceae	*Boronia octandra*	3KC-	W
Rutaceae	*Boronia oxyantha*	3RCa	W
Rutaceae	*Boronia pauciflora*	2R	W
Rutaceae	*Boronia penicillata*	3KC-	W
Rutaceae	*Boronia pulchella*	2KC-	W
Rutaceae	*Boronia revoluta*	2V	W
Rutaceae	*Boronia rivularis*	3RC-	Q
Rutaceae	*Boronia rubiginosa*	2RCa	N
Rutaceae	*Boronia* sp.1	2KC-	Q
Rutaceae	*Boronia* sp.2	2K	Q
Rutaceae	*Boronia* sp.3	2K	Q
Rutaceae	*Boronia* sp.4	2K	Q
Rutaceae	*Boronia subulifolia*	2RC-	N
Rutaceae	*Boronia tenuis*	3RC-	W
Rutaceae	*Boronia virgata*	2K	W
Rutaceae	*Bosistoa floydii*	2RCi	N
Rutaceae	*Bosistoa medicinalis*	2V	Q
Rutaceae	*Bosistoa monostylis*	3V	Q
Rutaceae	*Bosistoa selwynii*	3V	QN
Rutaceae	*Bosistoa* sp.1	2V	Q

Family	Species	Threat Code	States
Rutaceae	*Bosistoa transversa*	3VC-	QN
Rutaceae	*Correa baeuerlenii*	2VCi	N
Rutaceae	*Correa decumbens*	3RCa	S
Rutaceae	*Diplolaena andrewsii*	2K	W
Rutaceae	*Diplolaena ferruginea*	2KC-	W
Rutaceae	*Drummondita calida*	2K	Q
Rutaceae	*Drummondita ericoides*	2VCi	W
Rutaceae	*Drummondita miniata*	2R	W
Rutaceae	*Eriostemon coccineus*	2K	W
Rutaceae	*Eriostemon cymbiformis*	2RC-	W
Rutaceae	*Eriostemon ericifolius*	3V	N
Rutaceae	*Eriostemon falcatus*	1X	W
Rutaceae	*Eriostemon fitzgeraldii*	3K	W
Rutaceae	*Eriostemon nutans*	1E	W
Rutaceae	*Eriostemon obovalis*	3RCa	N
Rutaceae	*Eriostemon pinoides*	2RC-	W
Rutaceae	*Eriostemon wonganensis*	2V	W
Rutaceae	*Euodia* sp.1	2RC-	Q
Rutaceae	*Medicosma elliptica*	2V	Q
Rutaceae	*Medicosma glandulosa*	2RC-	Q
Rutaceae	*Medicosma obovata*	2V	Q
Rutaceae	*Medicosma riparia*	2K+	Q
Rutaceae	*Microcitrus garrawayi*	3RC-	Q
Rutaceae	*Microcitrus inodora*	2RC-	Q
Rutaceae	*Muiriantha hassellii*	2RC-t	W
Rutaceae	*Neobyrnesia suberosa*	2RC-	Y
Rutaceae	*Phebalium brachycalyx*	3K	W
Rutaceae	*Phebalium brachyphyllum*	3RC-	Sv
Rutaceae	*Phebalium carruthersii*	3RC-	N
Rutaceae	*Phebalium clavatum*	2R	W
Rutaceae	*Phebalium daviesii*	2X	T
Rutaceae	*Phebalium drummondii*	2K	W
Rutaceae	*Phebalium ellipticum*	2RCa	N
Rutaceae	*Phebalium equestre*	2E	S
Rutaceae	*Phebalium frondosum*	2R	V
Rutaceae	*Phebalium gracile*	2RC-t	Q
Rutaceae	*Phebalium hillebrandii*	2RC-	S
Rutaceae	? *Phebalium lachnaeoides*	1X	N
Rutaceae	*Phebalium lowanense*	3VC-	SV
Rutaceae	*Phebalium montanum*	3RCa	T
Rutaceae	*Phebalium obcordatum*	3RCa	NV
Rutaceae	*Phebalium obtusifolium*	2E	Q
Rutaceae	*Phebalium oldfieldii*	3RC-	T
Rutaceae	*Phebalium ralstonii*	2VCi	N
Rutaceae	*Phebalium rhytidophyllum*	2VCit	N
Rutaceae	*Phebalium sympetalum*	2VC-	N
Rutaceae	*Phebalium viridiflorum*	3RCa	N
Rutaceae	*Phebalium whitei*	2VC-	Q
Rutaceae	*Phebalium wilsonii*	2R	V
Rutaceae	*Rhadinothamnus euphemiae*	3RC-	W
Rutaceae	*Urocarpus niveus*	2E	W
Rutaceae	*Zanthoxylum rhetsa*	2K+	Q
Rutaceae	*Zieria adenophora*	2E	N
Rutaceae	*Zieria collina*	2VC-	Q
Rutaceae	*Zieria granulata*	2VC-	N
Rutaceae	*Zieria involucrata*	2VC-	N
Rutaceae	*Zieria murphyi*	2VC-	N
Rutaceae	*Zieria obcordata*	3E	N
Rutaceae	*Zieria rimulosa*	2V	Q
Rutaceae	*Zieria* sp.1	2E	N
Rutaceae	*Zieria* sp.10	2R	N
Rutaceae	*Zieria* sp.11	1K	T
Rutaceae	*Zieria* sp.12	1K	Q
Rutaceae	*Zieria* sp.13	2V	Q
Rutaceae	*Zieria* sp.14	2E	N
Rutaceae	*Zieria* sp.15	2E	N
Rutaceae	*Zieria* sp.2	3V	NV
Rutaceae	*Zieria* sp.3	2V	N
Rutaceae	*Zieria* sp.4	2V	Q
Rutaceae	*Zieria* sp.5	3RC-	QN
Rutaceae	*Zieria* sp.6	2RC-	N
Rutaceae	*Zieria* sp.7	2E	N
Rutaceae	*Zieria* sp.8	2RC-t	QN
Rutaceae	*Zieria* sp.9	2VCi	N
Santalaceae	*Dendromyza reinwardtiana*	2R+	Q
Santalaceae	*Leptomeria dielsiana*	1X	W
Santalaceae	*Leptomeria ericoides*	3K	W
Santalaceae	*Spirogardnera rubescens*	2VCi	W
Santalaceae	*Thesium australe*	3ECi+	QNVt
Sapindaceae	*Alectryon repando-dentatus*	2K+	Q
Sapindaceae	*Alectryon semicinereus*	3R	Q
Sapindaceae	*Alectryon* sp.1	2V	Q
Sapindaceae	*Arytera dictyoneura*	2V	Q
Sapindaceae	*Arytera macrobotrys*	3K+	Q
Sapindaceae	*Arytera* sp.1	2K+	Q
Sapindaceae	*Atalaya calcicola*	2R	Q
Sapindaceae	*Atalaya rigida*	3R	Q
Sapindaceae	*Cossinia australiana*	3E	Q
Sapindaceae	*Cupaniopsis dallachyi*	3K	Q
Sapindaceae	*Cupaniopsis shirleyana*	3V	Q
Sapindaceae	*Cupaniopsis tomentella*	3V	Q
Sapindaceae	*Dimocarpus leichhardtii*	1K	Q
Sapindaceae	*Diploglottis bracteata*	2RC-	Q
Sapindaceae	*Diploglottis campbellii*	2E	QN
Sapindaceae	*Diploglottis harpullioides*	3R	Q
Sapindaceae	*Diploglottis pedleyi*	2RC-	Q
Sapindaceae	*Diploglottis* sp.1	3K	Q
Sapindaceae	*Dodonaea biloba*	2R	Q
Sapindaceae	*Dodonaea ericoides*	3RC-	W
Sapindaceae	*Dodonaea glandulosa*	3KCi	W
Sapindaceae	*Dodonaea hackettiana*	2RC-	W
Sapindaceae	*Dodonaea hirsuta*	3RC-	QN
Sapindaceae	*Dodonaea megazyga*	3RCa	QN
Sapindaceae	*Dodonaea rhombifolia*	3RCa	NV
Sapindaceae	*Dodonaea rupicola*	2V	Q
Sapindaceae	*Dodonaea serratifolia*	2RC-	N
Sapindaceae	*Dodonaea* sp.1	2VC-	Q
Sapindaceae	*Dodonaea subglandulifera*	3E	S
Sapindaceae	? *Dodonaea tepperi*	3E	S
Sapindaceae	*Dodonaea trifida*	3RCi	W
Sapindaceae	*Dodonaea uncinata*	3RC-	Q
Sapindaceae	*Elattostachys megalantha*	2V	Q
Sapindaceae	? *Guioa chrysantha*	1K	N
Sapindaceae	*Guioa crenifoliola*	2K+	Q
Sapindaceae	*Guioa montana*	2RC-	Q
Sapindaceae	*Harpullia arborea*	2RC-+	Q
Sapindaceae	*Heterodendrum tropicum*	2R	Q
Sapindaceae	*Jagera javanica*	2VC-+	Q
Sapindaceae	*Lepiderema hirsuta*	2RC-	Q
Sapindaceae	*Lepiderema largiflorens*	2RC-	Q
Sapindaceae	*Lepiderema pulchella*	2RC-	QN
Sapindaceae	*Mischocarpus albescens*	2R	Q
Sapindaceae	*Sarcopteryx montana*	2RC-	Q
Sapindaceae	*Sarcotoechia heterophylla*	2RC-	Q
Sapindaceae	*Sarcotoechia serrata*	2RC-	Q
Sapindaceae	*Sarcotoechia villosa*	2R	Q
Sapindaceae	*Toechima monticola*	3RC-	Q
Sapindaceae	*Toechima pterocarpum*	2E	Q
Sapindaceae	*Tristiropsis canarioides*	2R+	Q
Sapotaceae	*Amorphospermum whitei*	3RCa	QN
Sapotaceae	*Chrysophyllum lanceolatum*	3RC-+	Q
Sapotaceae	*Planchonella eerwah*	3E	Q
Sapotaceae	*Planchonella euphlebia*	3R	Q
Sapotaceae	*Planchonella ripicola*	2RC-+	Q
Sapotaceae	*Planchonella singuliflora*	3RC-	Q
Sapotaceae	*Planchonella* sp.1	2K	Q
Sapotaceae	*Planchonella* sp.2	2K	Q
Schizaeaceae	*Schizaea malaccana*	2K+	Q
Scrophulariaceae	*Chionohebe ciliolata*	2RC-+	T
Scrophulariaceae	*Chionohebe densifolia*	2RC-t+	N
Scrophulariaceae	*Euphrasia alsa*	2RC-t	N
Scrophulariaceae	*Euphrasia arguta*	3X	N
Scrophulariaceae	*Euphrasia bella*	2ECi	QN
Scrophulariaceae	*Euphrasia bowdeniae*	2RC-t	N
Scrophulariaceae	*Euphrasia ciliolata*	2KC-	N
Scrophulariaceae	*Euphrasia orthocheila*	3VC-	QN
Scrophulariaceae	*Euphrasia phragmostoma*	3VC-	T
Scrophulariaceae	*Euphrasia ramulosa*	3RC-	N
Scrophulariaceae	*Euphrasia scabra*	3VCa	WsnVT
Scrophulariaceae	*Euphrasia semipicta*	2VC-	T
Scrophulariaceae	*Euphrasia* sp.1	1X	N
Scrophulariaceae	? *Limnophila kingii*	1K	W
Scrophulariaceae	*Limosella granitica*	2V	S
Scrophulariaceae	? *Lindernia pubescens*	1K	Y
Scrophulariaceae	? *Mimulus clementii*	1X	W
Scrophulariaceae	*Parahebe* sp.1	2RC-	N
Scrophulariaceae	*Rhamphicarpa australiensis*	3V+	YQ
Scrophulariaceae	? *Rhamphicarpa macrosiphonia*	2K	W
Scrophulariaceae	*Stemodia linophylla*	3K	W
Scrophulariaceae	*Torenia polygonoides*	2R+	Q
Scrophulariaceae	*Veronica parnkalliana*	2KC-	S
Simourabaceae	*Cadellia pentastylis*	3VCi	QN
Simourabaceae	*Quassia baileyana*	3RC-	Q
Simourabaceae	*Quassia bidwillii*	3RC-	Q
Simourabaceae	*Quassia* sp.1	2E	N
Simourabaceae	*Quassia* sp.2	3RC-	N
Simourabaceae	*Quassia* sp.3	2K	Q
Simourabaceae	*Quassia* sp.4	2K	Q
Sinopteridaceae	*Cheilanthes nudiuscula*	3K	YQ
Sinopteridaceae	? *Cheilanthes* sp.1	1KC-t	W
Sinopteridaceae	*Doryopteris ludens*	2K+	Q
Solanaceae	*Anthocercis angustifolia*	3RCa	S
Solanaceae	*Anthocercis anisantha*	3RC-	WS
Solanaceae	*Anthocercis fasciculata*	2RCat	W
Solanaceae	*Anthocercis gracilis*	2V	W
Solanaceae	*Anthocercis intricata*	3K	W
Solanaceae	*Anthotroche myoporoides*	3V	W
Solanaceae	*Anthotroche walcottii*	3RC-	W
Solanaceae	*Crenidium spinescens*	3K	W
Solanaceae	*Cyphanthera anthocercidea*	2RCa	V
Solanaceae	*Cyphanthera odgersii*	3RC-	W
Solanaceae	*Cyphanthera scabrella*	2RC-	N
Solanaceae	*Cyphanthera tasmanica*	3RCa	T
Solanaceae	*Grammosolen truncatus*	3R	S
Solanaceae	*Nicotiana burbidgeae*	2V	S
Solanaceae	*Nicotiana* sp.1	2K	Q
Solanaceae	*Solanum carduiforme*	2VC-	Q
Solanaceae	*Solanum cataphractum*	2K	W
Solanaceae	*Solanum dunalianum*	3V+	Q
Solanaceae	*Solanum hamulosum*	2RC-	Q
Solanaceae	*Solanum karsensis*	3RCa	N
Solanaceae	*Solanum leopoldensis*	2K	W
Solanaceae	*Solanum multiglochidiatum*	3R	Q
Solanaceae	*Solanum oedipus*	2K	W
Solanaceae	*Solanum sporadotrichum*	2R	Q
Solanaceae	*Solanum vansittartensis*	2K	W
Solanaceae	*Symonanthus aromaticus*	2VC-	W
Solanaceae	*Symonanthus bancroftii*	2E	W
Spigeliaceae	*Mitreola petiolata*	3K+	Q
Stackhousiaceae	*Stackhousia annua*	2RCa	S
Stackhousiaceae	*Stackhousia* sp.1	2KC-	W
Stackhousiaceae	*Stackhousia umbellata*	2RC-	W
Stackhousiaceae	*Tripterococcus sp.1*	3K	W
Stemonaceae	*Stemona angusta*	2V	Q
Sterculiaceae	*Argyrodendron* sp.1	2RC-	Q
Sterculiaceae	*Argyrodendron* sp.2	2RC-	Q
Sterculiaceae	*Brachychiton* sp.1	3V	Q
Sterculiaceae	*Brachychiton* sp.2	2R	Q
Sterculiaceae	*Brachychiton* sp.3	3R	Q
Sterculiaceae	*Brachychiton* sp.4	2RC-	Q
Sterculiaceae	*Brachychiton* sp.5	3RC-	Q
Sterculiaceae	*Brachychiton velutinosus*	3R+	Q
Sterculiaceae	*Commersonia* sp.1	2V	Q
Sterculiaceae	*Commersonia tatei*	3RC-	S
Sterculiaceae	*Firmiana papuana*	2R+	Q
Sterculiaceae	*Guichenotia apetala*	2V	W
Sterculiaceae	*Hannafordia kessellii*	2K	W
Sterculiaceae	*Heritiera littoralis*	1K	W
Sterculiaceae	*Lasiopetalum acutiflorum*	3K	W
Sterculiaceae	*Lasiopetalum bracteatum*	2RC-	W
Sterculiaceae	*Lasiopetalum cardiophyllum*	2K	W
Sterculiaceae	*Lasiopetalum compactum*	3RC-	W
Sterculiaceae	*Lasiopetalum dielsii*	2KC-	W
Sterculiaceae	*Lasiopetalum fitzgibbonii*	3V	W
Sterculiaceae	*Lasiopetalum glabratum*	2K	W
Sterculiaceae	*Lasiopetalum joyceae*	2RC-	N
Sterculiaceae	*Lasiopetalum longistamineum*	2VC-	N
Sterculiaceae	*Lasiopetalum maxwellii*	2K	W
Sterculiaceae	*Lasiopetalum membranaceum*	2K	W
Sterculiaceae	*Lasiopetalum micranthum*	2V	T
Sterculiaceae	*Lasiopetalum microcardium*	3KC-	W
Sterculiaceae	*Lasiopetalum oldfieldii*	2K	W
Sterculiaceae	*Lasiopetalum parviflorum*	3RC-	W
Sterculiaceae	*Lasiopetalum rotundifolium*	2E	W
Sterculiaceae	*Rulingia hermanniifolia*	3RCa	N
Sterculiaceae	*Rulingia magniflora*	3K	W
Sterculiaceae	*Rulingia procumbens*	3V	N
Sterculiaceae	*Rulingia prostrata*	3V	nV
Sterculiaceae	*Rulingia salvifolia*	2RC-	QN
Sterculiaceae	*Rulingia tratmannii*	1K	W
Sterculiaceae	*Sterculia shillinglawii*	3R+	Q
Sterculiaceae	*Sterculia tuberculatum*	2V	W
Sterculiaceae	*Thomasia brachystachys*	2K	W
Sterculiaceae	*Thomasia dielsii*	3K	W
Sterculiaceae	*Thomasia discolor*	2RC-	W
Sterculiaceae	*Thomasia formosa*	2K	W
Sterculiaceae	*Thomasia gardneri*	2K	W
Sterculiaceae	*Thomasia glutinosa*	2V	W
Sterculiaceae	*Thomasia laxiflora*	2K	W
Sterculiaceae	*Thomasia microphylla*	3VC-	W
Sterculiaceae	*Thomasia montana*	2VCi	W
Sterculiaceae	*Thomasia multiflora*	3K	W
Sterculiaceae	*Thomasia pygmaea*	3KC-	W
Sterculiaceae	*Thomasia quercifolia*	3K	W
Sterculiaceae	*Thomasia solanacea*	2KC-	W
Sterculiaceae	*Thomasia* sp.1	2VC-	W
Sterculiaceae	*Thomasia stelligera*	3KC-	W
Sterculiaceae	*Thomasia tenuivesta*	2K	W
Stylidiaceae	*Levenhookia octomaculata*	3V	W
Stylidiaceae	*Levenhookia pulcherrima*	3K	W
Stylidiaceae	*Stylidium aeonioides*	2KC-	W
Stylidiaceae	*Stylidium articulatum*	2V	W
Stylidiaceae	*Stylidium assimile*	3KC-	W
Stylidiaceae	*Stylidium barleei*	3K	W
Stylidiaceae	*Stylidium choreanthum*	3V	W
Stylidiaceae	*Stylidium claytonioides*	1K	W
Stylidiaceae	*Stylidium coroniforme*	2V	W
Stylidiaceae	*Stylidium corymbosum*	2RCa	W
Stylidiaceae	*Stylidium curtum*	1KC-t	Y
Stylidiaceae	*Stylidium expeditionis*	2RCat	W
Stylidiaceae	*Stylidium galioides*	2VCit	W
Stylidiaceae	*Stylidium glandulosum*	2K	W
Stylidiaceae	*Stylidium inaequipetalum*	3RCa	WY
Stylidiaceae	*Stylidium insensitivum*	2K	W
Stylidiaceae	*Stylidium inversiflorum*	2K	W
Stylidiaceae	*Stylidium laciniatum*	2K	W
Stylidiaceae	*Stylidium lepidum*	3V	W
Stylidiaceae	*Stylidium longicornu*	1K	Y
Stylidiaceae	*Stylidium merrallii*	1X	W
Stylidiaceae	? *Stylidium neglectum*	1X	W
Stylidiaceae	*Stylidium nominatum*	1K	Y
Stylidiaceae	*Stylidium plantagineum*	2V	W
Stylidiaceae	*Stylidium pseudocaespitosum*	2V	W
Stylidiaceae	*Stylidium pseudohirsutum*	2KC-	W
Stylidiaceae	*Stylidium pygmaeum*	1K	W
Stylidiaceae	*Stylidium rhipidium*	3V	W
Stylidiaceae	*Stylidium rigidifolium*	2RC-	W
Stylidiaceae	*Stylidium roseonanum*	2K	W

Family	Species	Threat Code	States
Stylidiaceae	*Stylidium rubriscapum*	1KC-t	W
Stylidiaceae	*Stylidium scabridum*	3E	W
Stylidiaceae	*Stylidium simulans*	1R	Y
Stylidiaceae	*Stylidium* sp.1	2K	W
Stylidiaceae	*Stylidium squamosotuberosum*	1K	W
Stylidiaceae	*Stylidium tenuicarpum*	2VC-t	W
Stylidiaceae	*Stylidium tepperianum*	2RC-	S
Stylidiaceae	*Stylidium utricularioides*	2E	W
Stylidiaceae	*Stylidium verticillatum*	2RC-t	W
Stylidiaceae	*Stylidium xanthopis*	2E	W
Symplocaceae	*Symplocos ampulliformis*	2R	Q
Symplocaceae	*Symplocos baeuerlenii*	2VC-	QN
Symplocaceae	*Symplocos crassiramifera*	2R	Q
Symplocaceae	*Symplocos hayesii*	2RC-	Q
Symplocaceae	*Symplocos hylandii*	2RC-	Q
Symplocaceae	*Symplocos* sp.1	3VC-	Q
Symplocaceae	*Symplocos* sp.2	2RC-	Q
Symplocaceae	*Symplocos* sp.3	3RC-	Q
Symplocaceae	*Symplocos* sp.4	2K	Q
Tetramelaceae	*Tetrameles nudiflora*	3R+	Q
Thelypteridaceae	*Amphineuron immersum*	3K+	Q
Thelypteridaceae	*Plesioneuron tuberculatum*	2KC-+	Q
Thelypteridaceae	*Pneumatopteris costata*	2KC-+	Q
Thelypteridaceae	*Pneumatopteris pennigera*	3RCa+	QNVT
Thelypteridaceae	*Thelypteris confluens*	3K+	QV
Thymelaeaceae	*Jedda multicaulis*	2V	Q
Thymelaeaceae	*Oreodendron biflorum*	2VC-	Q
Thymelaeaceae	*Pimelea cinerea*	3RCa	T
Thymelaeaceae	*Pimelea macrostegia*	2RC-	S
Thymelaeaceae	*Pimelea physodes*	2RCa	W
Thymelaeaceae	*Pimelea pygmaea*	2RCa	T
Thymelaeaceae	*Pimelea rara*	2E	W
Thymelaeaceae	*Pimelea* sp.1	2RC-t	V
Thymelaeaceae	*Pimelea* sp.2	2E	W
Thymelaeaceae	*Pimelea* sp.3	2KCi	W
Thymelaeaceae	*Pimelea* sp.4	3RC-	W
Thymelaeaceae	*Pimelea* sp.5	2RCa	Y
Thymelaeaceae	*Pimelea* sp.6	2RC-	N
Thymelaeaceae	*Pimelea spicata*	3E	N
Thymelaeaceae	*Pimelea umbratica*	2RC-	Q

Family	Species	Threat Code	States
Thymelaeaceae	*Pimelea venosa*	2V	N
Thymelaeaceae	*Pimelea williamsonii*	3RCa	Sv
Tiliaceae	*Brownlowia argentata*	2R+	Q
Tiliaceae	*Corchorus allenii*	1K	W
Tiliaceae	*Corchorus crassifolius*	3K	W
Tiliaceae	*Corchorus cunninghamii*	3E	QN
Tiliaceae	*Corchorus elderi*	3K	Y
Tiliaceae	*Corchorus hygrophilus*	3KC-	Q
Tiliaceae	*Corchorus rostrisepalus*	1K	Y
Tiliaceae	*Grewia australis*	3K	Q
Tiliaceae	*Triumfetta johnstonii*	1K	W
Tmesipteridaceae	*Tmesipteris elongata*	3RC-+	VT
Tremandraceae	*Tetratheca aphylla*	2V	W
Tremandraceae	*Tetratheca deltoidea*	2V	W
Tremandraceae	*Tetratheca elliptica*	1X	W
Tremandraceae	*Tetratheca fasciculata*	3X	W
Tremandraceae	*Tetratheca glandulosa*	2VC-	N
Tremandraceae	*Tetratheca gunnii*	2E	T
Tremandraceae	*Tetratheca harperi*	2V	W
Tremandraceae	*Tetratheca hispidissima*	2K	W
Tremandraceae	*Tetratheca juncea*	3VCi	N
Tremandraceae	*Tetratheca neglecta*	3RC-	N
Tremandraceae	*Tetratheca nuda*	3K	W
Tremandraceae	*Tetratheca parvifolia*	2K	W
Tremandraceae	*Tetratheca pilifera*	2RC-	V
Tremandraceae	*Tetratheca remota*	2E	W
Tremandraceae	*Tetratheca retrorsa*	3RC-	W
Tremandraceae	*Tetratheca similis*	2K	W
Tremandraceae	*Tetratheca stenocarpa*	2RCa	V
Verbenaceae	*Callicarpa brevistyla*	3K	Y
Verbenaceae	*Callicarpa caudata*	2K+	Q
Verbenaceae	*Callicarpa thozetii*	2R	Q
Verbenaceae	*Clerodendrum parvulum*	3KC-	Q
Verbenaceae	*Premna dallachyana*	2K+	Q
Verbenaceae	*Premna hylandia*	3K	Q
Violaceae	*Hybanthus volubilis*	2K	W
Violaceae	*Viola cunninghamii*	3RCa+	T
Violaceae	*Viola improcera*	3RC-	NV
Vittariaceae	*Antrophyum plantagineum*	3RC-+	Q
Vittariaceae	*Antrophyum* sp.1	2KC-	Q

Family	Species	Threat Code	States
Vittariaceae	*Antrophyum subfalcatum*	3R+	Q
Vittariaceae	*Monogramma dareicarpa*	3RC-+	Q
Winteraceae	*Tasmannia purpurascens*	2VC-t	N
Xanthorrhoeaceae	*Acanthocarpus humilis*	2K	W
Xanthorrhoeaceae	*Acanthocarpus parviflorus*	2RC-	W
Xanthorrhoeaceae	*Acanthocarpus rupestris*	2K	W
Xanthorrhoeaceae	*Chamaexeros* sp.1	2KC-	W
Xanthorrhoeaceae	*Lomandra brevis*	2RC-	N
Xanthorrhoeaceae	*Lomandra brittanii*	3KC-	W
Xanthorrhoeaceae	*Lomandra fluviatilis*	3RC-	N
Xanthorrhoeaceae	*Lomandra hermaphrodita*	3K	W
Xanthorrhoeaceae	*Lomandra nutans*	3RC-	W
Xanthorrhoeaceae	*Lomandra ordii*	2K	W
Xanthorrhoeaceae	*Lomandra patens*	3RCa	YN
Xanthorrhoeaceae	*Lomandra rigida*	3RC-	W
Xanthorrhoeaceae	*Lomandra spartea*	3K	W
Xanthorrhoeaceae	*Lomandra teres*	2RC-	Q
Xanthorrhoeaceae	*Romnalda grallata*	2RC-	Q
Xanthorrhoeaceae	*Romnalda strobilacea*	2E	Q
Xanthorrhoeaceae	*Xanthorrhoea acanthostachya*	3K	W
Xanthorrhoeaceae	*Xanthorrhoea brevistyla*	3KC-	W
Xyridaceae	*Xyris* sp.1	2VCi	W
Zamiaceae	*Macrozamia diplomera*	3RC-	N
Zamiaceae	*Macrozamia macdonnellii*	3VCa	Y
Zamiaceae	*Macrozamia platyrhachis*	2RC-	Q
Zamiaceae	*Macrozamia stenomera*	2RC-	N
Zannichelliaceae	*Zannichellia palustris*	3R+	SN
Zingiberaceae	*Alpinia hylandii*	3R	Q
Zingiberaceae	*Amomum dallachyi*	3R	Q
Zingiberaceae	*Amomum queenslandicum*	2RC-	Q
Zingiberaceae	*Etlingera australasica*	3RC-	Q
Zingiberaceae	*Globba marantina*	2R+	Q
Zosteraceae	*Zostera mucronata*	3K	WS
Zygophyllaceae	*Tribulopis affinis*	1K	W
Zygophyllaceae	*Tribulopis curvicarpa*	1K	W
Zygophyllaceae	*Zygophyllum crassissimum*	3K	S
Zygophyllaceae	*Zygophyllum humillimum*	3K	SN
Zygophyllaceae	*Zygophyllum hybridum*	3R	S
Zygophyllaceae	*Zygophyllum kochii*	3R	S
Zygophyllaceae	*Zygophyllum* sp.1	3K	W

APPENDIX V

What You Can Do –
Conservation Group Contacts

The National Threatened Species Networks (NTSN)

In 1990, with help from the Federal Government's 'Endangered Species Advisory Committee', eight key conservation organisations around Australia established State, Territory and national 'Threatened Species Networks'. The overall aim in developing these grassroots networks is to enhance community support for the conservation of threatened species, and the current National Endangered Species Program.

They will operate within the community at all levels to distribute information on matters affecting threatened species and habitat conservation, promote the issue of wildlife conservation in the media, and participate in a range of campaigns directed at conserving the hundreds of species listed in this book.

The Threatened Species Networks have been designed to involve you and other members of the public in this critical fight, and a call to any of the organisations listed below will give you further information on how to participate.

Each and every Australian citizen can and must help to ensure that our marvellous wildlife heritage remains intact for centuries to come. There are many ways in which this help can be given, and even the smallest effort by yourself and your friends can often mean the difference between survival and extinction, be it a flower, insect or mammal.

Participating in the networks will provide you with the means to help – and help you must – for without your long-term support and understanding Australia's biological magnificence will tragically disappear.

National Groups

THE AUSTRALIAN CONSERVATION FOUNDATION
340 Gore Street
Fitzroy VIC 3065
Phone: Melbourne (03) 416 1455
             Sydney (02) 247 1497
Interests: All environmental issues affecting the nation.

FRIENDS OF THE EARTH
4th Floor, 56 Foster Street
Surry Hills NSW 2010
Phone: Melbourne (03) 419 8700
             Sydney (02) 211 3953
Interests: Conservation, restoration and rational use of the ecosphere

GREENPEACE AUSTRALIA
Suite 14, 37 Nicholson Street
Balmain NSW 2041
Phone: Sydney (02) 555 7044
Interests: Wildlife conservation, pollution, marine conservation, uranium mining, nuclear disarmament

THE WILDERNESS SOCIETY
130 Davey Street
Hobart TAS 7000
Phone: Tasmania (002) 34 9366
             Sydney (02) 267 7929
Interests: Preservation of wilderness areas

WORLD WILDLIFE FUND AUSTRALIA
National Co-ordinating body of the Threatened Species Network
GPO Box 528
Sydney NSW 2001
Phone: Sydney (02) 261 5572
             Melbourne (03) 650 7011
Interests: Conservation of Australia's native endangered species

RAINFOREST INFORMATION CENTRE
PO Box 368
Lismore NSW 2480
Phone: (066) 21 8505
Interests: Rainforest conservation

Guide to Conservation Councils and Environment Centers in the United States

AMERICAN FORESTRY ASSOCIATION

1516 P St., N.W.
Washington, DC 20005
Phone: (202) 667 3300

CENTER FOR HOLISTIC RESOURCE MANAGEMENT

P.O. Box 7128
Albuquerque, NM 87194
Phone: (505) 242 9272

CHARLES DARWIN FOUNDATION FOR THE GALAPAGOS ISLES

National Museum of Natural History
Tenth and Constitution Ave., N.W.
Washington, DC 20560
Phone: (202) 357 2670

CONSERVATION INTERNATIONAL

1015 18th St., N.W., Suite 1002
Washington, DC 20036
Phone: (202) 429 5660

NATIONAL ASSOCIATION OF CONSERVATION DISTRICTS

509 Capital Ct., N.E.
Washington, DC 20002
Phone: (202) 547 6223

NATIONAL AUDUBON SOCIETY

950 Third Ave.
New York, NY 10022
Phone: (212) 823 3200

NATIONAL WILDLIFE FEDERATION

1400 16th St., N.W.
Washington, DC 20036
Phone: (202) 797 6800

STUDENT CONSERVATION ASSOCIATION

Box 550
Charlestown, NH 03603
Phone: (603) 826 5206

TREEPEOPLE

12601 Mulholland Dr.
Beverly Hills, CA 90210
Phone: (213) 273 8733

WORLD WILDLIFE FUND

1250 24th St., N.W.
Washington, DC 20037
Phone: (202) 293 4800

APPENDIX VI

Bibliography

References used for species research

Archer, M., Flannery, T. and Grigg, G. 1985, *The Kangaroo*, Weldon.

Augee, M.L. 1988, *Marine Mammals of Australia*, The Royal Zoological Society of New South Wales.

Barker, J. and Grigg, G. 1977, *A Field Guide to Australian Frogs*, Rigby Limited.

Blakers, M., Davies, S.J.J.F. and Reilly, P.N. 1984, *The Atlas of Australian Birds*, Melbourne University Press – Royal Australasian Ornithologists Union.

Burbidge, A.A. and Jenkins, R.W. (eds) 1984, *Endangered Vertebrates of Australia and Its Island Territories*, Council of Nature Conservation Ministers, ANPWS, Canberra.

Burton, J.A. and Pearson, B. 1987, *Rare Mammals of the World*, William Collins Sons & Co Ltd.

Cogger, H.C. 1988, *Reptiles and Amphibians of Australia*, Reed, Sydney.

Croxall, J.P., Evans, P.G.H. and Schreiber, R.W. (eds) 1984, Status and Conservation of the World's Seabirds, *ICBP Tech. Publ.* 2.

Cupper, J.L. 1981, *Hawks in Focus – A Study of Australia's Birds of Prey*, Jaclin Enterprises.

Dawson, S. 1985, *The New Zealand Whale and Dolphin Digest*, Brick Row Publishing Co Ltd.

Greenslade, P. 1989, *An Assessment of the Situation Regarding Threatened Australian Invertebrates in Both Protected and Non-protected Areas*, Prepared for the ACIUCN Threatened Species Conference, December 1989.

Grigg, G., Shine, R. and Ehmann, H. 1985, *Biology of Australasian Frogs and Reptiles*, Royal Zoological Society of New South Wales.

Hall, L.S. 1983, *A Study of the Status, Habitat Requirements and Conservation of Rare and Endangered Australian Rats*, World Wildlife Fund Australia – Project 33.

Harris, J.H. (ed) 1987, *Proceedings of the Conference on Australian Threatened Fishes*, Australian Society of Fish Biology and Dept Agriculture New South Wales.

Harris, J.H. (ed) 1988, *Australian Threatened Fishes – 1988 Supplement*, Australian Society for Fish Biology.

Hermes, N. 1985, *Birds of Norfolk Island*, Wonderland Publications, Norfolk Island.

Hyett, J and Shaw, N. 1980, *Australian Mammals – A Field Guide for New South Wales, Victoria, South Australia and Tasmania*, Thomas Nelson, Australia.

Hutchins, B. and Swainston, R. 1986, *Sea Fishes of Southern Australia*, Swainston Publishing.

IUCN/Conservation Monitoring Centre, 1988, *1988 IUCN Red List of Threatened Mammals*, World Conservation Union, Cambridge.

IUCN/SSC Tortoise and Freshwater Turtle Specialist Group 1989, *Tortoises and Freshwater Turtles – An Action Plan for Their Conservation*, World Conservation Union, Switzerland.

Koopman, K.F. 1984, Taxonomic and Distributional Notes on Tropical Australian Bats, *Am. Mus. Novit.* 2778:1-48.

Jenkins, R.W.G. 1989, *The Conservation Status and Requirements of Threatened Australian Reptiles*, Prepared for the ACIUCN Threatened Species Conference, December 1989.

Lidicker, W.J. (ed) 1989, *Rodents – A World Survey of Species of Conservation Concern*, World Conservation Union, Switzerland.

Lindsey, T.R. 1986, *The Seabirds of Australia*, National Photographic Index of Australian Wildlife, Angus and Robertson.

Macdonald, J.D. 1973, *Birds of Australia*, A.H. & A.W. Reed Pty Ltd.

Merrick, J.R. and Schmida, G.E. 1984, *Australian Freshwater Fishes: Biology and Management*, J.R. Merrick, Sydney.

Michaelis, F.B. 1985, *Threatened Fish, A Report on the Threatened Fish of Inland Waters in Australia*, Report Series No 3, ANPWS, Canberra.

Michaelis, F.B. 1989, *Conservation of Australian Fish and Australian Marine Mammals*, Prepared for the ACIUCN Threatened Species Conference, December 1989, ANPWS, Canberra.

Ovington, D. 1978, *Australian Endangered Species: Mammals, Birds and Reptiles*, Cassell, Australia.

Perrin, W.F. (compiler) 1988, *Dolphins, Porpoises, and Whales – An Action Plan for the Conservation of Biological Diversity: 1988-1992*, IUCN Gland, Switzerland.

Pizzey, G. and Doyle, R. 1980, *A Field Guide to the Birds of Australia*, William Collins Sons & Co Ltd.

RAOU, 1989, 'Background Paper Prepared by the Conservation Committee of the RAOU for the ACIUCN Threatened Species Conference, December 1989', Royal Australasian Ornithologists Union.

RAOU 1988, 'List of Birds Being Considered for Inclusion in the RAOU's Annotated List of Rare, Endangered and Extinct Birds of Australia and Its Territories', Second Draft, Royal Australasian Ornithologists Union.

Reader's Digest 1988, *Complete Book of Australian Birds*, Reader's Digest Services Pty Ltd.

Ride, W.D.L. 1980, *A Guide to the Native Mammals of Australia*, Oxford University Press, Melbourne.

Schodde, R., Fullager, P. and Hermes, N. 1983, *A Review of Norfolk Island Birds: Past and Present*, ANPWS, Canberra.

Simpson, K. (ed) 1986 2nd edn, *The Birds of Australia – A Book of Identification*, Lloyd O'Neil Pty Ltd.

Thornback, J. 1982, *The IUCN Mammal Red Data Book*, International Union for Conservation of Nature and Natural Resources.

Total Environment Centre 1983, *Our Wildlife in Peril*, A.H. & A.W. Reed Pty Ltd.

Tuck, G. and Heinzel, Hermann 1980, *A Field Guide to the Seabirds of Australia and the World*, William Collins Sons & Co Ltd.

Tucker, M. 1989, *Whales and Whale Watching in Australia*, ANPWS, Canberra.

Tyler, M.J. 1984, *There's a Frog in my ~~Throat~~ Stomach*, William Collins Pty Ltd.

Tyler, M.J. 1989, *Australian Frogs*, Viking O'Neil Penguin Books.

Walton, D.W. (ed) 1988, *Zoological Catalogue of Australia, 5*, Mammalia, AGPS.

Watson, L. 1981, *Sea Guide to Whales of the World*, Hutchinson & Co.

Our Biological Heritage

Australian Heritage Commission 1986, *Tropical Rainforests of North Queensland – Their Conservation Significance* – A Report to AHC by the Rainforest Conservation Society of Queensland, AGPS.

Australian National Parks and Wildlife Service 1989, 'An Australian National Strategy for the Conservation of Species and Habitats Threatened with Extinction', Draft for public comment, Canberra.

Burbidge, A.A. and McKenzie, N.L. 1989, 'Patterns in the Modern Decline of Western Australia's Vertebrate Fauna: Causes and Conservation Implications', *Biological Conservation* 50:143-198.

Burgin, S. (ed) 1984, *Endangered Species – Social, Scientific, Economic and Legal Aspects in Australia and the South Pacific*, Total Environment Centre.

Johnson, K.A., Burbidge, A.A. and McKenzie, N.L. 1989, 'Australian Macropodoidea: Status, Causes of Decline and Future Research and Management', in *Kangaroos, wallabies and rat-kangaroos*, (eds) Grigg, G., Jarman, P. and Hume, I., Surrey Beatty and Sons, Sydney.

Kennedy, M. 1989, 'Biodiversity – Can We Preserve Life's Riches?', *Habitat* 17:3.

Kennedy, M. 1989, 'Threatened Species Legislative and Management Imperatives', in *National Parks Journal*, Vol 33, No 2, NPA, Sydney.

Kennedy, M. (compiler) 1990, *An Action Plan for Australasian Marsupials and Monotremes*, World Conservation Union, Switzerland, (in press).

Kennedy, M. and Burton, R. (eds) 1986, *A Threatened Species Conservation Strategy for Australia – Policies for the Future*, Ecofund Australia.

McNeely, J. 1988, *Economics and Biological Diversity: Developing and Using Economic Incentives to Conserve Biological Resources*, IUCN, Switzerland.

Morton, S.R. 1989, 'The Impact of European Settlement on the Vertebrate Animals of Arid Australia: A Conceptual Model', in *Proceedings of the Ecological Society of Australia*, 16.

Recher, H.F. and Lim, L. 1989, 'A Review of Current Ideas of the Extinction, Conservation and Management of Australia's Terrestrial Vertebrate Fauna', in *Proceedings of the Ecological Society of Australia*, 16.

Wilson, E.O. (ed) 1988, *Biodiversity*, National Academy Press, Washington.

Invertebrate Conservation

Fry, I. and Robinson, M. 1986, 'The Threatened Invertebrates', in Kennedy, M. and Burton, R. (eds), *A Threatened Species Conservation Strategy for Australia*, Ecofund Australia, Manly, pp 1-67.

Hill, L. and Michaelis, F.B. 1988, 'Conservation of insects and related wildlife', Occ. Paper, No 13, ANPWS, Canberra, pp 1-40.

Key, K.H.L. 1978, 'The conservation status of Australia's insect fauna', Occ. Paper No 1, ANPWS, Canberra, pp 1-24.

New, T.R. 1987, 'Insect conservation in Australia: Towards rational ecological priorities', in Majer, J.D. (ed), *The Role of Invertebrates in Conservation and Biological Survey*, WA Dept Conservation and Land Management Report.

New, T.R. 1987, *Butterfly Conservation*, Entomological Society of Victoria, pp 1-50.

Riek, E.F. 1969, 'The Australian Freshwater Crayfish (Crustacea; Decapoda: Parastacidae), with descriptions of new species', *Aust. J. Zool.* 17: 855-918.

Taylor, R.W. 1983, 'Descriptive Taxonomy: Past, Present and Future', in Highley, E. and Taylor, R.W. (eds), *Australian Systematic Entomology: A Bicentenary Perspective*, CSIRO pp 1-47.

Australia's Threatened Plants

Barlow, B.A. 1981, *The Australian Flora: Its Origin and Evolution in Flora of Australia*, 1, Introduction, pp 25-77, Bureau of Flora and Flora, AGPS, Canberra.

Barrallier, F. 1802, *Journal of the Expedition into the Interior of News South Wales*, Marsh Walsh Publishing, Melbourne, 1975.

Benson, J.S. 1983. 'Rare and threatened plants', Paper 36 in Review of Policies, Priorities and Programs for Nature Conservation in New South Wales, NSW NPWS, Sydney.

Benson, J.S. 1989, 'Establishing priorities for the conservation of rare or threatened plants and plant associations in New South Wales', Proc. National Conference on the Conservation of Threatened Species and their Habitats, ACIUCN, Sydney.

Bowman, D.M.J.S. and Brown, M.J. 1986, 'Bushfires in Tasmania: A Botanical Approach to Anthropological Questions', *Archaeol. Oceania* 21:166-171.

Briggs, J.D. and Leigh, J.H. 1988. *Rare or Threatened Australian Plants* (1988 Revised Edition), Special Publication 14, ANPWS, Canberra.

Briggs, J.D. and Leigh, J.H. 1985, *Delineation of important habitats of rare or threatened plant species in the Australian Capital Territory*, Ecological Society Australia.

Cramston, D.M.C. and Valentine, D.H. 1983, 'Transplant experiments on rare species from Upper Teesdale', *Biol. Cons.* 26 No 2:175-191.

Ehrlich, P.R. and Ehrlich, A.H. 1982, *Extinction: The Causes and Consequences of the Disappearance of Species*, Victor Gollancz Ltd, London.

Good, R.B. and Leigh, J.H. 1982, 'Guidelines for the formulation of uniform flora legislation in all states', Unpublished report to CONCOM.

George, A.S. 1981, 'Background', in *Flora of Australia*, 1 Introduction, pp 3-25, Bureau Flora and Fauna, AGPS, Canberra.

Harper, J.L. 1977, *Population Biology of Plants*, Academic Press, London.

Hopper, S.D. and Rye, B.L. 1981, 'A guide to the gazetted rare flora of Western Australia', Report No 42, Dept. Fisheries and Wildlife, Perth.

Hynes, R.A. and Chase, A.K. 1982, 'Plants, sites and domiculture: Aboriginal influence upon communities in Cape York Peninsula', *Archaeol. Oceania* 17:38-50.

Johnson, L.A.S. and Briggs, B.G. 1981, 'Three old southern families – Myrtaceae, Proteaceae and Restionaceae', in A. Keast, *Ecological Biogeography of Australia*, W. Junk, The Hague.

Jones, R. 1969, 'Fire-stick farming', *Aust. Natural History* 16:224-228.

Lassack, E.V. and McCarthy, T. 1983, *Australian Medicinal Plants*, Methuen Australia Pty Ltd.

Leigh, J., Boden, R. and Briggs, J. 1984, *Extinct and Endangered Plants of Australia*, Macmillan, Melbourne.

Leiper, G. 1984, *Mutooroo: Plant Use by Australian Aboriginal People*, Eagleby South State School, Eagleby. Queensland.

Morley B.D. and Toelken, H.R. (eds) 1983, *Flowering Plants in Australia*, Rigby, Adelaide.

Myers, N. 1979, *The Sinking Ark: A New Look at the Problems of Disappearing Species*, Pergamon Press, Oxford.

Myers, N. 1983, 'A priority-ranking strategy for threatened species?', *The Environmentalist* 3:97-120.

Sampson, J.F., Hopper, S.D. and Coates, D.J. 1989, *Eucalyptus rhodantha: Western Australian Wildlife Management Program No 3*, Dept Conservation and Land Management, Perth.

Specht, R.L., Roe, E.M. and Broughton, V.H. 1974, 'Conservation of major plant communities in Australia and New Guinea', *Aust. J. Botany* Supp. Series, 7.

Strahan, R. 1984, *Why save endangered species and which ones do we save?* Proc. Endangered Species Conference, Total Environment Centre, Sydney.

Went, F.W. 1963, *The Plants*, Time-Life Books, New York.

White, M.E. 1986, *The Greening of Gondwana*, Reed, Sydney.

Captive Breeding of Endangered Species

Conway, W. 1967, 'The opportunity for zoos to save vanishing species', *Oryx* 9:154-160.

Foose, T.J. 1883, 'The relevance of captive populations to the conservation of biotic diversity', pp 374-401 in *Genetics and conservation: a reference manual for managing wild animal and plant populations*, ed by Schonewald-Cox, C.M., Chambers, S.M., MacBryde, B. and Thomas, L., Benjamin/Cummings, Menlo Park, California.

Frankel, O.H. and Soule, M.E. 1981, *Conservation and Evolution*, Cambridge University Press, Cambridge.

Myers, N. 1979, *The Sinking Ark: A New Look at the Problem of Disappearing Species*, Pergamon Press, Oxford.

Olney, P.J. (ed) 1988, 'Conservation Science and Zoos', *International Zoo Yearbook* 27:1-230, Zoological Society of London: London.

Wildlife Trade and Exploitation

Anon 1976, *Trafficking in Fauna in Australia: Second Report of the House of Representatives Standing Committee on Environment and Conservation*, Commonwealth of Australia, Canberra.

Anon 1987a, *Management Plan for Brushtail Possum (Trichosurus vulpecula) (Kerr), in Tasmania 1988*, Department of Lands, Parks and Wildlife, Hobart.

Anon 1987b, *Management of the Short-tailed Shearwater (Puffinus tenuirostris) in Tasmania*, Department of Lands, Parks and Wildlife, Hobart.

Anon 1987c, 'Australian Shell Trade', *Traffic Bulletin* 9 (1): 5.

Anon 1988, 'Wildlife Prosecutions in Australia', *Traffic Bulletin* 10 (1/2): 12.

Anon 1989, *Convention on International Trade in Endangered Species of Wild Fauna and Flora, Annual Report for Australia 1988*, ANPWS, Canberra.

Antram, Frank 1986, 'The Australian Sea Snake Industry', *Traffic Bulletin* 8 (3): 51.

Antram, Frank 1988, 'Wildlife Prosecutions in Oceania Region', *Traffic Bulletin* 9 (4): 78-79.

Antram, Frank 1989, 'Australian Sea Snake Utilization – an Update', *Traffic Bulletin* 10 (3/4): 31.

Bottom, Bob 1985, *Connections – Crime Rackets and Networks of Influence Down-Under*, Macmillan (Sun Books), Melbourne.

Callister, Debbie 1989, *Trade in Australasian Marsupials and Monotremes*, A report prepared for the IUCN/SSC Australasian Marsupial and Montreme Specialist Group – Action Plan for Australasian Marsupials and Monotremes, unpublished.

Fitzgerald, Sarah 1989, *International Wildlife Trade: Whose Business Is It?* World Wildlife Fund, Washington, DC.

Grant, T.R. 1989, 'Ornithorhynchidae', in Walton, D.W. and Richardson, B.J. (eds) 1989, *Fauna of Australia*, Mammalia, Canberra, AGPS Vol 1B x pp 401-1227.

Hume, I.D., Jarman, P.J., Renfree, Marilyn B. and Temple-Smith, Peter D. 1989, 'Macropodidae', in Walton, D.W. and Richardson, B.J. (eds) 1989, *Fauna of Australia*, Mammalia, Canberra, AGPS Vol 1B x pp 401-1227.

Lyster, Simon 1985, *International Wildlife Law*, Grotius Publications, Cambridge.

Messel, H. and Vorlicek, G.C. 1986, 'Population Dynamics and Status of *Crocodylus porosus* in the Tidal Waterways of Northern Australia', *Aust. Wildl. Res.* 13:71-111.

Skira, I.J. 1987, 'Socio-economic aspects of muttonbirding in Tasmania, Australia', *ICBP Tech. Publ.* 6:63-75.

Thomson, J.M., Long, J.L. and Horton, D.R. 1987, 'Human Exploitation of and Introductions to the Australian Fauna', in Dyne, G.R. and Walton, D.W. (eds) 1987, *Fauna of Australia*, General Articles, Canberra, AGPS Vol 1A x 339.

Wells, Susan M. (1981), 'International Trade in Ornamental Corals and Shells', *Proceedings of the 4th International Coral Reef Symposium*, Manila, Vol 1, pp 323-330.

APPENDIX VII

The Authors

Frank Antram

Frank Antram has been researching wildlife trade for over ten years in Australia and the UK. An amateur naturalist and keen bird-watcher for many years, he first became professionally involved in wildlife conservation in 1980 when he joined TRAFFIC (Trade Records Analysis of Flora and Fauna in Commerce) International in London.

At that time TRAFFIC was the Trade Specialist Group of IUCN's Species Survival Commission. Frank moved to Cambridge when the TRAFFIC International office became part of IUCN's Wildlife Trade Monitoring Unit. In 1983 he took a break from trade research for a year and moved back to London to manage the London office of Greenpeace.

In January of 1984, he accepted a job in Sydney setting up an Australian TRAFFIC office. Under Frank's direction, the office is now responsible for most of the South Pacific region.

Frank has extensive experience in the Convention on International Trade in Endangered Species of Wild Fauna and Flora (CITES) and was an official adviser to the Australian Government's delegation at the Sixth CITES Conference in 1987, and to the Papua New Guinea Government's delegation at the Seventh CITES Conference in 1989.

John Benson

John Benson graduated from Macquarie University with majors in Botany and Zoology in 1976. Since that time he has worked extensively on flora conservation with both the New South Wales National Herbarium and with the National Parks and Wildlife Service, where he co-ordinates the Service's rare and threatened plants program.

For the last decade, John has steadfastly attempted to increase awareness within both the government and the public about the need to protect a representative range of habitats and in particular, rare plant species.

He has been involved in the establishment of numerous conservation reserves in New South Wales and has carried out flora surveys throughout the State. John is a member of the World Conservation Union's Australasian Plant Specialist Group, and through his representation on other national committees and his travels around Australia, he has developed a wider appreciation of the threats to our native flora.

Graeme G George

Graeme George spent 13 years in Papua New Guinea, teaching in remote highland schools for six years. For seven years Graeme was Superintendent of the Baiyer River Sanctuary in the Western Highlands where he began captive-breeding programs for cuscuses and tree-kangaroos, developing contacts with zoos around the world. During this period part-time studies of the zoogeography, taxonomy and evolution of Australasian marsupials began which have since taken him to the major museums in the USA, UK and Europe.

From 1975 Graeme was Director of the Healesville Sanctuary in Victoria, where he initiated breeding programs for rare Australian native species. While at Healesville he convened a scientific meeting of the Australian Mammal Society to review current knowledge of the captive management requirements of Australasian mammals, drawing on the accumulated experience of zoo keepers and curators, wildlife biologists and university researchers.

Since 1983, he has been the Regional Co-ordinator of the Species Management Program of the Association of Zoo Directors of Australia and New Zealand, co-ordinating breeding programs among the major zoos, establishing a regional computerised database, compiling studbooks and developing Species Management Plans.

Graeme is also a member of the IUCN/ SSC Australasian Marsupials Specialist Group and the Captive Breeding Specialist Group, and has attended many international conferences on the breeding of endangered species in captivity.

Michael Kennedy

Michael Kennedy has been a professional environmentalist since 1978, when he became the Co-ordinator of Friends of the Earth New South Wales. In 1981, Michael took up the position of Campaign Director for The Fund For Animals Ltd, Australia, one of the country's largest membership conservation organisations. In 1986, he accepted the position of personal environmental adviser to the Federal Minister for the Environment.

He has been published widely on the issue of threatened species conservation, including a major policy work entitled *A Threatened Species Conservation Strategy for Australia*, produced by Ecofund Australia in 1986. Michael has also been involved in the global conservation of wildlife and habitats, serving as an adviser to four Australian Government Delegations at meetings of the Convention on International Trade in Endangered Species of Wild Fauna and Flora (CITES).

Over the past few years, he has concentrated on consultancy work dealing directly with species conservation, including the development of an *Action Plan for Australasian Marsupials and Monotremes*, published by the World Conservation Union (WCU) in Switzerland. He is also a Regional Member of the Union's Species Survival Commission.

Michael played an instrumental role in the establishment of the National Endangered Species Program, and helped initiate the present negotiations for a Convention on the Conservation of Biological Diversity. He is currently contracted to World Wildlife Fund Australia, where he works as a threatened species campaigner, and co-ordinates the National Threatened Species Network.

Professor Norman Myers

Norman Myers is a consultant in environment and development working in Oxford, England, and is the recipient of many prestigious international awards, including the United Nations Environment Program 'Global 500 Roll of Honour'; the 'Gold Medal and Order of the Golden Ark', World Wildlife Fund International; the 'Gold Medal of the New York Zoological Society', and the 'Distinguished Achievement Award' of the Society for Conservation Biology.

He is a consultant to a large number of international institutions and agencies, such as the World Bank, United Nations, European Economic Community, the World Commission on Environment and Development, World Wildlife Fund US, and the World Conservation Union.

Professor Myers is perhaps best known in the public arena as the author of several books on the conservation of threatened species and rainforests, including *The Sinking Ark* (1979, Permagon Press), *Conversion of Tropical Moist Forests* (1980, National Resources Council), *A Wealth of Wild Species* (1983, Westview Press), *The Primary Source – Tropical Forests and Our Future* (1984, W.W. Norton & Co.) and *The Gaia Atlas of Planet Management* (1984, Pan Books).

Geoff Williams

Geoff Williams is a Research Associate at the Australian Museum in Sydney. His research work has involved publications on invertebrate taxonomy, biology and distribution, animal nutrition and rainforest rehabilitation. He is also experienced in researching the impacts of fire on natural ecosystems.

Geoff has played an important role in helping develop a 'Coastal Wetlands and State Environmental Planning Policy' for Littoral Rainforest Surveys (habitats that are especially important for invertebrate conservation), in co-operation with the New South Wales Department of Planning and Environment.

He has also written several Nature Reserve Proposals for the north coast of New South Wales, and is keenly interested and concerned for the conservation of invertebrate fauna of rainforest remnants, maintaining a particular interest in forest ecology.

Index

Scientific Names

Common Names